Joseph de Maistre
An Intellectual Militant

Joseph de Maistre is the first full biography in English of one of the founders of conservatism, and the first to have benefited from access to the family archives. Richard Lebrun shows that understanding the dynamics of Maistre's political evolution contributes not only to our knowledge of Continental conservatism as it emerged from the crucible of the French Revolution but also to a better understanding of the roots of modern conservatism.

Even in France, where his stature as a great stylist generally has been acknowledged, Maistre is often dismissed with a brief remark about his scandalous comments on bloodshed and war. Lebrun argues that this dismissal is unwarranted: study of Maistre's life and thought is worthwhile in itself and provides useful insights into the factors that encourage the formulation and acceptance of conservatism or reactionary ideologies.

Lebrun shows how Maistre became a renowned defender of throne and altar by detailing the formative influences – the Savoyard roots, religious heritage, and predominant intellectual influences – of Maistre's experience before 1794. The Joseph de Maistre revealed here is a more complex figure than either the bloody-minded apologist for conservatism portrayed by his liberal critics or the steadfast Church Father of his traditional Roman Catholic admirers. Maistre was a scholarly magistrate in the tradition of Montesquieu, a man who had been open to the trends of his time but was profoundly shaken by the violence of the French Revolution. Appalled by the prospect of chaos, he used his rhetorical skills as a lawyer to defend monarchical institutions and traditional Catholicism. Lebrun argues that only with the opening of the family archives and the discoveries in recent studies are we able to appreciate Maistre's struggles to understand the upheavals of his time, his doubts and hesitations, and his reasons for taking the public positions he chose.

Richard A. Lebrun is a member of the Department of History, St John's College, University of Manitoba, and the translator of Joseph de Maistre's *Considerations on France*.

Joseph de Maistre

An Intellectual Militant

RICHARD A. LEBRUN

McGill-Queen's University Press
Kingston and Montreal

© McGill-Queen's University Press 1988
ISBN 0-7735-0645-4

Legal deposit second quarter 1988
Bibliothèque nationale du Québec

Printed in Canada on acid-free paper

This book has been published with the help of a grant from
the Canadian Federation for the Humanities, using funds
provided by the Social Sciences and Humanities Research
Council of Canada.

Canadian Cataloguing in Publication Data

Lebrun, Richard A. (Richard Allen), 1931–
   Joseph de Maistre
   Includes index.
   Bibliography: p.
   ISBN 0-7735-0645-4

   1. Maistre, Joseph, comte de, 1753–1821—Biography.
   2. Philosphers—France—Biography. 3. Authors,
   French—19th century—Biography. I. Title.
   PQ2342.M28 1987   194   C87-090318-7

To my wife

Contents

Introduction

Joseph de Maistre has had a rather paradoxical place in European intellectual history. On the one hand he is usually recognized as one of the founders of conservatism, but on the other hand he has not been well understood. Even in France, where his stature as a great French stylist has generally been acknowledged, Maistre[1] has too often been dismissed with a brief citation of his scandalous comments on bloodshed and war. Part of the reason for this is that his political, philosophical, and religious thinking focused on topics about which the French have remained profoundly divided. The political and ideological presuppositions of his admirers as well as his detractors have created an aura of uncertitude and suspicion that has mitigated against objective assessment and appreciation of the depth, complexity, and significance of his work.

Maistre has often been characterized as the French Edmund Burke, but compared to Burke, Maistre is scarcely known in the English-speaking world, and compared to the impressive corpus of Burkean scholarship, Maistrian scholarship is still in its infancy. Maistre deserves to be better known because of his considerable influence on European thought, and because his opposition to the Enlightenment and the French Revolution can help us understand the weaknesses as well as the strengths of the liberal intellectual and political traditions that have generally predominated in the Western world since the eighteenth century. Moreover, at a time when neo-conservative theorists and politicians are winning increasing popular support, when conservative religious fundamentalism appears to be gaining influence in the Protestant world (as well as in the world of Islam), and when we are witnessing a renewed exercise of papal authority in the Roman Catholic Church, a better understanding of the roots of modern conservatism is certainly something to be desired. Maistre was an intelligent and articulate spokesman for a tradition that has been denigrated and poorly understood by the liberal tradition. Study of his life and thought is worthwhile in itself and may provide useful insights into the factors favouring the formulation and acceptance of conservative or reactionary ideologies.

All this argues for the relevance of new Maistre studies. In particular, there has been a need for a scholarly English-language biography. Until recently, there simply were no book-length biographical studies of Joseph de Maistre in English.[2] There are a number of biographies in French, but most of them are either quite old or of the popular, unscholarly variety. The exception is a comprehensive study by Robert Triomphe.[3] While invaluable for the specialist, the utility of Triomphe's book for an English-language readership is limited by its language, its length (over 600 pages), and the author's hostility to his subject. Moreover, the approach is that of the literary scholar rather than that of a historian.

Two circumstances make this an opportune time to attempt a new biography of Joseph de Maistre. Recent work on the social history of Savoy in the eighteenth century provides extraordinarily detailed information on Maistre's native milieu.[4] The other important thing that has happened in Maistrian scholarship is the establishment, in 1975, of an Association des Amis de Joseph et Xavier de Maistre to promote Maistre studies, and of an Institut des études maistriennes the following year. This institute, to which I belong, has negotiated access to the family archives containing the original manuscripts of most of Maistre's works, his notebooks, and a considerable body of his correspondence. In addition to sponsoring a new critical edition of Maistre's works, the association organizes Maistre colloquia and puts out the *Revue des études maistriennes* (ten issues between 1975 and 1987). The review publishes previously unpublished Maistre manuscripts, the proceedings of the Maistre colloquia, and other studies based on newly available archival materials. It is my hope that an English-language biography, based on primary source materials unavailable to previous biographers, synthesizing recent French, German, and Italian scholarship, and focusing on his intellectual development, will prove a useful contribution to improved understanding in the English-speaking world of one of the most original and influential authors writing in reaction to the Enlightenment and the Revolution.

What I have tried to do in this biography is provide an explanation of how Maistre became such a renowned defender of throne and altar. Since I have written elsewhere on the thought of the mature author,[5] I have tried to avoid repeating myself. The emphasis here is on the "making" of Joseph de Maistre. It is my contention that he had made up his mind on the important issues by the summer of 1794, and that he stated his position on most of these issues in his first important work, *Considérations sur la France*, which was published in early 1797. Consequently, I have gone into considerable detail on Maistre's Savoyard roots, his religious heritage, his intellectual development prior to the Revolution, and his immediate reaction to events in

France and Savoy in the period from 1789 to 1796.[6] However for the sake of providing a complete biography for English-language readers, the account has been carried through to Maistre's death in 1821 and something has been said as well about his posthumous fortunes.

The reader should be aware that in preparing this book I have tried to follow four practical guidelines. In the first place, while recognizing that it would have been impractical to treat the origins or substance of Maistre's thinking on all the subjects he chanced to write about, I have included what has helped me understand the distinctive features of his thought and his place in European intellectual history. Second, in quoting from my subject, I have been generous with citations from unpublished manuscript materials and hard-to-find printed sources, and parsimonious in citing easily-found published materials (especially where these are available in English translation). Third, where I had available both the archival original and the printed version of a particular document, I have cited the latter whenever possible. And finally, in the firm belief that a book written in English should be fully comprehensible to those who read only that language, translations have been provided for all quotations from other languages.

Unless otherwise indicated, all translations are my own. It was Joseph de Maistre's belief that he was difficult to translate,[7] and consequently this task has been approached with some trepidation. In translating Maistre's prose I have aimed for accuracy of meaning, but have not attempted to remain literal. Word order, punctuation, and capitalization have all been treated freely. Saint-Beuve's admonition to Maistre editors was: "Let the man speak. Joseph de Maistre is indeed plain enough, clear, vibrant, and clean enough in tone, to explain himself."[8] My goal has been to translate Maistre into readable English that will distract as little as possible from what he had to say, without, however, obscuring the evolution of his style from the sometimes pompous and pretentious phraseology of his youth to the flowing freshness of the mature author. To help the reader remember that he was writing in French, I have left terms of address in his letters, such as Monsieur, in the original language. Perhaps readers who have some French will be inspired to explore for themselves Maistre's marvellous French prose.

It should be noted that Russia still used the Julian calendar during the years Joseph de Maistre spent in St Petersburg (now Leningrad). Most of his Russian letters carry the Julian date, which was twelve days behind Western Europe, as well as the Gregorian date. To simplify matters, I have cited only the Gregorian dates.

Acknowledgments

This book has been in gestation for a very long time, and consequently there are probably more people to thank that I can hope to remember. I first began thinking about a biography of Joseph de Maistre in 1962 when I was at the University of Minnesota completing a doctoral dissertation on Maistre's religious and political thought. I am grateful, in the first instance, to Professor John Bowditch for the suggestion that Joseph de Maistre was a figure deserving more study, and to Professor John B. Wolf for encouraging me to write something on Maistre's life.

I have been gathering materials for this project ever since that time. Recognition is thus due to the institutions that over the years have funded my research here and in France and Italy, paid for a considerable body of microfilming, and made possible my attendance at conferences and colloquia where my thinking about Maistre was stimulated and challenged. In many cases the immediate purpose of the grant was a particular study that has since been published (with appropriate acknowledgments), but since the larger project was always in mind, the assistance of all these funding bodies should be recorded here as well. The Canada Council's support took the form of a Doctoral Fellowship (1962) and Research Grants (1967, 1971, and 1974). The Social Science and Humanities Research Council of Canada (SSHRCC), the Canada Council's successor in funding research in the humanities, provided a Research Grant (1980) and supplemented and administered an award under a French government program for the Exchange of Research Scholars in the Humanities and Social Sciences (1977). SSHRCC also funded grants awarded by the University of Manitoba and SSHRCC Grants Committee (1978 and 1979). I am grateful as well for grants provided by the University of Manitoba Research Grants Committee (1980, 1981, and 1983). The University of Manitoba must also be thanked for Summer Research Fellowships (1969 and 1970), a Sabbatical Leave (1967), an Administrative Leave (1977–8), and a Research Leave (1984–5). Without the uninterrupted time for research and writing provided by these leaves, this study could never have reached timely completion.

The individuals who have assisted me in this project in one way or other include Mr H.H. Jacobs of the university's Office of Research Administration, who helped me obtain funding; my colleagues of the Institut des études maistriennes (especially Jean-Louis Darcel, Maître de Conférences at the Université de Savoie, whose patience and co-operation were particularly helpful), the late William Hawkins of the Service International de Microfilms of Paris, and my colleagues of the Department of History at the University of Manitoba. I appreciate the encouragement and support of successive department heads, especially Professors J.L. Finlay and J.E. Kendle. My thanks go as well to Professor O.H. Gerus for translating Russian-language materials, for calling my attention to an important article in the *Slavic Review*, and for reading what I wrote about Maistre and Russian domestic politics, to Professor D.N. Sprague for encouraging and assisting my initiation into the mysteries of word-processing on the university computer, and to the late Reverend L.C. Braceland sj of St Paul's College for his assistance in identifying and translating certain Latin passages.

I owe a very special debt of gratitude to Count Jacques de Maistre and his charming wife for their unfailing kindness and hospitality; they transformed an intellectual adventure into a warm personal experience. By facilitating my membership in the Institut des études maistriennes, by his full co-operation in my microfilm projects, and by allowing me free access to the rich family archives, Count de Maistre made this study possible. His support will never be forgotten.

I would also like to thank those who have read my book in manuscript for their comments and suggestions. Readers include Professors David M. Klinck of the University of Windsor and John Hellman of McGill University, the anonymous readers used by McGill-Queen's University Press and the Aid to Scholarly Publications Programme of the Canadian Federation for the Humanities, and McGill-Queen's copy-editor Jean Wilson, whose vigilance and critical eye caught countless misspellings, typographical errors, and stylistic inconsistencies. I acknowledge my responsibility for the interpretation and for the remaining errors and faults.

Lastly, I want to thank my wife and my children for accommodating my preoccupation with Joseph de Maistre these many years.

Joseph de Maistre: An Intellectual Militant

CHAPTER ONE

Savoyard Roots

The first forty years of Joseph de Maistre's life and career were lived out in the restricted provincial environment of Savoy, then a part of the Kingdom of Piedmont-Sardinia. Despite his eventual status as a great "French" author, Maistre never lived in France and visited Paris only once, in his sixty-fourth year. In his mature works, he never hesitated to discuss problems of European dimensions. Maistre would prescribe restoration of the French monarchy (*Considérations sur la France*, 1797), provide solicited advice to the émigré Count de Provence (the future King Louis XVIII) and to the Russian tsar on their policies and pronouncements, deluge his own monarch with his views on European international relations during the Revolutionary and Napoleonic eras, offer unsolicited counsel to all European monarchs on the folly of written constitutions (*Essai sur le principe générateur des constitutions politiques et des autres institutions humaines*, 1814), publish books urging ultramontane views of the papacy on European Catholics (*Du Pape*, 1819) and telling the French in particular how to manage church-state relations (*De l'Eglise Gallicane*, 1821), and leave other works exploring the most profound theological and philosophical questions (*Les Soirées de Saint-Pétersbourg*, 1821, and *Examen de la philosophie de Bacon*, 1836). Maistre's theorizing came to embrace problems of European and even cosmic significance, but to appreciate what went into the formation of his views and to understand the evolution and complexities of his thought, we must begin by placing him in his native milieu.

FAMILY

Born in Chambéry on 1 April 1753, Joseph de Maistre was a native of a province that was French in language and culture but politically a part of a northern Italian kingdom. Savoy's ties to Italy were of great importance for the Maistre family. Joseph's father, François-Xavier Maistre,[1] had come to

Chambéry from Nice, also a part of the Kingdom of Piedmont-Sardinia, where he had been born in 1706. There is some confusion about the more remote origins of the Maistre family. Joseph de Maistre himself believed that the family's distant ancestors were of noble French blood,[2] but the best documentary evidence suggests that the family was of humble local origin in Nice.[3] Going back to the early seventeenth century, there are records concerning a certain Jean Maistre (or Maÿstre – which probably reflects the Italian pronunciation of the name).[4] Jean Maistre was an illiterate mule driver who became a miller, prospered, and acquired property. Jean's grandson, François (Joseph's great-grandfather), died a prosperous cloth merchant, leaving a modest fortune. François' son, André (Joseph's grandfather), was educated in Turin and entered the lower ranks of the legal profession. Despite a rich dowry from his wife, André appears to have suffered financial setbacks during the French occupation of Nice in 1708–9. Nevertheless his social ascension included service as a municipal official (*syndic*). It was André Maistre who adopted the coat of arms and the motto Joseph inherited (*Fors l'honneur nul souci*). This kind of social mobility, from trade to commerce, from commerce to law, and then from law to public office, followed a pattern that was not that unusual in Europe in this period. The culmination of this ascent, incorporation into the nobility, was the achievement of Joseph de Maistre's father, François-Xavier Maistre.

Like his father, François-Xavier received his legal education in Turin. His entry into the law was delayed by the necessity of directing the family business for a few years after the death of his father, but after providing a dowry for his sister, he accepted appointment in March 1730 (at the age of twenty-five) as Substitut au Bureau de l'Avocat des Pauvres in the Senate of Nice. In effect, he became an official in an office providing state-subsidized legal aid for the poor. Initially, advancement was slow. He served in this first post for seven years, and then, in 1737, was named Substitut Avocat Fiscal Général (ie, an assistant in the office of the public prosecutor) in the same Senate. His real success came in 1740 when the king transferred him to the Senate of Savoy with the rank of Senator.

The Senate of Savoy in the eighteenth century may be thought of as more or less the equivalent of a provincial French parlement in the same period. The high court of the province of Savoy, a proud body with a distinguished history, the Senate had served from its creation in the sixteenth century as a kind of parliament as well as a high court. The geographic extent of its jurisdiction had included not only Savoy, but Bresse and Bugey (areas later lost to France) and the Val d'Aosta. The Senate had been responsible for the administration of the duchy, charged with the supervision of morals, religion, education, and economic life. By the early eighteenth century, its competence had been restricted, for the most part, to juridicial matters. However, it still possessed, like a French parlement, the right of remonstrance. It could delay the registration of royal edicts until receipt of a third letter of demand (*lettre de jussion*) from the king. But tensions between the king and the Senate were never as serious as the conflicts between the French kings and their parlements since the Senators prided themselves on being both defenders of the population of the province and loyal servants of the crown. By the time François-Xavier Maistre joined the company in 1740, the centralizing tendencies of the government had limited its old pretensions, and a governor and an intendant resided in Chambéry as direct instruments of royal absolutism. Nevertheless, the Senators remained highly respected by the local population and they took their status and their work very seriously indeed. In contrast to the French parlements, posts in the Senate of Savoy were not venal. To be named a Senator was a great honour, and the rank carried with it "personal" (ie, non-transmissible) nobility.

It was not unusual at this time for high officials in the Kingdom of Piedmont-Sardinia to be named to positions in other than their provinces of origin. In order to try to assure the unity of the realm and to counteract particularism in what was a rather disparate kingdom, the monarchy regularly named Piedmontese to serve in Savoy and Savoyards to serve in Piedmont – and sometimes, men from Nice to serve in Savoy.[5] So it was that François-Xavier Maistre, at the age of thirty-four, left warm Mediterranean Nice to spend the rest of his long life as a magistrate in the sub-Alpine city of Chambéry.

The elder Maistre's career as a Senator must be described as successful and distinguished. Two years after his arrival in Chambéry, the city was occupied by Spanish troops, an incident in the War of the Austrian Succession. During the six-year Spanish occupation (1742–8), the Senate, although forced to swear allegiance to the Spanish king, did its best to deflect Spanish demands, and one of François-Xavier Maistre's closest colleagues was imprisoned as a result. With the return of peace, King Charles-Emmanuel III rewarded the Senators for their loyalty. Maistre's colleague was named First President of the court and François-Xavier was named to the post of *avocat fiscal général* (ie, public prosecutor), a position regarded as the third most prestigious in the Senate. A few years later in 1756, when there were rumours in Chambéry that the king might transfer Maistre elsewhere, the city granted him Lettres de Bourgeoisie (ie, granted him all the privileges of citizenship).[6]

In addition to his regular work in the court, Maistre was given special assignments by the Crown. In October 1761, he was called to Turin for four months to work on an important edict that liberated peasants in the realm from some of the more degrading vestiges of serfdom. The king was so pleased with Maistre's contribution that he rewarded him with a substantial annual pension, and two years later, in 1764, named him Second President of the Senate, a post he would occupy until his death in 1789.[7] In 1768, Maistre was also appointed president of a three-man commission of public instruction charged with overseeing all aspects of higher education in the province. Of even greater significance was Maistre's role in codification of the laws of the realm, the Royal Constitutions, which received their definitive form in 1770. The six "books" of this code included sections delineating the religious and judicial institutions of the kingdom, codes of civil and criminal procedure, a criminal code, and a civil code (based on Roman law). The first version of the Royal Constitutions had appeared in 1723; Maistre and his colleague, Jacques-Philibert Salteur, First President of the Senate since 1764, played important parts in editing the 1770 revised version. In the last stages of its redaction, Maistre was called to Turin to work with a commission that had been established in the capital. The king was so impressed with Maistre's contributions that he entrusted the Chambéry magistrate with the final editing.

Maistre's loyal and able services were rewarded by promotion, honours, and increased remuneration. His most significant honour came in September 1778, when by royal letters patent he was awarded hereditary nobility (*à part entière*) with the title of count.[8] This was a signal distinction: of thirty-seven commoners who entered the Senate of Savoy between 1700 and 1792, only sixteen were granted this status, and only three of the sixteen by letters patent rather than by purchase of a fief.[9] In addition, Maistre was further rewarded in 1785 by being named Conservateur Général des Apanages des Princes en Savoie, a post carrying substantial extra remuneration. In considering the influences that shaped Joseph de Maistre's royalism, surely due weight must be given to his father's successful and well-rewarded career.

François-Xavier Maistre had still been a bachelor when he came to Chambéry. It was only in 1750, when he was already forty-four years old, that he married Christine Demotz, a young woman of noble family twenty-two years his junior. Christine's father, Joseph Demotz, was a learned magistrate, a *juge-mage* (judge of a court immediately below the Senate in jurisdiction) and an honourary Senator.[10] Despite the difference in ages, the marriage appears to have been harmonious and happy. It was certainly fruitful. Joseph was the first child to survive to adulthood. He was preceded by two sisters who died quite young and followed by four brothers and five more sisters who survived infancy.[11] Christine Demotz was, by all accounts, a pious, well-educated woman and a beloved wife and mother.[12] Her sudden death from pneumonia in 1774 at the age of only forty-six was an unexpected and severe blow for the entire family.[13]

As the first child to survive and as the eldest son, Joseph de Maistre always enjoyed a special place in the family. According to Rodolphe, Joseph's son, the relationship between Joseph and his mother was particularly intimate: "Nothing equalled the veneration and love of the Count de Maistre for his mother. He was accustomed to say: 'My mother was an angel to whom God lent a body; my happiness was to guess what she wanted of me, and I was in her hands like the youngest of my sisters'."[14] Rodolphe also recounts another anecdote that illustrates Christine Demotz's piety and her influence on her son. When Joseph was about nine years old, news reached Chambéry of the edict expelling the Jesuits from France. The boy was playing noisily in his mother's room when she told him: "Joseph, don't be so merry, a great misfortune has occurred." As Rodolphe tells it, "the solemn tone in which these words were pronounced so struck the young child that he remembered them until the end of his life."[15] More direct evidence of how much Joseph de Maistre's mother meant to him can be found in his correspondence. For example, in a letter to his brother Nicolas in 1805, he reminisced: "At six hundred leagues distance, ideas of family, memories of childhood ravish me with sadness. I see the sacred figure of my mother walking in my room, and in writing to you about it I am crying like a child."[16]

Maistre's letters also reveal that his mother had a significant influence on his literary tastes. Writing to his daughter Adèle, he described how his mother put the "inimitable Racine" into his head: "I did not understand him when my mother repeated him to me at my bedside, putting me to sleep with her beautiful voice and that *incomparable* music. I knew hundreds of verses before I knew how to read; and so my ears, having *drunk* that ambrosia at a young age, have never been able to suffer cheap wine."[17] Indirect evidence of Joseph's memory of his mother can be found as well in his literary works, where he wrote eloquently of the role of mothers in the moral education of their children.[18] It seems reasonable then, to credit Joseph de Maistre's mother with a strong and profound influence on his development. Her acceptance, love, and support contributed significantly to the robust self-assurance that would carry him through all the vicissitudes of life.

Before turning to Joseph's relationship to his father, it should be noted that his maternal grandfather also played an important role in his formation. Joseph Demotz had only daughters, and perhaps because of this, lavished attention on his grandson. The learned *juge-mage* loved literature and fine books and possessed a rich library. From the age of about five, Joseph's tutor took him twice a day to his grandfather's office so that his progress could be carefully monitored.[19] Even when the boy was at his grandfather's place in the country, he was expected to recite his lessons.[20] Joseph Demotz was very attached to the *pénitents noirs,* a confraternity whose members pledged themselves to a Christian life and to practical charitable activities such as helping the sick in hospitals, burying the dead, and comforting condemned criminals.[21] As long as he lived, Joseph de Maistre remembered that when he was fifteen years old his grandfather had sponsored his membership in this association.[22] On his death in 1769, Joseph Demotz left his entire library (bookcases included) to his grandson.[23] Clearly, the grandfather appreciated Joseph's remarkable intellectual gifts and nurtured their development.

Maistre's biographers have disagreed about the personal qualities of Joseph de Maistre's father and his influence on his son. In contrast to his tributes to his mother, Joseph's writings and letters are nearly silent when it comes to his father. Some historians have made much of a couple of family anecdotes that seem to portray François-Xavier as a fear-inspiring paterfamilias. According to the first, told by Joseph's son Rodolphe, when recreation was over and the study hour had arrived, Joseph's father had only to appear at the garden gate without saying a word, and Joseph would drop his toys immediately in response to his father's wish.[24] In the second, passed on by Maistre's daughter Constance, the children had made a bet among themselves to touch one of the curls of the old magistrate's wig as he napped in an armchair. The bravest approached, but at the last moment withdrew, too frightened to disturb him.[25] There is also a surviving bust of François-Xavier (made when he was over seventy-five years old) that portrays his features in a way that suggests a severe and formidable personality.[26] These bits of evidence, however, are probably misleading. Jean Rebotton, who discovered and published a considerable number of François-Xavier's letters, paints a very different picture of Joseph's father and of the relationship between him and his children.[27]

The hard-working and successful magistrate was also, Rebotton's study shows, a sociable colleague, a tender and thoughtful spouse, and a fond and proud father. A man of this sort would, it might be presumed, have a different kind of relationship to his son than would a severe autocrat.

Joseph de Maistre would follow a legal career himself and would even lecture the Senate about the "external character" of the magistrate.[28] What kind of a role model did his father offer? The Senators as a group have been portrayed by their historian as "grave, sober, profoundly religous, and generally scrupulously respectful of the highest demands of conscience."[29] Like his colleagues, Maistre's father was profoundly convinced of the importance and dignity of his functions. Moreover, he brought to these tasks "a lively intelligence, a vast judicial culture, and an exemplary devotion."[30] Blessed with robust good health and capable of a vast amount of work, Maistre "loved his work and did it well." His administrative letters show that he carried out his duties with painstaking care, firmness, moral rectitude, and absolute integrity. He was, Rebotton concludes, a "great magistrate."[31] Joseph de Maistre had only to look to his father to find a living example of the virtues that should characterize a judge. Which is not to say, as we shall see in following Joseph's personal development, that there was no possibility of tension and ambiguity in his attitude towards the legal profession.

François-Xavier Maistre's administrative correspondence reveals a man of easy sociability. He was, after all, a "stranger" when he joined the Senate in 1740. Yet his official letters to his fellow magistrates serving in the Val d'Aosta under the supervision of the Senate show that his relationship with these men was one of genuine friendship. The letters often included personal notes relating family news, sharing confidences, and expressing deep personal concern over the trials and tribulations of his colleagues and their families. They testify that their author was a man of sensitivity and generosity who could be a witty and charming companion. He was courteous, affable, and even obliging towards his colleagues, with an honesty and simplicity that sprang from a fundamental goodness. There is evidence, nonetheless, of a vivacious "southern" temperament that could find expression in vigorous repartee. But these disagreements would soon be forgotten. This is a quality that Joseph de Maistre evoked in one of his few epistolary asides about his father. Writing to his brother Nicolas, he remarked: "If there has ever been any coolness between us, I would like you to remember well my father's sublime sally – Ah! The silly man thinks that I remember."[32] François-Xavier was a man who enjoyed the company of friends, and who had a particularly close relationship with his wife's family.[33]

Evidence that the sociable magistrate was also a tender spouse is found in his actions when rumours began circulating in Chambéry that he might be promoted to a higher position outside Savoy. Madame Maistre was apparently extremely devoted to her mother, her sisters, her friends, and her native city. Responding to her concerns about a possible transfer, Maistre wrote to friends in Turin for assurance that he would not be moved.[34] When his wife died in 1774, he had to write to his son Nicolas who was absent in the army to announce the sad event. His letter reveals both his great sorrow at his loss and his concerns for his family:

The month of July, which has just passed, has been very sad for us, my dear son. I have lost the best of wives and you have lost the tenderest of mothers ... I need the particular graces of heaven to sustain me in my affliction. I ask for them every day, more for my family than for myself. I sense how much I am necessary for them and God knows this more than I do. This is what makes me hope that He will be pleased to prolong my days until your establishment and that of Joson [Joseph] and André; as for the others I must not delude myself about seeing them established – they are too young and I am too old. Meanwhile I must thank the Lord that in this unfortunate circumstance my health has not been affected ... I have only the consolation of seeing them [my children] ever more strengthened in the sentiments of religion and honour, always united by a perfect friendship, and always eager to help one another in every occasion that may present itself.[35]

This letter testifies as well, of course, to the elder Maistre's deep religious faith.

But was the magistrate an overly severe father? The two anecdotes told by his grandchildren might suggest that this was the case. Moreover, there are a couple of remarks in Joseph de Maistre's letters that may perhaps be interpreted to support this supposition. In one he said that he had been "delivered early to serious and thorny studies."[36] In another he wrote of having been "raised in old-fashioned severity."[37] But these anecdotes probably show no more than that the elderly man (as he was by the time his younger children had arrived) disliked having his much-needed rest disturbed, and that he tried to inculcate in his children a decent respect for the employment of time.[38] Joseph's remarks about his education are general, and may refer to his experience with his teachers rather than to his father.

We have better evidence of François-Xavier's attitude towards his children, and towards Joseph in particular, than second-hand anecdotes. The magistrate's letters to his colleagues provide helpful insights, because in them he often referred to his family. His correspondence shows that he was especially fond of little "Joson," as Joseph was called as a small boy. He described the "little man" at eighteen months as being noisy and somewhat reckless, but nevertheless obedient. By four, Joseph's prodigious gifts of memory were already evident; he knew by heart all the capitals of the world. These epistolary comments only take us up to the time when Joseph was nine years old, but they reveal that the father was obviously proud of his son's intelligence, application, and strong character.[39] He may have taken for granted that the impetuosity should be disciplined, that the gift of intelligence should be intensely cultivated, and that the boy should be prepared for a judicial career, but there is no evidence that such expectations were ever resented by the son.

Joseph de Maistre's feelings about his father may have been too intense to be shared casually. The only surviving letter in which he wrote about the elder man in any detail is one to his brother Nicolas a few months after the death of their father. The relevant lines evoke his deep sense of loss:

Like you, I am always thinking of our good papa. His round wig, his dressing gown *which is never soiled,* his black cane, his coffee, his soup, and his "sit there." An inconceivable childishness, which I have never shared with anyone but you, is that I cannot accept seeing him buried. I would like to have his *relics* near me in some airy little cave. It seems to me that the earth is stifling him, and this idea comes to mind a hundred times a day.[40]

These remarks in turn evoke a very early entry in a private notebook. In a page that can be dated to 1768 or 1769 (when Joseph would have been fifteen or sixteen), he had written: "When, by some great misfortune, my father is taken from me, I would hope with all my heart to be permitted like an Eygptian to embalm his body and keep it with me."[41] The same entry describes the Egyptian practice as "the last retrenchment of filial love." Together, these two passages, separated by some twenty years, suggest that Joseph de Maistre loved his father with a deep and abiding affection.

The evidence, then, shows that François-Xavier was probably a firm father, but not abrupt or cold. Other testimony comes from Joseph's brother, Xavier, who spoke of the senior Maistre as "the most virtuous of men" and "the best of fathers."[42] As a child, Xavier had been dreamy and lazy, and for the sake of his education and health his parents had finally placed him with a country priest a few kilometres from Chambéry. It was on a visit to Xavier, in fact, that Madame Maistre contracted her fatal illness. That this temperamental son (a temperament revealed in his literary works) thought so highly of his father is surely significant. We can note too, that Joseph de Maistre himself cherished the memory of family life in his father's house as "a little republic, one and indivisible."[43]

Any account of the evolution of Maistre's beliefs, attitudes, and ideas must begin with the circumstances of his family and milieu. The family background described here could be characterized in various ways. One could stress its bourgeois character – the origins in the world of commerce, the upward mobility through the traditional avenue of law and public service, and the supposedly "bourgeois" traits of belief in education and careful financial management. But perhaps the emphasis should be placed on the "patriarchal" character of the Maistre household. Joseph's memories of family seem always to have combined recollections of spiritual unity and paternal authority. A passage in a letter to his favourite sister, Jenny, illustrates how these two qualities of childhood experience remained linked in his mind: "One thing never changes, and that is the spirit of family and the memory of the years of our youth. You must approve my heartfelt feelings about this. Who knows whether we will ever again find anything like that old patriarchal life?"[44] Unity under paternal authority. One finds here the roots of one of the underlying themes of Maistre's political and religious thought.

EDUCATION

The evidence concerning Joseph de Maistre's education is remarkably scanty. The roles of his mother and maternal grandfather have already been noted, as has the anecdote about his tutor bringing him twice a day to his grandfather's office. It was the custom in such families for a tutor to be engaged to prepare children for entrance to secondary school.[45] Most biographers have assumed that Joseph's tutor was a Jesuit and that the Jesuits had a dominant role in his education.[46] On closer examination, however, the presumed importance of the Jesuits on Maistre's development is hard to document or to describe in any detail.

In later life, Maistre would refer to the Jesuits as the "friends and instructors of my youth."[47] During his years in St Petersburg, he associated with the Jesuits, lobbied the Russian government on their behalf, and wrote in their defence. There are passages in a couple of his letters dating from 1816 (when the Jesuits were losing favour in Russia) that appear to support the belief that the Jesuits had been important in his education. In a letter reporting the expulsion of the Jesuits from St Petersburg, Maistre wrote: "I feel very sorry for these gentlemen, who nurtured [ont élevé] my youth, and to whom I owe not having been an orator in the Constituent Assembly."[48] There is also an often-cited passage in a letter to his brother-in-law, Alexis de Saint-Réal. Maistre had been provoked by some uncomplimentary remarks about the Jesuits in Saint-Réal's letters, and his letter of reply, devoted to a passionate defence of the order, concludes with this ringing statement: "Finally, my dear friend, there is nothing I like better than family spirit; my grandfather loved the Jesuits, my father loved them, my sublime mother loved them, I love them, my son loves them, and his son will love them if the king permits him to have one."[49] But these passages, written forty years after Maistre had completed his education, offer no particulars.

Was Joseph de Maistre's tutor a Jesuit? Family tradition seems to suggest that this was the case.[50] There is no contemporary evidence to either support or reject the tradition.[51] Whether or not Joseph ever attended a Jesuit school is also problematical. We know that the *collège royal* in Chambéry, which Maistre likely attended, was no longer a Jesuit institution in his time. The college had been founded by the Jesuits in the sixteenth century, but it had been reorganized as a royal institution in 1729, with the Jesuits excluded from instruction. Nevertheless, the Fathers continued to exercise considerable influence in Chambéry through a boarding school (*internat*), which they operated in their large quarters, and through their direction of religious confraternities.[52] We also know that Joseph de Maistre was enrolled in one of these confraternities in 1760 (when he would have been no more than seven years old).[53] The confraternity Joseph entered, the Congrégation Notre-Dame de l'Assomption, had been founded by the Jesuits in 1611, and continued to flourish in Chambéry until it was dismantled in 1793. This association was also known as the Grand Congrégation des Nobles et des Messieurs, an appellation reflecting its élite character and distinguishing it from other confraternities for artisans. Joseph's father had been a member since the 1740s and his brother Xavier would be enrolled in 1780. There were, in fact, different sections for students and for adults. According to the statues of the Congrégation, Joseph would have been admitted to the student section, the Minor Congregatio the Jesuits had established for their *internat* students.[54] Joseph's early membership in this confraternity constitutes our only evidence that he may actually have attended the Jesuit boarding school. In any case, whatever the role of the Jesuits in Maistre's intellectual formation, his involvement in their Congrégation suggests a significant Jesuit influence on his religious development.

Maistre's formal education most likely included attendance at the *collège royal,* perhaps after preparatory training with the Jesuits.[55] The college did not have a particularly good reputation at this time and there were complaints about both the lack of discipline and the poor quality of instruction.[56] The curriculum appears to have emphasized literary exercises – discourses, apologues (didactic moral tales), and disputations. But there were attempts to modernize; chairs of mathematics and physics had been added in the 1750s, as well as the teaching of design and a pre-law course.[57] Whether from the

Jesuits or the *collège*, Maistre achieved mastery of Latin and a solid foundation in rhetorical and literary skills.

In 1769, with his secondary education completed, the sixteen-year-old Joseph was sent to the University of Turin for his legal training, following in the footsteps of his father and grandfather. The University of Turin in this period was a relatively vigorous if conservative institution. Instruction was in Latin, of course. The curriculum Maistre followed would have included, in addition to professional courses in civil and canon law, courses in philosophy and theology.[58] Joseph proved himself a brilliant and assiduous student. He completed the entire program in less than three years, passing his examinations for the *licence* on 29 May 1771, and for the doctorate on 29 April 1772 (less than a month after his nineteenth birthday).[59] It is difficult to assess how significant these years in Turin were for Maistre's intellectual development. Rodolphe de Maistre, in his pious biographical notes on his father, tells us that "during the whole period Joseph spent in Turin following the law course at the University, he never permitted himself to read a book without writing to his mother or father in Chambéry to obtain their authorization."[60] Maistre himself seems never to have mentioned his university training in either his works or his correspondence. The only evidence to be found of his student experience in Turin are comments in his notebooks that suggest he had been scandalized by the "Jansenism" he encountered there.[61] But Rodolphe's portrait of a young man still completely submissive to parental authority may be doubted. By 1769, the year he entered the university, Joseph had already inherited his grandfather's large library. Moreover, we know from his notebooks that by 1770 he was reading such authors as Mirabeau and Voltaire.[62] Perhaps he did return from Turin, as one author suggests, "very open to the philosophy of the century, ever so little liberal," and in reaction against the rigid traditionalism of his early education.[63] But before examining this possibility, more must be said about the religious traditions to which Joseph de Maistre would have been exposed before going to Turin.

The Catholicism of Joseph's parents, François-Xavier Maistre and Christine Demotz, was of an undoubting, deeply held, traditional kind. Madame Maistre was known for a piety that found expression in practical charity – helpfulness to neighbours, the sick, and the poor. François-Xavier lived the kind of spirituality taught by St Francis de Sales – a profound faith in providence, a confidence that God does what is best for our interests, and that He knows better than we do what we need. This was a faith characterized by the humility of the sinner as well as stoic calm.[64] The elder Maistre's last will and testament exemplified traditional Christian piety. It began with the following paragraph:

I, François-Xavier, Count Maistre, Second President of the Senate of Savoy, wishing to dispose of the goods Providence has been pleased to give me, have made my will as follows. But before beginning the act that recalls my last end, I ask pardon of God, my Creator, for all my sins, in the hour of my death humbly begging him not to judge me according to the rigour of his justice, but giving me the benefit of his infinite mercy in which I put all my hope, imploring for this end the merits of the passion and death of our Lord Jesus Christ and the intercession of the Blessed Virgin Mary, of St Francis Xavier, my patron, and of all the saints in heaven.[65]

In short, Joseph de Maistre's father, like his mother, was a sincere and traditional Catholic. It would be surprising if the Catholicism of his parents had not had a significant influence on Joseph's religious development. Their confidence in providence may, in fact, have had a special significance with respect to their eldest son, whose life had been threatened by a serious illness when he was nine years old. The father described Joseph's recovery in these terms: "The Lord has graciously willed, by a particular grace, to preserve my eldest son. He had been reduced to the last extremities, he had received extreme unction, when by a happy revolution, we observed a diminution of the illness just when we thought he was going to expire. He is not yet without fever, but he is out of danger."[66] If the cure was perceived as miraculous, the incident could only have strengthened the parents' piety – and perhaps have had an effect on their attitude towards their son, and, in time, on his attitudes as well.

Both father and son, as members of the Congrégation de Notre-Dame de l'Assomption, would have been exposed to the spirituality taught by the Jesuits. The Fathers maintained a retreat house in Chambéry where members of the confraternity were expected to make an annual retreat. The spirituality encountered there would have been based on the *Spiritual Exercises* of St Ignatius, with emphasis on such practices as daily examination of conscience. There may have been a time when the Jesuits merited Pascal's sarcasm for their "laxity" and their perhaps excessive confidence in human nature. But this was not the case in the eighteenth century, when their emphasis appears to have been on human iniquity. The literature they produced for use by members of the confraternity as well as official statements about their educational strategy (documents produced in the 1760s) suggest a "pedagogy of faith based on terror."[67] Jesuit teaching in this period proceeded from a pessimistic view that assumed that human nature had been almost completely vitiated by original sin. Contemporary Jesuit pedagogical practices, which Maistre himself would later describe and praise,[68] called for constant supervision of their charges (lest they fall into solitary vice), protection from contamination from the corruptions of the world, strict obedience, and plenty of hard work (idleness being the mother of all vice). The approach used with adults reflected a similar mentality. A 1768 book of offices and prayers produced for use by members of the Congrégation presented an image of a "death's head" with a meditation stressing the terrifying choice between "penitence" and damnation.[69] The Jesuits defended these traumatizing methods as cures for "deranged conduct."[70] This was a spirituality that often seemed obsessed with guilt, punishment, and fear of God, a spirituality that exhibited characteristics usually associated with Jansenism. It may be ironic, for Joseph de Maistre would always be a fierce critic of Jansenism, but it appears that eighteenth-century Savoyard Catholicism generally (and not merely that of the Jesuits, who may have been compensating for earlier charges of laxity) was impregnated by a "Jansenist rigorism."[71] This was not a matter of conscious acceptance of Jansenist doctrine, but of a subtle influence on mentalities. The historian who has studied this "Jansenist" influence most closely describes how Savoyard priests too often resorted to the inculcation of guilt: "For a naïve piety, confident and blossoming in love, the inconsiderate severity of their direction substituted a stiff, narrow devotion darkened by fear. For the sake of evoking the inexorable justice of God, their cold and distant preaching allowed His infinite mercy to be forgotten. This was what little by little threw sinners into discouragement and despair."[72]

There were contrasting and even contradictory currents, then, in the Catholicism in which Joseph de Maistre grew up. On the one hand, one finds evidence of the influence of the gentle St Francis de Sales, his deep trust in providence and confidence in a divine love freely pouring out the grace of salvation. On the other hand, there is also evidence of a harsher spirituality stressing the terrible justice of God, and a rigorous "Jansenist" mentality inculcating guilt and fear. In fact, these currents were often intermixed in ways that today seem incomprehensible. The *pénitents noirs,* to which Joseph's grandfather Demotz had belonged and into which Joseph was initiated in 1768, had been co-founded by St Francis de Sales in 1594. Its original focus had been on sanctification through practical Christian charity, but as in other confraternities of the time, there was also a preoccupation with death.[73] Its iconography included the black hoods the members wore in procession and similar symbols of death in their chapel and devotional literature. The *memento mori* (reminder of death) and the *ars bene moriendi* (the art of dying well) were familiar parts of the spirituality of the *pénitent.* We do not know the extent to which Joseph de Maistre may have participated in the activities of this confraternity – after all, he departed for university the year of his entrance. It seems too that this particular confraternity was losing its vitality in these years – with membership becoming a badge of social status and a laicized philanthropy displacing the traditional values of contemplation, death to self, and recognition of the sufferings of Christ in those of the poor.[74] In contrast to the Jesuit-inspired Congrégation, which continued to flourish in Chambéry until the Revolution, the *pénitents noirs* seem to have become something of an anachronism after about 1770. So of the two, it seems likely that the Jesuits had the greater influence on Joseph de

Maistre's religious mentality. In either case, it is not hard to see in the sombre Christianity of Maistre's later works a reflection of the largely pessimistic assumptions and attitudes of the Catholicism he had known as a boy.

Starting with Rodolphe's biographical note, most of Maistre's biographers have portrayed him as having been an unwavering Catholic from his youth. Robert Triomphe, however, has challenged this view and argued that Maistre must have gone through a stage of adolescent rebellion against the traditional Catholicism of his family and his milieu.[75] Mining Maistre's works for his views on impiety, guilt, remorse, education, and conversion, Triomph built a circumstantial case for an antireligious crisis (occurring at about the time he left for the University of Turin), followed by a sudden "conversion" in Turin. According to Triomphe, only this hypothesis can explain the doctrine and the character of the adult writer. Two recent scholars have rejected Triomphe's hypothesis,[76] while another, Jean-Louis Darcel, acknowledges the possibility that the young Maistre may have experienced adolescent doubts, but believes that these were soon resolved with a Pascalian "wager" on faith.[77] Triomphe's interpretation, which appears to be built on a rather tendentious reading of scattered remarks in works Maistre wrote many years later, seems less well-founded than Darcel's, which is based on entries from Maistre's notebooks dating from the years in question.

These notebooks, which Maistre began keeping at about the time he entered university, provide invaluable evidence for tracing his religious and intellectual development. Since the notebooks are a primary source of great importance which will be cited frequently in this study, it seems appropriate at this point to interrupt the narrative to provide a brief description of these documents.[78]

The Maistre family archives contain seven bound volumes of Joseph de Maistre's "*registres de lectures*" (also referred to by Maistre and scholars who have consulted them as "*recueils*" or "*cahiers*"). Maistre himself, in the person of the "Count" of the his *Soirées de Saint-Pétersbourg,* described these notebooks in a famous passage that suggests their importance for the biographer. Near the beginning of the "ninth dialogue" the Count calls to the attention of his friends the "immense volumes" lying on his desk and tells them:

There is where, for more than thirty years, I have written all the most striking things I have encountered in my reading. Sometimes I limit myself to simple references; other times I transcribe essential passages word for word; often I accompany these with notes, and often too I put down my thoughts of the moment – those *sudden illuminations* that would remain fruitless if their light was not captured by writing. Carried by the revolutionary whirlwind to various countries of Europe, I have never abandoned these notebooks; and so you must believe me when I tell you of my great pleasure in paging through this great collection. Every passage awakens in me a multitude of interesting ideas and melancholy memories a thousand times more agreeable than what are usually called *pleasures*. I see there pages dated Geneva, Rome, Venice, Lausanne.[79]

These notebooks are an immense collection, totaling more than 5,000 pages, of extracts, commentaries, unedited notes, and essays. There are references to more than 760 works, with citations in eight different languages (French, Latin, Greek, English, Italian, Spanish, Portuguese, and German). His notebooks testify that Maistre was a serious scholar, an *érudit* as the French would say, and no mere propagandist.

Unfortunately, these materials are not as helpful as one might wish for Maistre's early years. Only two of the seven volumes contain entries dating from the period prior to 1793, and none of them contain dated entries for the period from July 1776 to May 1793. Moreover, while much of the material dating from the 1770s can be dated from that era by the handwriting, many of these early entries are not dated precisely. On the other hand, the value and usefulness of the earliest passages are enhanced by Maistre's habit of rereading at later dates and adding dated marginal notes and commentaries on his earlier thoughts.

Returning now to the questions of Joseph de Maistre's early religious development and Triomphe's hypothesis of adolescent rebellion followed by "conversion," let us see what can be learned from his notebooks. It turns out that the two earliest entries that can be dated are both relevant. Both, curiously enough, can be dated by Maistre's later self-critical comments, and both deal with burial customs.

It is impossible to say which of the entries was written first, but the one that occurs first in the notebook in question is headed "tombs" and reads as follows:

Only wicked men or those of common virtue should be buried pell-mell in a church or a cemetery. Every citizen of distinguished virtue should be buried, not in what is called consecrated earth – something useful neither to the dead nor the living – but in his fields or even in a public place if he was a man of extraordinary merit. These tombs would not be loaded with emblems, torches, and ornamental statuary. There would only be a stone elevated a bit above the earth bearing a simple and noble epitaph. One would read, for example, "Here lies a virtuous man who was a friend of his god and his country. His fellow citizens in according him an honourable burial have wanted to eternalize his memory in the hearts of all passers-by! Imitate his virtues and you will have the same reward." We forget our dear dead too soon, says the good and lovable St Francis de Sales: he is certainly correct; we do not understand how respect for the dead influences the morals of a people. It is often asked why love of country is no longer as vital as it once was. I answer that the way in which we bury the dead has contributed to enfeebling it. I do not say that this is the sole cause, that would be absurd. But it is one, and I say that citizens who had in their fields and before their eyes the tombs of their fathers would be more attached to their native country. Listen to a Roman general haranguing his troops on perilous occasions: "Romans! You go to fight for your wives, for your children, for your temples, and for the tombs of your ancestors." Imagine in turn a modern general commencing his harangue thus: "Soldiers, you go to fight for the Church of St Francis, for the Church of St Dominic."[80]

In 1772, Maistre underlined the remark, "what is called consecrated ground —something useful neither to the dead nor the living," and added the following note:

Foolishness [*sottise*] of a young man. When I read this fine article, I see there speculations void of sense – words, phrases, vain ideas, two or three impertinences, and a few gleamings of good sense, for one must be just to the illustrious author. I remember that when I composed this piece (it was, I think, in 1768 or 1769), I was prouder than Pythagoras when he measured the square of the hypotenuse; I came out of my room content with my person, penetrated with esteem for myself. When I saw that I was such a prodigious philosopher, I began to respect myself very much.[81]

Whatever the passage tells about Maistre's religious views at fifteen or sixteen, the commentary shows that at nineteen or twenty he already possessed the sense of irony that would characterize his later works!

The second entry is also interesting from the point of view of Maistre's relationship to his father:

The dead (respect for) – universal among all peoples who have covered the earth since the creation; this is proof perhaps that they all have a vague knowledge of another life, knowledge that they have gotten from the patriarchs when all humankind was only one family on the plains of Sennaar, knowledge that may well have been enfeebled by the passage of time, the revolutions of empires, the fanaticism of priests, etc., but that has never been effaced entirely. Witness initiation mysteries, the hell of Orpheus, etc.

Among the Egyptians respect for the dead still derived from the love they had for their parents. After a son had exhausted in vain all the healing arts to prolong his father's life, after he had to close his eyelids, he embalmed his body, he carefully preserved his cherished vestments. He seemed to want to fight against the death that took from him what he held most dear. Embalming was so to say the last retrenchment of filial love.

Among us we hasten to throw the dead into a hole, and since what does not strike a man's senses makes only a mediocre impression, our parents are as soon forgotten as buried. The ancient practice pleases me greatly; only rascals need be buried, while all bodies that were animated by souls of great virtue should be carefully preserved. The life of a father who was an honest man would be a living lesson for his son. When by some great misfortune my father is taken from me I would hope with all my heart to be permitted like an Egyptian to embalm his body and keep it with me. I would look at it every day with that kind of sorrowful pleasure known only to sensitive souls; I would be nourished by my sadness. But what does it matter? I would learn to wait, I would become more sensitive, more human, more sympathetic to the sorrows of others. I have often thought that affliction which has its source in a virtuous motive inspires virtue in the man so affected. A son, for example, who has just wept at the bedside of his sick father or even beside his corpse will not go out from there and do something bad, on the contrary ... Unfortunate the man who never cries. See tombs.[82]

The entry is followed by this brief dated comment: "I was fifteen or sixteen when I wrote this. It shows it. I dreamt continually then and much more during the day than at night. Nice, 24 September 1772."[83]

Jean-Louis Darcel cites these entries as evidence of a "probable religious crisis appearing towards the end of adolescence," and of "provisional doubting of familial piety and beliefs,"[84] and points out that these passages show young Maistre to be in conflict with traditional Christian custom and belief in two ways. In the first place he ignores or rejects the symbolic meaning of traditional Christian burial customs. In contrast to the practices of antiquity, the Christian custom of burying the dead in the church or in consecrated earth in its shadow symbolized both the community of the living and the dead, and Christian acceptance of death as a prelude to the final resurrection of the body. Second, Joseph's view that traditional burial was good enough for the wicked and those of common virtue but that those of extraordinary virtue should be "eternalized" in memory for the inspiration of the living could have some rather startling implications. Reserving the comforts of religion to common humanity would make of it "a religion deprived of all transcendence, a religion whose most apparent purpose is the conservation of society and the consolation of the unfortunate and the lowly."[85]

Maistre's youthful musings may reflect the changing perception and experience of death that has been traced in eighteenth-century France,[86] but it may be doubted that the fifteen- or sixteen-year-old lad had thought through the implications of his "philosophizing." His appended note of three or four years later ("Foolishness of a young man") suggests that any heterodox impulses in this matter were soon checked and of minimal significance for his later thinking. Nevertheless, these notebook entries reveal a precocious intelligence ready to question and eager to philosophize. One sees too an interesting mixture of acceptance and at least implied rejection of traditional values – respect for the "good and lovable St Francis de Sales" along with the impertinent remarks about "consecrated earth" and the "fanaticism of priests." And the suggestion that universal respect for the dead among all peoples might be proof of "a vague knowledge of another life" (immortality surely) can be read as opposing the apparent neglect of the transcendent in other parts of the entries. In fact this interest in univeral customs and the possibility of citing such customs in support of the truth of revealed religion testifies to a remarkable continuity in Maistre's approach to such questions – later works such as *Du Pape* and *Les Soirées de Saint-Pétersbourg* will employ this strategy again and again. Nevertheless, these two notebook entries, and others that can be dated from the early 1770s, show us a young man whose inherited certainties were being shaken. Nothing in these entries testifies to a "loss of faith," but they indicate that he was reading the philosophes, and experimenting, so to say, with the new secular morality of the Enlightenment.

To illustrate some of these early intellectual adventures, let us look as some other entries for the period through 1772, the year Maistre completed his course at the University of Turin. An entry for 1770, for example, displays his enthusiasm for the elder Mirabeau:

L'Ami de l'homme is one of those rare books that greatly honour the human mind. Posterity will pardon the eighteenth century for *Candide*, *La Pucelle*, *Le Sophia*, etc. in favour of *L'Ami de l'homme*; there is not a line of this work that does not inspire esteem for its author. It is a temple elevated to virtue, you can perceive the intention of the architect even in the smallest detail of ornamentation. [deleted sentence] The illustrious, lovable Mirabeau will be venerated among honest men in all times and all places. [deleted phrase].[87]

Young Maistre's naïveté may be amusing, but it is interesting to note that his admiration for the physiocratic writer was in contrast to his obvious distaste for the author of *Candide*. Hostility towards Voltaire will be another constant in Maistre's intellectual posture.

Joseph's questioning attitude at seventeen is evident in another 1770 entry, this time in his comments on a citation from Cardinal de Polignac's *Anti-Lucretius* (1747). This work, an "interminable didactic poem,"[88] was a refutation of antique "materialism" Maistre would later cite with approval.[89] But in this youthful note, he rails against Polignac's Cartesian *esprit de système*, ridicules his use of the term *esprits vitaux*, and concludes with the ironic remark that "when a man of honour, and especially a Cardinal, certifies something positively, I do not see how one can be right in doubting it."[90]

An entry dated April 1771 provides an interesting example of an "experiment" in the new morality. This entry is in the form of twenty-five propositions and corollaries on the nature of man and human happiness.[91] From the first proposition, which proclaims that "Man is a sensible being," the argument is developed in a straightforward utilitarian fashion. Statement number 12, for example, sounds like something from Bentham: "Man being a sensible being, susceptible to agreeable and painful sensations, the sovereign good for him is to be absolutely exempt from pain and to experience all the agreeable sensations of which he is susceptible." The argument is pushed to an extreme position that would do credit to the Marquis de Sade: "Therefore man, in his quality as a sensible being, must do everything that pleases himself, and abstain from anything that would make him suffer. Therefore he can and he must commit a crime when the crime pleases him and if he does not in committing it expose himself to any unwelcome outcome; and if he did otherwise he would be a fool" (statements 21 and 22). But then the whole argument is made to support traditional belief in immortality and divine justice as a necessary sanction for moral law: "But, if the crime must lead to a terrible and inevitable punishment, he must abstain from it. From which it follows that only belief in immortality gives a sanction to morality, and that any law which presupposes neither pains nor rewards ceases to be a law" (statement 23). The same argument about the necessity of a higher will to enforce obedience to natural law will be found in Maistre's *Essai sur le principe générateur des constitutions politiques*.[92] Another example of continuity?

The tendency to resolve troubling questions with what Darcel has characterized as a Pascalian "wager" on faith is evident in another 1771 entry. Here Maistre begins a reflection on the topic of "the eternity of torments" by acknowledging that the mind is revolted by the idea of "infinite duration." After a rather rambling argument in which it is suggested that "perhaps" eternity and duration are "contradictory ideas," the reflection concludes with these remarks:

I always say *perhaps*, for in this matter and in all others where the senses are not the sole judges, where is the man with enough temerity to think that he has demonstrated his opinion? Would not this be to say to God: that is it and You cannot have done it otherwise? [deleted sentence]...whether there is or whether there is not duration in eternity, all is well since You have made all. I adore you without understanding."[93]

This is not the passage Darcel cites in support of his suggestion of a "wager" on faith, but it certainly provides evidence in support of the idea. Unfortunately, the entry Darcel uses does not carry a precise date, only "Chambéry, 177...," but it is nevertheless worth quoting because we find in it an interesting notion of "intellectual intuition": "A true proposition is not one against which one cannot bring an objection, but one that makes in our heart an impression we cannot prevent, so that we understand that our heart says *yes* when our mind says *no*: even though it seems that our mind has good reasons for saying *no*, and even though it does everything it can to get the heart to say *no*."[94] Maistre will always remain faithful to this notion of the truth of intuition; in the *Soirées*, for example, he will say that "It is one of my favourite ideas that an upright man is often enough alerted, by an interior feeling, to the truth or falsity of certain propositions prior to all examination."[95]

But to return to the specific question of the young Maistre's religious beliefs at about the time he was completing his education, there are two dated notebook entries for 1772 that provide fairly certain evidence of his belief in the uniqueness and validity of the Christian revelation. In the first, dated "Nice, June 1772" (ie, after his graduation from the university but before he began his legal career), Maistre noted that Plutarch and other Greek writers of antiquity had at best only a confused concept of immortality of the soul. The entry concluded rather dramatically: "A dense veil robbed the world of its vision of divinity, and man, who knew not God, could not know himself. All of a sudden, twelve Jewish fishermen appeared; they ordered the veil to fall, and man saw God."[96] In the second, also dated "Nice, 1772," Maistre recorded his reaction to Cicero's *De Natura Deorum*. He came to the conclusion that despite the title, Cicero really said no more than that there were gods, and was unable to say anything about their nature. Maistre concluded: "analyze the ideas of all the philsophers of antiquity. I defy you to find more than this: God is an I do not know what."[97] Again, there is the implied uniqueness of revealed religion.

Finally, there is another entry, undated but from the 1770s to judge by the handwriting, that reflects both Maistre's acceptance of the truth of the gospels and the grave outlook of the Catholicism in which he had been raised. Reacting to some of Rousseau's remarks about revelation, Maistre entered the following comments:

Either you believe in Revelation or you do not. If you do not accept it, I would be proud to prove to you that you know nothing of your nature, and I will undertake to overthrow one after another all the truths that you would like to establish. If, on the contrary you accept it, note well that this same religion that teaches you so many consoling things about everything that it is important to know, teaches you at the same time that the weaknesses you allow yourself every day will be punished by eternal tortures. Oh man! How unfortunate you are. If you reject the Gospel you know nothing; if you accept it you learn dreadful truths that will cause you to live in continual apprehension if you still have good sense.[98]

Insisting on the hard truths of religion as he saw them would be a leitmotif in much of Maistre's mature writings.

Questioning, attraction to the writings of at least some of the philosophes, wide-ranging curiosity, a penchant for adventuresome theorizing, and a readiness to fall back on intuition and faith are traits that characterized Maistre's personality his whole life long. Openness and adventuresomeness were more dominant prior to the French Revolution, insistance on the importance of revealed truth after. But to sum up the situation at the point where Maistre had completed his formal education and was about to begin his career, the evidence of the notebooks reveals a basic continuity of development rather than rebellion and conversion.[99]

For twenty years, from 1772 to 1792, Joseph de Maistre followed a legal career that was, outwardly at least, typical for his time, place, and social status. Assuming that his professional experience and the milieu in which he lived and worked were among the influences that shaped the thought of the mature writer, I want to trace his progress in his profession and to situate his experience within the social, economic, and political circumstances of Savoy in the latter decades of the eighteenth century.

After receiving the prerequisite degrees at the University of Turin, and a holiday visiting relatives and improving his Italian in Nice,[100] young Maistre began his legal career in late 1772 as an unpaid assistant in the Bureau de l'Avocat des Pauvres in the Senate of Savoy. The laws of the kingdom required two years of service in this office for all lawyers who aspired to plead before the Senate.[101] With the completion of his two-year stint, Joseph was named Substitut Surnuméraire in the Bureau de l'Avocat Général; in effect, he became an extra assistant (still unpaid) in the public prosecutor's office. Joseph's early career was very much under the aegis of his father. The king's letter of nomination of 17 December 1774 indicated that the appointment was being made because the king was persuaded that Joseph would "try to imitate in everything the good example of his father who has so distinguished himself in the various judicial posts he has filled, and who is presently a President of the Senate."[102] It was only in November 1777, when he was twenty-three years old, that Joseph was awarded a salary of 600 livres per year.[103] A little over two years later, in February 1780, he was named a full-fledged Substitut (deputy public prosecutor). He worked in this position in the public prosecutor's office until the eve of the French Revolution, serving as the Doyen des Substituts from 1785 until 1788 when he was named a Senator. Even at these later stages of his career, the sponsorship of his father appears to have remained important – at least in the eyes of the government in Turin. In January 1787, when he was appointed to replace his father on the Conseil de Réforme des Etudes, the royal letter of nomination referred both to Joseph's "zeal for the public good and his other laudable qualities" and to his father's "very long and distinguished services."[104] Similarly, when he was named Senator in May 1788, the royal letter indicated that the king had conferred the office because he was "persuaded that in following the example of his father the President, who has never ceased to give proofs of his zeal for our service and the public good, he

[Joseph] will continue to acquit himself of his duties with all the diligence and exactitude the service of justice requires."[105]

It has been suggested that Maistre's advancement was notably slow and that perhaps his promotion was held back by his Masonic activities and liberal opinions.[106] There does seem to be some evidence that the police in Turin maintained a secret dossier detailing Maistre's Masonic activities and reformist views.[107] But the fact is that Maistre's promotion was not unduly slow. Advancement in the Senate of Savoy followed a strict seniority; the number of places was limited (there were never more than twenty Senators during this period) and normally vacancies occurred only when incumbents died. For the period from 1766 to 1790, it appears that most *substituts* served over ten years before promotion to Senator, and that the average age on promotion was about forty-five.[108] Joseph de Maistre served only eight years as Substitut and was only thirty-five years old when he attained the rank of Senator. Given these facts, one must conclude that if there were doubts in Turin about Joseph's suitability, they were overridden – perhaps out of deference to his father.

Historians who have examined the archives of the Senate of Savoy for evidence of Maistre's professional activity all agree that he was a competent jurist; even Robert Triomphe, usually a severe critic, concludes that Maistre "must have been a good magistrate."[109] Perhaps it was an accident of history the magistrates of the Chambéry court were called "senators," but the title had a certain appropriateness. Not that the Senate was a representative body in any modern sense, but its activities tended to involve its personnel in almost every aspect of the life of the province. The record of Joseph de Maistre's legal opinions and judgments, as well as his official correspondence with the secretary of state during these years (especially after he became a Senator in 1787), show that his work would have given him an opportunity to acquire an extensive knowledge of the province's legal, fiscal, economic, and social realities. He was involved in all branches of the law – not only civil and criminal law, but constitutional, administrative, and canon law as well. He had to deal with questions involving the relationship of church and state, and he appears to have become something of an expert on fiscal questions, undertaking comparative studies of the French and the local tax systems. As a member of the Conseil de Réforme des Études, he had the opportunity to study public education from an administrative point of view. He was also involved in the administration of a local hospital, and proposed reorganization of its administrative structure.[110] In short, Maistre's work as a magistrate involved him in questions of justice, finance, education, and social welfare.[111] The theorizing of his major works was informed by broad practical knowledge as well as erudition. To appreciate fully what Maistre may have learned as a magistrate, and to follow the evolution of his thinking during this period, it is important to understand the dimensions and contours of Savoy in the latter decades of the eighteenth century.

Joseph de Maistre would one day become a figure of European stature, but the first forty years of his life and career were lived out in the restricted environment of the small provincial city of Chambéry. Although the largest city of the province and its capital, Chambéry had only 10,000 to 12,000 inhabitants at this time. Savoy itself had a population of around 400,000 in 1790, while the population of the entire Kingdom of Piedmont-Sardinia was about four million.[112]

A little larger than the state of Connecticut, the province of Savoy measured about 145 kilometres in its north-south dimension and about ninety-five kilometres in its east-west dimension. Most of the population was concentrated in the valleys and lowlands. Savoy was, in a sense, dominated by geography. The mountainous terrain made local communications difficult, but on the other hand its situation made it a kind of European crossroads. On the major land route between France and Italy, it felt the influences of both. At the same time, the main lowland area (Chambéry included) opened naturally towards Geneva, which constituted an important market for the province's agricultural production. Through Geneva, the outpost of the "Protestant" continent, came the influences of the central European world.

Savoy's political position was also, at least in part, a heritage of its geography. The House of Savoy, which dates from the eleventh century, had made the best of the crossroads position of its duchy. Over the centuries the dynasty had enhanced its power by balancing the Empire against the papacy, Spain against France, and France against Austria. A combination of military prowess and shrewd pursuit of balance of power politics had won the dynasty new lands and titles – culminating with Victor-Amadeus II (1675–1730) who secured the title of King of Sardinia in the aftermath of the War of Spanish Succession. But with their successes, the centre of gravity of their domains had shifted to northern Italy, and by the sixteenth century the capital had been moved from Chambéry to Turin. These developments had inevitably introduced new cross-currents into the life of the old duchy – tensions arising from the minority position of French-speaking Savoyards in the kingdom as well as those imposed by the difficulties of trans-Alpine communications.

Eighteenth-century Savoy was in many ways typical of the European old regime. The distribution of population between the capital and the remainder of the province points to the predominant place of agriculture in its economy. At the beginning of the century, economic, social, and political structures were all dominated by the landed nobility. Nicolas counts 795 noble households (about 3,000 individuals) in 1700.[113] The nobility thus accounted for about 1% of the population. The holdings and residences of the nobility were concentrated in the valleys and lowlands, with more than a quarter having residences in Chambéry itself.[114] The patterns of noble life, privileges, holdings, and revenues in eighteenth-century Savoy were generally similar to those in France, with the exception that the percentage of nobles who saw military service was astonishingly high. In 1700, one out of every two male adult nobles were either presently in service or were veterans.[115] A number of factors contributed to this phenomenon: the militaristic character of the monarchy, the persistence of "chivalric" traditions, the desire to maintain noble status and the associated tax exemptions, financial pressures reflecting the relatively meagre revenues obtained from noble holdings, ambition to advance in the service of the Crown, and fear of losing noble status through derogation. As in France, tradition and legal restrictions limited "business" opportunities for Savoyard nobles to exploitation of the soil and the subsoil – ie, mines, forges, and glassworks were permissible. This left military service, government, and the church as noble career options. The strength of these traditional élite career patterns was reflected in the career choices made by rising bourgeois and recently ennobled families. Of François-Xaiver Maistre's five sons, for example, three went into the army, one the church, and one, Joseph, the law.

The extent and pattern of noble landed wealth varied considerably from one part of Savoy to another, reflecting the province's geography. Geographic constraints were also reflected in the fact that almost half of the appropriated lands of Savoy remained "communal property." In the mountainous areas (where communal grazing lands were extensive), the percentage of common lands ran as high as 72%, but in the plains areas the percentage dropped to as low as 23%.[116] Reflecting this topographic variation, the percentages for lands held directly by the nobility in the early eighteenth century ranged from a low of about 9% in mountainous areas to as high as 32% around Chambéry. For the province as a whole the figure was approximately 20%. Net revenues from noble lands as a percentage of total net revenue from all appropriated lands (as measured by tax officials for purposes of noble exemption from the *taille*) reflected a similar pattern, averaging some 17%, with a high of 24% in Savoy "proper" (the tax district in which Chambéry was located) and dropping to a low of less than 4% in the most mountainous tax district.[117]

These more or less objective measures of the property and income of the nobility, however, do not take into account the prestige accorded to noble status or the advantages noble seigneurs reaped from exploiting various kinds of "feudal" rights and privileges still existing in Savoy at the beginning of the eighteenth century. Despite the fact that in Savoy, as in southern France, the law presumed that land was allodial unless proven otherwise, most appropriated lands were parts of at least one seigneurie and most inhabitants (except a few people in remote mountain areas) were affected by feudal impositions.[118] As in France, these "feudal" impositions involved an amazingly complex variety of annual and "casual" dues, monopolies, rights of supervision and taxation over such things as roads, bridges, markets, and judicial privileges. In Savoy the importance of seigneurial "rights" as a source of income for the landed nobility is known because the government made arrangements for such rights to be bought out. From the consequent "emancipation contracts" (*contrats d'affranchissement*) (1771–92), it has been determined that these revenues had constituted (with great local variation) some 16% to 21% of their "landed" income.[119] Mention of this governmental initiative points to important social and economic changes that were occurring in the course of the century. As magistrates of bourgeois origin, François-Xavier Maistre and his son were very much involved in developments aimed at restricting anachronistic privileges of the old landed nobility for the sake of modernization of the economy.

The still dominant social position of the nobility in Piedmont-Sardinia was apparent in their near monopoly of the highest positions in the army, the royal court, the church, and the high courts (such as the Senate). Diplomatic posts, in particular, were reserved for old noble families. It was assumed that members of such families would have the requisite polish, travel experience, independent income (necessary because such posts could be ruinously expensive), and linguistic skills (French in particular, which gave an advantage to the Savoyards), and that the prestige of an old name and title would ensure effective representation at foreign courts. Joseph de Maistre, as ambassador to St Petersburg, will not fit the traditional pattern. For Savoyard nobles, Turin and service at the royal court was expensive and presented other hazards to established wealth as well – such as the rage for gambling in fashion at the court. For the Maistre family in the period prior to the Revolution, even the temptation was probably beyond their means or ambition. But in his later career, Joseph de Maistre would experience the trials and tribulations of an ambitious and able parvenu trying to establish a place at court for himself and his family.

The church in Savoy was neither as wealthy nor as powerful as its French counterpart. The Savoyard clergy at the beginning of the century included some 2,500 to 3,000 individuals – less than 1% of the population. The church appears to have held only about 5% of the appropriated land of the province, but its revenues included as well a considerable income from seigneurial "rights," the tithe, urban property, and interest on accumulated liquid capital.[120] As in France, the nobility was well represented in the higher ranks of the clergy. For the one diocese for which statistics are available at mid-century, nobles made up 21% of the higher and middle clergy, 5.5% of the lower clergy, and 13.8% of the regular clergy, with an average of 8.9% overall.[121] Savoyard bishops drew only modest revenues compared to some of the princes of the church in France, but nevertheless enjoyed notable prestige. Higher places in the church were avidly sought out, and there were veritable dynasties of noble families in particular bishoprics and cathedral chapters. The relatively high percentage of nobles in certain monasteries and convents indicates that these houses served the social strategy of noble families who used them as places to install younger sons and daughters and thus conserve the family estates by avoiding the higher costs of dowries or placement in other professions. On the other hand, the church remained an avenue of social mobility in an hierarchical society.

In the Kingdom of Piedmont-Sardinia, as in many other "Catholic" kingdoms in the eighteenth century, the church as an institution was under the firm control of the monarchy. The pattern had been established during the reign of Victor-Amadeus II. The concordats of 1726 and 1727 had acknowledged governmental support for religious orthodoxy, but Rome had explicitly or tacitly to accept a number of limitations on earlier pretensions: limitations on ecclesiastical immunities, the practical suppression of the Inquisition, the exclusion of foreign clerics, and royal administration of vacant benefices.[122] This royal "Gallicanism" was seconded in Savoy by the Senate, which had the responsibility of examining all papal bulls, briefs, and mandates to ensure that they contained nothing contrary to the rights of the king, the nation, or the public interest.[123] Joseph de Maistre would become a severe critic of Gallicanism, but he had once been, as he himself acknowledged in a letter to a friend, an accomplice in its workings: "I sat for twenty years in a Gallican Parlement (or Senate) in a Gallican country. *I have known, studied, and executed the liberties of the Gallican Church.*"[124] Maistre's conversion from Gallican to ultramontane principles will constitute an important part of his reaction to the Revolution.

If the nobility and the clergy constituted the traditional élites of Savoyard society, the eighteenth century saw their dominance challenged by bourgeois "notables." Nicolas estimates that at the beginning of the century the "bourgeoisie" (as a more or less ill-defined social class rather than a legal category) would have numbered about 7.5% of the population.[125] Within the general category, distribution among sub-categories reflected the relatively undeveloped state of the province's economy. Nicolas believes that about 25% of those he has identified as belonging to the "bourgeoisie" would have been "men of law" (from notaries through Senators). Merchants would have accounted for less than 10%, doctors and surgeons about 2%. Manufacturers (*fabricants*), "intellectuals," and artists accounted for even smaller percentages. Over half the Savoyard "bourgeoisie," in fact, were proprietors whose income came primarily from rents on their land holdings.[126]

As with the nobility, the pattern of bourgeois land ownership varied considerably from one part of the province to another, but their holdings were most significant in the neighbourhood of urban centres such as Chambéry. Given the lack of legal differentiation between "bourgeois" and peasant ownership, it is difficult for historians to come to an accurate estimate of the land holdings of the non-noble élite, but it appears that in the first decades of the century the non-noble élite of bourgeois "notables" held about the same proportion of land as the nobility – ie, about 20%.[127] Of course the nobles were not proprietors "like the others"; they enjoyed the advantages of all kinds of "feudal" and "seigneurial" rights and privileges. Such privileges were an important source of tension between the landed nobility and the bourgeois notables. The 1771 edict of "emancipation," which provided obligatory procedures for communities to indemnify seigneurs for extinguished seigneurial rights, is clear evidence of a shift towards accommodating the concerns of the more dynamic bourgeoisie at the expense of the traditional landed nobility.

The leading position of members of the legal profession within the pre-Revolutionary Savoyard bourgeoisie hardly needs stressing. Senators of bourgeois origin, such as François-Xavier Maistre, ranked at the very top of the bourgeois élite. Moreover, Maistre's incorporation into the hereditary nobility exemplifies attainment of the traditional ambition of that élite.

Bourgeois dynamism was only one of the forces of change at work in eighteenth-century Savoy, and probably not the most important. Jean Nicolas, whose study provides a comprehensive treatment of the evolution of social and economic relationships in Savoy in this period, stresses the importance of "exterior" factors.[128] He identifies climatic perturbations, war and occupation by foreign military forces, the centralizing and modernizing activities of the monarchy, and exterior cultural influences (in particular, the French Enlightenment) as important forces impinging on Savoyard society. Climatic accidents could be especially devastating in sub-Alpine regions only marginally suitable for agriculture at the best of times. Savoy experienced long periods of occupation by French armies in the years from 1690 to 1696 and from 1703 to 1713, and then by Spanish forces from 1742 to 1748. But Nicolas puts major emphasis on the activities of the monarchy.

The intrusion of the activities of the central government into the life of the province was especially evident during the long reign of Victor-Amadeus II (1675–1730).[129] The immediate stimulus behind his reform activities was the impact of war, especially the exhausting experience of the War of the Spanish Succession in which his kingdom was caught between France and Austria. In the years following the war, from 1717 to 1730, this wily and able monarch embarked on a wide-ranging program of changes inspired, apparently, by the dynastic absolutism of Louis XIV. Stuart Woolf describes the reforms of this period as practical changes designed to strengthen the state for war:

The reforms were intended to eliminate the most evident weaknesses in the administrative and legal structure of the state, to limit the encroachments of privilege, to provide a firm basis for taxation, to stimulate industry and commerce, to assert the sovereign's control over the Church, to break the ecclesiastical monopoly of education, to create a broad administrative class of new men alongside the nobility, to forge a large and efficient diplomatic service and army.[130]

The reforms of Victor-Amadeus II applied, of course, to the entire kingdom, but there were specific measures that particularly affected Savoy and the lives of the Maistre family.

The royal administration was reorganized along French lines; in addition to clearer allocations of responsibility, with the Secretariat of State divided into separate departments for internal affairs, foreign affairs, and war, the central government's effective authority in the provinces was strengthened by the introduction of intendants and by closer supervision of municipal officials. The Royal Constitutions of 1723 (it will be recalled that Joseph's father was involved in the 1770 revision of this legislation), while not innovative in the Enlightenment sense, eliminated contradictions of earlier legislation, "simplifying and occasionally modifying in favour of royal authority the chaotic jurisdictions inherited from the past."[131] Other measures had the effect of disciplining the old landed nobility. In 1720 the royal demesne confiscated fiefs that had been illegally acquired during the periods of regency in the seventeenth century, and two years later resold them at considerable profit to newly ennobled newcomers. The general cadastre finally published in 1731, one of the great projects of the period, provided a new measurement and valuation of the appropriated land of the province and thus laid a sound base for the land tax. Feudal and ecclesiastical exemptions were restricted to properties with proven title to their privileged status.

The administrative bureaucracy was strengthed by the recruitment of new men (such as François-Xavier Maistre) and by educational reforms. The University of Turin was reorganized and given a monopoly of higher education, while provincial colleges, such as the *collège royal* in Chambéry, were removed from clerical control and endowed with scholarships to provide for the training of future civil servants. We have already noted the concordats of 1726 and 1727, which assured the state's authority over the church. The government also created a well-trained diplomatic service and a standing army of 24,000 men, which could be increased to 43,000 in time of war.[132]

It is important to appreciate the absolutist and pre-Enlightenment character of the reforms of this period. Victor-Amadeus II and his son Charles-Emmanuel III (1730–73) were monarchs who were ready to amplify and develop all the possibilities of monarchical institutions while rejecting the least limitations on the exercise of their authority.[133] The monarchy's self-image in some ways remained "feudal." Private property was considered as a revocable delegation from the sovereign's rights of eminent domain. Victor-Amadeus II in his letters of instruction to the governor of Savoy in 1721 insisted on his own "despotic authority."[134] Nor should the monarchy's recruitment of new men of bourgeois origin be thought of as a matter of maintaining an equilibrium between equally influential groups. Rather the monarchy should be seen as crowning a unified and hierarchical noble structure into which bourgeois notables were assimilated one by one as executive agents.[135] Both Nicolas and Woolf emphasize the "Prussian" character of the monarchy and its civil service. As Woolf puts it, Victor-

Amadeus II's reforms "made the sub-Alpine kingdom the most efficiently organized, bureaucratic-militaristic state in Italy, with a genuine tradition of loyalty to the dynasty among the ruling classes."[136]

One must also stress the point that these reforms were carried out in the first decades of the century. These were reforms pushed through by a paternalistic absolutism under the pressures of war and its aftermath, reforms that predated Enlightenment optimism about the possibility of reforming society according to the criteria of the philosophy of reason. Victor-Amadeus II's successor, Charles-Emmanuel III, appears, for the most part, to have been content with perfecting the system his father had created. The 1770 version of the Royal Constitutions, the "reformed" code François-Xavier Maistre helped edit, was condemned by contemporary "enlightened" opinion as retrogressive in the light of Cesare Beccaria's *Dei delitti et delle pene* of 1764.[137] Even the great "emancipation" edict of 1771, which prescribed and enjoined procedures for buying out seigneurial rights and privileges, seems to have aimed primarily at more efficient tax collection and administration.[138] The fate of the religious and educational reforms is also revealing. Once royal control over the church had been established, "heretical" thinkers were forced into exile; once the clerical monopoly of education had been broken, the government itself enforced strict limits on freedom of the new professors.[139] There may even be a sense in which the success of the earlier reforms blocked opportunities for a more "enlightened" reform movement later in the century. In the forefront of Italian states in the 1720s, by the 1750s and 1760s Piedmont-Sardinia appears to have become increasingly isolated from the new ideas circulating elsewhere. As Woolf puts it: "In this highly centralized state, in which nobles and bureaucrats vied with each other in their loyalty to the crown, there were few possibilities for an independent and critical intellectual class to emerge and develop."[140]

Joseph de Maistre's legal career coincided with the reign of Charles-Emmanuel III's successor, Victor-Amadeus III (1773–96). This monarch has been described as a "reactionary, bigoted" king,[141] but in the early years of his reign the direction he would take was not clear. One of his first acts was to heed noble complaints about the "emancipation" edict of 1771 and suspend its implementation, but the "pause" lasted only two years, and the process of "emancipation" continued uninterrupted until the French invasion of 1792.[142] The new monarch subsidized the establishment of a theatre in Chambéry in 1775, and a thermal spa at Aix-les-bains in 1783.[143] It also appears that Victor-Amadeus III was less hostile to Freemasonry than his father had been, and the early years of his reign saw a rapid increase in the number of lodges in Savoy.[144] Joseph de Maistre himself, in his youthful *Eloge de Victor-Amédée III* of 1775, expressed confidence in the new monarch in these words: "Gothic institutions are going to disappear. Victor will lead true philosophy by the hand; he will order it to snuff out all the old formulas; and ignorance, pursued, chased, and insulted all over Europe, will no longer be able to boast that we are its last subjects."[145]

The young magistrate's optimism about the character and possibilities of the new reign would be disappointed. The monarchy continued its efforts to modernize property relationships, but philosophy, especially that of the French Enlightenment, met a decidedly hostile reaction in Piedmont-Sardinia. The absolutist system of Victor Amadeus II, with both its strengths and its weaknesses, remained in place until the Revolution. As summarized by his most recent biographer, this king's heritage continued to guide his successors:

Uncompromising statism exacted a high standard of obedience and self-sacrifice from subjects and officials alike, but it stifled their initiative and discouraged any independence of thought ... These qualities made Piedmont-Sardinia one of the most justly and intelligently governed states in Europe ... But the state's political and intellectual culture remained backward ... By the end of the century, for want of new men and new ideas to revivify the deadening political structure, the state had degenerated into a brittle, formalistic shell that easily succumbed to the shock of revolution.[146]

Joseph de Maistre's early reputation for "liberalism" has to be measured against a stubbornly absolutist regime.

The political and social status of the Maistre family can now be delineated more precisely. Politically, François-Xavier Maistre was always a loyal servant of the monarchy. Socially, he belonged to the class of bourgeois notables recruited to strengthen the royal bureaucracy. Although eventually "co-opted" into the hereditary nobility, he was never a member of the fief-holding landed nobility. Nicolas identifies him as one of the group of administrators and Senators who played a key role in the genesis and execution of the 1771 edict of emancipation.[147] These men had a clear understanding of the necessity of modernizing property relationships; their reports to the king spoke of the need to adapt to changing times and of the benefits of property held without feudal encumbrances.[148]

Joseph de Maistre's legal opinions and judgments as a young jurist in the office of the Public Prosecutor reveal a similar modern point of view. To quote only one example from a number cited by Nicolas, in a case involving a tithe in which the plaintiff's claim rested on a title dating from 1296, Maistre contrasted the past and the present in this way: "in place of the Enlightenment, Order, and Tranquility that reigns today, one must recall the troubles, anarchy, and devastations of the Middle Ages, one must remember the ferocious independence of the nobility, the unlimited influence of the clergy, the nullity of the people, and the ignorance of all parties."[149] We know that in March 1791 Maistre submitted a major report on matters relating to the "emancipation" of fiefs,[150] and we know too that a report on the tithe, which he submitted to the First President of the Senate on 24 July 1791, was later sent on to the Secretary of State for Internal Affairs in Turin.[151] Although we do not know the contents of these reports, there is no reason to doubt Joseph's continued adherence to his father's "modern" views on property.

The Maistre family's economic status within Savoyard society may also be established with considerable confidence. Nicolas has categorized "levels of fortune" for both the nobility and the bourgeoisie in this period, and we have precise information on the salaries earned by both François-Xavier and Joseph.

For the period 1750–92, Nicolas provides the grid shown in Table 1 for the nobility.[152]

For the bourgeoisie in the same period, the information provided by Nicolas produces the grid shown in Table 2.[153]

Nicolas provides information on bourgeois dowries by profession, but does not try to provide averages for the class as a whole. The average dowry for lawyers in Chambéry in the period 1781–91 was 8,613 livres.[154]

We can plot the financial fortunes of the Maistre family against these grids. When François-Xavier was appointed to the Senate of Savoy in 1740, it was with an annual salary of 1,200 livres. This was raised to 2,000 livres in 1749 when he became Avocat Fiscal Général. But from this, he had to pay some 580 livres for the rent and maintenance of his office. In 1761 he benefited from an exceptional gratuity of 3,000 livres, and then in 1762 he was granted an annual pension of 1,000 livres. When he was named Second President in 1764, his salary was increased to 3,000 livres per year, but he had to give up the pension he had been granted in 1762. The appointment as president of the Conseil de Réforme des Etudes in 1768 brought in another 600 livres per year. But President Maistre continued through most of these years to complain to Turin about the insufficiency of his salary, and later in 1768 he was granted a pension of an additional 400 livres. Finally, in 1785, his appointment as Conservateur Général des Apanages brought in another 1,200 livres per year.[155]

As we have already noted, Joseph's first salary as an assistant in the office of the Public Prosecutor in 1777 was 600 livres. It was not until 1786, when he took over his father's position on the Conseil de Réforme des Etudes, that an extra 400 livres per year was added. On promotion to Senator in 1788 his salary was raised to the same 1,200-livre level his father had received in 1740.

Apparently as long as the senior Maistre lived, the two men kept a common purse. In any case, in 1788 Joseph drew up the statement shown in Table 3 of the family's annual revenues.[156]

Table 1
Noble fortunes in Savoy, 1750–92

Elite nobles
  (a) very large fortunes
      patrimony   more than 300,000 livres
      annual revenue   more than 9,000 livres
      dowries   from 30,000 to 200,000 livres

  (b) large fortunes
      patrimony   from 100,000 to 300,000 livres
      annual revenue   from 3,000 to 9,000 livres
      dowries   from 15,000 to 50,000 livres

Average nobles
      patrimony   from 30,000 to 100,000 livres
      annual revenue   from 750–1,000 to 3,000 livres
      dowries   from 7,500 to 30,000 livres

Lesser nobles
      patrimony   less than 30,000 livres
      annual revenue   less than 750–1,000 livres
      dowries   less than 7,500 livres

Table 2
Bourgeois fortunes in Savoy, 1750–92

Wealthy families
      patrimony   from 30,000 to 100,000 livres
      annual revenue   more than 2,000–3,000 livres

Average familes
      patrimony   7,000 to 30,000 livres
      annual revenue   700 to 2,000 livres

Least wealthy families
      patrimony   7,000–8,000 livres
      annual revenue   from 500 to 700 livres

Assuming a return of between 3% and 5%, an income from property and interest of over 5,000 livres per year would imply a "patrimony" of somewhere between 100,000 and 170,000 livres. It is also of interest to note that when Joseph married Françoise-Marguerite de Morand in 1786, the amount of the dowry was 22,000 livres.[157]

Table 3
State of my family's revenues in 1788

1) Revenues on my father's account:	
Appointment as president	3,000 livres
Appointment as Conservateur Général	1,200 livres
Casuel from his position as president	1,200 livres
His pension (on the king's purse)	400 livres
2) Revenues on my account	
My appointment as senator	1,200 livres
My appointment as Réformateur	400 livres
3) Family revenues	
Property, interest, etc.	5,030 livres
	12,430 livres

It seems reasonable to conclude from all this that the Maistre family's financial status on the eve of the French Revolution was at the top of the scale for a rich bourgeois family, and equal to that of an élite noble family with a "large fortune." Since Savoy remained a relatively poor and backward province, the Maistre family fortune was not particularly large by French standards. Moreover, we must recall that François-Xavier had ten children to place and marry, and that Joseph had to assume some of this responsibility on his father's death. Nevertheless, the political, social, and financial position of the Maistre family clearly placed it high among the élite of the province. Given their circumstances, it would have been unusual if its members had not been found among the opponents of revolutionary change.

CHAPTER TWO

Adventures of the Mind

Joseph de Maistre once declared, in the person of the Count of the *Soirées de Saint-Pétersbourg*, that his life had been "a life entirely consecrated to serious studies."[1] He may have been indulging in a bit of hyperbole, but even as a young lawyer he displayed an unusual commitment to broad and serious intellectual pursuits. His life as a magistrate was only one part of his experience during the years from 1772 to 1792. He was also devoting long hours to the acquisition of languages, reading extensively in both classical and contemporary authors, and trying his hand at composition. In addition, he was very involved in Masonic activities in Chambéry and nearby Lyon.

Maistre's success as an author would come relatively late in life – he would be almost forty-four when the work that made his literary reputation appeared in early 1797. But in a sense he had been preparing for that success from the time he returned from the University of Turin in 1772. *Considérations sur la France* was the work of a mature author. It was a deeply felt reaction against the French Revolution, but the dimensions of that reaction cannot be understood without taking into account the author's personal and intellectual development during the preceding twenty years.

Perhaps too we can uncover clues to help us understand Maistre's decision to flee Chambéry ahead of an invading French army on 22 September 1792. It was an unusual decision that made all the difference; he gave up his comfortable life of position, abandoned his property (including most of his beloved library), and began the adventure that would eventually make him a figure of European stature. There were eighteen Senators on the Chambéry court in September 1792. Only three chose not to stay, and two of those who left were of Piedmontese origin.[2] Joseph de Maistre was the only Senator of Savoyard origin to decide to leave, breaking all the personal, family, and professional ties that might have kept him in Chambéry. A symbolic decision perhaps, a decisive break in his life no doubt. Within months of his departure he would begin a new career as a counter-revolutionary propagandist. One would like to understand why he made the break as well as what he brought to the new career.

Maistre's notebooks were cited earlier as evidence of his religious views at about the time he completed his university training. Other notebook entries dating from the 1770s provide invaluable insights into his interests and his thinking during his early professional years. In particular, they provide evidence of a curious, questioning, and at times, "liberal" mind, of the breadth of his interests, of a deep and continuing concern with religious questions, and of his personal character. By using a quantitative approach to the titles of the works cited in these early entries, it is also possible to find something of a pattern in his interests.

Maistre's curiousity about a wide range of subjects is especially apparent in his lifelong infatuation with periodical literature. His notebooks over the years contain hundreds of entries from a wide range of newspapers, reviews, and learned journals. In an early entry (undated but probably in the mid-1770s), he made this avowal:

I love journals: I go there looking for the little truths that can be encountered in them. Ordinarily, works of this kind are done by animals. On the contrary, I would prefer they were done by men of genius and written in a country where liberty of the press has been established. If I had a collection of twenty thousand real journals, printed in London or Amsterdam, I would prefer it infinitely to *L'Esprit des lois*, or any other book of politics that one can imagine.[3]

By 1792, Maistre's library contained 43 volumes of Fréron's *l'Année littéraire*, 230 volumes of the *Journal encyclopédique*, and 180 volumes of the *Mémoires de l'Académie royale des Sciences*.[4] Eventually his notebooks included citations in five languages from over ninety different periodicals.

Facility with languages was a gift that gave Maistre access to a vast amount of literature of all kinds. His native French was of course of the utmost importance in the age of the French Enlightenment. His schooling had given him a solid grounding in Latin; his notes, letters, and works would be strewn with Latin tags and quotations. Next to works in French, works in Latin were most often cited in his notebooks. Maistre also became fluent in Italian. In addition to the three years he spent at the University of Turin, we know he made a special effort to improve his Italian while visiting his relatives in Nice in the fall of 1772.[5] Italian words and phrases also appear in Maistre's correspondence (although all his official correspondence with the Piedmontese government was in French). Evidently Maistre learned to speak Italian reasonably well; later in his life he lived and worked in Turin and Cagliari without difficulty or embarrassment.

There is a remarkable sixteen-page entry in one of Maistre's notebooks in which he described, simply for his own satisfaction apparently, how he taught himself to read English. The entry is dated 11 July 1776 – an appropriate month and year to be learning English! It is tempting to quote extensively from this fascinating document, but the introductory and concluding comments at least deserve to be cited for what they reveal of Maistre's habits of work and mind:

Since I have a natural disposition for learning languages, I am curious to explain to myself what happens in my mind when I translate (without a dictionary, following my custom).

For some time I have had it in mind to learn English, but in the month since the idea came to me, the duties inseparable from my position have so engrossed me that I have only been able to devote fifteen and sometimes only ten or twelve minutes a day to this study – and that only two or three times a week. So that in about a month I have only gone over rapidly and once, in Berry's grammar,[6] the articles, pronouns, nouns, and declensions.

Yesterday, I enjoyed a moment's respite. I profited from it to copy the verb *have* (avoir) and the different meanings of these singular terms: *can, may, will, shall, would*. This did not take me very long, because it is really only the second person that changes; so that I wrote, for example: *I can have; thou cans't have; he, she, we, you, they can have*, and so on for the others.

Besides, by dint of reading books of all kinds, I have encountered here and there some translated English citations, and in comparing the text and the translation I could not fail to guess and retain some words.

I even recall a long time ago having looked at a couple of old English grammars, but since I scarcely got further than the rules of pronunciation and that without really thinking seriously about learning English, I recalled nothing. It could be, however, that some words stuck in my memory without my having the least idea of what they were about.

With these overtures, yesterday I took it in mind to translate. Here now with the greatest exactitude is the way I reasoned. The book I translated had been given to me by one of my friends who told me that it dealt with *bees*. Here is how it was entitled: *A Treatise on the Management of Bees*. I had read in the first pages of my grammar that *a* is the definite article *un*. *Treatise* resembles *traité* a little; moreover a book on a certain subject matter is called a *traité*. Therefore put *traité*.[7]

Maistre then goes on word by word, phrase by phrase, through the first sentence of the book, explaining how he managed to decipher the English and produce a fairly accurate French translation. After some fourteen pages of word-by-word detail, he concludes his self-examination with these comments:

Now I understand the author's idea; and as there are still some words I do not understand, I write between the lines what I imagine to be their most probable meaning. One sees that to translate perfectly it is only up to me to continue my reading to the point where I can figure out the sense of all the words by their context. But this task, which would only be an amusement, would take me too far. It suffices for me to have given an account of my way of proceeding and to have followed with the greatest exactitude all the operations of my mind.

Someone would say, undoubtedly, if they saw all this, that the method is prodigiously long. I agree that it is long on paper, but in the mind it is very short. Reasonings that fill several pages proceed like lightning and occupy the mind for only a second.

It is fairly demonstrated that one can find out the sense of a word perfectly by its context. But here is the problem: *How many words is it necessary to know to be in a position to know all?* I would like to have the time to examine the question.[8]

Intelligence, curiosity, and readiness to philosophize are all evident here; so too is an interest in psychological and epistemological questions. Maistre's facility in reading English improved rapidly after 1776. His notebooks and early writings up to 1792 contain citations from at least a dozen English authors; his reading included great literary figures such as Francis Bacon, Pope, and Swift, historians, and religious controversialists such as William Warburton. Over his lifetime, English works consulted in the original language would constitute nearly 12% of the titles cited in his notebooks.[9]

The notebook entries in the 1770s contain only a few Greek words and phrases, but Maistre's catalogue to his first library lists some twenty works in Greek, and his account books show that in the period from 1788 to 1792 he was purchasing Greek titles.[10] Maistre eventually developed an excellent knowledge of Greek. From 1794 on, Greek quotations become abundant in his notebooks; overall, almost 6% of the titles cited there were read in Greek.[11] Maistre attempted German only later in life, and although he would one day work his way through heavy volumes of philosophy and religious controversy in the language, he was never really comfortable in it. His later notebooks also contain a few citations in Spanish and Portuguese; these languages apparently posed few problems for a reader fluent in Latin, French, and Italian. Maistre's flair for languages was one of the things that broadened his horizons far beyond the conventional interests of a Savoyard lawyer.

Maistre's reading in these years included a considerable amount of history, a discipline bound to broaden his perspectives. His interests embraced ancient, medieval, modern, and ecclesiastical history.[12] That Maistre's reading in history awakened a sense of historical relativism is quite clear in a 1774 notebook entry. After citing Monstrelet's contemporary account of the Hundred Years War at the point where the chronicler attempts to justify the assassination of the Duke d'Orléans by the Duke de Burgundy, Maistre adds this note: "That is how they reasoned in 1400. In four or five centuries, some man amusing himself like me by studying men of all times, will make extracts from the works of our present-day philosophers and he will write at the end: that is how they reasoned in 1770."[13]

He was becoming aware of how difficult it is to achieve an objective understanding of ancient or exotic cultures. Another entry from the same time reads: "It must be confessed that the Chinese owe great obligations to the Jesuits, who tried by all sorts of means to give us a lofty idea of this ignorant, weak, superstitious, and roguish people. But finally scholars protested, and Mr de Pauw among others has just imposed silence on the admirers of the Chinese."[14]

Reading history also led Maistre to question some of the established pieties of his youth. The works of Sarpi, for example, offered new perspectives on the Jesuits. A notebook entry from the 1770s contains these critical reflections:

Paul Sarpi was assuredly a very great man. His letters please me very much. I like him especially in his chapter on the Jesuits and the pretentions of the court of Rome. As to his religion I can only think [deletion] ... One cannot deny that one finds in his letters, and elsewhere, certain barbs that would not have been disavowed at Wittenberg or at Geneva ... I would however be tempted to believe that he was really Catholic, but that the injuries he had received from the court of Rome sometimes drove him beyond the bounds of moderation, and tore from him statements dictated more by anger than by conviction.[15]

Maistre was especially interested in Sarpi's treatise on benefices; in 1774 he made some forty pages of notes on the work, paying particular attention to Sarpi's historical treatment of the gradual extension of papal control over the wealth and offices of the Church in the West. Occasional comments suggest that Maistre was fascinated and appalled by what Sarpi revealed about the abuses of papal authority in the later Middle Ages. On the matter of "reservations" – the practice whereby the papacy "reserved" for itself nominations to benefices all over Europe – Maistre found Sarpi's details "curious" and commented: "The popes played with us for four or five centuries: since then we have taken our revenge, perhaps even with too much animosity."[16] Another note reads:

Excellent ideas on the power of the popes. If the pope has such ample authority, who gave it to him? If he has this authority, why did his predecessors not exercise it for more than a thousand years? How come neither councils, nor the fathers, nor canons, nor older historians said anything about it? Since the popes began to exercise absolute power, the Christian princes have always offered some opposition constraining the popes to moderation – which they undoubtedly would have been unable to do ... if the pontifical authority came from God. (Of course we are not speaking of the spiritual authority that comes from above, and that suffers neither more nor less.)[17]

One senses Maistre's discomfort concerning Sarpi's anti-papal and even anti-ecclesiastical views.[18] A page later, after recording Sarpi's complaint about the extent of ecclesiastical property, Maistre appends this footnote: "See Father Mamachi's book strongly opposing these anti-ecclesiastical opinions [*Del diritto libero della Chiesa de acquistare et possedere Beni, etc.*]."[19] But Maistre's notes on Mamachi's book reveals that he could be critical of that author too; an extract from the latter's book concludes with these ironic comments: It is a pleasure to hear the reasoning of our politicans. They tell us that children never die of hunger provided that they are willing to use their hands, work, live frugally, etc. There is nothing easier for our savants, who are for the most part celibate, than to arrange the world from the depths of their studies. But their reasonings are almost always fine speculations that prove nothing.[20] Maistre's notebooks show that he was usually a critical and even sceptical reader.

Although he may have been sceptical about some of the things he read, he does not appear to have been seriously tempted by scepticism as a philosophical or religious stance. There are, however, early notebook entries that suggest a kind of doubting agnosticism in the face of phenomena that could not be satisfactorily explained by the science of the time. In a 1774 entry, for example, Maistre records an anecdote reported in a work of Hermann Boerhaave about a four-year old child who went into convulsions on hearing the Lord's Prayer. Maistre speculates about the probable reaction of an eighteenth-century philosophe to such a tale, and concludes:

there is, however, as much narrow-mindedness in believing nothing as in believing everything; wisdom consists in doubting. When I see something marvelous, or when some such thing is reported by a scholar who has seen, touched, and examined it, I will do like s'Gravesande, who when he saw the machine of Ossireus, said simply "Here is something beautiful, but I understand nothing of it." Messieurs les philosophes! Cure yourselves of this strange malady of denying everything that goes beyond your petty intelligence: see rather if there is not some way of explaining what you find easier to deny.[21]

On the second page following, after recording another anecdote about a birthmark supposedly caused by the pregnant mother being frightened by a caterpillar, Maistre remarks: "If a woman gives birth to a monster, I would do like Maupertuis: I would rather believe it a crime than a miracle. As to simple birthmarks ... one cannot force the mind to believe what is forever being proposed that is most repulsive to reason."[22]

From an early date, Maistre was particularly suspicious of theories that appeared to "degrade" man by attempting to explain all human behaviour in purely material terms. In another notebook entry from this period, Maistre complained that the system of the "illustrious" Buffon treated love simply as a physiological phenomena. The entry continues: "I cannot believe that. I believe that there is a morality in love and this morality pleases me. If this is an illusion, I prefer the illusion to the contrary hypothesis that appears to me debasing for humanity. All systems tending to degrade man find me obstinately incredulous."[23] Maistre's later "philosophical" works, *Les Soirées de Saint-Pétersbourg* and the *Examen de la philosophie de Bacon*, reveal the same incredulity and present the author's mature arguments against "degrading" materialism.

If the philosohical comments of Maistre's early notebooks are in some ways unexpectedly conservative, his political sentiments could be more "liberal." In 1774, for example, he entered an extrait from the *Gazette de Berne* reporting a speech in the English House of Commons in favour of the Anglo-Americans. Maistre's comment shows his sympathies were with the colonists: "I am only angry that there are to be found in that country people vile enough to want to subjugate these poor Americans."[24] Another story in the same newspaper a few days later reported the opening of a new theatre in Poland; the journalist stressed that there were declared partisans of the theatre among the Polish magnates. After recording the item, Maistre made this entry: "When I read news of this kind, I sense the blood boiling in my veins; I am beside myself. What then! When all of Poland is on fire, when foreign sovereigns are crushing brave republicans without reason and without pity, when the King of Prussia [deletion] is advancing right to the gates of Warsaw, operas are put on in this capital, and Polish magnates are the ones demanding and protecting them!"[25]

One can hardly imagine the post-Revolutionary Maistre so concerned about the fate of brave republicans. On the other hand, Maistre would never abandon his early agreement with physiocratic ideas. We have already noted his approval of Mirabeau's *L'Ami des hommes*. He read Guibert's *Discours sur l'état actuel de la politique et de l'art militaire en Europe* (Geneva 1773) the year it appeared and found it an "excellent piece" fully in agreement with "Mirabeau and all his *brother* economists."[26] Another 1774 entry records his view that Colbert had "ruined France."[27] In the preface of his *Essai sur le principe générateur des constitutions politiques* (1814) Maistre still cites physiocratic free trade doctrines as proven.[28]

The wide range of young Maistre's interests should be apparent from the notebook entries already cited: languages, history, science, philosophy, and contemporary politics are all represented. Poetry should also be added. The extracts in Maistre's notebooks include quite a number of poems in different languages as well as speculations on the origin and nature of poetry. In a very early entry (1772), there is a little six-page essay on these questions.[29] Maistre's penchant for indulging in biting, witty judgments of highly renowned works was also evident at an early date. Noting Chesterfield's admission that he found much of Milton practically unreadable, Maistre entered his own opinion of *Paradise Lost* – to the effect that it was "not one of the least disadvantages of original sin to have produced that poem."[30]

Religious questions seem always to have fascinated Joseph de Maistre. His notebook entries from the early 1770s on suggest a particular interest in the tougher philosophical problems raised by belief in revealed religion. One finds, for example, that when Maistre made extracts from Rousseau's *Profession de foi du Vicaire savoyard* his notes show that he was especially upset by what he saw as the contradictions between Rousseau's admission that there was "something divine" in the Gospels and his simultaneous claim that the same Gospels "were full of things repugnant to reason." Maistre professed to find Rousseau's position absurd:

Do you say you will admit the Gospel truths that appear reasonable to you and reject the others? But you have no more reason to believe one part of the Gospel than another. Is it not the same book, composed by the same persons, revealed, taught, and published in the same way? Is there a single chapter that carries a particular character of authenticity? Show me the rule, the touchstone you use to distinguish the true from the false in a book containing only facts ... I say therefore that it is absolutely impossible that God would have permitted his adorable oracles to be found confused in the same book with impudent lies invented and sustained by scoundrels who called themselves apostles. Therefore either I believe nothing of the Gospel or I believe it all.[31]

Maistre's position with respect to the Gospels may have been all or nothing, but when it came to other Catholic "authorities," from the Church Fathers to contemporary apologists, he was always disposed to question and to argue his own point of view. There is a very early notebook entry (1771), for example, in which he took issue with certain Church Fathers on their views of the spirituality of the soul:

In general it appears to me that the ancients did not have absolutely sane ideas on the spirituality of the soul. Abstractions frightened them. Those who accuse the Holy Fathers of having made the soul material and those who claim to absolve them can equally find passages in their support because the Fathers never explained themselves as clearly as our modern metaphysicians ... The perpetual failing of several of the ancients was to have had a rage for chasing after positive ideas in speaking of the soul. They feared, if I may be permitted the expression, they feared to find themselves with only nothingness ... they did not notice that there is an infinity of possible substances. The soul is one of these substances, and the sole reasonable idea that we can form of it is to be persuaded that we can have no idea of it. I confess that the soul has consciousness of its own existence and that is the sole way in which the mind can be known by the mind in a positive manner. As for its intimate nature, it can have no positive idea until it is quit of its [earthly] shackles. So if someone asks me what the soul is, I reply that it is something that is not matter. All other definitions signify nothing. I do not say that the Fathers had ignored that definition, I only say that they have been accused of it, and I hope with all my heart that the contrary can be proved.

When it is a question of condemning such respectable personages it is necessary to look closely. For myself, I naïvely confess that I am too young and not enough of a scholar to decide a question of this importance. All I have just written is only an assemblage of desultory and unpretentious ideas, and I even hope to be wrong on many points.[32]

As Rebotton remarks, "All Maistre is here, already sure of his truth, peremptory, insolent even ... but, finally, restrained and guarded, despite his outbursts, by his prudence and his fidelity to the Church."[33]

The same awareness of the difficulties inherent in using human language to speak of spiritual realities is evident in some very interesting notebook entries relating to the problem of speaking about God. One entry records Maistre's agreement with his "good friend Charron" on the unknowability of God.[34] Referring to a passage in which Charron had stated, among other things, that "the true knowledge of God is a perfect ignorance of him," and that "to praise him eloquently is to remain silent in astonishment and dread, and in silence to adore him in one's soul," Maistre commented: "His discourse on the knowledge of God is admirable from one end to the other. I was flattered to find there several ideas that have been in my mind for a long time and that I naïvely believed mine ... This is precisely the idea that I had formed of the adoration of God; this is just what I had in mind and I have found no other author who expressed it with so much energy."[35]

Maistre cited Charron's statement that "God, eternity, omnipotence, infinity, these are only words pronounced in the air and nothing more for us," and commented: "That is a little sharp; however it is sure that he is correct, or nearly so."[36] And in comments provoked by reading Rousseau's *Profession de foi du Vicaire savoyard*, there are similar reflections:

Whenever we speak to or of God we must create, so to say, a new language: our speeches must breathe humility and annihilation, they must be simple, denuded of all elaborate ornament. Moreover, our expressions must retain a certain religious terror that one senses better than one can define; and especially we must guard against wanting to be witty, for it is only pride that seeks wit, and foolish pride must be silent when we pray to God or speak of him. The best prayer is to adore in silence, and if we sometimes break this silence, only love, zeal, and veneration have the right to evoke language from us.[37]

Maistre's attitude expressed in these passages could be called a kind of "agnosticism," but only if this is understood as a special kind of "religious agnosticism" of wonder before the mysteries of God. The same attitude may be found in many passages of his *Soirées de Saint-Pétersbourg*. Once again one is struck by continuity in fundamental concerns and approaches between the young magistrate's notebooks and the works of the mature writer.

A quantative approach to the titles cited in Maistre's notebooks provides another way establishing the pattern of his interests. One way to do this is to categorize the titles by subject matter. Insofar as particular subject categories have been utilized to analyze Maistre's library holdings,[38] we have a grid that can be used for this purpose and for looking for possible evolution in the pattern of Maistre's interests over the years. Table 4 shows the schema Jean-Louis Darcel used to classify Maistre's library holdings and provides and general headings and subject-matter content for each heading.

Using this grid to classify the titles cited in Maistre's notebooks for the years from 1768 to about 1780, here are the results one gets: belles-lettres, 33%; arts and sciences, 38%; history, 15%; law, 0%; and theology, 13%.

It is also possible to perceive some development in the pattern of Maistre's interests by putting these subject-matter percentages for the titles in his notebooks in these early years in the context of similar statistics covering his notebooks as a whole, and for subject-matter classifications of his library holdings and book purchases. In Table 5, "A" categorizes notebook titles for the years from 1768 to 1780; "B" represents titles read by Maistre in the period from 1768 to 1792 (information deduced from his notebooks, correspondence, diary, and writings in this period); "C" categorizes titles acquired in the period 1788-92 (from Darcel's study); "D" classifies titles in Maistre's "first library" (from Darcel's study); "E" categorizes titles in the "second library" Maistre put together after fleeing Savoy in 1792 (from Darcel's study); and "F" categorizes all the titles cited in all Maistre's notebooks during his life.[39]

At least two things should be noted about the general pattern that emerges from Table 5. The first is Maistre's apparent disinterest in the law! Except for the titles in his "first library" (D), which included titles inherited from his grandfather (who had also been a magistrate, it will be recalled), this category is practically absent from the table. Maistre would have had to read and use legal books in his professional work, but it is obvious his real intellectual interests lay elsewhere. The second interesting thing about the overall pattern is the relatively equal distribution between "belles-lettres" and "arts and sciences," with "history" and "theology" only a bit behind. One is again impressed by the breadth of Maistre's interests. With respect to changes over time, a comparison of the percentages for his "first library" (D) and for his notebooks as a whole (F) suggests a growing interest in religious questions in his later years – but this was an interest that was clearly present all through his life. To be sure, these are relatively crude ways of measuring our author's interests, but the figures are nevertheless suggestive.

Maistre's notebooks also contain entries that provide clues to his personality and moral character. There are, for example, passages that suggest awareness of his intellectual superiority. In 1774 (when he was twenty-one) he copied an inscription for a fountain as a "model of simplicity"

Table 4

Classification of Library Holdings

Belles-lettres	History
poetry	secular history
oratory	ecclesiastical history
grammar and philogy	geography, travel literature
dictionaries	Law
novels	jurisprudence
miscellaneous literary works	civil law
Arts and sciences	canon law
physics	Theology
mathematics	Sacred Scripture
natural sciences	theology
political economy	patristics
philosophy	religious controversy
metaphysics	

Table 5

Classification of Titles in Maistre's Notebooks and Libraries

Categories				Titles							
	A		B		C		D		E		F	
Theology	13	14%	23	17%	7	12%	71	8%	40	13%	179	24%
Belles-lettres	35	33%	38	28%	15	25%	336	36%	169	55%	183	24%
Arts and sciences	40	38%	53	38%	28	47%	220	24%	48	16%	256	34%
History	16	15%	25	18%	9	15%	194	21%	48	16%	141	19%
Law	0	0%	0	0%	2	4%	121	13%	2	.1%	4	.5%

A = notebook titles for the years 1768 to 1780
B = titles read by Maistre from 1768 to 1792
C = titles acquired by Maistre from 1788 to 1792
D = titles in Maistre's "first library"
E = titles in Maistre's "second library"
F = notebook titles for all of Maistre's life

and added this note: "I doubt there are three persons in Chambéry capable of appreciating this inscription."[40] Again from the same year are these comments provoked by reading Guibert's *Discours sur l'état actuel de la politique et de l'art militaire en Europe*:

I noticed in this work an egoism that did not displease me. This is not a stupid egoism, the property of insolent mediocrity, but the confidence of a genius who senses his powers. The pronoun *one* is only made for fools[41] ... But men made to instruct their fellows must not have false modesty. I love to hear them speak in the first person, and I willingly pardon them for saying like Montesquieu "*Ed io anche son Pittore.*"[42]

Was Joseph de Maistre already dreaming of joining the ranks of those called to instruct their fellow men? A decade later, in a letter to an acquaintance who requested his opinion of Jacques Necker's *De l'administration des finances de la France* (Paris 1784), Maistre defended the "egoism" of the Genevan banker in just about the same terms: "Let heaven send us such egotists often! ... it is at once an injustice and an absurdity to want to condemn a genius to ignoring himself. Pride consists in estimating oneself at more than one is worth, and there is none in rendering justice to oneself interiorly."[43]

It is ironic, since Maistre would make his reputation with his pen, but from an early date he professed a preference for "men of action" over "men of words." Again in 1774, he copied an anonymous poem on cowardice and in his marginal notes made these comments:

I always distrust fine talkers. The truly courageous man does not talk, he acts; he does not amuse himself by making windy speeches, he goes onto the field of battle to kill or be killed. When I hear a man using pompous phrases to exhalt grandeur of soul and courage, I begin to believe he is a coward ... A hand that has never wielded anything but a pen has not the skill to seize a dagger. Never will the tyrant fall to the blows of a scholar.[44]

The mature Maistre will repudiate all attempts to tumble tyrants, but will nevertheless continue to disdain mere scholars. In his *Considérations sur la France*, for example, he will maintain that the "one basic characteristic of true legislators" is that "they are never what are called scholars."[45] The point is reiterated in a footnote on the following page: "Plato, Zeno and Chrysippus made books, but Lycurgus acted."[46] It is true that Joseph de Maistre was never a professional scholar, that he made his living as a magistrate, and then as a diplomat – but it is still the case that he is remembered primarily as a maker of books. His instincts, habits, and interests were in many ways those of the scholar. Tension between his belief in the superiority of the man of action and his passionate involvement with ideas, books, and authorship must have been a source of deep conflict.

The first formal "composition" we have from Maistre's pen is the *Eloge de Victor-Amédée III* that he wrote and published in September 1775 on the occasion of a royal visit to Chambéry by the new king. At this point young Maistre had just begun his career in the Senate of Savoy (he had been appointed an unpaid extra assistant in the Public Prosecutor's Office less than a year previously). We know too that he was at this time Grand Orateur of a local Masonic lodge called the Trois Mortiers.[47] Maistre's Masonic career will be traced in more detail later, but the affiliation is mentioned here because some scholars have suggested a "double reading" of his first publication.[48] In the first reading, Maistre is simply a loyal servant of the king, praising his sovereign in the declamatory style of the time. In the second, he is seen as a spokesman for the "reformist" political ideals popular in Masonic circles. The problem with the second reading is that we really do not know anything about the circumstances surrounding the work's composition and printing. Was young Maistre encouraged and supported by the lodge or his father? Given the cost of printing (which was carried out in Lyon), some such possibility seems likely, but has not been proven. Whatever the circumstances of its composition, the *Eloge de Victor-Amédée III* is of interest today only for what it reveals about Maistre's thinking at this early stage of his career. The style is generally jejune and pompous, although there are flashes that hint at what is to come. The young author knowingly chose a particularly difficult literary genre; the epigraph and the introductory paragraph both spoke of the dangers of flattery, and the text explicitly disclaimed all hopes of material advantages for praising the monarch. Maistre's compliments may strike the modern reader as cloying and exaggerated, but it is hard to know whether to attribute the overblown style to contemporary rhetorical fashion or to a conscious design on Maistre's part to render his political advice to the new monarch more palatable.

There are certainly passages in the piece that suggest Maistre's sympathy for bourgeois ideals and goals. Referring to the most contentious local political issue, the famous "emancipation" edict of 1771, Maistre characterizes it as "a political operation that will annihilate the last vestiges of feudal government in Savoy."[49] While acknowledging the delicacy of the operation and listing the interests and concerns of the parties involved, Maistre's purpose in raising the issue appears to be praise for the consultative procedures the monarchy used in dealing with the question. The paragraph concludes with these lines on the advantages of such exchanges of views: "Is it not from the clash of opinions that the truth is born? With such precautions, if we have the misfortune of not discovering it, man is condemned to encounter it only by chance. God requires sovereigns not to give exclusive confidence to a single man or to just a few. Liars will be silent only when they are convinced the prince will consult everyone."[50]

After recounting how the king has spent three months visiting every part of the province to find out the real needs of his people, Maistre goes on to describe what he believes will be the fruits of this royal concern:

[With respect to the education of youth] we see a revolution we had only dared hope for. The stranger who comes to offer his talents is welcomed, protected, and honoured. Gothic institutions are going to disappear. VICTOR will lead true philosophy by the hand; he will order it to snuff out old formulas; and ignorance, pursued, chased, and insulted all over Europe, will no longer boast that we are its last subjects.

Soon a public library will open ... At the gates of the capital a magnificent road is being opened through the rocks, and our city, previously unapproachable, is becoming a convenient entrepôt for the commerce of Switzerland and Italy. Solid bridges, constructed in several places, reassure the traveller ... The reconstruction of the palace and other public works occupies a crowd of workers, who now find subsistence near their homes.[51]

Maistre's "bourgeois" point of view is also evident in his comments on the government's military policy. After stating that "large armies are a frightful plague for humanity," he suggests that "it is in encouraging the military spirit that VICTOR makes the best of a numerous nobility," and asks: "Would it more be more prudent to dismiss them to their old châteaux where they would pass the time destroying game and tormenting people?"[52] Finally, near the conclusion of the piece, in reflecting on the general situation of a Europe threatened by social conflict and war, Maistre speaks also of the situation in America: "Liberty, insulted in Europe, has taken its flight to another hemisphere; it soars over the ice of Canada and arms the peaceable Pennsylvanian; and from the middle of Philadelphia, it cries out to the English: *why have you outraged me, you who have bragged of being great only through me?* "[53] Whether inspired by Masonry, or simply by youthful enthusiasm, these are passages suggesting a far more liberal Joseph de Maistre than the post-revolutionary apologist of throne and altar.

But these citations should not be read in isolation; other portions of the same work display Maistre's characteristic monarchism and religious concerns. The whole piece, of course, is written from the perspective of a loyal subject of the monarchy. But there is also an explicit avowal of monarchist principles. After describing the progressive reforms he expects from the new regime, Maistre goes on: "Let us ... look to at the administration as a whole, and we will find it has all the perfection of which a monarchy is capable; and statesmen generally agreeing that the monarchical state is the most perfect of all, we have nothing to envy any other people."[54] He praises the Sardinian monarchy for its moderation, but makes clear that moderation does not preclude firmness: "For see how we have known how to assure ourselves against some of the dangerous opinions that are agitating minds in certain states. As soon as error raises its voice, royal authority claps its hand over its mouth. In awaiting God's judgment in the other world, it has to remain silent in this one: and this is a masterpiece of prudence."[55] There are numerous passages that leave no doubt that in Maistre's mind the most dangerous opinions are those that tend to undermine traditional religion.

In praising the king's respect for religion, Maistre stresses its importance for the stability of society and the state. In lines not very different from the position he will take in his mature works, he writes: "How cruel are these dangerous men who have tried to take religion away from us! Tell us, miserable philosophers, when you have annihilated the hope of the good man and the terror of the wicked, what will be put in its place?"[56] As in his later writings, Maistre insists that religion is "still the most powerful of political forces and the true sinew of states; it is under this point of view that it enters into the political regime and needs the protection of monarchs."[57] Maistre praised the king for the way he played the Constantinian role of "external bishop," following a policy "equally removed from the excess of laxity and the excess of severity."[58] In contrast to his later defence of the Inquisition, Maistre here professes indignation that there are countries where extravagance and cruelty are pushed to the point of burning at the stake and bloodletting in the name of God. But the following paragraph makes it clear that he was far from advocating a policy of toleration:

Other countries present a totally opposed and no less condemnable excess. There one can say and write anything with impunity, there all that is most sacred is insulted with the greatest impudence, there the foundations of human society are boldly sapped, for society will be no more than a chamber of horrors if people are persuaded that virtue is only a word. Yet the government closes its eyes, or if it investigates the guilty, it is with a mildness that announces its indifference clearly enough. Here, we know not the assaults of incredulity; in whatever form it presents itself, it is unmasked and punished ... if someone dares insult religion it is a capital crime the sovereign avenges without pity. I am not ignorant of the fact that unbelievers loudly claim *freedom of thought*, but this is a gross misuse of words. Who prevents them from thinking? Never has the Monarch imagined the power to subjugate intelligence; man is essentially free in his thought ... It is discourses, it is writings that VICTOR prohibits, and rightly so. And I dare to entreat him, in the name of his people, to redouble, if it is possible, his untiring vigilance to preserve them from the ravages of scepticism. Our religion is the most beautiful present of heaven to earth, and the maintenance of this religion is the most signal benefit Sovereigns can accord their subjects.[59]

This could hardly be described as a "liberal" position.

There is however, one passage in young Maistre's *Eloge* that may suggest a bit of anticlericalism. This occurs in a paragraph in which the king is advised to maintain a perfect equilibrium between the various orders in the state:

it is necessary that a priest, that a warrior, that a magistrate, etc., bé persuaded that he enjoys the esteem of the master when he fulfils his duties; this is the great secret of administration, to protect all the orders in the state, to protect none to the prejudice of others. If the Monarch abandons the cares of the throne for those of the sanctuary, and if he has the culpable weakness to want to meddle in the functions of Aaron, soon the priests will cede him the censor provided he cedes them the scepter, and this monstrous exchange will shatter the state.[60]

Perhaps it would be misleading to make too much of this passage; despite his later reputation as an apologist of throne and altar, Maistre would never advocate theocracy.

Maistre's *Eloge* was published with the "approbation" of the Abbé Panisset, the professor of rhetoric and prefect of studies of the royal college in Chambéry. Father Panisset certified that he had found nothing in the piece "contrary to faith, morals, or the truth."[61] Maistre presented copies of his little work to close friends,[62] but it seems to have had no effect on his fortunes.

Two years later, on 1 December 1777, Maistre had another opportunity to display his literary and oratorical talents when he was invited to deliver the annual "opening discourse" to the Senate of Savoy. This was always a formal and decorative occasion, with the entire company gathered in full regalia in the refectory of the Dominican monastery (the Senate occupied rented quarters in one wing of the old monastery). Young Maistre, now twenty-four years old and garbed in his red robe of office, chose to speak on "virtue." His colleagues apparently felt that his address was a notable success, although it seems banal enough to the modern reader.[63] The vocabulary, literary style, and celebration of "sensibility" all appear to reflect Rousseau's influence. In a passage decrying Stoic "indifference," for example, we find this celebration of nature and tears:

It is a false and atrocious philosophy that teaches us to suppress the movements of nature: all that it has made is good, and since it has given us tears, undoubtedly they do not demean us ... let us be men, and let us not be afraid to be seen as such; unfortunate the insensible being whose eyes have never moistened with tears of sentiment, who has never experienced soft shudders of pity, and who, armouring himself with a ferocious insensibility, puts his glory in not being a man.[64]

But apart from these tributes to contemporary intellectual fashion, the discourse also suggests themes Maistre will make peculiarly his own.

His fascination with the theodicy problem and with the existence of violent conflict both find expression in the discourse. Evoking the problem of evil, he exclaims: "Gentlemen, let us not blaspheme the Being of beings! Let us complain of nothing, since He made all; evil is necessary since it exists."[65] The vocabulary echoes contemporary deism, but the theology remains orthodox. Another passage later in the discourse dramatizes the conflict between virtue and vice: "What is society, gentlemen? A battlefield, a scuffle, where good men on one side and the wicked on the other attack each other, resist each other, clash and overturn each other, where we cannot rest for an instant without giving the advantage to the opposite party."[66]

Maistre's discourse on "virtue" also contains a seemingly Rousseauistic portrayal of the origins of society:

Undoubtedly, gentlemen, all men have duties to fulfil; but these duties differ in the their importance and their extent. Picture for yourselves the birth of society; see these men, around the sacred altars of the country just being born; all voluntarily abdicate a part of their liberty; all consent to allow their particular wills to be curbed under the scepter of the general will; the social hierarchy is taking shape. Each position imposes its duties; but does it not seem to you, gentlemen, that more is demanded of those who must have a more particular influence on the destinies of their fellow men, that a particular oath be required of those who have with trembling been confided with the power to do great evil.[67]

Maistre then goes on to speak of the particular responsibilities of "ministers of the altar" and of magistrates. Now to be sure, the image of a social contract could have been borrowed from Rousseau, but it should be noted that Maistre explicitly repudiates the egalitarian implications of the concept. He assumes that the social hierarchy was born with society itself, and puts his emphasis on the different responsibilities of the various orders in society. Even in his later works, Maistre will remain ready to entertain naturalistic "anthropological" hypotheses about the origins of society. He will simply differ from his more liberal contemporaries on how the "natural history" of man should be read; he will insist that political authority and social hierarchy have been "natural" features of all human societies.

In December 1779, it was the turn of Maistre's close friend, the Chevalier Roze, to give the "opening discourse" to the Senate. These exercises were the terror of the young *substituts*, since it was always difficult to find a suitable topic and to develop it in a way that would honour both the assembly and the orator. In this case, Roze produced a first draft while on his vacation in the country, and then sent it for comment to his friends and *substitut* colleagues, Maistre and Jean-Baptiste Salteur (son of the First President of the Senate). Their reply has survived, and it allows us to catch another glimpse of Maistre's serious commitment to literary and oratorical excellence.[68] Their letters describe how the two friends had sat at the square table in Salteur's study and gone through the draft line by line, Salteur reading it aloud and

Maistre recording their advice. Their comments touched on a multitude of matters, including general structure, imagery, word choice, French usage, and logic, and reveal an acute sensitivity to questions of taste as well as style.

In their comments, Maistre and Salteur also displayed an astute sense of political realities. For example, Roze had celebrated the magistrate's prerogative of defending the public good before the throne in these terms: "The courtisans who surround it [the throne] are vile adulators ... We alone know how to tell the truth to kings." His friends advised him to delete the sentence on the grounds that "this exclusive privilege of telling the truth to kings belongs to us neither in law or in fact."[69] Roze's draft also contained an enthusiastic endorsement of the "emancipation" edict of 1771. He was warned that his remarks would needlessly provoke the nobles who still opposed the legislation:

Why scratch an unhealed wound without reason and make yourself enemies for nothing? If, in a political treatise, you said coldly that the emancipations were useful, you would be right; but in a discourse on the spirit of the magistrature, you would offend the first order of the state, which appears to us neither prudent, or even decent. Complaints are made about the efforts of the nobility to push down the magistrature; do not justify, even in part, their antipathy ... *Offend no one without reason* appears to us to be an incontestable axiom. The great art of an honest man is to know how to walk firmly between weakness and recklessness without leaning to one side or the other. As for us, here is our profession of faith: to fear to displease when justice and truth are demanded is the depth of baseness; to displease from lightheartedness is unpardonable carelessness.[70]

Roze apparently accepted his friends' advice in good part since the discourse he finally delivered before the Senate incorporated nearly all their suggestions.[71]

Maistre's next important composition, his "Mémoire au Duc de Brunswick" of 1782, was entirely devoted to Freemasonry, and cannot be understood apart from his involvement in Masonic activities. Since this Masonic experience was of such significance in the life of our author, this aspect of his story deserves to be treated separately.

THE MASONIC ADVENTURE

For almost twenty years, from 1773 to 1792, Joseph de Maistre's affiliation with Freemasonry was an important part of his life. Moreover, since these Masonic activities led the government in Turin to suspect his political and ideological loyalty, the consequences affected his later career as well. An examination of the nature and extent of Maistre's Masonic adventure should be helpful, not only for an appreciation of the "Mémoire au duc de

Brunswick," but also for an understanding an important dimension of his intellectual and political life.

The first direct evidence we have of Maistre's membership in the Trois Mortiers lodge of Chambéry are portions of a letter dated 13 October 1774, from that lodge to the mother lodge in London.[72] Maistre is identified among the authors of the letter as the lodge's Grand Orateur. (His friend, Jean-Baptiste Salteur, is identified as Deuxième Surveillant.) Since Maistre is found playing a role of some importance in the lodge in October 1774, it may be assumed that he had been initiated sometime after his twentieth birthday in April 1773 (twenty being the minimum age for admission).[73] The letter in question is of interest since it may have been at the origin of some of Maistre's difficulties with the Turin government, but before looking more closely at this particular document, perhaps it would be useful to speculate on his reasons for joining the lodge.

We are reduced to speculation because Maistre himself was particularly reticent on his topic. The closest he ever came to identifying his reasons for involvement is a suggestion that it was the fashionable thing to do; in a 1793 letter he told a friend that he too would have been a Mason at that time if had "lived among us."[74] Undoubtedly this is part of the answer. Many of his colleagues were members, and the lodge was a place to socialize and to meet men of other professions and social origins.[75] But there was probably more to it than this. Jean Rebotton, who has studied the matter most closely, suggests a number of other reasons why Maistre would have been attracted to Freemasonry. He may have been seeking to satisfy his lively curiosity and his taste for new ideas; the lodges were "always receptive to currents of ideas."[76] The presiding officer of the Trois Mortiers lodge at this time was a Dr Joseph Daquin, a pioneer in medical research in Europe and a very cultivated and public spirited individual.[77] Maistre would not have been insensible to such intellectual prestige. Daquin's example and leadership would have given the lodge an image of moderate reformism that would also have been attractive to young Maistre.

Rebotton thinks too that Maistre's religious faith would have pushed him towards Masonry. At first blush, this suggestion might sound a bit bizarre – after all, Maistre was a practising Catholic and popes had twice condemned Freemasonry.[78] Nevertheless, Rebotton may well be right. Papal authority was little heeded in the eighteenth century; in 1773, the very year Maistre became a Mason, Europe's Catholic kings had bullied Pope Clement XVI into suppressing the Jesuits. In Savoy, France, and elsewhere, Catholic clergymen as well as laymen continued to participate in the lodges. On the positive side the Masonic practice of benevolence offered Maistre a modern way of carrying out the Christian duty of charity. As a *pénitent noir* and a *congréganiste* he would have been devoted to "works of mercy." But the old confraternities, it seems, were increasingly felt to be ill suited to the modern mentality.[79] One can understand how "Maistre would have been interested in a philanthropic organization permitting him ... to live in a more modern way the charitable obligations of the believer."[80] Moreover, it seems likely that Maistre was attracted to Freemasonry precisely because he found in it a providential counterforce to incredulity and atheism. The Trois Mortiers lodge had been founded as an offshoot of English Masonry and this variety of Masonry remained "resolutely Christian."[81] That this was Maistre's perception seems clear from his later explanation of his Masonic activities: "It is as surprising as extraordinary that at the moment when scepticism appeared to have extinguished religious verities all over Europe, there should everywhere have arisen societies having no other purpose than the study of religion."[82] The Trois Mortiers lodge was full of practising Catholics, many of them *congréganistes*.[83] It seems, in short, that the lodge was experienced as a complement to the Church, not something opposed to it. So it is understandable that young Maistre, concerned about the century's rising tide of irreligion, solidly loyal to the Church but troubled by the difficult questions posed by contemporary rationalism, should have been lured by a movement offering new approaches to service to humanity and the search for truth.

Whatever Maistre's motives for joining the Trois Mortiers lodge, the 1774 official letter cited above provides substantial evidence of the political ideas he encountered there. The letter in question was a protest against an action taken by the mother lodge in London. To understand what was involved it is necessary to go back to the origins of the Trois Mortiers lodge. In 1739, Jean-François de Bellegarde, Marquis de Marches, received from the Grand Lodge in London patents as Grand Master of Masonry in all the states of the Kingdom of Piedmont-Sardinia, and returned to create the Trois Mortiers lodge in Chambéry – which became, in effect, the mother lodge of the realm. In 1765 this lodge had sponsored the creation of a daughter lodge, La Mystérieuse, in Turin. A few years later the Turin lodge, arguing that it had been abandoned by Chambéry, requested authorization from London to elect a provincial Grand Master. This request had been granted 3 April 1774. The Chambéry lodge, hurt by this infringement of its place of honour, decided to ask London to reverse the decision. The letter of 13 October 1774, which Maistre co-signed as Grand Orateur, implemented this decision.

The Chambéry lodge's arguments, insofar as they can be reconstructed from the surviving fragments of the letter, are interesting from a political point of view. The first argument, which answered the Turin lodge's complaint of neglect, stressed the problems faced by Masons living under an absolutist government:

You who have never heard the thundering voice of an absolute government! You who can, it is said, do everything that is not unjust! Think about a world full of men who have free wills only because no one knows how to enslave them. In London, when the Sovereign raises his arm, you put Magna Carta between you and him; his sceptre is broken on that shield, or if not, it is your own fault.

But elsewhere, as soon as the Master has spoken, all who do not bend the knee are crushed and there are no more remonstrances to make nor distinctions to propose: glory is in obedience and the least contravention becomes dangerous.

Is it a question of convoking an assembly against the king's orders? The Freemason – magistrate, military officer, or priest – will fear to lose his position and his peace; the man who is not protected by his office dreams only of prison and chains, so that lodge meetings are decided on only with difficulty.

Assemblies, become very rare, do not permit much business to be done ... Would it not be unduly harsh ... to require of a society that groans under oppression as much exactitude as from one that enjoys inalterable calm?[84]

The second argument reflects old jealousies between Savoyards and Piedmontese: "Would a sensitive mother force her children to be adopted by a foreigner?"[85] To be deprived of the Grand Mastership, and to be subordinated to La Mystérieuse in Turin, was "a new vassalage added to so many others."[86]

London's decision was not changed. Perhaps the letter never got to its destination, perhaps it was confiscated by the police before it ever left Piedmont-Sardinia.[87] If this is indeed what happened, and if Joseph de Maistre was aware that this was the case, his *Eloge de Victor-Amédée III* of the following year may have been, at least in part, an attempt to clear himself with the government. An interesting possibility, but no more than that unless more documentary evidence is uncovered.

Membership in the Trois Mortiers lodge was only the beginning of Maistre's Masonic adventure. He was soon attracted to a new current of Freemasonry centred in Lyon. In 1774, three Masons from Chambéry (including Dr Daquin) had gone to Lyon and received authorization from the leaders of the "reformed Scottish rite" Masons there to establish a Scottish rite lodge, La Sincérité, in Chambéry. In 1778, Joseph de Maistre and some fifteen of his companions from the Trois Mortiers lodge transferred their allegiance to La Sincérité. But two years before this, in November 1776, Maistre had already gone to Lyon himself, and had been made a Chevalier Bienfaisant de la Cité Sainte of the new rite under the name Josephus a Floribus.[88] This affiliation with Lyon-centred Scottish rite Masonry involved Maistre in an esoteric and "illuminist" variety of Freemasonry quite different from the simple "blue Masonry" of the Trois Mortiers lodge.

Scottish rite "reformed" Masonry of Lyon was largely the creation of one man, Jean-Baptiste Willermoz (1730–1824). A bourgeois cloth merchant, Willermoz had, on his initiation into Masonry in 1750, an intuition that Freemasonry "veiled rare and important truths."[89] He was convinced that God had made a primitive revelation to our first parents, and that these truths about man and his relationship to the spiritual world constituted a deposit of transcendent knowledge transmitted from age to age through a secret élite of initiates. The recovery of this message became his life's goal.[90] He was sure he had found what he sought when, in 1767, he met the mysterious Martinès de Pasqually.[91] Perhaps a converted Jew of Spanish or Portuguese origin, part charlatan, part genuine mystic, Martinès claimed to possess the ultimate Masonic secret of celebrating the true divine cult and of communicating with the next world. To perpetuate his teachings and celebrate these mysteries Martinès had created a very restricted order of Elus Cohen (elected priests) within a couple of provincial Masonic lodges.[92] It was into this order that Willermoz was initiated in 1768 with the elevated rank of Réau-Croix. From this time on he devoted himself to spreading his newly acquired enlightenment within Freemasonry. After a couple of false starts, and the creation of his own lodge, called the Grande Loge de Lyon, Willermoz allied himself in 1774 with the German Stricte Observance Templière (SOT). This branch of Freemasonry claimed uninterrupted filiation with the medieval Templars and an inheritance of hermetical secrets reserved to the highest "Scottish" ranks of the order. Utilizing the SOT for his own purposes, Willermoz managed to become head of the order's Province de Auvergne (of which Lyon was the capital) and then undertook his own "reform" – which meant interpreting the form, ritual, and medieval vocabulary of the SOT in an allegorical sense appropriated from the mystical teachings of Martinès de Pasqually. From this Réforme de Lyon was born the Rite Ecossais Rectifié (RER), which was recognized by the three French directories of the SOT at a "convent of the Gauls" in 1778. The new order had an impressive hierarchy of grades, beginning with the symbolic grades of Apprentice, Companion, and Master, followed by three higher grades of Maître Ecossais de Saint-André, Ecuyer Novice, and Chevalier Bienfaisant de la Cité Sainte (CBCS). These last two grades formed an "interior order." And then above this interior order was a very secret class of Profès and Grands Profès. Other members of the RER, even those who belonged to the "interior order," were not supposed to know of the existence of these two highest grades. From among the Grands Profès, Willermoz chose those who to him seemed "most worthy to enter more deeply into the knowledge of Martinism and the practice of the cohens."[93] These chosen few would receive the full teachings that Willermoz had elaborated from what he had learned from Martinès de Pasqually.[94]

Among the members of the new Sincérité lodge in Chambéry, only Joseph de Maistre and three others belonged to the secret group of Grands Profès having the full confidence of Lyon. In addition to his visit to Lyon in 1776 when he had become a Chevalier Bienfaisant de la Cité Sainte, Maistre appears to have made another visit in 1779 to receive the grade of Grand Profès.[95] We know that one of the four Grands Profès of La Sincérité, Maistre's friend Marc Revoire, was chosen by Willermoz as a secret cohen.[96]

There appears to be no surviving contemporary evidence as to whether or not Maistre himself was ever initiated into this innermost sanctum. The Count of the *Soirées,* however, does make this intriguing comment: "I have had the occasion, more than thirty years ago in a great French city, to satisfy myself that a certain class of these illuminés had secret grades unknown to the initiates admitted to their regular assemblies; that they even had a cult and priests called by the Hebrew name of cohen."[97] Even if Maistre was not a cohen himself, he at least knew of the existence of Willermoz's most secret group.

Maistre became a disciple of Jean-Baptiste Willermoz, but he turned out to be a sceptical and questioning follower. Among the papers surviving in the Maistre family archives are three letters to Joseph de Maistre from Willermoz and his close colleague, Gaspard de Savaron, letters in which the masters attempted to answer the disciple's insistent questions about their teaching.[98] Maistre's letters to the RER leaders in Lyon have not been found, but from their replies it is easy enough to deduce the general nature of his reservations. But to appreciate Maistre's questioning, we must go into Willermoz's secret teachings in a little more detail.

These secret teachings are now known since they have been discovered and published.[99] As set forth in the "Instruction secrète des Grands Profès" delivered to Joseph de Maistre by Gaspard de Savaron some time in the second half of 1779, what Willermoz taught was a kind of theosophy combining "*martinésisme*" and traditional Catholic doctrine. (Willermoz was and remained a practising Catholic all his life.) Briefly, the main outlines of his teachings were as follows.[100] In the beginning there was a realm of pure spirits emanating from God. Then there was a revolt of some who wanted to usurp the divine power. The Creator punished them by imprisoning them in matter. Then man appeared, with an immortal soul and prodigious powers, charged with guarding and redeeming the rebellious angels. But Adam betrayed his mission, going over to the perverse forces he was supposed to contain. He was punished in turn by being imprisoned in a corruptible body and deprived of the beatific vision. As a consequence, having suffered an "intellectual death," man was doomed to all sorts of evils and to perpetuating his miserable existence through his condemned descendants and to expiating his crime until the end of time. But despite his fallen state, characterized by the abnormal alliance in him of a "spiritual being" and a "material animal," man retained the mark of his original grandeur. By right, he disposed of powerful means to approach the state of glory in which Adam, before his fall, contemplated God and participated in the divine wisdom. It was this precious knowledge, enfeebled to be sure, but not completely destroyed, that Adam transmitted to his posterity. Eventually Noah became the trustee of this teaching. But after one of his sons abused the trust and returned to the crimes that had been effaced by the deluge, Wise Men in the following generation decided that in the future this precious knowledge must be entrusted to a small circle of initiates. The "Instruction secrète" traced the various initiations that passed the secret message down through the ages until it was finally lost through human iniquity. Then God revealed Himself again through King David, giving him the mysterious plan of the Temple of Jerusalem. Constructed by his son Solomon, the Temple was an image of man and the universe, which were also temples of the Holy Spirit. Thus, man learned again how to know himself, relearned "his origin, his destination and all the facts that he had unfortunately forgotten."[101] This is why Masonic initiation, which cultivated the symbolism of the Temple, invited the novice to reconquer this wisdom that would lead towards an intimate vision of the spiritual principle of all creation. Remember, the Grand Profès was told, that "the error of primitive man hurled him from the Sanctuary to the Porch and that the sole goal of Initiation is to lead him to reascend from the Porch to the Sanctuary."[102] But the ascent towards the light could never reach fulfilment without the aid of Christ, who has come to perfect the work of reconciling God and man. Christ is the infinitely powerful Repairer who has come to rescue man from his fatal fall and to restore him to his original destiny. Willermoz thus included Christ in his scheme, but only vaguely and briefly. The stress remained on a symbolic interpretation of the role of Masonry in reconstructing the Temple – understood allegorically as "enlightening man on his nature, his origin, and his destiny."[103]

Joseph de Maistre's reaction to these teachings, as reflected in the letters by which the masters responded to his questions, appears to have been that of a respectful but rather sceptical disciple requesting better textual evidence and more details on the logic of the system. What he got by way of reply were exhortations to meditate more deeply on the teachings that had already been transmitted to him. In his lengthly letter of 3 December 1780, Willermoz told Maistre:

I see that you have seen and painted in black everything concerning the interior order and that, distrusting too much the particular purpose of the secret instruction for the Grands Profès, you have only envisioned it as a system displayed for anyone's censure. What has happened to you will happen to all who are admitted too hastily into this class and without having been duly prepared by being made to sense each truth one after another so that the whole strikes them irresistibly by the connection of the parts ... My Dear Brother, as long as you examine these instructions with the mistrust that a simple system naturally inspires, you will not understand them, you will not feel them, and until you feel them all your research will be in vain ... light and wisdom are promised not to scholars who run after science but to those who have the simplicity of children and who make all their science, all their study, consist in conserving and cultivating this simplicity.[104]

Willermoz was less insistent that Maistre accept the supposed historical connection between the medieval Templars and modern Masonry, and even conceded that "if in the end the system of filiation proves dangerous, it would be advisable for our common safety to modify it so that, covering it with a thick veil without absolutely snuffing it out, there is no more danger."[105] If this correspondence shows some differences between Willermoz and Maistre, there is no evidence of any rupture in their relationship.[106] Maistre continued to participate in the Lyon-affiliated La Sincérité lodge; his "Mémoire au Duc de Brunswick" of 1782 provides ample evidence of this continuing link and of his personal adherence to the teachings of Willermoz.

Maistre's memoir was written in response to a general questionnaire circulated to all the provinces of the SOT by its head, Duke Ferdinand of Brunswick.[107] Without going into all the Masonic politics involved, we should note that Brunswick had requested opinions on the following questions:

(1)   Does the Order have its origins in an ancient society, and what was that society?
(2)   Have there really been Unknown Superiors, and who were they?
(3)   What is the true goal of the Order?
(4)   What is the purpose of the restoration of the Order of the Templars?
(5)   In what way should the ceremonial and rite be organized to be as perfect as possible?
(6)   Should the Order occupy itself with secret sciences?[108]

Maistre's lodge made a collective response with which he was associated, but since the circular had solicited individual as well as collective replies, he went ahead and prepared a lengthly personal response as well. As a Grand Profès, but unknown as such to the general membership of his lodge, Maistre had more to say than "could be explained freely in a letter edited with the advice of the whole chapter."[109] His memoir, in fact, went far beyond simple answers to the questions Brunswick had posed; what Maistre offered was a grand vision of what Freemasonry could become. Since the discovery of this hitherto "secret" document, "one can no longer write Maistre's history without keeping in mind the portrait presented by this document."[110]

After an introduction praising the Duke of Brunswick for inviting comments on questions so important for the future of Masonry and humanity, Maistre turns to the question of the origins of Freemasonry. The supposed link with the medieval Templars is contemptuously dismissed. Who cares about their destruction? "Fanaticism created them, avarice destroyed them, that is all."[111] Citing the English historian, Robert Henry, Maistre opts for the view that Freemasonry may have had its origins in the guilds of stonemasons involved in the construction of the great medieval cathedrals.[112] But the question is a matter of "pure curiosity": "Can we not be useful and virtuous without predecessors? We are all united in the name of Religion and humanity; we can answer for the uprightness of our intentions. Let us boldly place the edifice on its foundations; instead of renewing, let us create!"[113]

The post-Revolutionary Maistre will, of course, be much more pessimistic about human capacities for creating viable institutions and much more respectful towards historical origins and precedents.

Brunswick's question about Unknown Superiors is answered with a curt "no," but the question about a possible link to secret societies in antiquity provokes a dazzling display of erudition. Maistre cites a multitude of ancients (both pagan historians such as Plutarch and Herodotus and Church Fathers such as Eusebius and Clement of Alexandria) and moderns (such as Pluche, Cudworth, and Warburton) to demonstrate that the secret cults of pagan antiquity possessed no truths of any value and that it is ridiculous to try to find the origins of Freemasonry in Greek or Egyptian initiations.[114] Instead, Maistre argues, if Masons feel the need for historical roots, they should look to the Judeo-Christian tradition:

Let us prove that we are not *new men*, but let us make ourselves a genealogy that is clear and worthy of us. In short let us attach ourselves to the Gospel and set aside the madness of Memphis. Let us go back to the first centuries of the holy law; let us search eccelesiastical antiquity, let us question the Fathers one after the other; let us bring passages together and confront them, let us prove that we are Christians. Let us go even further. True religion is more than eighteen centuries old.

It was born the day the days were born.[115]

Let us go back to the origin of things, and let us show by an incontestable filiation that our system brings together the primitive deposit and the new gifts of the great repairer.[116]

The notion of a tradition going back to Adam and the reference to Christ as the "great repairer" are easily recognizable as ideas Maistre appropriated from Willermoz.

Maistre also shows himself to be in basic agreement with Willermoz on the question of the general purpose of Freemasonry. Maistre asserts that there are two preliminary propositions no instructed Mason would contest:

(1)   The most scholarly brothers in our Order believe that there are solid reasons for believing that true Masonry is only the *science of man* par excellence, that is to say, knowledge of his origin and destiny …
(2)   Whatever the success of our research on the origins of Freemasonry, we are no less decided about boldly occupying ourselves with these sublime truths … with fixing them, and with propagating them within the order for the happiness of humanity.[117]

So even though Maistre continued to disagree with Willermoz on questions of historical detail, he professed adherence to his mentor's lofty vision of the goals of the order.

In some ways Maistre's detailed prescriptions for the future of Masonry appear to follow the practices Willermoz had worked out for Scottish rite

Masonry in Lyon; in other ways his proposals reveal "an astonishing originality."[118] Maistre retained the scheme of a hierarchy of grades with different activities for each, and with the lower grades viewed as probationary steps. As he put it, "it is necessary to give our society secondary purposes that can occupy men of different characters and put us in a position to judge them."[119] More interesting are Maistre's proposed purposes for three general classes of Masons. The first class would undertake benevolent acts and the study of morals and politics; the second would aim for the reunion of Christian sects and the instruction of governments; and the third would seek the "revelation of revelation" – ie, the "sublime knowledge" that constitutes "knowledge of man" at its highest level.[120] Maistre differs from Willermoz (and much of Masonry of his time) in not suggesting fanciful titles for his levels. While he writes of three "grades," what he appears to have in mind is a plan for three general classes and specific grades within each class. For example, with reference to the first group he writes of the "simple blue grades."[121]

For each of these three general classes of Masons, Maistre had quite definite ideas about entrance requirements and prescribed activities. He criticized existing practices concerning entrance for not being selective enough, arguing that it was better to have stricter admission requirements than to try to discipline or expel bad choices. He also wanted more precise and meaningful criteria of religious belief both for admission and for advancement to higher grades. According to Maistre, candidates who were ready to take their initiation oath were suddenly being presented with a copy of St John's Gospel and being asked if they believed in it. He thought such a demand an "unpardonable imprudence and the response that follows often a crime."[122] For the entering novice, he thought it enough for the candidate to sign the following deistic profession of faith: "I certify on my honour that I firmly believe in the existence of God, the spirituality of the soul, and the punishments and rewards of a future life, without exclusion of the other truths of my religion about which I am not being questioned."[123] Maistre felt that it was necessary to have some assurances about the candidate's religious sentiments, but that in the eighteenth century it was unwise to assume or expect too much. If the applicant doubted one of these dogmas, it was better to heal his wounds than to reject him.

Before spelling out his ideas on the particular duties of each of the three classes he has proposed, Maistre comments on other matters covering all the grades. His response to Brunswick's question about ceremonial and rite probably reflects his experience as a member of the Senate of Savoy, a body that took its rituals very seriously. He stresses the point that "the forms and apparatus of ceremonies strike the wisest men, impressing them, and serving to keep them in order."[124] He also advices retention of the Masonic oath for similar reasons, and disagrees with theologians who had tried to prove the oath illicit. And if the prince disapproves or proscribes the association? Here

Maistre gives an ambiguous response: "That is another question whose solution must be left to the conscience of each brother, according to different circumstances."[125]

Turning to the activities of newly admitted Masons (his first class), Maistre suggests three modifications to current practice: the extension and tightening of bonds of fraternity between members; more active benevolence; and more serious study of morality and politics. In Maistre's view, "any unfortunate or suffering Mason has a formal *right* over the power, talents, and affections of all his brothers."[126] In addition to fraternity within the local lodge, Masons should be able to count on the friendship and assistance of their Masonic brothers in foreign countries; as a practical measure to make this possible, Maistre proposes a "short and enigmatic" letter of recommendation to be carried by all traveling Masons.[127]

Maistre's recommendations for improving Masonic "benevolence" appear to be based on his experience in religious confraternities. He suggests that each lodge establish "a *benevolence committee* particularly charged with informing itself of all the good that can be done and the means for doing it,"[128] and insists that mere almsgiving is not enough. Young members in particular must engage personally in acts of charity: "To send a piece of gold to a suffering family is only an alms; to carry it there yourself is an act of kindness. Moreover, acts of this sort contribute powerfully to our moral perfection. Man is not created to speculate in an armchair; and in doing good one acquires a taste for it."[129]

In recommending the study of morality and politics, Maistre does so in terms that are markedly different from those used in his later speculations. In this memoir he writes: "In politics one should never lose oneself in vain systems, for the metaphysics of this science, and in general everything that is not clear and practical, is only good for amusing schools and cafés."[130] In contrast, in the 1814 preface to his *Essai sur le principe générateur des institutions politiques* Maistre will commend the Germans for having invented the term "metapolitics" to "express the metaphysics of politics, for there is such a thing, and this science deserves profound attention."[131] As we shall see, Maistre will lose confidence in purely human political activity apart from divine action. But in 1781 he sought heightened political consciousness – at least among Masons. He thought that the special goal of novice Masons should be "to obtain for themselves a deeper knowledge of their country, what it possesses and what it lacks, the causes of its distress, and the means of regenerating it."[132]

In Maistre's proposed system, the second class of Masons would have the dual goals of the "instruction of governments" and the reunion of the Christian churches. The first of these objectives was based on the explicit presupposition that princes and those entrusted with their power want to do what is right and are only prevented from doing so by being mistaken. Whether or not this avowal represents Maistre's true sentiments after observing his monarch's tour of Savoy in 1775,[133] the assumption is used to justify a "behind-the-throne" role for Freemasonry: "In those delicate occasions where the passions so often divert the most clear-sighted equity, a society devoted by its most sacred motives to ensuring the triumph of the truth can render the most essential services, either by indirectly transmitting it to the agents of authority, or by entering into correspondence with them if they happen to be members of the order as can easily happen."[134]

Maistre would not have these activities of his second class of Masons limited by state boundaries. He realizes that this proposal might be subject to abuse (and consequently appear alarming to authority) and so suggests three safeguards: no Mason could be elevated to this class before his thirtieth birthday, nor have a deliberative voice before his thirty-fifth; every Mason admitted to this class must swear solemnly never to refuse the advice of his Masonic brothers no matter what his office – but always with the understanding that he remain the judge of what to do with this advice since "he is a citizen and public man before being a Mason"; and the society must never accord its protection to a member's ambition or become involved in cabals.[135]

Maistre also thinks that it would be appropriate for one Mason or even the order to recommend the appointment of other Masons to Masons in positions of power, but again cautions that this practice would have to be used soberly.

It is hard to assess Maistre's motives and seriousness in proposing such explicitly political activities for this class of Masons. At least one commentator, Robert Triomphe, has portrayed this part of Maistre's scheme as the heart of the whole memoir – what was really involved was his ambition to play an important role in government. In this interpretation Maistre is seen as too intelligent to be duped by all the mystical nonsense of people like Willermoz, but ready to use international Freemasonry's unprecedented promise of political renovation as a ladder for his own extravagant ambition.[136] However, if one is to judge by the relative lack of emphasis given to this part of the memoir (both in terms of length and intensity of literary style), this interpretation appears strained. Maistre may have been intelligent, able, and ambitious, but there seems no good reason to believe that his interests and goals at this time were primarily political.

The reunion of the different Christian sects, the second objective of the second class of Masons in Maistre's scheme, appears to have been a cause that was particularly close to his heart. It was certainly a more original proposal. Political reformism was common enough in eighteenth-century Masonry, but the notion of using the fraternal ties of Masonry for ecumenical purposes seems to have been Maistre's own. Willermoz, for example, appears to have been indifferent to this issue.[137] But the most eloquent pages in Maistre's entire memoir are those in which he advocates the cause of Christian unity as a goal for Freemasonry.

Maistre's argument for Masonic involvement in the ecumenical cause is based on need; eighteenth-century scepticism and indifference are threatening all Christians:

It is high time, my lord, to efface the shame of Europe and the human mind. What is the use of possessing a divine religion since we have torn *the seamless robe*, and Christ's adorers divided by the holy law are carried to excesses that would make Asia blush? Mohammedanism knows only two sects; Christianity has thirty of them; and, as if we were destined to dishonour ourselves in turn by opposite excesses, after slaughtering each other over dogmas, we have fallen, in everything concerning religion, into a stupid indifference we call *tolerance*. Humankind is debased, earth has divorced heaven. Our supposed wise men, ridiculously proud of some childish discoveries, write learnedly about fixed air, volatize the diamond, teach plants how long they must last, swoon over a tiny petrifaction or the proboscis of an insect, etc.; but they take care not to condescend to asking themselves once in their lives what they are and what is their place in the universe ... Carried away be a fanaticism a thousand times more criminal than that against which they never cease to decry, they strike indifferently at truth and error, knowing no other way of attacking superstition than by scepticism.[138]

In this state of things, Maistre proposes "the advancement of Christianity" as one of the goals of Masonry. The project would have two parts, "for it would be necessary for each communion to work on itself and to work at approaching the others."[139] The time, he suggests, is peculiarly favourable, since "the poisoned systems of our century have at least produced the one good result that minds, more or less indifferent to the controversy, can come together without colliding."[140]

Maistre acknowledges that politics (since every state has an established religion) and theological pride are formidable obstacles that make fruitful public discussion of reunion unlikely. So what he proposes are "committees of correspondence made up especially of the priests of the different communions that we will organize and initiate."[141] With Masons working quietly behind the scene, modern Christians will suddenly be surprised to find themselves reunited. Since Masons of this second class will be working for the advancement of religion, the profession of religious faith required for admission must be more rigorous than for the first: no Mason should be admitted to this group "without having openly confessed the divinity of Christ and the truth of the revelation that follows from this."[142] Whatever the practicality of Maistre's proposal, it should be noted that ecumenism was a cause he would continue to champion later in his life.

The third class of Masons in Maistre's scheme would have as their goal "transcendent Christianity." They would have "as the object of their studies and their most profound reflections, factual research and metaphysical knowledge."[143] More particularly, Maistre argued that these studies would furnish new motives for the credibility of Christianity, "searching proofs of our doctrine in the very nature of things."[144] In this part of the memoir, in contrast to the first section where he had ridiculed Masonic allegories and types supposedly pointing to more remote or exotic origins of the order, Maistre now calls for research into the "sacred allegories" of the religious writings of antiquity. "All is mystery in the two testaments, and the elect of the one law and the other are only true initiates."[145] Both ancient and modern writers (including English Protestant divines) are cited to show the absurdities that can arise from literal interpretations of Scripture.

Opinions about Maistre's intentions in this part of the memoir are quite divided. According to Dermenghem, these passages show that Maistre "saw in the esoteric sciences a means to explain, to justify, or to deepen the dogmas of the Catholic religion."[146] Triomphe doubts whether Maistre believed this "mystical childishness." In his view, "Maistre very certainly hoped that there would be the greatest possible number of *mystics* lost in the clouds so that a small number of *politicians* could direct the destinies of society to their own taste."[147] Triomphe claims that it was only later, in Lausanne and St Petersburg, that Maistre's interest in mysticism deepened and became more sincere. This interpretation has a certain plausibility, but given all we now know (especially from his notebooks) about Maistre's early and continuing concern with religious matters, it remains unpersuasive.

In the next section of his memoir, Maistre offers recommendations for the internal governance of the order. Reviewing the possibilities, he dismisses the absolutism of one man on the grounds that contemporary Masons would reject it. Many Masons, he acknowledges, lean towards democratic forms. But since democracy can only work in small states and since the Masonic order embraces vast distances and a diversity of languages, cults, and usages, this form would be impracticable. Maistre concludes that to avoid "the dangers of tyranny and those of anarchy, it would appear wholly suitable to opt for a government of a single person modified by other powers."[148] The government of the Catholic Church, in fact, is what Maistre recommends as the most appropriate model for Freemasonry: "If one wanted an excellent model of a regime of this kind, one would find it in the authority the pope exercises over the Catholic churches; one cannot believe that it would be possible to imagine anything better. Of course, one speaks only of countries where this power is kept within just bounds, such as France, Austria recently, and the country where this is written."[149] Although this passage provides evidence that Maistre held Gallican views in 1781, it would probably be a mistake to exaggerate the contrast with his later ultramontanism.[150] As Rebotton has pointed out, Maistre's Gallicanism, like that of the Senate of Savoy, was of a generally moderate character.[151]

Maistre's other recommendations are of lesser interest, but include a suggestion for a permanent Masonic headquarters in Germany and for a code of Masonic regulations to be edited in French, "the language of the world."[152] Maistre's elitist proclivities are evident in his advice not to lower admission fees or annual membership dues.[153] The memoir concludes with an interesting note on "a most delicate moral question," the Masonic oath of secrecy. Citing Pope Benedict xiv's anti-Masonic bull of 1751, Maistre puts the question this way: "can we lawfully swear *to hide something, even to the civil power that interrogates us in court?*"[154] While Maistre acknowledges that the pope has "attacked the place by its weak side,"[155] he nevertheless advances "natural law" arguments in favour of the licitness of the oath of secrecy. He argues that natural law is anterior to civil law and that secrets are a part of natural law since trust is the very basis of human society. Moreover, since Masons are in conscience sure that the Masonic secret contains nothing contrary to religion or country, it pertains only to natural law, and consequently Masons are no more obliged to reveal its secrets than they would be to reveal the secrets of their friends. The passage is significant because this was one of the few times Maistre ever used a natural law argument.[156]

In summary, the "Mémoire au duc de Brunswick" is a remarkable document, characteristically Maistrian in both content and style. Twenty-nine years old, Joseph de Maistre offers a comprehensive plan for the future of Freemasonry. The order could become a transforming power in society, "an intermediary institution between church and state, palliating the insufficiencies of the one and the other, aiding the one and the other without substituting itself for them."[157] It was a hardy project aiming at creation of a more harmonious world, a utopia not unworthy of the eighteenth century. Rebotton muses: "In reading this text written seven years before the Revolution, one can perhaps dream of the good that would have been permitted, the evils that would have been avoided, if Maistre had been heard and followed."[158]

But Maistre's text remained practically unknown. It is not even sure that it was transmitted to the Duke of Brunswick. Maistre sent the memoir to Gaspard de Savaron in Lyon with the expectation that Savaron, who had been named to represent their "province" at a planned meeting at Wilhelmsbad in Germany, would bring it to Brunswick's attention. Savaron acknowledged receipt of Maistre's "interesting work," but hinted that it was too late and that Brunswick would probably lack the leisure to read it.[159] Given the many ways in which Maistre's proposal departed from the teachings and practice of Willermoz, it is entirely possible that Savaron simply silenced the Savoyard upstart by neglecting to forward the document.[160]

Although 1782 was probably the high point of Maistre's enthusiasm for Masonry and of his involvement in the world of the lodges, we have no direct evidence of disillusionment following the lack of response to his memoir. The Wilhelmsbad meeting, which Brunswick had called in the hope of regenerating the divided Stricte Observance Templière, failed in its purpose.[161] Maistre later dismissed the meeting as useless.[162] There is no record of further correspondence between Maistre and the RER leaders in Lyon, but this is not surprising because in 1783 the Sincérité lodge in Chambéry agreed to transfer its affiliation from the Lyon-centred "province of Auvergne" to the Turin-centred "province of Italy."[163] Maistre continued to participate in the activities of this lodge until 1791, when its meetings were suspended (at the king's request). Government suspicion of Masonry intensified with the coming of the Revolution, and Maistre later had to try to explain away his affiliation. But there is no doubt about his continuing interest and involvement in the years between 1782 and 1791.

We know too that Maistre continued to be attracted by the mystical currents of thought he had encountered in Lyon. In particular, he remained enthusiastic about the writings of Louis-Claude de Saint-Martin. A disciple of Martinès de Pasqually (who had left Europe for the West Indies in 1772), Saint-Martin was also known as the "unknown philosopher." His first book, *Des Erreurs ou de la vérité* (1775), had condemned the philosophes for undermining religious faith. In his next important work, *Tableau naturel des rapports qui existent entre Dieu, l'homme et l'univers* (1782), he had proposed to hasten the coming of the reign of Christ by meditation on the Bible. His *L'Homme de désir* (1790) maintained the view that it was man's desire and that of God to achieve mystical unity. Maistre had all three of these books in his library,[164] cited the second in his "Mémoire au duc de Brunswick,"[165] and defended the third against his sister's scepticism. In the very year that *L'Homme de désir* appeared, we find him writing to her in these terms: "So you say this prophet appears to you as sometimes sublime, sometimes heretical, sometimes absurd. The first point suffers no difficulty. I formally deny the second and promise to support his orthodoxy on all major points … On the third I have nothing to say to you, or, if you wish, I will tell you that it is very certain that with a rule of three one cannot make an angel, or even an oyster."[166] Maistre's fascination with Saint-Martin survived the revolutionary upheaval. He read Saint-Martin's *L'Homme nouveau* (1792) in February 1793,[167] and in November 1797 spent "38 hours and 13 minutes" copying in his own hand three anonymous pieces by the same author.[168] He would continue to defend Saint-Martin in his works and in his correspondence; in the *Soirées de Saint-Pétersbourg* Saint-Martin is characterized as "the best-instructed, the wisest, and the most elegant of modern theosophists."[169] We know too that Maistre was personally acquainted with the man. In 1793 he told a friend that "Mr de Saint-Martin is a French gentleman 35 or 40 years old, of very gentle manners, and infinitely likable. I know him."[170] Many years later, he described meeting Saint-Martin (apparently in about 1787):

I once happened to spend an entire day with the famous Saint-Martin, who passed through Savoy on his way to Italy. Someone having asked him *what he thought of me*, he replied: *This is excellent soil, but it has not yet received the first cut of the spade.* I did not know then that anyone had *ploughed* me; but I was no less enchanted to know how these Gentlemen *ploughed*. Moreover ... although I was only *fallow*, still the good Saint-Martin had the kindness to remember me and to sent me compliments from afar.[171]

Triomphe thinks Saint-Martin's comment proves Maistre a sceptic at the time of their interview,[172] but this seems far-fetched. Saint-Martin may have been a bit put out by Maistre's questioning attitude or by his characteristic irony, yet there seems no reason to doubt Maistre's real sympathy and admiration for the "unknown philosopher."

There is one last curious bit of evidence concerning Maistre's involvement in esoteric activities during these years. In February 1787, a renowned scholar and Freemason named Friedrich Münter passed through Chambéry and recorded the event in his diary.[173] Münter described how he was taken to meet "a certain Count Maistre, an assistant of the Senate, a young man and well-informed, who has devoted himself particularly to the philosophy of language."[174] They apparently spent two evenings together. Münter writes: "We recognized each other as brothers, ate together at an inn, and talked of Masonry and other things." The second evening was spent at Maistre's home where "since we were among brothers, most of the conversation was about Masonry."[175] The following morning Münter was present when Maistre "magnetized" a friend who suffered from gout. This is the only evidence we have that Maistre was interested in magnetism, but there is no reason to doubt its veracity. Magnetism was fashionable at the time and we know that one of Maistre's friends, Dr Sebastien Giraud, also a high ranking Mason, was a great advocate of the practice.[176]

In a dossier labeled *Illuminés* in the Maistre family archives there is a note in Joseph de Maistre's hand dated 10 December 1816, in which he summed up his experience in the world of mystical Masonry: "I once consecrated a good deal of my time to getting to know these gentlemen. I frequented their assemblies, I went to Lyon to see them at first hand; I maintained a certain correspondence with some of their principal personages. But I remained in the Catholic, apostolic, and Roman Church; not however without having acquired many ideas from which I have profited."[177] In retrospect, of course, it is easy to say that traditional Catholicism and Freemasonry embodied two quite divergent cultures – yet Joseph de Maistre lived in both simultaneously and with no great sense of tension. Perhaps his hopes of enriching the one by the other were quixotic, but reflection on his experience can also deepen our appreciation of the complexities of both "cultures" in the eighteenth century.

To the Eve of Upheaval

Between 1782, the high point of his Masonic adventure, and 1792, when the French invasion launched him on a dramatic new adventure, Joseph de Maistre continued the life of a cultured provincial magistrate. Promotion to Senator in 1788 signalled success in his professional career, but did not satisfy his ambition. Apart from his profession and Masonry, these years saw Maistre enjoying the company of close friends, holidays at their country estates, and long tramps to his vineyard properties in nearby villages. His social life included dances, plays, and dinner parties; social skills were honed that would enable him to succeed charmingly in the sophisticated salons of Lausanne and St Petersburg. This is the decade in which Maistre married and became a father. Time also brought inheritances, and the responsibilities and rewards of proprietorship. Books retained their fascination; with bequests and purchases Maistre was building one of best private libraries in Savoy. Nor was he satisfied with reading what others had written; authorship was an increasingly tempting possibility. Maistre's intellectual horizons had long since expanded beyond provincial Chambéry; the approach of the revolutionary crisis now riveted his attention on France.

From the summer of 1789 to the fall of 1792, events in France and their repercussions in Savoy became more and more the dominant topic of Maistre's meditation, conversation, and correspondence. When the Revolution exploded into Savoy with the French invasion in September 1792, his immediate decision to leave reflected an already well thought-out opposition to all it stood for. In tracing the personal, social, and intellectual dimensions of his life through the decade from 1782 to 1792, I will be trying to elucidate the origins and nature of that hostility. The first section of this chapter will highlight the personal and social aspects of Maistre's life through 1792, and try to delineate his political and intellectual position on the eve of the French Revolution. The question of how his attitudes and ideas evolved from 1789 to 1792 in response to the Revolution will be taken up in the second section.

THE SAVOYARD GENTLEMAN

Chambéry may have been a relatively small provincial centre, but it was not that remote from the fads and fashions of the larger world. In 1784 the fashion was hot-air balloons. The previous June the Montgolfier brothers had flown the first successful hot-air balloon at Annonay in France. In the following months imitators in France and elsewhere began to experiment with the new device. Among the enthusiasts was Joseph's brother, Xavier de Maistre – now an army cadet stationed with his regiment in Chambéry. Beginning in January 1784, he and some other young gentlemen began organizing a project to launch Savoy's first balloon. Joseph was sent to Geneva to consult Benedict de Saussure, a celebrated physicist, on the technical details, and was also drafted to write a "Prospectus" to enlist subscribers to finance the project.[1] A first attempt on the 22nd of April failed, but on the 6th of May, Xavier and Louis Brun, the technical organizer of the ascent, went aloft for about twenty-five minutes. The launch was witnessed by a large crowd, and after their success the young heros were feted at a gala dinner hosted by President Maistre and Mme Brun, which was followed by a ball. A few days later Xavier's description of "Chambéry's aerostatic experiment" appeared from the press of the local printer.[2] Perhaps it was no more than a high-spirited escapade by bored young gentlemen, but for Xavier it presaged a writing career that would include descriptions of other adventures, and in 1805 in St Petersburg, an appointment as director of the scientific department of the admirality (an establishment with a library, a museum, and a physics laboratory).

Chambéry's cultural life included a theatre (initiated with royal sponsorship in 1775) and Joseph de Maistre appears to have been a regular patron. His correspondence includes a letter written in 1786 assessing at length the talent (or rather general lack of talent) of a visiting French actress; he found "her reputation prodigiously exaggerated, like everything that comes from France."[3] In the same letter Maistre describes another social affair, an "English day," which was a subscription event beginning at noon and ending at four o'clock the following morning. Tea, coffee, chocolate, parlour games, and a concert were followed by a lavish banquet and a ball. As one of the subscribers who hosted the fete, he professed to be scandalized by the cost, but his evident enthusiasm in telling about the event suggests that he had enjoyed himself immensely. Maistre also liked to hunt and fish on the estates of his friends and relatives.[4] We know too that he belonged to a "noble club," Le Casin de Chambéry, which had been founded in 1784.[5] But perhaps what he enjoyed most of all, besides his beloved books, were long conversations with his friends.

Friends were always very important to Joseph de Maistre. Throughout his life he displayed a remarkable capacity for forming deep and lasting friendships with men and women of quite diverse views. In these pre-revolutionary years there were three men with whom he was particularly close. Two of them, Gaspard Roze and Jean-Baptiste Salteur, we have already met as fellow Substituts on the Senate of Savoy. Like Joseph de Maistre, both of these men were Freemasons and sons of Senators. The third, by Maistre's own account his most intimate life-long friend, was the Marquis Henry Costa de Beauregard.

The Chevalier Roze belonged to an old non-noble robe family from Saint-Genix, a small town on the Rhone some thirty kilometres west of Chambéry. He has been described as a generous and sensitive young man, rather infatuated with the ideas of justice, liberty, and humanity, yet independent and shrewd in his observations. With Maistre and Salteur, he was part of a liberal group of young magistrates "sincerely and steadfastly attached to the religion of their fathers, to the principles of order and authority, but aspiring to reconcile classes by a more equitable distribution of the advantages and favours of power."[6] A loyal servant of the Crown, he remained cold to royal pomp and circumstance. As a magistrate, he demonstrated inflexible integrity. An accomplished and elegantly attired figure in society, he was known for a wit that was sharp but devoid of any maliciousness. Joseph de Maistre often visited Roze at the family's large comfortable home in Saint-Genix. Roze was named a Senator in April 1789, a few months after Maistre. He stayed in Savoy through the French occupation, returned to the magistrature in 1816, and became a president of the Senate of Savoy in 1821. There is no evidence of any correspondence between Maistre and Roze during the years from 1792 through 1815, but contact was renewed after the Restoration.[7]

Viscount Jean-Baptiste Salteur was the only son of Count Jacques-Philibert Salteur, First President of the Senate and a colleague and friend of Joseph de Maistre's father. Like Roze, young Salteur was an elegant figure with a reputation as a brilliant conversationalist. He had his father's grand air and could appear cold. But when Maistre and Roze chided him with being at the North Pole when they were at the Equator, he replied: "If it were possible to realize all the dreams nurtured in my imagination you would both see that nature has not given me a cold heart. But it is sure that to be happy, one must neither be a slave to one's heart nor enchain its liberty."[8] One of the most literary of the young magistrates, Salteur had made a special study of French legislation and its history. His correspondence with Roze on this topic reveals his hostility to absolutism.[9] He had begun his career in the Senate as a Substitut a few months after Joseph de Maistre, but was promoted to Senator in May 1785, three years before Maistre. One can assume that his father's status and influence assisted his career.

The Salteur residence was just across the Place de Lans from President Maistre's residence in Chambéry, and Jean-Baptiste had a large study with windows overlooking the square. There the two young magistrates would sit opposite each other at Salteur's large square table, discussing a vast range of topics, with recourse as appropriate to the family's notable library.[10] There is good reason to believe that the opinions expressed by Maistre's friend in these discussions were more liberal than his own. In 1790, the conservative new First President of the Senate, in a confidential letter to the minister of internal affairs in Turin, described Salteur as a good jurist, but "full of bad philosophers and of everything presently coming from the French presses ... [and] ordinarily in the society of cultivated men of letters of the third estate."[11]

Salteur, like Roze, elected to remain in Chambéry in 1792. Under the Consulate, the electoral council of the Department of Mont-Blanc named him as a candidate for the French Senate, and he was later decorated with the Legion of Honour by Napoleon. Salteur died in October 1812.[12] In Salteur's case, Maistre remained in correspondence with his old friend and colleague during these years of separation.[13] He appears to have been closer to Salteur than to Roze. After Salteur's death, Maistre wrote to his other intimate friend, Henry Costa: "I have had two friends in my life (that is a prodigious number), the good Salteur and you. Although not your equal in elevation of mind or in depth of feelings, he was, however, an excellent man who I will never cease to regret."[14]

Unlike the other two, Henry Costa was not a magistrate but an officer in the topographic section of the army. A descendant of a distinguished noble family, Costa had been raised at the Château de Villard, about twenty-four kilometres northwest of Chambéry, but later established his family at the Château de Beauregard on the shores of Lake Geneva in the part of Savoy that lies directly across the lake from Lausanne. His father, Marquis Alexis-Barthélemy Costa, had been an enthusiastic physiocrat, who in 1773 had published an essay on the amelioration of agriculture and had experimented with innovative practices on his own estates.[15] Costa's sister was married to Baron Claude-François de Morand and it seems likely that Maistre and Henry met at the Morands' since the Baron was a brother of Maistre's future wife.[16]

Maistre and Costa were almost exactly the same age, but Costa had married in 1777, almost a decade before his friend, and Maistre greatly enjoyed the company of the young couple and their children when he joined them at the Château de Beauregard during the Senate's annual autumn holiday. We catch a glimpse of these happy times in a letter from Maistre to Costa in December 1789, written at a time when the thoughts of both were becoming preoccupied with French politics. In the course of a long narration of news from France, Maistre breaks off to evoke happier memories:

It is pleasant to come down from the region of storms to that of peace. My imagination, continually a fellow citizen of your amiable household, brings me back there a thousand times a day. Sometimes, while I spend long and sad evenings looking for the just and the unjust through the shrubbery of chicanery, I dream of those patriarchical evenings, so well and so agreeably employed ... It is then that my thoughts visit you and ask a place around the large green table ... I will faithfully remember those October days, passed so agreeably, when we said so many nothings, so many things, always in an agreeable way.[17]

Years later, Maistre would still recall Beauregard with great affection: "It was there that I passed days of my life that were so full, so happy; it was there that I composed in 1784 the *senatorial* discourse of which I still possess a copy ... followed by your animadversions, very carefully bound at the end of the work ... Good God, what persons! What evenings! What conversations.[18]

His relations with the Costas would be particularly close during the years from 1793 to 1797, since they too took refuge in Switzerland. In 1794, the death of their oldest son, Eugène, from wounds suffered serving as a soldier against the French, inspired Maistre to write his "Discours à Mme la Marquise de Costa," in which one finds for the first time the distinctive providential interpretation of the Revolution that will be elaborated in his later works.

In the happy years before the Revolution disrupted their lives, Henry Costa was an even more liberal spirit that Roze or Salteur. Of an artistic temperament, he had painted in his youth and even visited Greuze in Paris in 1767, showing the celebrated French painter his youthful efforts and meeting Diderot at the artist's studio.[19] Costa's wife was French, from Grenoble, and he remained fascinated by things French. As the crisis developed in France in 1789, Costa continued to hope for the best long after Maistre had become disillusioned with the prospects for constructive reform. But this is to get ahead of our story.

Maistre's three closest friends in these years had a number of things in common. They came from wealthier families than his own. Men of high intelligence and broad interests, they shared his delight in good conversation. All three appear to have been more open to the Enlightenment and more optimistic about the possibilities for reform than Maistre himself. One can only speculate on their influence on his thinking. But if there were disagreements among them, the exchanges still would have stimulated Maistre to think through his own positions more clearly. And quite apart from substance, Salteur and Costa were knowledgable critics who encouraged and supported Maistre's literary efforts.

After his 1782 memoir on Freemasonry (which of course remained unknown), Maistre's next significant piece of writing (in addition to correspondence and legal opinions written in the course of his work) was the "opening discourse" of 1784. His topic this time, "the exterior character of the magistrate or the means of obtaining public confidence,"[20] was in some ways little more than the development of the theme of his 1777 discourse on "virtue." In the first, he had argued that "not only are we obliged to be virtuous, we must also appear to be so."[21] The point of the second was that "if our first duty is to be just, our second is to appear so."[22] Despite the commonplace topic, the discourse provides interesting evidence of Maistre's literary style as well as of his thinking.

The discourse was written at the Château de Beauregard, and as we have seen, Maistre cherished the manuscript and Henry Costa's comments on it. His friend's judgment remains pertinent today:

Your work, my dear friend, appears to me full of profound thoughts, good and useful to bring to the light of day, and developed with warmth and nobility. The subject is well chosen, well presented. The style, especially, is in my opinion superior to anything else of yours that I have read. It is habitually forceful, picturesque and simple at the same time. And this is true eloquence – one sees clearly that you have sometimes fought against an imagination that is difficult to discipline ... If you make some use of the notes I am sending you and if, as a consequence, you find them appropriate, I will be proud to be in agreement with you. I will tell you then that there are some superfluous epithets and some recherché turns of phrase that appear to me from time to time to take away from the forceful gravity of your style and produce an unevenness that would be easy to efface ... There are likewise some passages that appear to me to lack clarity and even exactness.[23]

The freedom and tenor of Costa's comments suggest how helpful he must have been to Maistre in his efforts to achieve an effective literary style.

At the head of his discourse Maistre placed the following epigraph (in English) from the *Essays* of Francis Bacon: "Do not only bind thy own hands, or thy servants' hands from taking but bind the hands of suitors also from offering: for integrity USED doth the one, but integrity PROFESSED and with manifest detestation of bribery doth the other."[24] With Bacon, Maistre spoke of the "dignity of the magistrate, of the imposing character that certifies the virtues of the public man and captivates universal confidence."[25] This theme, developed at length in this discourse, provides an important clue for understanding a distinction Maistre would always make between public pronouncement and private conversation or correspondence. Ever since some of Maistre's correspondence was first published in the mid-nineteenth century, commentators have been struck by the apparent dichotomy between the intransigence of his published works and the openness and liberality of his private correspondence. This discourse provides evidence that the apparent discrepancy stems, at least in part, from Maistre's conviction that public personages, and magistrates in particular, have a special responsibility to be prudent in public discourse.

Public men generally, Maistre argues here, have a responsibility to uphold moral values: "We are rightly expected to have more fixed and more severe moral principles than other men: if we, in our discourse, do not know how to respect everything that deserves respect, we make ourselves suspect to those who imitate us."[26] Private doubts that might endanger public morality must be rigorously repressed: "Let us watch over ourselves with an indefatigable severity! The *man* will say nothing that the *magistrate* could repent."[27]

Evidence that this stance was a well thought-out and deeply held belief on Maistre's part can be found in his later correspondence. In 1793, for example, still before any of his major works were written, he acknowledged to a friend that he felt obliged to utilize a distinctive style for public consumption:

You have seen that when I have spoken in public, I have always taken a tone of approbation and confidence; in my opinion this is a duty and I have never violated it. Let us stick to this if you have faith in me; but as to private communications, let us beware those trenchant systems that make us regard as lepers those who have the misfortune not to think as we do.[28]

Similar acknowledgments can be found in other private letters.

But to return to the discourse on the "exterior character" of the magistrate, there is another interesting passage combining this theme of the necessity of maintaining public confidence in authority with the concept of sovereign political authority:

It will always be necessary that there be in the judicial order as in the political order a power that judges and is not judged. This power (which will always be somewhere) resides in you, gentlemen. Alone, by yourselves, you *study the law*; together on the Court, you *discuss the law*; but to the eyes of the world, *you are the law*. So, gentlemen, you owe it to yourselves never to forget your rights: the Oracle does not dispute, it pronounces. And if you see a member of the high Court casting his opinions before the critic and descending to contest them, the astonished eye seeking the Magistrate will see only a jurist.[29]

These notions about the nature and responsibilities of political authority will find much more extensive development in Maistre's later works.

There is one last passage on this same theme from this 1784 piece that deserves to be cited for what it reveals about Maistre's attitude towards the Enlightenment:

These principles, gentlemen, which are for all time, acquire a particular importance in the century in which we live; this century, which has done and prepared so many great things by bad means, has distinguished itself from all ages by a destructive spirit that spares nothing – it has attacked all, shaken all, and the havoc will extend to boundaries we do not yet perceive.[30]

In these circumstances, Maistre avers, "the wise man, truly worthy of the name and ashamed to take his opinions from fashion, knows the point where he must abandon his contemporaries."[31] Just where and to what extent Maistre had "abandoned his contemporaries" in the mid-1780s is not clear from this discourse, but other evidence from the time suggests that he continued to share more contemporary assumptions than he would later have cared to admit.

Evidence for Maistre's general agreement with reformist ideas of the time can be found in a letter he wrote just a few weeks after delivering this discourse to the Senate. A French acquaintance, a Baron de Rubat who was the Lieutenant of the Bailliage of Belley, had requested his opinion on the introduction Jacques Necker had placed at the head of his three volume *De l'administration des finances de la France*.[32] Maistre's long letter of response provides a very interesting glimpse of his general attitude towards the French political situation in 1785.[33] Enthusiasm for Necker, his person, his literary style, and his efforts to reform the finances of the French monarchy characterize the whole letter. Maistre comments on more than a dozen particular points from Necker's introduction, but he returns a number of times to the question of public opinion.

Necker's own views on public opinion, at least as expressed in this piece, were somewhat ambiguous. He recognized that public opinion "reigned" in France in a quite extraordinary new way and seems to have felt that in the long run its "authority" would be salutary. But he also complained that increased public enlightenment rendered the tasks of administration, especially those of finance, "infinitely more difficult and more laborious."[34] Maistre's comment on this complaint is quite unsympathetic:

There is much one could say on this topic, and undoubtedly one can still find among us a great number of men who would make observations about the immense inconveniences of reasoners who agitate men's minds and who often impede the course of administration by taking away public confidence in it. Without entering into a long dissertation on the topic I will only observe that this enlightenment (good or bad) is naturally too disseminated for governments to wipe it out or even to stop its propagation; so, if by chance the reasoners are to be feared (which I do not at all believe), there would be no other remedy than to satisfy them.[35]

On the same theme, commenting on Necker's remark that in France an administrator's course is lit by the light of public opinion, Maistre phrases his agreement in these terms: "In effect, leaders of peoples and their first agents can no longer, in our days, excuse their mistakes with the difficulty of perceiving the truth; one has only one answer for them: *Let them write and read*."[36] And Necker's description of public opinion as a "court of honour" is a characterized as a "superb expression."[37]

Maistre also tells his friend that he had been flattered to find in Necker's introduction "some of my own ideas, and sometimes, so to say, my own expressions."[38] He proceeds to cite his own 1784 Senate discourse to demonstrate their similarity of views on the necessity for public men to uphold the highest moral values and to be prudent in their choice of acquaintances. Maistre praises Necker's ideas on effective administrative techniques, but criticizes him for glossing over the question of government borrowing. (Necker's first term as finance minister, 1777–81, had been characterized by massive borrowing to finance France's involvement in the War of American Independence.) Maistre also notes a passage in Necker's introduction that shows "the author has lost neither the desire nor the hope of re-entering the administration."[39] But despite these minor criticisms, Maistre generally approved Necker's program for the reform of the French monarchy. Maistre's reformist sentiment comes out too in his characterization of Louis XIV as a sultan and of Turgot as an "excellent man" (if too impatient).[40]

And finally, there is Maistre's marvellously suggestive commentary on Necker's dictum never to hurry things in administration:

It is true that great revolutions in internal politics are like dissonances in music in that they must be *prepared* (in the language of the art). Every old institution has thrown out deep roots that ordinarily extend much farther than one thinks, and that must not be uprooted before having cut these long filaments one after the other, and, if possible, quietly, so that when the great blow is struck there is not too much clatter nor too great tears.[41]

Organic analogies abound in Maistre's later works, but there the emphasis is on allowing institutions to grow naturally, like great trees, rather than on strategies for uprooting them! Despite his hostility to some of the destructive manifestations of the Enlightenment, the Savoyard magistrate of 1785 still shared its optimistic hopes for liberal political reform.

Another letter written the same year to a life-long Italian friend, the Marquis de Barol,[42] provides clear evidence that Maistre at this time felt torn between his heavy professional responsibilities and his ambition to write. Since this letter reveals so well Maistre's interests, attitudes, and aspirations on the eve of the Revolution, it seems appropriate to reproduce the entire document:

Chambéry, 24 July 1785

On my return from the country, Monsieur le Marquis, I found your charming letter. Send me this kind of *chatter* often, I beg you; and you can be sure that it will be well received. I will experience a double pleasure in lending you books, Monsieur, if you have the goodness to return them accompanied by your judicious reflections, even though I must pay for this pleasure by the little humiliation of seeing with what perfection you write my language while I stammer in yours. I am struck by your judgment of Count Carli,[43] and from appearances some time will pass before I get involved in giving you mine. For in my position, what one can do is a minimum compared to what one would like to do, and everyday I wake up with a thousand projects. The *mania to write* [*scribomanie*] possesses me; I sense it in my head, and sometimes my heart, inflated; but I can achieve nothing, and, so to say, undertake nothing. In the evening I find that obligations have taken all my time; it is necessary to go to sleep without having been able to follow any of my views. You undoubtedly have a very clear idea of this torment. The need to produce without any possible explosion! Something is going to burst. Can you imagine the fermentation? It is Papin's machine exactly. Sometimes to quiet myself I think (sincerely, on my honour) that these kinds of inspiration that agitate me like a pythoness are only illusions, the puffed-up foolishness of human pride; and that if I had all my liberty it would result, to my shame, in a *ridiculus mus*.[44] Other times I vainly exhort myself as well as I can to reason, modesty, and tranquility: a certain force, a certain indefinable gas lifts me like a balloon, despite myself. I lose myself in the clouds with Monsieur empyrean, I would *do it*: I would – my faith, I do not know too much what I would do. Perhaps, however, circumstances will want me in the end to do one thing. Pulled one way by philosophy and the other by law, I believe *I will escape by the diagonal.* One can try something this way.[45]

This letter could elicit a long commentary. Paillette thought it showed that "Joseph de Maistre knew his vocation before he was able to follow it."[46] Many have made the obvious comment that the French Revolution proved to be Maistre's "diagonal." For the moment perhaps it is enough to note his frustration, torn as he was between learning and his legal career, and his emotional intensity, an intensity that will later animate his published diatribes against the Revolution and the thinkers he blamed for inspiring it.

    Interestingly enough, one finds little evidence of this emotional intensity in his relationship with Françoise-Marguerite de Morand, whom he married in 1786. This may be because practically none of his letters to her have survived,[47] but the few remarks he made about her in letters to others leave the impression of affection rather than passion. A few days before his wedding Maistre wrote to his friend, Henry Costa, to thank him for sending best wishes and congratulations:

Yes, my dear Costa, I have cause to believe this marriage will be happy, and it is true the *preliminary* of which you speak is an inestimable advantage: one man in a million has the happiness to know intimately and to frequent casually, for seven years, the woman he is going to marry.

Monsieur de Morand has given me a great mark of esteem in never opposing the least obstacle to my relations with his daughter: at last I can show him my gratefulness by working for the happiness of my loved one. Moreover, my dear friend, you easily believe that marriage, for a man the least bit wise, like salvation, is worked out *with fear and trembling*. Oh! How many hostages one gives to fortune the day one says yes, if that wicked lady wants to amuse herself by harassing us! But that is not what one must think about now. My plan in my new career is short and simple, it is to help myself to the advantages fortune has given me. I am the first and only attachment of the woman I am marrying; this is a great good that must not be allowed to escape. My occupation at all times will be to imagine all the ways possible to make myself agreeable and necessary to my companion, so as to have always before me a being made happy by me. If something resembles what one can imagine of heaven, it is this.[48]

Robert Triomphe was struck by how this letter appeared to be "dominated by the pronoun of the first person" and he used it as evidence of Maistre's alleged "religious egoism."[49] One not need agree with Triomphe to feel that Maistre's approach to marriage appears rather cool and calculating. A seven-year courtship does seem somewhat dilatory. Perhaps Maistre felt constrained by his modest financial situation,[50] perhaps Françoise was already behaving in the way that later earned her the nickname "Madame Prudence" and was reluctant to commit herself. Whatever the case, it was certainly no whirlwind romance.[51]

Françoise de Morand was the daughter of a retired army officer, Jean-Pierre Morand, Baron de Confignon.[52] Her brother, Claude-François Morand, who was married to Henry Costa's sister, was also an army offier. The Morands had been ennobled in the fourteenth century. Françoise was born 1 November 1759, and so would have been twenty-seven at the time of her marriage – six years younger than Joseph, who would have been thirty-three. The wedding was celebrated 17 September 1786 in the cathedral church of Saint-François de Sales, Chambéry's newest and most elegant church, with Joseph's brother, Abbé André Maistre, officiating. The ceremony has been described as a major social event, with "all Chambéry," including Joseph's eighty-year-old father and two brothers in brilliant army uniforms, in attendance.[53]

Despite a dowry that was promising in the long term, the couple's financial situation was "far from being brilliant." They began their married life in a house "repaired and furnished" with a 3,000 livre loan borrowed by President Maistre from a cousin.[54] But until the French invasion disrupted their lives in

1792, their marriage appears to have been tranquil enough. Joseph's promotion to Senator in 1788, and his inheritance from his father, who died in 1789, would have eased any financial problems. The first two children were born before the invasion: Adèle on 16 June 1787, and Rodolphe on 22 September 1789. But by the time their last child, Constance, was born, 26 January 1793, circumstances would have changed dramatically, as we shall see.

"Madame de Maistre was not, certainly, her husband's equal in intelligence."[55] Nor is there any evidence that she shared his broad intellectual interests. But on the other hand, there is no reason to doubt that it was a solid marriage or to believe that Joseph de Maistre was anything but a loyal and faithful husband. Most references to her in his correspondence are brief and conventional, but there is one letter, written in 1806 while he was in St Petersburg and she was in Turin, in which he drew a delightful picture of the contrast between her and himself. This letter, which is to a Genevan lady the couple had come to know during their years of exile in Switzerland, also testifies to his respect for his wife's maternal abilities:

I am not surprised that you have not been able to learn anything from Madame Prudence (how I laughed at this name!) in Turin. Even if you were there, there is no way you could get her to talk of me, or even to admit that she had received a letter from me. I am, as you may have found out, the *easy-going senator*, and above all, very free in saying what I think. *She*, on the contrary, will never affirm before noon that the sun has risen for fear of committing herself. She knows what must be done or not done on 10 October 1808, at ten o'clock in the morning, to avoid some difficulty that will otherwise occur on the night of 15–16 March 1810 ... She is my supplement, and when I find myself separated from her, as I am now, I suffer absurdly from being obliged to think about my own affairs; I would rather have to chop wood all day. My children should kiss her feet; as for me, I have no talent for education. She has what I regard as the eighth gift of the Holy Spirit: that of a certain loving persecution by which *it is given her* to torment her children from morning to night *to do, to refrain*, and *to learn*, without ceasing to be tenderly loving. How does she do it? I have always watched without understanding it.[56]

There are also conclusions that can be drawn from his one letter to her that has survived in a copy in Maistre's letterbook. This is a long confidential letter, written in early June 1808, in which Maistre describes his situation in St Petersburg and discusses the prospects for their children and their reunion.[57] This letter will be cited later for what it reveals about Maistre's feelings towards his king, but for the moment what should be noted is its testimony to his complete trust in his wife. He writes to her in detail, and without the slightest trace of talking down to her, of all the difficulties of his situation, of their financial situation, and of the possibilities of "placing" their children in the uncertain circumstances of

Napoleonic Europe. The letter is replete with terms of endearment: "my very dear friend," "my dear Françoise," and "my dear friend." After explaining why reunion appears impossible in the forseeable future, he remarks: "I turn this way, I turn that way, and always I see that we are two victims sacrificed to our children." And finally, his closing words: "Farewell, my very dearest [*ma très chère*], here is a lot of words: but I assure myself that my letter will not appear too long to you. I embrace you and I love you with all my heart." Perhaps the Maistre marriage lacked passion, but the relationship displayed great strength in surviving some very difficult circumstances. Late in his life, Maistre wrote of his wife to his editor in Lyon who had just met her: "Under the simplest of exteriors and the most diminutive stature, you will have met a heroine of courage and activity, of forgetfulness of self, of tenderness and piety, who I can never cherish and respect enough."[58] This was a spontaneous tribute, written to a man Maistre himself never had the opportunity to meet.

As for Joseph de Maistre's relationship with his children, all the evidence shows that he was a loving, even doting, father who was always deeply concerned for their welfare. Letters to his sisters when the children were small babble on about their least accomplishments. Letters to his daughters in Turin from St Petersburg are full of humorous but delicate discussions of a wide range of topics, including their education, their reading, and the role of women in the world. Letters to his son Rodolphe, both during the years when Rodolphe was serving in the Russian Imperial Guard and later when they were both back in Italy and it was a question of arranging his marriage, testify to the complete openness and trust of the father towards the son with respect to their political and financial circumstances. Other letters to his brothers, sisters, and close friends show, however, that he was also well aware of the faults and weaknesses of his offspring. But his affection for them was unconditional; one of his major concerns always was to provide them with an adequate patrimony. Whether a "patrician" or "bourgeois" trait, this sense of the importance of building, conserving, and transmitting a family heritage (in terms of both financial and social status) would seem to be one source of Maistre's bitterness against the Revolution that had disrupted his domestic life and confiscated his property.

But to return to the happier years preceding the revolutionary upheaval, it was perhaps his new responsibilites as a husband and father that led Maistre to travel to Turin in the spring of 1788 to solicit promotion to the rank of Senator.[59] King Victor-Amadeus III, now aged, was surrounded by familiar old counsellors, and Maistre apparently had to spend a considerable amount of time making useful visits to his protectors and paying court to the powerful. Waiting for a response to his initiatives, he used his time to work on two "memoirs," one on venality of office and the other on the French Parlements.[60] The first, which contained a tirade against the entrenched gerontocracy, concluded: "Old age learns nothing, corrects nothing, establishes nothing. To grow old is not to grow wise, says Charron."[61] Finally, on 2 May 1788, Maistre was named a Senator, and he forthwith returned to Chambéry.[62]

Achieving the coveted rank of Senator, however, did not satisfy Maistre. Despite the theoretical professions about the dignity of the magistrature found in his discourses to the Senate, there are passing remarks in his correspondence during these years that suggest he found judicial work drudgery – one letter refers to his slavery.[63] There was still the ambition to write, expressed so forcefully in the 1785 letter to the Marquis de Barol. In retrospect, he would recall this period as a time of boredom and frustration. In 1805, in a letter to his brother Nicolas, he evoked rather bitter memories:

I remember those times when, in a small city that you know, my head resting on another dossier and seeing around me only our narrow circle ... of little men and little things, I said to myself: "Am I thus condemned to live and die here like an oyster attached to its rock?" I suffered much then; I had a head burdened, fatigued, *flattened*, by an enormous weight of *nothing*.[64]

We know that in 1791 and 1792 Maistre thought seriously of changing professions. Diary entries for 6 July and 9 July 1791 record letters requesting the post of "intendant general" of Savoy.[65] In early 1792 he requested Henry Costa's support in case the Sardinian ambassador to Geneva, who was reported very ill, should die and his post become vacant.[66] Maistre's ambition for something else or something better should be counted among the factors that influenced his crucial decision in September 1792. He had been thinking of other possibilities, something less restless or less ambitious colleagues would not likely have done.

The death of President Maistre in January 1789 left Joseph with additional responsibilities. He was the oldest son, and his father placed on him the role of becoming head of the family. The pertinent section of President Maistre's will reads as follows:

I appoint as my universal heir Joseph Marie, my very dear eldest son ... and I recommend to him his brothers and sisters, especially the latter. The tender friendship that he has given sincere signs of showing them up to the present and the respectful attachment he has always had for me, make me hope that he will not belie the confidence I have in him and that he will take the place of a father to them after my death.[67]

Joseph took this charge very seriously. Three of his sisters (Anne, Jenny, and Thérèse) were still unmarried at the time of his father's death, and so he acted as the father of the family in making the arrangements for their marriages.

Until 1792 his home remained the family hearth, the place where everyone gathered for holidays and special occasions.[68] We know too, from his diary, that he sent sums of money to his brothers who were serving in the army.[69] And during the years following 1792, he would maintain frequent correspondence with all the members of the family in an effort to ensure their unity.[70]

Joseph de Maistre may have inherited the considerable responsibilities of an extended family, but the patrimony was respectable. In 1788, as we have seen, income from property and investments came to over 5,000 livres per year. Maistre's real estate holdings included his house on the Place Saint-Léger (worth 10,080 livres),[71] two apartments (worth 9,591 livres and 301 livres respectively), rural property at La Trousse (which Maistre sold in 1791 for 59,910 livres),[72] another piece of property at Talissieu in Bugey (in France),[73] vineyards at Arbin and Cruet (worth 8,700 livres), and some vines in the renowned vineyard at Montmeillant.[74] There was also the property that had been part of his wife's dowry – some land at Vernay and a "prairie" near the village of Bissy on the western outskirts of Chambéry.[75] In addition, Maistre had a considerable inventory of silver serving pieces,[76] and an extensive library.

Maistre's papers reveal the meticulous "bourgeois" habits of his paternal grandfather, the Nice cloth merchant. In his diary, for example, the numerous references to the rental or sale of properties, and to the borrowing and lending of various sums, are always precise to the last penny. The entries only begin 6 November 1790, but they are as noteworthy for what they reveal of Maistre's attitudes towards financial matters as for what they tell us about his finances. His abiding concern for building the family patrimony, for example, comes out clearly in entries recording the disposition of a debt he had owed to a Countess de Gilli since February 1785. On 22 February 1792, he proposed cancellation of the 9,000-livre debt for lifetime free rent of an apartment he owned and she occupied. On the 5th of March, after recording her reply, which was simply to cancel the debt without taking up his offer of rent-free accommodation, he made this entry: "My son, you know nothing of this, but you have had a good day."[77] For the period from 1790 to 1792, it is also interesting to observe that these records of loans, debts, and buying and selling, while interspersed with entries noting the increasingly tense political situation, seem to bear no relation to the approaching crisis. On 23 June 1792, for example, just three months before the French invasion, Maistre records inquiring about the possibility of purchasing a piece of land at Carouge.[78] There are also a great many entries recording the purchase, exchange, and lending of books.

Joseph de Maistre had inherited a substantial library from his maternal grandfather, Joseph Demotz, in 1769. He inventoried his library in July 1788 and noted that it contained approximately 1,400 volumes and was worth about 5,200 livres.[79] We do not know how many of these books had come from his grandfather's library and how many he had purchased himself in the years between 1769 and 1788. In August 1791, he inherited an additional bequest of another 1,132 volumes worth 3,680 livres from the Abbé Joseph Victor.[80] In addition, Maistre's account book shows that between July 1788 and 8 June 1792, he purchased some 61 titles (amounting to 156 volumes) at a cost of a bit over 724 livres.[81] Since his salary as a Senator was only 1,200 livres per year, these purchases represent an important sum. Jean-Louis Darcel, who has published the list of these purchases as well as the catalogue Maistre compiled of his library (to 1792) and who has analyzed both with care, concludes that Maistre was "an informed and passionate bibliophile, on the lookout for any occasion – exchange of books, estate sales – that would permit him to enrich his library, occasionally with manuscripts and incunabula, more often with rare or important editions."[82] By the eve of his flight from Savoy in 1792, his catalogue listed 937 titles comprising 2,621 volumes.[83] The total value would have been over 9,000 livres. Jean Nicolas, who reviewed all that is known about private libraries in Savoy in the eighteenth century, ranked Joseph de Maistre as the "holder of the most important collection of those inventoried."[84] According to Darcel, it was one of the two or three largest libraries in the province and worthy of being compared to those of the principal robe families of Lyon, Toulouse, or Bordeaux.[85]

Consideration of the contents of Maistre's library and the pattern of his book purchases in these years also helps us assess his intellectual interests and political position in the shadow of political crisis. We have already cited Darcel's analysis of the subject categories in Maistre's "first library," which shows the following distribution: belles-lettres, 36%; arts and sciences, 24%; history, 21%; law, 13%; and theology, 8%.[86] In comparison with what is known of other private libraries in Savoy at the time, Maistre's library was distinctive not only for its size, but for its remarkable equilibrium and encyclopedic quality.[87] But insofar as the bulk of Maistre's holdings at this time were acquired by inheritance, it is the listing of his purchases from 1788 to 1792, rather than his catalogue, that is more revealing of his interests and concerns. Darcel's study provides the following subject-matter categorization of Maistre's purchases: belles-lettres, 25%; arts and sciences, 47%; history, 15%; law, 4%; and theology, 12%.[88] The high percentage under the category "arts and sciences" reflects a number of purchases in the areas of political economy, philosophy, and metaphysics. But what is most surprising is that in contrast to his friend Salteur, who was so enamoured of contemporary French publications, Maistre gave high priority to England. Almost half the works in the category "arts and sciences" concerned England or were by English authors; in the "history" category, five out of nine titles were by English historians.[89] What is just as interesting is that the only works directly concerned with the French Revolution that Maistre purchased between 1789 and 1792 were radically hostile to it. These were Burke's *Reflections on the Revolution in France*, purchased 20 September 1791, and an anonymous work, *Les Crimes constitutionnels de France*, acquired in 1792.[90] The only other work directly addressing contemporary issues, Frossard's work on Negro slavery, was given to Maistre by the author's father.[91] Darcel's conclusions appear well justified:

It all happened as if the reformist sympathies of Joseph de Maistre had been quickly cooled by the first revolutionary manifestations that were going to lead, not to the reform of abuses, but to a more and more radical upheaval of the political, social, and religious structures of the old France ...

In the absence of explicit confidences, one can consider his Anglomania, revealed in his choice of books, as denoting a need for an ideological and political antidote: to chose Newton, Cudworth, the school of the English Platonists, and finally, Burke, was to disavow, in a certain sense, Bayle, Voltaire, Diderot and the *Encyclopédie*, and even Montesquieu.[92]

The clues provided by Maistre's acquisitions are important to us, because the evidence for tracing the evolution of his thinking from 1788 through 1792 is all too scanty.

The unfinished memoirs he wrote in Turin in the spring of 1788 reveal that he was still, at that time, a partisan of moderate reform. The memoirs dealt directly with contemporary French issues just at the time when the Assembly of Notables called by Calonne had repudiated his proposed reforms and his successor, Loménie de Brienne, was trying to force the Parlement of Paris to register a similar program. Both memoirs testify to Maistre's identification with the political position and ideas of the French parlementaires.

In the one document, which is dated March 1788, Maistre set himself the seemingly unrewarding task of developing a defence for the French system of venality of office. Although defended by Montesquieu, venality was generally thought to be an abuse that lowered the esteem of the parlements in the court of public opinion. Maistre begins his memoir by acknowledging that he had long shared the view that venality of office was the "opprobrium of the government of France."[93] But further reflection on how the system works in practice under a monarchy has led, he writes, to a number of reflections in its favour.

Against the argument that venality substitutes wealth for merit and knowledge as prerequisites for public office, Maistre points out that the system in fact provides a reasonable alternative to patronage (which he seems to assume to be the only other option). Wealth, he argues, has always been considered a relevant qualification for office. He cites Greek and Roman systems that classified citizens by wealth, and points to contemporary English practice that imposed property qualifications for the franchise and required an independent income for eligibility for election to Parliament. The system of venality provides a dignified avenue of advancement for wealth and amibition, and renders "an inestimable service" by "suppressing an almost incalculable number of intrigues." Even in a small state like Savoy where it is not impossible for the prince to have detailed knowledge of situations and persons, Maistre argues, "the equitable distribution of appointments strains their resources if it does not exceed them!" How many times have they seen the "weight of cabals and the irresistible influence of intrigue force them to ask themselves if they are sovereigns."[94] (It is instructive to remember that Maistre was developing these arguments at the same time as he was paying court to the powerful in Turin in the hope of being named Senator.) In a large country like France, of course, these arguments against patronage are all the more relevant. But it is amusing to find Maistre citing the "sparkling Mirabeau" and the "eloquent Rousseau" on the dangers of a monarch trying to do too much himself.[95]

On the question of merit and ability, Maistre develops a curious argument to the effect that not that much is required for most offices:

To return to the great question of merit necessary for the exercise of certain offices, it must not be forgotten, following an almost general rule that nothing necessary is difficult, that few offices in society exceed the ordinary resources of the human mind. Good sense and uprightness are generally sufficient to make the political machine go, and it is not extremely rare to see genius hinder its progress.[96]

As for the technical knowledge required for certain positions, such as the magistrature, Maistre points out that existing regulations do set minimum requirements, and that if these are neglected it is an abuse and not the fault of the system itself. But, he asks, "is it to be thought that English juries, which every day decide the most important questions in civil and criminal cases, have a profound knowledge of the laws?"[97] He notes too that in France, where a son is sure to succeed his father on the bench, family pride and tradition ensure adequate preparation. In contrast, in Savoy, the father's labours are lost when the son opts for another career: "the father's learning is shut up in his tomb; books, memoirs, the most precious collections, all become useless, all are scattered by heirs who take no more interest in them."[98]

Maistre develops two other arguments that are more pertinent to the developing political crisis in France. In the first, he praises venality for having produced "the inestimable benefit for humanity" of procuring political representation for the people. In developing this argument, Maistre characterizes existing European governments in a way that no leaves no doubt about his reformist political sentiments or his hostility towards the old feudal nobility:

It must be admitted to our shame that all European governments are only a collection of parts, without political unity, the fortuitous result of the clash of different interests, a shapeless mélange of the debris of the feudal colossus knocked down by royal power; the people, crumpled between these two enormous masses, has not yet recovered from its annihilation. This state of war has produced a mutual defiance that is the radical vice of our governments; jealous political authority regards minor political discussions as offences of lese majesty, and it is a crime for people to believe they have rights.[99]

In France, where the royal power had taken advantage of unfortunate circumstances to suspend the "august" Estates-General, the "nation" would have been lost if it had not been for venality of office, which allowed the Parlements "to represent the nation until happier times."[100] The nation would have been sacrificed, Maistre argues, "but with the system of venality of office, the total price of offices formed an enormous mass whose reimbursement always frightened the administration."[101] So, if there have been abuses with the system, "the nation has been very well repaid since it has procured some kind of representation, and the true maxims propagated and defended by the Parlements have finally shown peoples the certain epoch of the re-establishment of the Estates."[102]

Maistre's last argument is that venality helps prevent the evils of gerontocracy by "carrying young people into all offices." Again, the argument displays Maistre's reformist attitude: "But as every human institution carries in itself a germ of corruption, and must continually be renewed if one does not want to see the edifice crumble, it follows that public affairs absolutely cannot dispense with youth. The roles are fixed by nature; that of young people is to do good and that of the old is to prevent the evil."[103] As was suggested earlier, the argument probably reflects Maistre's impatience with old men entrenched in high position in Piedmont-Sardinia.

All in all, Maistre's little memoir on venality is a rather remarkable document; a defence of one of the "abuses" of the old regime, it also reveals its author's fundamentally reformist political outlook.

The second 1788 memoir is in two portions, the first dated "Turin, May 1788," and the second dated "September 1788," but the entire document simply develops the thesis that "the Parlements of France were once what the Parliament of England is at present."[104] It adds little to our understanding of Maistre's attitude towards political reform, but the way what is essentially an historical argument is developed reveals some other interesting aspects of his thinking and attitudes.

Maistre's admiration of the English and English political arrangements comes out quite clearly. The English, he writes, "wiser, happier, or better placed (which amounts to the same thing), have retained their ancient institutions, the French have let theirs slip away."[105] In England, he believes, the consequence of the admission of the Third Estate to Parliament was that monarchy was "irrevocably limited," and in contrast to the situation in France, "the people, more thoughtful, wiser, more energetic, early sensed its rights and its resources."[106] The French nation, on the other hand, went to extremes in favouring the royal prerogative against the tyranny of the barons, with the result that after striking down feudalism, the royal authority "fell on the nation."[107]

In Maistre's version of the story, the history of the French Parlements diverged from that of the English Parliament at the point where Philip the Fair detached the Parlement of Paris from his person and settled it in Paris. Until then, the "Court of Peers" had been the king's necessary council, "the nation was constantly represented and its representatives were really an integral portion of the sovereignty."[108] Gradually, the barons and prelates abandoned the Parlement, and it was left with only legists who judged, and "the nation was lost." Quite apart from the accuracy of Maistre's history, it should be noted that his interpretation rather denigrates the judicial function. And yet the memoir ends with the observation that this substitution of legists for peers explains the military nobility's "monstrous prejudice" against the nobility of the robe.[109] One senses some ambiguity in Maistre's attitude towards his own position as a noble magistrate – perhaps, as Triomphe suggests, an ambiguity reflecting political ambition.[110]

In addition to the indications provided by these two uncompleted memoirs, further hints about Maistre's thinking on the eve of the French Revolution may be found in an untitled "dialogue" in his hand discovered among his papers in the family archives.[111] The manuscript is undated, but internal evidence suggests that it must have been written between 1786 and 1789. It takes the form of a dialogue between "Mr Dennis," an Englishman who defends freedom of the press with arguments from natural law and utility, and "the President" (of a French court, presumably), who ends up setting aside the appeal to natural law and attributing to the sovereign the kind of authority Maistre will ascribe to sovereigns in his published works. This document provides valuable insights into Maistre's understanding of natural law concepts and into his reasons for not using traditional natural law phraseology in his later works.[112] But apart from the question of natural law, the dialogue is of interest because of the arguments in defence of freedom of the press attributed to "Mr Dennis."

Maistre appears to have written his little dialogue in response to a specific dispute that had arisen in France. In 1786, Charles Dupaty, a member of the Parlement of Bordeaux who was becoming known as an advocate of legal reform, published a "*mémoire justificatif*" protesting the innocence of three men condemned to be broken on the wheel. As a consequence of Dupaty's intervention, the verdict was reversed by a higher court, but then the Parlement of Paris got involved in the affair and had Dupaty's memoir burned by the public executioner. The Parlement's condemnation, written by its Advocate-General, Antoine-Louis Séguier, was subsequently published. Séquier was well known as an opponent of the philosophes and had been involved in attempts to suppress the *Encyclopédie*.[113]

Maistre's dialogue opens with Mr Dennis angrily berating the arrogance of Séquier's condemnation of Dupaty. Séguier had argued that the law prohibited any such public questioning of a court's judgment, and had, in the words of Mr Dennis, "thundered against freedom of the press."[114] In defending this freedom, Mr Dennis develops two lines of argument. The first is an argument from natural law to the effect that mere human laws cannot prohibit the denunciation of unjust legal decisions or unjust laws. The second is a utilitarian argument to the effect that freedom of the press promotes knowledge, safeguards mankind against injustice, and ensures reforms.

The bulk of Maistre's dialogue is devoted to a question that arises out of the first line of argument. Mr Dennis argues, on the basis of natural law, that a magistrate should not enforce a law that he believes to be unjust. The President, in response, sets aside the natural law argument on the grounds that its prescriptions are too vague to be practical, and argues, from the unitary nature of political sovereignty, that magistrates must enforce existing laws (no matter what their private beliefs about their justice). The argument expresses essentially the same view of the nature of sovereignty that Maistre will develop in his published works:

THE PRESIDENT

If there is anything evident in politics, it is that in every possible kind of constitution there must always be a power that is accountable to no one and that can neither be stopped nor even opposed in its determinations. This power is the sovereign ... If there is not a power that can make itself obeyed invincibly, there is no more society and we have to return to the woods.[115]

From the evidence of this passage it seems safe to conclude that Maistre's characteristic stance on the nature of sovereignty was not the result of reaction to the French Revolution, but a position he had adopted prior to and independently of that event.

But to return to the utilitarian arguments advanced by Mr Dennis in favour of freedom of the press, what is interesting is that Maistre's "President" makes no serious effort to refute them. The way Maistre has the dialogue develop is really very intriguing; from what we know of his thinking from his earlier writings, and from the kinds of positions he will take in his later writings, we have the feeling that we are eavesdropping on a self-dialogue. The arguments and phrases he gives to Mr Dennis echo some of his own earlier writings, and in the course of the dialogue those arguments are not so much defeated as subjected to a bit of irony and then passed over as the discussion turns to the question of the enforcement of unjust laws. Let us listen in on some snippets of the dialogue:

MR DENNIS

Let all opinions show themselves freely and clash with each other as they will. This is the true way to prevent any of them from becoming dangerous: there will be no more contagious errors, no more party chieftains, no more fanatics. For from an equal and universal reaction, repose will necessarily result.

THE PRESIDENT

What then, sir, you would put no bounds to licence. The nation's religion, its laws, the reputation of its citizens, would cease to be sacred things, and you would permit the first fool ...

MR DENNIS

Yes, sir, but take note that wise men will also be permitted to write against the fools. What deceives you are your tyrannical prejudices that do not permit you to see beyond the first moment of fermentation that will necessarily follow granting the freedom to write everything to a slave people who will at first abuse it prodigiously. But first of all, I do not ask for a law, since all abrupt changes are worthless in politics; it is enough to follow the natural inclination of the century, to close one's eyes, and to chastise only as a last resort ... The truth has nothing to fear in any case; if it could succumb it would no longer be the truth. Free discussion is a fire that separates the gold from the dross that surrounds it ... You have just spoken about religion. Do you not know that the irreligious fever that has troubled Europe for some years would have passed sooner if ...

THE PRESIDENT

Which is to say, according to you, that it has passed. Permit me, my dear friend, to congratulate you on your discovery.

MR DENNIS

Do not laugh, my dear President. Yes, it has passed; there is a great *weakness* that remains as a consequence, but this is a convalescence. Since no physical or moral change can be accomplished by leaps, it was necessary that mankind, having fallen from credulity into scepticism, pass by indifference to arrive at a reasonable faith. But you have distracted me; I wanted to say to you that this fever would have been far less ravaging under a regime of freedom of the press. Too much attention has been paid to irreligious books: proscribing them with all the force of public authority has given them an incalculable weight in the opinion of the multitude. Persecuting free thinkers has made them famous, and instead of opposing them with contempt or reasoning, we have the awkwardness of offering them a martyr's glory ... It would even be easy for me to prove to you that the government has nothing to fear from writers and that the only way to render lampoons powerless is to permit them to multiply; but with you I believe details are useless.

THE PRESIDENT

You cajole me to seduce me, my friend, but I am on guard.[116]

As the dialogue proceeds, Mr Dennis concedes that magistrates should display respect for existing laws, at least when they are speaking in court and as magistrates, but he argues that it would be absurd and inhuman to require unjust laws to be respected in purely philosophical writings. When he refers to a passage in Condorcet's recently published life of Turgot as decisively supporting his position, he elicts this response:

THE PRESIDENT

I know the passage; but this book contains, it seems to me, a number of false or exaggerated opinions. This is said without the least disrespect for the spirit of Turgot, without contradiction one of the greatest men who have ever honoured France. The Voices that are presently celebrating his Maxims and his procedures announce that the Century progresses with great steps towards the truth. But while waiting for him to be universally known and esteemed as much as he deserves, I have made my particular apotheosis. I have just consecrated his portrait in my study and written beneath it *ostendent Gallis tantum neque ultrà/esse sinent.*[117]

But Maistre has the irony work both ways. At the end of the dialogue he has the President conclude his argument with these sanctimonious remarks:

THE PRESIDENT

The legislators must think about it [ie, the justice of their laws]. If they do not know how to weigh crimes and measure punishments, if from lack of enlightenment or too much haste they take sins for crimes, if they cause human blood to flow too lightly, it is a terrible misfortune. But let us pray God to enlighten them.[118]

Mr Dennis is permitted to deliver an appropriate one word answer: "Amen!"

Maistre would not use the dialogue format again until late in his life when he wrote *Les Soirées de Saint-Pétersbourg*. This seems a pity, since it is a literary form well-suited to his genius. He was a very complex man, curious, extremely intelligent, and quite capable of seeing the various facets of an issue. His response to the intellectual currents of his time – the Enlightenment, the "illuminist" ideas he encountered in Freemasonry – was often one of simultaneous attraction and repulsion. These tensions, his sense of irony, and his rich intellectual gifts could all find adequate expression in the dialogue form – as his masterpiece, the *Soirées*, shows so well. Perhaps one of the ironies of Maistre's relationship to the French Revolution is that by provoking him to devote his literary energies to more polemical genres it distracted him from a form that might have ensured earlier literary renown.

If one phrase had to be chosen to characterize Joseph de Maistre's intellectual and political position on the eve of the French Revolution, perhaps the most appropriate choice would be "enlightened conservative." He was "enlightened" in his familiarity with the thought world of the Enlightenment and the world of Freemasonry, in his love of learning and the attraction he felt for freedom of the press, in his moderate Gallicanism, in his opposition to the absolutism of a Louis XIV, in his belief in the ideal of a moderate monarchy limited by "intermediate bodies" such as the Parlements or the Senate of Savoy, in his distrust of the Sardinian monarchy's militaristic and centralizing policies, in his admiration of England and its political system, and in his openness to the possibility of political reform. He remained "conservative" in his adherence to traditional Christian values and Roman Catholicism, in his belief in the fundamental excellence of monarchical institutions generally and in his loyalty to the Sardinian monarchy, in his fear of the excesses of popular democracy, in his assumption that the natural élite of educated and better-off subjects (of which he was obviously a member) had a special claim and responsibility to participate in the exercise of political power, in his belief in the indivisible character of sovereignty, in his feeling for the slow organic growth of human institutions, and his conviction that reforms must be rooted in tradition and introduced prudently and slowly. It was a position that invited distrust and misunderstanding, both by his contemporaries and by historians.

For those who held power by inheritance and tradition, the Sardinian kings and the hereditary military nobility, for those who unthinkingly assumed the validity and appropriateness of traditional values and institutions, a man like Joseph de Maistre, a man of insatiable curiosity, of broad cosmopolitan interests and learning, ready to take seriously the challenge of the Enlightenment, a man who adventurously involved himself in the faddish and suspect Masonic movement, a man with an independent mind and a talent for the articulate enunciation of ideas, a man whose powerful intelligence and imagination could scarcely be restrained from witty and ironic expression, was a man who would always remain suspect. Maistre was impatient with the dull, narrow-minded, selfish, and unthinking sort who had simply inherited their power and position, and attracted to the company of intelligent, open-hearted, "liberal" young colleagues, to the exciting intellectual ferment of the Enlightenment, and to the exotic lure of "illuminist" Freemasonry. Conscious of his intellectual superiority and abilities, he was ambitious for power and status. Perhaps he could have gone either way in the crisis of the Revolution; he was equipped by native talent, imagination, education, experience, and friendships to seek success in either camp. In the event, his loyalty to traditional Catholicism and the monarchy that had facilitated his family's social ascent, his sense of order, his consciousness of caste, and his patriarchal concern with family patrimony weighed most heavily in his decision. He opted to throw his support to traditional political and religious values and institutions and to seek his fortune in their service, but not without retaining a nostalgic loyalty to the friends and enthusiasms of his youth.

How historians and biographers have perceived his position has depended on their own presuppositions. Conservative and Catholic admirers of the later Maistre have tended to explain away his earlier attraction to the Enlightenment, his Gallicanism, his dabbling in Freemasonry, his hostility to absolutism, and his aspirations for political reform as youthful aberrations that were soon cured by his experience of the Revolution. Critics in the tradition of nineteenth-century liberalism, appalled by Maistre's later defence of what they regarded as hopelessly obscurantist and reactionary institutions, have tended to assume that Maistre was simply unable to escape his Jesuit indoctrination – despite some youthful impulses towards rationalism and good sense. Other critics of a more Marxist bent tend to explain Maistre's political position and political choices largely in terms of his membership in a particular socio-economic class, and to explain away his intellectual positions as hypocritical rationalizations of class-bound interest. More recent and more sympathetic Maistrian scholars, such as Jean-Louis Darcel, while not disdaining the insights offered by earlier admirers and critics, tend to stress the uncomfortableness of Maistre's position as the Revolution approached Savoy. As events belied the possibility of achieving his political ideal of traditional monarchy tempered by historic "intermediate bodies" and strengthened by prudent reforms, Maistre's reaction was a predictable evolution from reserve to fear, and then rather quickly to reprobation and horror. And yet Maistre was too enlightened, too aware of the abuses and weaknesses of the old regime, to give mute uncritical support to his government's panicky reaction to the dangers posed by revolutionary events in France. He could not refrain from offering moderate unwelcome advice to Turin – with the consequence that he remained the object of incomprehension by the very authorities he chose to support.[119]

Moderates never find it easy in a time of revolutionary upheaval. In France, the moderates, "liberal aristocrats" like the Marquis de La Fayette and anglophile lawyers like Jean-Joseph Mounier, were soon caught between the radicals and their deepest convictions and forced to choose, and choosing, fled. Across the frontier in Savoy, the choice was not posed so sharply or so soon. It was only with the French invasion in September 1792 that Joseph de Maistre was put in the position where he felt obliged to make an "irrevocable" decision – and even then, as we shall see, in coming back to Chambéry for a few weeks in January 1793, he appears to have been tempted by the possibility of reversing that choice. But let us explore the dynamic of events and response that in the end led Maistre to his vocation as spokesman for throne and altar.

IN THE SHADOW OF THE REVOLUTION

In the spring and summer of 1788, Joseph de Maistre had been an enthusiastic partisan of the French *parlementaires* and endorsed their compaign to force the calling of an Estates-General. There is even reason to believe he may have considered seeking election himself. Years later, when the Jesuits were being expelled from St Petersburg, he would suggest as much in one of his letters: "I feel sorry for these gentlemen ... to whom I owe not having been an orator in the Constituant Assembly."[120] Whimsical exaggeration? In the absence of contemporary evidence, it is impossible to say. But election to the French Estates-General was not beyond the realm of possibility. With his property at Talissieu in the French province of Bugey, he perhaps could have met the eligibility requirements for election as a deputy of the Second Estate for the Bailliage of Belley. He was an old friend of the Lieutenant of the Bailliage, Baron de Rubat. A classmate from the University of Turin, the Marquis de Clermont Mont-Saint-Jean, was elected a noble deputy from the same constituency. Maistre's numerous Masonic connections at Lyon and elsewhere might have encouraged and supported his candidacy if he had decided to stand.[121] But of course he did not. Still, when we try to find out just when he lost hope in the Estates-General, we are faced with an embarrassing lack of evidence.

This lack makes it difficult to trace Joseph de Maistre's immediate response to events in the early months of the French Revolution. His diary – at least the journal that has survived – has no entries prior to 6 November 1790. As for his correspondence, we have nothing between a letter written in September 1788 to the secretary of state for internal affairs in Turin and a letter to his brother Nicolas dated 18 August 1789. Then there are portions of two letters to Henry Costa, one undated but from internal evidence apparently written in September, the second dated 7 December 1789, and that is all we have of Maistre's own letters for 1789. Luckily, we do have a letter from Henry Costa to Maistre of 15 June 1789, from which we can infer that the latter is already pessimistic about events in France. But unless and until further evidence is unearthed, it appears that we will never be able to do more than speculate about the exact timing of Maistre's loss of faith in the regeneration of France by the Estates-General. It seems likely, though, from what we know of his later views, that the campaign for the "doubling of the Third" and the sudden appearance on the scene of an aggressive reform party demanding considerably more than the traditional Estates-General meeting and voting in the traditional way (developments that occurred after September 1788) were the crucial factors involved in Maistre's change of attitude.

Henry Costa's letter of 15 June 1789 provides indirect but unmistakable evidence that Maistre was shifting his position even before the Tennis Court Oath and the transformation of the Estates-General into the National Assembly:

My dear friend, why are you so cold about the future? Believe me, these Versailles discussions, which upset you so much, can only produce a happy levelling among these men who, *despite you*, desire the good of France. In this deluge of misfortunes that you announce to our poor world, in my opinion, the only ones to be counted unfortunate are the poor men Providence has cast so abruptly outside their sphere and dragged into a theatre where they are forced to play an unusual role.

You say that deputies must have an uncommon strength of soul to stiffen themselves against the current, to isolate themselves from the crowd, to sustain themselves against the seductions of what you call a too easy popularity. But tell me, my dear friend, where in all this truth ends and error begins.

Dogma should not invade politics; in this sphere of ideas, principles owe nothing to revelation.[122]

Even though we do not have the letter to which Costa was replying, there can be no doubt about the stance Maistre must have enunciated. He opposed "vote by head," feared popular pressures on the deputies, and predicted "a deluge of misfortunes." With the Estates indulging in demagoguery, his hopes for reform of traditional institutions were evaporating, perhaps abandoned. Costa's closing comment suggests too that Maistre may already have begun to "dogmatize" his opposition to the direction of developments at Versailles.

In his letter to his brother Nicolas on the 18th of August, Joseph de Maistre reports "interesting news" from France, passing on what he has heard about an oath "to King and the nation" being imposed on French troops, and about harsh measures being taken to restore order in the countryside. He adds: "I do not know what the result of all this will be; however, I am always betting on the king."[123] Other comments in this letter suggest that Maistre has not yet sensed any threat to his personal life as a consequence of events in France. After telling his brother that he too misses their father (who had died eight months previously), Joseph goes on: "My affairs are always the same ... *I go on living* and our republic [ie, the family] will all be here until some happy event puts us in a more agreeable situation. This event is not only in the order of the possible, but, it seems to me, in that of the probable. Hard work, a steady irreproachable life, and some friends, will lead, I hope, to something."[124] Whether or not Maistre's ambition was focused on "something" specific at this point is impossible to say.

Some time after the famous night session of 4 August at which what was now the National Assembly abolished "feudalism" in France, Maistre wrote to Costa in terms that leave no doubt as to his intense emotional reaction to what was happening:

In writing two pages on politics to me, my dear friend, you have thrown a red-hot ball into a powder magazine. I am heated up beyond expression on this question, and I even see here before me twelve or fifteen written pages that would call forth more. But I am alone, poorly situated, discouraged; I find around me only coldness, ignorance, and that hateful envy of the *powerless* against a man who ...

After breaking the sentence midway, Maistre continues:

Sometimes, and even often, I tell myself that I am nothing, that I lack everything, and that professional obligations paralyze me. I even believe this for a day, a week, an entire month; but then I experience twinges, exaltations where all this seems not altogether false. So it is that, tossed between the stupor of disgust and outbursts of enthusiasm, I see nothing clearly, except that I know what I am. There is only you, my dear and lovable friend, who electrifies me *more*. Others sustain my fire; elsewhere I find envy without assistance, – near you I have help without envy; it is you who are rich enough not to envy your neighbour's *little coins*.

Who knows if, towards the beginning of October, you will not see me arriving at your place with Montesquieu, Bacon, and Mably wrapped up in four folders – and some scraps of paper that I will read to you to know what you think? While waiting – look, here is a tirade that just fell from my pen:

"It is however this session of August 4th that they dare to call an *Immortal Session*. – *Look*, they say, *what the National Assembly has done*, IN AN EVENING, *for France and humanity!* Alas! One can, undoubtedly, make great mistakes *in an evening;* but it takes years ... "[125]

Again Maistre breaks off, as if in frustration. The legislation of 4 August may well have cost him seigneurial income from his property at Talissieu, but one senses that Maistre's reaction was a consequence of something more fundamental – he was shocked by the rapidity and wholesale nature of the changes. That his opposition should take literary form is something he seems to have taken for granted. But for the moment, it was still to the writers cherished by the Enlightenment – Montesquieu, Bacon, and Mably – that he looked for support in judging the National Assembly.

In his letter of 7 December 1789, after complaining that the opening of the new court session meant that "reading, conversations, and meditations" were now over until September 1790, Maistre went on to report that he had passed an entire evening with a good friend of Jean-Joseph Mounier, who had told him of the details of what Mounier had witnessed at Versailles the night of 5 October. (Mounier had been the presiding officer of the National Assembly when the women of Paris had arrived to demand bread and had been an eye-witness of many of the events of the famous "October Days" that had seen the women invade the palace, the killing of members of the royal bodyguard, and then, with the arrival of La Fayette and the National Guard, the forced march of the royal family back to Paris.) Maistre was obviously shaken by what he had heard of these events:

Would you believe it, my dear friend? Mounier saw, saw with his own two eyes, women of Paris, who had just taken bread from the King's kitchens, soak this bread in the blood of the slaughtered bodyguard and then eat it. The charming people! ...

But this is what I find most conformable to the Declaration of the Rights of Man, which also includes those of women, in virtue of natural equality. The ... of the third[126] and of the people must begin to show themselves at Versailles; for too long those of the mighty, and great ladies, have alone enjoyed acknowledged representation there.

What can I say to you, my dear friend? My faith is shaken. Help! Assist me! My head is forever fermenting with all these affairs to the point that sometimes I cannot sleep. Never has a more interesting spectacle struck mankind ... [127]

But if Maistre was upset, and perhaps angered, by this report of the October Days, he was also able to see another side to the story and to view it in broader philosophical perspective. The letter continues: "You know that I am no friend of popular factions; however, I take a great interest in this terrible sermon Providence is preaching to kings. Yes, it is well worth the trouble of being listened to attentively, and so much the worse for those who do not profit from it."[128] Finally, after comments on Necker's unenviable situation and pessimistic predictions for the future, Maistre concludes his remarks on politics (and turns to domestic news) with these words: "Let us quit Paris! Let us quit Paris! Let us quit this filthy abyss where Mirabeau squalls like a veritable Lucifer."[129]

This letter exhibits an important dimension of Joseph de Maistre's reaction to the events of the French Revolution – his visceral revulsion in the face of its bloody violence. A man of vivid imagination, he was deeply moved by eye-witness accounts of the blood and violence of the revolutionary process. The French royal family was intermarried with the House of Savoy, and Turin was the initial destination of some of the earliest noble émigrés. Chambéry was on one of the main émigré routes and served as well as a centre of refuge until 1792. Maistre would have had ample opportunity to hear first-hand accounts of the bloodshed of the Revolution. The hallucinatory visions of carnage that haunt the pages of his later works, the themes of blood being spilled out endlessly on the earth, of the sufferings of the innocent, of expiation, "were they not imposed on his sensibility, on his imagination in the first months of the French Revolution?"[130] With many of his contemporaries, Maistre was shocked by the "sudden irruption of irrationality into the century of rationality, of savagery and inhumanity into the century of civilization and philanthropy."[131] At first, as this letter of December 1789 testifies, the emotional shock tended to derange attempts at rational analysis ("My faith is shaken. Help!") Since there is no evidence that his religious faith was shaken at this time, we may assume that Maistre was referring to blows to this faith in monarchy and perhaps as well to a lingering belief in Enlightenment-inspired hopes for rationalistic political reforms. But even at this early date, his impulse was to interpret events in providential terms – although at this stage in his evolution Maistre saw the sermon as preached to kings rather than to the people.

We have even less contemporary evidence for Maistre's thinking and reactions during 1790 than for 1789. There is a letter to the secretary for state for internal affairs in Turin, which Maistre wrote as the chairman of the administrative board of the general hospital of Chambéry and which requested approval for proposed changes in the institution's administration.[132] The letter contains no direct reference to the Revolution, but there is one sentence that seems to reflect sensitivity to the government's increasing conservatism. Maistre assured Turin that "it is certainly not the spirit of cabal nor the spirit of innovation that has inspired our wish for change in the administration of our hospital."[133]

Also surviving is a short brief in Maistre's hand dated 22 June 1790 and headed "to the Senate."[134] We do not know if Joseph de Maistre ever delivered these remarks, but they are nevertheless significant for what they reveal of his views on the developing crisis and the way to deal with it. After noting that "minds are agitated enough to inspire alarm and to authorize a body like the Senate to suggest some measures to the sovereign," Maistre asserts that when authority speaks on such an occasion there are two things to consider: "1. How to command. 2. What to command." On the first question he offers this advice:

On the first article: it appears that the king will gain by having the Senate act instead of acting directly himself. This will be a means of rendering the authority of the sovereign milder and more venerable without taking away any of its strength, and of effacing more completely from the minds of the people any idea of arbitrariness ...

In a word, I would ask that one act today to repress political troubles precisely as one did two centuries ago to pacify religious troubles.

(This is Maistre's first surviving mention of a perceived analogy between the French Revolution and the Reformation.) On the second question, Maistre advises no new penalties, pointing out that there are existing laws against riots, lese-majesty, extortion, and carrying arms. At most one might consider stiffer penalties, with less rigorous requirements for proof, for offences such as refusing to pay the tithe. He recommends an amnesty for subjects who may have gotten into trouble prior to the date of the proposed manifesto, and concludes: "It seems to me, gentlemen, that it is up to us to be protectors of those who have none, who are poor, abandoned, and who cannot send representatives to Turin." Delivered or not, this was moderate enough advice.

The only other relevant document we have for 1790 is a letter from Joseph de Maistre to his sister Thérèse with a postscript with a "poor little word on politics."[135] Maistre's political comment concerns the festivities planned for 14 July, the famous Fête de la Fédération which was to be held on the Champs de Mars on the first anniversary of the fall of the Bastille, an event a modern historian has characterized as "perhaps the greatest day of the whole Revolution."[136] From Maistre's postscript, one can surmise that he was viewing events in Paris through the eyes of the Sardinian ambassador to the French government: "The king's ambassador in Paris has shown little enough regret at not seeing the festival of the 14th; he arrives tomorrow or the day after and is passing through Switzerland. The only one that remains with the august assembly, I believe, is the English ambassador. Those who have departed detest it; those who remain mock it."[137] Maistre's diary entries begin 6 November 1790, but there are no entries reflecting political concerns prior to 15 March 1791.

When we come to 1791, we have better evidence for tracing the evolution of Maistre's attitudes and thinking concerning events in France and their impact on his native Savoy. Towards the end of January 1791, we find him writing to Henry Costa and sharing his reactions to authors he has been reading on the situation in France as well as his concerns about what is happening locally:

Have you read Calonne, Mounier, and the admirable Burke? What do you think of the way this rude senator treats the great gambling-den of the Manège and all the *baby* legislators? For myself, I am delighted, and I do not know how to tell you how he has reinforced my anti-democratic and anti-Gallican ideas. My aversion for everything that is being done in France becomes horror. I understand very well how systems, fermenting in so many human heads, are turned into passions. Believe me, this abominable assembly cannot be too much abhorred. See how thirty or forty rascals accomplish what the Black Prince and the League were unable to do: massacres, pillaging, fires are nothing, it only takes a few years to heal all that; but public spirit annihilated, opinion vitiated to a frightening degree; in a word, *France putrefied*, that is what these gentlemen have done. And what is really deplorable, is that the sickness is contagious and our poor Chambéry is already well tainted.[138]

Maistre goes on to relate a local incident that had caused unnecessary bitterness, and then indicates his disapproval of the way the government is reacting to the situation:

In short, my dear friend, I tell you with the greatest regret that power is retreating every day, even when it wants to advance, for it is being applied badly; our good master is being given incomprehensible advice. A number of people in this province and in Turin are entertaining strange suspicions on this matter; as for me, I am suspending judgment. It is certain however that a certain subterranean spirit is working against authority and dictating the most perfidious advice. The government is in a very misplaced attitude of terror, and when it is trembling, can it make others tremble?[139]

Maistre reveals himself to be pessimistic about the local situation, but knowing Costa remains more optimistic, he also requests reassurance:

When I see so many faux pas, so many risks run voluntarily, I am sometimes like the Misanthrope:
It throws me into a melancholy humour, a profound chagrin.[140]
Other times I try to reassure myself, but a little sermon on your part would not be useless ... So, my dear friend, I exhort you to exhort me; I have so much more need of it because it is a time of sadness. What a night! What a storm! Yesterday I made a mark on my barometer, with the date, as a monument to *Baseness*, for I imagine I will never see the mercury there again.[141]

Several points in this important letter require commentary. The reference to Edmund Burke has, of course, been duly noted by all Maistre scholars since this letter was first published in 1884; most have concluded that Joseph de Maistre was greatly influenced by his reading of Burke's *Reflections on the Revolution in France*. Darcel, for example, says that it is "no exaggeration to say that all Joseph de Maistre's reflection on the Revolution rests on the analysis of the great English politician."[142] However, when one tries to delineate the nature and extent of Maistre's debt to Burke, the issue is not so clear-cut. In the first place, apart from this letter, there are very few references to Burke in Maistre's published works – or even for that matter, in his private notebooks.[143] Without denying that one finds similar themes in the thought of these two great conservative theorists, it would be a mistake to conclude that Maistre's ideas are simply derived from Burke. The relationship appears to be much more complex; Maistre was too imaginative and powerful a thinker simply to reproduce someone else's theories. Read carefully, this 1791 letter to Henry Costa reveals something of the essential dynamic of what was involved.

"I am delighted [*j'en ai été ravi*] ... My aversion becomes ... horror." Reading Burke reinforced Maistre's emotional reaction to the Revolution. If Isaac Kramnick's interpretation of Burke is anywhere near the mark, deep "rage" was an essential component of the English conservative's response to the revolution in France.[144] Without suggesting that the same pyschological mechanisms were at work in the two men (the mechanisms were probably quite different, in fact), it still seems reasonable to interpret Maistre's reaction to Burke's *Reflections* as an instinctive acclamation of an emotional revulsion similar to his own. One suspects that this emotional dynamic may well have been more important than any of the particular ideas he found in Burke.

On the level of ideas, Maistre's own words suggest the essentials of the relationship: "I do not know how to tell you how he has reinforced my ... ideas." Joseph de Maistre, as we have already seen from his reactions to Charron and Necker, often responded most enthusiastically to authors who expressed ideas he already held. In this case, as Holdsworth has pointed out, Burke's position was not strictly "anti-democratic" or explicitly anti-Gallican.[145] Burke never advocated abolition of popular representation as provided in the existing English system, nor, as an Anglican, did he uphold papal authority. Now it is not that difficult to see how Maistre could have interpreted Burke's ideas in such a way that they could be made to support his own anti-democratic ideas and his doubts about even the moderate Gallican position he had held in the past,[146] but the important point is that Burke may have been little more than a stimulus to Maistre's own thinking. Holdsworth appears to have captured the relationship nicely when he concludes that "even when Burke's ideas furnished the point of departure of Maistre's political thought, the latter gave them so much larger a range that one cannot find there the trace of a really fruitful literary and philosophical influence."[147]

In addition to reinforcing anti-democratic and anti-Gallican ideas, this letter also suggests that reading Burke helped Maistre appreciate how systems (of ideas, presumably) can turn into passions. This understanding may have strengthened his hostility to the sceptical, destructive side of the thought of the Enlightenment, but Maistre had worried about this danger before reading Burke. The *Reflections* may also have helped Maistre recognize the crucial role of a determined and active minority ("thirty or forty rascals") in a period of political crisis. If a small minority could annihilate public spirit and vitiate opinion, the appropriate counter-revolutionary strategy will be an equally vigorous campaign to rectify public opinion. At least this is the course Maistre will follow.

Turning now to Maistre's remarks to Costa on the situation in Savoy, Triomphe has suggested that the phrases about "strange suspicions" and "a certain subterranean spirit" probably refer to rumours being circulated about the possible role of Masonry in undermining royalty.[148] Maistre's comment about suspending judgment lends credence to the suggestion. He will never accept the conspiracy theory that blamed the whole Revolution on a Masonic plot, but the time was quickly approaching when his record of affiliation with the lodges would prove a serious embarrassment in his relations with Turin. Perhaps he had more than one reason for asking Henry Costa to cheer him up.

Maistre's complaints about the mistakes being made by the Sardinian government in dealing with unrest being stirred up by French revolutionary propaganda continue in another letter to Henry Costa the following month. Maistre describes how the government had reacted to the circulation of a pamphlet entitled *Le Premier Cri de la Savoie vers la liberté*. According to Maistre, this well-written piece of propaganda had obviously been published in Paris (judging by the quality of the type and the paper), but it had carried the false imprint of the local printer. The pamphlet had, Maistre writes, "produced on the part of the government one of those acts of political silliness that try my patience."[149] Instead of refuting the pamphlet, which Maistre says would have been easy enough, the government commanded the local printer to disavow it. Maistre's comment: "*Quos Jupiter vult perdere prius dementat.*"[150]

A month later Maistre himself had the opportunity to deal with a local manifestation of unrest. Some students at the local college had insulted and harassed three French émigré nobles on the street in front of their institution. As a member (and acting chairman, apparently) of the Conseil de Réforme responsible for the supervision of higher education in Savoy, Maistre was involved in investigating the incident and taking action to try to prevent similar occurrences in the future. In his letter reporting all this to the secretary of state for internal affairs in Turin, Maistre acknowledged that there were rumours circulating in the city to the effect that "French maxims" had been insinuated into the college, that some of the professors favoured them, and had even expressed approval for the Civil Constitution of the Clergy. After relating the incident, Maistre described how he called in one of the principal professors and impressed on him the importance of maintaining "good maxims." The professor had protested his "political orthodoxy" and that of his colleagues; Maistre indicated that he was inclined to believe the man since "when spirits are heated everything gets exaggerated."[151] The Conseil de Réforme then decided to post a declaration warning staff and students to respect the "laws of hospitality towards respectable foreigners living peacefully under the protection of His Majesty," and promising expulsion, and for those of legal age, criminal prosecution for disturbing the peace, if there were any repetitions of the incident.[152] In a follow-up letter a few days later, Maistre added this comment on the nature of the situation:

The great popular thesis is that every act of repressive authority is an act of tyranny or imprudence, and that power is preserved by not acting or by doing so showing all the symptoms of fear. This system, preached for two years by the ignorant who believe it and by some intelligent people who want it believed, has produced the effects that Your Excellency, who is in charge of affairs, can judge better than anyone.[153]

Maistre was warning the minister in Turin against allowing the government to be confined to the paralyzing alternatives of inaction or repression.[154]

In another letter to the minister written the same day, Maistre took the initiative in recommending a more active method of meeting the threat posed by revolutionary propaganda emanating from France. He forwarded a pamphlet produced in Grenoble that gave a "French version" of a brawl that had occurred in Chambéry a few days earlier.[155] In his own account of the incident, Maistre blamed "the maneuvring or even the gold of the Jacobins," and went on to say: "I take this occasion to repeat to Your Excellency what I have already told our leaders here a number of times, which is that if the King wants to know the way in which we are being worked on and the instruments that are being used, it is not here that spies and intelligence are needed, but in France, and in the first place, in Grenoble."[156] He advised the minister that it would be sufficient to plant someone with their eyes open in two or three clubs in Grenoble to discover a great deal. His own initiative, he explained, had produced some interesting results: "By simple interest for a government which I love and to which I owe everything, I asked some questions of a French friend, a good royalist, and this produced for me the letter from which the interesting attached extracts are taken."[157] The extracts offered hearsay evidence that the recent brawl in Chambéry had indeed been instigated by the Jacobins of Grenoble.

The minister's reponse to Maistre's letter was encouraging, and three weeks later, Maistre wrote again, appending a "Memoir on the Jacobin Club" in which he offered his analysis of the purposes and strategy of the French Jacobins, passed on detailed information that he picked up on the French Jacobin involvement in the incident in Chambéry, and again proposed planting an informant in Grenoble. Jacobin propaganda, according to Maistre, had two motives: to force the Sardinian government to chase out

French royalists who had sought refuge in Savoy; and "to sow everywhere corruption and unrest so as not be diverted from their great work."[158] Maistre's analysis of the situation of the National Assembly foreshadows in some respects the interpretation that will appear in his later works: "the National Assembly ... knows very well that its strength is only a relative strength founded on circumstances that are doubtless the result of special degree of Providence, since human reason understands them so little."[159] With respect to the situation in Savoy, Maistre's analysis suggests that he has been meditating on the causes of revolution: "Prudent people believe that they can flatter themselves that there is no danger in this province, but if there were, certainly it would not be from what are called *the people*. For it is vanity and thirst for power that make Revolutions or that begin them, and when the people have bread they desire nothing."[160] Maistre warned that Lyon, Grenoble, and Geneva were danger points that needed to be watched since they were being used as bases for revolutionary propaganda in Savoy, and concluded his memoir with the advice that "it is necessary to be afraid but not to show it."[161]

From Maistre's next letter to the minister, it appears that the minister had proposed that Maistre himself take on the task of coordinating espionage in Grenoble. But Maistre begged off with a number of excuses:

I have thought a great deal about the last letter that Your Excellency has done me the honour of writing to me, and I am convinced that I am not the right person to fulfil your intentions concerning the people that must be sounded out in Grenoble. First, it would take a lot of spare time for enterprises of this kind. It would be necessary to write, to talk, to get involved in activities, and when Your Excellency considers the ordinary work of the Senate, as well as my work on Reparations and the Tithes,[162] and other things, he will not accuse me of exaggeration when I assure him that I have no time to look after my own domestic affairs. In the second place, I would not want to compromise either myself, or for very good reasons, the government, and this is what I would expose myself to by involving myself in things that I do not understand at all, intrigue being for me a foreign country.[163]

Triomphe suggests that Maistre's polite refusal hid a desire for a more illustrious role than that of secret agent.[164] Perhaps this was the case; it was in the following months that Maistre canvassed the possibilities of becoming "intendant general" of Savoy or Sardinian ambassador in Geneva. Whatever Maistre's real motives, there would be no active or official involvement in espionage until he settled in Lausanne in 1793.

But if Maistre declined the task of organizing an intelligence net, he continued to reflect on the meaning and significance of the ongoing revolution in France. In July 1791 we find him sharing these reflections with another friend, Baron Vignet des Etoles,[165] and drawing an explicit analogy between the French Revolution and the Reformation: "The situation is dreadful. I tell you frankly, I fear for the eighteenth century a political shock just like the one the sixteenth experienced in religion. The revolution is advancing rapidly." Maistre confessed to his friend that he found everyone affected by the revolutionary contagion: "Alas, which is the healthy side? I am aware of some strange things on this point; in truth I do not know what delirium has seized everyone." His confidences to Vignet des Etoles also reveal a deepening pessimism: "we are weak, and our pastime is to devour each other instead of facing the enemy."[166]

There were, in fact, good reasons for pessimism concerning the propects for Savoy. French politics were becoming ever more radical and neighbouring states were feeling increasingly threatened. The Civil Constitution of the Clergy (approved in July 1790) and the imposition of an oath on the clergy (in early 1791) had led to a schism in the Church that strengthened both the forces of counter-revolution and the determination of the revolutionaries to defend their achievements. King Louis XVI had become increasingly hostile to the Revolution, and had tried to flee Paris in June 1791. He had been brought back from Varennes (and the fiction adopted that he had been abducted by enemies of the people) and reinstated in September with the adoption of the new constitution and the opening of the Legislative Assembly. But the Brissot faction that increasingly dominated the new assembly sought popularity and political power by demanding vigorous action against the counter-revolution at home and abroad. By November, the Assembly decreed that all Frenchmen assembled beyond the frontiers would be declared traitors unless they returned by the end of the year. The king had vetoed this act, but there were increasingly violent threats against neighbouring states that harboured émigrés. These threats were directed primarily towards the Elector of Trier (in whose territories lay Koblentz, the major gathering place for counter-revolutionary émigrés), but the Kingdom of Piedmont-Sardinia was threatened as well.

When the Legislative Assembly voted for war, 20 April 1792, it was for a declaration of war against Austria and Prussia, with nothing said about Piedmont-Sardinia. But Marie-Antoinette had secretly warned Turin in March that the new minister of external of affairs in Paris, Dumouriez, intended to declare war on the king of Sardinia.[167] As a consequence, King Victor-Amadeus III reinforced the garrisons in Savoy. Dumouriez declared that he regarded these preparations as a cause for war, there was an incident involving the French ambassador to Genoa who was refused entrance to the Sardinian kingdom, and for a moment war between France and Piedmont-Sardinia seemed imminent. It is just at the height of this crisis, towards the end of April 1792, that we catch our next glimpse of Joseph de Maistre's reactions to these developments.

In the middle of April, Maistre had crossed into France to visit his property at Talissieu and "to fight the assignats," and on his return found a letter from Henry Costa awaiting him. His long reply to Costa discusses the French threat and the Sardinian response at some length. Maistre tells his friend that he had been "sick, literally" on reading of Dumouriez's threat in the French "democratic papers," but relieved to learn that their king's response had been "what it had to be, that is to say, decently misleading."[168] Maistre obviously regretted the necessary diplomacy of a small kingdom, for he followed this remark with an envious comment about the English: "Tell me about my good friends the English who are demanding satisfaction from France for a frigate that was taken. They are the right sort! Happy are the powerful!"[169] In the course of relating the incident concerning the French ambassador to Genoa, Maistre breaks out: "There is no question of reason with these gentlemen, or even of reasoning, but of canons and bayonets."[170] And yet Maistre fears war, fears that despite the reinforced garrisons the defences are insufficient ("no citadels"), and that Savoy will be the battlefield. (It should be noted that Chambéry was only about fifteen kilometres from the French frontier.) He concludes that "A balance of terror [un repos de terreur] on the part of the one and the other would perhaps be best. This wish cannot be sublime, but I believe it prudent."[171]

In closing his letter Maistre reports a rumour that "the poor king of the French has been killed by three stab wounds"; he discounts the news, but goes on to share his reflections on French conduct at this point in their revolution: "What a century, good God, or better, what a nation! Compare the conduct of the English with regard to the unfortunate Charles I: you will see that the French are inferior to their rivals in their crimes as well as in their great deeds, and that the first is to the second (in categories of badness) as the hyena is to the lion."[172] Maistre reports as well that local French authorities had had women beaten for trying to cross the bridge at Seyssel to make their Easter duty at their former parish church in Savoy. But he breaks off in the middle of his narrative, and writes: "There is no way to write about that. The abominable executioners! ... Murders would not revolt me more."[173] Joseph de Maistre's revulsion in the face of what was happening in France was deepening in the fourth year of the Revolution.

In the months following the April 1792 war crisis, Maistre's life went on much as before. In February, he arranged the marriage of his sister Thérèse to the Chevalier Constantin de Moussy. On 5 August there is a diary entry to the effect that he lent two of his brothers (both serving as officers in the Sardinian army) 500 livres each "for the needs of war, real or imagined."[174] On 20 August another entry reports: "Rumour of an imminent invasion by the French: people ridiculously frightened."[175] But apart from these two entries, Maistre's diary for these months records only social occasions, financial transactions, and the books he has read. Despite family, social, and professional obligations, from January to September 1792, he comments on finishing the following works: 24 March, Prideau's *L'Histoire des Juifs et des peuples voisins* ("learned work, which justifies, however, Daguesseau's renowned comment 'the English do not know how to make a book'"); 9 April, a book entitled *De l'Origine des abus, des l'usage, des quantités de la foi et de la raison*[176] ("Good God"); 23 July, a history of Bengal ("in 1717 the Mogul gave the English seventeen acres of land around their factories; in 1792 the Company has 12,000,000 subjects. That is tolerably good work."); and on 28 August, Necker's *Du Pouvoir exécutif chez les grandes nations* (no comment).[177] Since we have no letters from the period from 27 April (the letter to Henry Costa) until after the French invasion, these little notes are the only immediate evidence we have of Maistre's thinking during these months.

The crisis came at the end of September 1792. The Sardinian government had apparently been warned in advance that a French attack was coming.[178] On 19 September Maistre recorded in his journal that the Senate had been pressed for the immediate registration of an edict authorizing a large issue of paper money to meet the needs of the emergency. Many of the Senators were frightened by the size of the issue; Maistre took the lead in questioning the action and said that "the government was putting its existence on one card."[179] Given the circumstances, he did not ask for resistance or a remonstrance prior to registration, but he did want the Senate to warn the government of the "fatal consequences" of the edict. The First President said that he was far from approving the edict, but that the money was absolutely required and that there was no other means of getting it. Addressing himself particularly to Maistre and Salteur, who were leading the opposition, he intimated that they had enough wit and knowledge to manage affairs, but that unfortunately they had not been consulted. On which Maistre turned to Salteur and said laughingly, "let us register the compliment." Maistre's diary entry concludes: "we went to dinner. For the present, it only remains to commend ourselves to Providence."[180]

The government's response to the French threat seems not to have gone beyond the edict to issue paper money; the local military commander was charged only with maintaining order.[181] On the 20th, Maistre's diary entry reads: "Departure of my wife and my children for Moutiers, on the rumour of an imminent French invasion. She is carrying my money, my silver, and some linen."[182] Two days later, on 22 September, Maistre wrote: "Saturday, French invasion, horrible rain. Dishonourable flight of our troops. Treason or stupidity of the generals, a rout that is incredible and even a little mysterious, according to some persons. This is the eternal shame of the government and, perhaps the annihilation of the military state."[183] Borrowing his brother-in-law's horse, Joseph de Maistre left Chambéry on horseback, followed his wife and children to Moutiers, and thus began an entirely new adventure.

Our direct evidence dating from the period prior to 22 September 1792 has only partially elucidated Maistre's decision to leave Chambéry. Clearly it was not the consequence of a high estimate of the wisdom or effectiveness of the Sardinian monarchy in meeting the French threat. Perhaps, as Darcel has suggested, "the call to adventure would have been heard sooner by the young man, if his education and the austere discipline of the familial and social milieu had not taught him to master an impulsive and dominating nature."[184] The French invasion may have offered Maistre the opportunity he craved, perhaps unconsciously, to break with the drudgery of his profession and to seek his fortune on a larger stage. Looking back many years later, Maistre himself offered a somewhat different explanation. Writing to the king after the Restoration in 1814 (in a letter requesting tangible rewards for his loyal years of service in St Petersburg), he said: "I left my country and turned my back on the Revolution to satisfy myself and because all they were doing shocked me."[185] If this retrospective comment is to be believed, it was antipathy to the French Revolution rather than loyalty to the House of Savoy that counted most in Maistre's decision to flee Savoy in September 1792.

CHAPTER FOUR

Lausanne

The next four years, 1793 to 1797, were probably the most important years of his life for Joseph de Maistre's intellectual development. Within a few months of his flight from Chambéry in September 1792, he launched himself into a new career as a counter-revolutionary pamphleteer and by the spring of 1797 he had published his *Considérations sur la France*, the work that won him a European reputation as a defender of throne and altar. This "sublime pamphlet," as Saint-Beuve called it, revealed a mature writer sure of his doctrine and in full command of a powerful literary style. *Considérations* was an occasion piece evoked by the particular circumstances in which it was written in the last half of 1796 and early 1797, but it was also a work that embodied all Maistre had become. If it reflected many facets of his life prior to 1793, it was also the more immediate product of the evolution of his thinking in response to his reading, to his experiences in Piedmont, revolutionary Savoy, and the émigré milieu of Switzerland, and to his perception of the climax of the revolutionary upheaval in France and the impact of these events on Europe. These were years in which Maistre gained experience as a writer, produced counter-revolutionary tracts of various kinds, composed two treatises on political theory (which remained incomplete and unpublished), wrote other occasional pieces, and carried on an enormous official and private correspondence.

In contrast, then, to the paucity of evidence for Maistre's thinking in the period from 1788 to 1792, we have abundant material to use in tracing his development from 1793 to 1797. The evidence includes works he published at the time, unpublished manuscripts (some published in the nineteenth century, some only recently), his diary, his notebooks (in which the dated entries begin again in May 1793), and a sampling of his correspondence.[1] The intensity of his life during these years seems to have engraved the memories of this period on Maistre's mind, since his later correspondence from St Petersburg contains vivid and often fond recollections of his sojourn in Lausanne. In addition to this direct evidence from Maistre's own hand, scholars have done some excellent detective work on this period of his life. In short, it should be possible to follow Maistre's evolution closely enough to understand something of the dynamics of his transformation from refugee Savoyard magistrate to European-rank counter-revolutionary theorist and propagandist.

FLEEING THE WHIRLWIND

When Joseph de Maistre fled Chambéry on the day of the French invasion, he took the road north to Annecy, where he slept the first night; he then turned southeast through Faverges and rejoined his family at Moutiers at nine o'clock on the morning of 24 September 1792. His wife, two children, his brother, André, and his servants were on the point of departing, so they all left the same day for Italy. After a difficult crossing of the Little St Bernard Pass (Maistre noted that his wife and children "suffered much"), they reached the safety of Aosta on the 26th.[2] Years later, in describing these events to a friend, Maistre recalled warning his wife of the implications of their flight: "When the French entered Savoy in 1792 and I crossed the Alps to follow the fortunes of the king, I said to the faithful companion of all my vicissitudes good and bad, beside a boulder I can still see from here: *my dear friend, the step we are taking today is irrevocable; it decides our lot for life*."[3] Maistre may have remembered saying something like this in 1792, but his actions during the next four or five months suggest that loyal service to the Sardinian monarchy may not have been the only possibility he had been willing to envisage.

After installing his family in Aosta, Maistre left on horseback at noon on 29 September, and despite terrible rains and flooded roads arrived in Turin on the afternoon of the 30th. The next day he dined with Baron Favrat (a long-time member of the Senate now resident in Turin, Favrat was also a brother Mason who had made the journey to Lyon in 1777 and had helped found the Sincérité lodge in Chambéry), and then began a round of visits to important ministers and people who were influential at court. He dined with Count de Hauteville, minister of foreign affairs, and Count Graneri, minister of the interior, and then, on 5 October, had an interview with the king. On the 8th, after having lunch with Dr Giraud (the royal physician but also an eminent Freemason), Maistre left Turin to return to Aosta.[4] A few days after his return, he had an interview with the Duke de Montferrat, the king's brother and commander of the Piedmontese forces stationed in the Val d'Aosta.[5] But whatever Maistre's hopes may have been, all this frenetic activity produced nothing.

The sad fact was that the refugees from Savoy were not very welcome in Piedmont. They were accused of not having known how to defend their province. The bitterness and discouragement of the Savoyards accentuated long-standing tensions between the refugees and the Piedmonetese.[6] Maistre later complained of the "scandalous reception" they had received.[7] And yet at the time in the Savoyard community in Aosta there was an almost fevered atmosphere of loyalty to the monarchy and the cause of reconquering Savoy from the French.

Maistre's closest friend among the Savoyards in Aosta was the Marquis de Sales, who had distinguished himself during the retreat of the royal forces from Savoy. Like Maistre, he had been deeply involved in Freemasonry. A man of mystical and earnest temperament, he now returned to the practice of Catholicism and reproached himself for having been lax in the past in his defence of throne and altar. Eager to redeem his previous faults, he swore that he would not return to Savoy until he had reconquered it with his sword.[8] Events in Savoy soon put this resolve to the test.

The French invasion of Savoy had been something of a promenade and the "liberators," as they thought of themselves, at first showed themselves to be the most considerate of conquerors. Composed for the most part of volunteer battalions from the Midi, this was the first French army to score such an easy success since the French had gone to war in the spring of 1792. It was an army overflowing with fraternity for their French-speaking Savoyard brothers. French Jacobins travelled the countryside promising the peasants abolition of the salt tax, corvées, the tithe, and militia obligations, and respect for their religion (with their pastors paid by the state). They had only to ask to become French and seek union with the French Republic.[9] Even before the invasion, French propaganda and a natural interest in what was happening in France had won many to the new cause. The French had no difficulty in arranging for the election of deputies from all the districts of Savoy to an Assemblée nationale des Allobroges, which met in Chambéry on 21 October. This assembly voted almost unanimously to petition the new national Convention in Paris for incorporation into the French nation. The Chambéry assembly separated after a few days, leaving the government in the hands of an executive committee whose first acts were to order an inventory of church property and the confiscation of the property of the clergy and of all émigrés (ie, all who had left Savoy since the French invasion) unless they returned before 1 January 1793 (later changed to 31 January). On 18 November 1792 the Convention promulgated a decree uniting Savoy to the French Republic as the Department of Mont-Blanc.[10]

News of the threatened confiscation of their property caused division in the Savoyard community in Aosta. Although the king counselled the nobles to obey the decree to save their property, the Marquis de Sales and his party felt such a course would compromise honour. They objected to the way the decree treated them as émigrés, since as Maistre would maintain in his first counter-revolutionary pamphlet, "we had absolutely nothing in common with the French émigrés to which they tried to assimilate us."[11] Unlike the French émigrés, the Savoyards served a king who was still on his throne even though he had lost one province of his kingdom. In leaving Savoy, the Savoyards felt they had followed the path of honour by continuing to serve the sovereign to whom they had sworn allegiance. Obedience to the revolutionary government's decree would imply recognition of that government's legitimacy. As the Marquis de Sales wrote in a letter from Aosta at the time, "on re-entering [our country] we would be offering assent to the manner of thinking of those who occupy it. Such is my opinion. Count Maistre thinks like me."[12] For the moment, Maistre stood firm with his friends. On 10 November he forwarded a doctor's certificate to Chambéry establishing that it was impossible for his wife to travel to Savoy given her pregnancy and the season.[13] While waiting for something to turn up, he spent much of his time reading.[14]

Then growing impatient, Maistre returned to Turin for another round of visits with relatives, influential friends, and government officials (13 to 28 December). On the 17th he submitted a memoir (which has not survived) to the Count de Hauteville, the minister of foreign affairs – which suggests that Maistre was soliciting a diplomatic appointment. A new position might have been worth the risk of losing his property in Savoy – but none was offered. On the morning of the 28th, he left Turin to return to Aosta. When he arrived there on the evening of 29 December, he found that his wife had left for Savoy.[15]

Since the circumstances of Madame de Maistre's departure and of her husband's subsequent action have been the subject of some disagreement among his biographers, we should take careful note of his diary entry for 29 December 1792:

forced march to embrace my wife and children sooner, whom I found departed, my oldest sister having come to look for us through Switzerland and having written to us from St Maurice, where she waited for us with a carriage. Feeling pains that made her fear an earlier delivery than she had expected, she decided to leave on the 27th. She had a good journey; on her departure, everyone had feared for her and my two children, one five years old and the other three. They crossed the Great St Bernard in baskets carried by men.[16]

Maistre's diary entries also show that he himself did not leave Aosta until 4 January, that he took the route through Switzerland via Lausanne, that he spent two days in and around Geneva, and that he did not arrive in Chambéry until the evening of 12 January.[17]

The confusion arises because this account reconstructed from Maistre's diary is hard to reconcile with what appears in his son's "biographical notice." In Rodolphe's version (which has been accepted by many of

Maistre's biographers), Madame de Maistre, wanting to save their property and knowing that her husband would risk losing it rather than expose her to the hazards of winter travel in the ninth month of her pregnancy, took advantage of his absence in Turin and left without his knowledge. Finding her absent on his return, Maistre followed immediately ("trembling to find her dead or dying in some little cabin in the Alps"), and arrived in Chambéry shortly after her.[18] The discrepancies between these accounts raise questions about Maistre's motives in returning to Savoy. If, as Rodolphe's account implies, it was only concern for the safety of his wife and children, his loyalty to the Sardinian monarchy and to the stand taken by his friends in Aosta would not be put in question. But the diary account reveals that he did not follow his family as immediately or as closely as exclusive concern for their safety would have dictated. Moreover, the diary account leaves open the possibility that his wife's decision to return to Savoy was not as sudden or unexpected as Rodolphe's narrative appears to imply.

Maistre's two married sisters and their husbands had remained in Savoy at the time of the French invasion. Marie-Christine (the eldest) and her husband, Pierre-Louis Vignet (who was also a Senator), had remained in Chambéry. Thérèse and her husband, François-Hyacinthe de Constantin (a country gentleman and a reserve officer in the Sardinian army), had remained at their country estate at Truaz (located just across the frontier from Geneva). Maistre's diary shows that he had remained in constant communication with these two families from the time he had left Chambéry.[19] This correspondence must certainly have included discussion of the threatened confiscation and the possibility of return. We know too that Maistre wrote to his wife three times during his short December visit to Turin.[20] The wording of his 28 December diary entry leaves open the possibility that he was well aware that Marie-Christine would be waiting for them at St Maurice – and that the only surprise was his wife's departure on the 27th without waiting for his return from Turin to begin together a journey that was already agreed upon. There is, moreover, additional evidence that suggests that Maistre's motives for returning to Savoy might have included (in addition to the wish to follow his wife and children) the desire to save his property from confiscation, the intention to see for himself whether or not life could be tolerable under the new regime, and the hope of inspiring and organizing opposition to it.

Something of Maistre's frame of mind on his arrival back in Chambéry can be caught in his first two diary entries following his return. On 12 January, the date of his arrival, he wrote: "dinner at Chambéry where I went to present myself to the municipality on arrival. *novus rerum nascitur ordo.*"[21] The second entry, dated 20 January, reads: "I stand my first guard at the town hall, a nice question would be to know if I will stand a second."[22] There may have been irony in the bit about a "new order," but the readiness to accept guard duty even once suggests some willingness to try co-operation. Evidence of Maistre's disillusionment with his stay in Piedmont and with any hopes of arousing opposition to the new regime in Savoy appears in letter to the Marquis de Sales written from Geneva on 2 April (after his second flight from Chambéry):

It cost me much to abandon the city of Aosta; but having taken counsel with myself, I saw that there were no means of remaining on the other side of the Alps. Sometimes I am stupid (this is not just a way of speaking), but my pride never is, and since it saw that it had nothing to gain in the country where I was, it led me back to Savoy, not without regret, however, at seeing that the cowardice and the *baseness* of our weak compatriots did not permit me to accomplish plans that I could not carry out alone ... [23]

And finally, in a letter to the Count de Hauteville, Maistre wrote of returning to Savoy "to see if there was not some way to live."[24]

Whatever Maistre's motives for returning to Savoy in January 1793, and clearly they were mixed, he soon found living under the new regime more than he could stomach. The weeks he spent in Chambéry, from 12 January to 22 February, were weeks when the revolutionary fever was running high in France. Following Valmy and the invasion of Savoy, the war was going well for the new French Republic that had been proclaimed in September 1792. But the trial of Louis XVI and his execution on 12 January 1793 greatly heightened political tensions. When Maistre returned to Chambéry he did indeed find a whole new political order. The old ducal château was occupied by General Kellerman and his staff, and French civil authority was represented by the Convention's deputy on mission, Hérault de Séchelles. The Ursuline convent had been taken over for military purposes and Sister Eulalie, Joseph's sister, had been turned out to live again as Marthe de Maistre. Of his old friends, Salteur was under house arrest and Roze had retired to Saint-Genix. Even the names of the streets had been changed; the old central square, the Place Saint-Léger, for example, had become the Place de la Liberté.[25] A transformation that had taken four years in France was being imposed on Savoy in as many months.

Joseph de Maistre scarcely bothered to feign acquiescence in the new order. Rodolphe reports that his father refused to make a "voluntary contribution" in support of the war, saying "I will give no money to kill my brothers who are serving the king of Sardinia." Perhaps for this reason, perhaps because he disdained to hide his opinion on the condemnation of Louis XVI, the Maistre residence was subjected to an armed visit from the local "security committee" on the evening of 25 January. According to Rodolphe's account, the shock of this incident triggered Madame de Maistre's labour pains.[26] In any case, Maistre's youngest daughter,

Constance, was born the next day. Her baptism was an almost clandestine ceremony compared to the kind of celebration that been customary previously.[27] This was just the time when the clerical oath was being imposed on the Savoyard clergy.[28] A few days after the birth of Constance, his friend Salteur's father, the retired First President, died, and Maistre was greatly scandalized by the funeral. His diary entry noted that the service in the cathedral had included pikes, the revolutionary red cap, and the singing of the Marseillaise.[29] Years later, he would still recall the incident with distress. Writing to Turin in 1814, he explained his decision to leave Chambéry a second time in these terms: "Savoy ... was invaded in the midst of the great paroxysm; one had to see churches closed, priests chased out, the king's portrait paraded in public and stabbed; one had to listen to the Marseillaise sung at the elevation (I heard it); my heart was not strong enough to put up with all that."[30] There seems little reason to doubt that Joseph de Maistre's revulsion for the French Revolution was significantly strengthened by this brief experience of living under the revolutionary regime.

Following the birth of his daughter, Maistre began preparations to leave Chambéry a second time. He may even have thought of fleeing to Germany.[31] In any case, he arranged to have a friend at Talissieu write requesting his presence there "so that no one would doubt my presence in France."[32] With this cover, he left his wife and children in the care of his relatives (his mother-in-law and his sisters) and again took the road north through Annecy. But he seems for a time to have been uncertain as to just what he should do. He left Chambéry on 22 February, but it was not until 13 April that he settled in Lausanne. During the intervening weeks he wandered restlessly between Truaz (where he stayed with his sister and brother-in-law), Talissieu, Seyssel, and Geneva.[33] His reading during these weeks, duly noted in his diary, also suggests an agitated and hesitant state of mind. The day before he left Chambéry he noted he had finished reading Saint-Martin's *L'Homme nouveau*. In the days that followed he read the Apocalypse, the prophets Nahum and Isaiah, the epistle of Jude, and the *Théologie de l'eau* of Johann Albert Fabricus. More secular reading included a work on Newton and Chastellux's *Voyages dans l'Amérique septentrionale*.[34] Was he thinking of extended travels?

It was during this same period that Maistre completed his first counter-revolutionary pamphlet, his "Adresse de quelques parents des militaires savoisiens à la Convention Nationale des Français."[35] The piece as published carried the date 1 February 1793, but it was only towards the end of that month that he wrote to Mallet du Pan, the well-known Swiss publicist, to request his assistance in its publication.

The pamphlet takes the form of an appeal to the Convention against the injustice of confiscating the property of Savoyard nobles and military personnel who continued to serve the king of Sardinia. But as Maistre admitted in his letter to Mallet du Pan, the address to the Convention was "only a framework and no more." His real purpose, so he told Mallet, was "to exhibit nobly and *dexterously* our way of thinking."[36] "Talking sense to his compatriots" as he put it in a preface to a later edition,[37] Maistre offered a reasoned defence of the pre-revolutionary regime in Savoy and urged continuing loyalty to the Sardinian monarchy.

But if the pamphlet expressed rational confidence in the royalist cause, Maistre's letter to Mallet du Pan reveals his tortured and discouraged emotional reaction to recent events:

Since the great crime,[38] all my philosophy abandons me. As soon as I think of this unfortunate France, of its guilty capital, of its parricide legislators, of its bloody folly, I dream only of hot irons, wheels, and gibbets. What a century, Monsieur, and what will become of us? Has sovereignty received an irreparable blow, or will we be forced to throw ourselves into the arms of despotism in order to obtain a little of that repose Newton calls *rem prorsu's substantialem?*[39] Perhaps only after long and terrible convulsions will men fold their arms and say with that other Englishman:

"For forms of government let fools contest!

Whatever is best administered, is best."

(Pope)

For that it would scarcely be worth shaking Europe, cutting off so many heads, burning so many châteaux, and assassinating an excellent king![40]

With respect to his reasons for writing, while Maistre may well have thought of himself as labouring for the "public good" (as he assured Mallet du Pan), closer examination of the circumstances surrounding the writing and publication of this pamphlet suggests that his effort may have been inspired by personal interest as well as by concern for the commonweal.

If, on leaving Chambéry a second time, Maistre still hoped for the opportunity of serving the Sardinian monarchy (perhaps with his pen), a good example of what he could do would both demonstrate his royalism and show that he was worth the hire. Maistre had, in fact, reason to fear that Turin was more than a little suspicious of his political orthodoxy. He knew that Freemasonry was now regarded with great disfavour; he knew as well that as a Senator he had been thought independent and liberal. In addition, Maistre may very well have felt compromised by the fact that his brother-in-law, François-Hyacinthe de Constantin, had collaborated with the new regime.[41]

At the time of the French invasion in the fall of 1792, Constantin had been on active duty as an officer with a reserve regiment that had been called up in the face of the French threat and stationed at Carouge (just opposite the frontier from Geneva). When the French approached Carouge, the regular units of the Sardinian army had been withdrawn without a shot being fired, and Constantin's reserve unit had been disbanded and the officers and men sent back to their homes. So Constantin, in contrast to his Maistre brothers-in-law, had not followed the Sardinian colours over the mountains to Piedmont. He had returned to his estate at Truaz and, co-operating with the new republican regime, accepted election as a municipal officer and secretary of the council of the Commune of Arthaz (the local government).

As already noted, Maistre had remained in close correspondence with his sister and brother-in-law, and it would indeed be surprising if Constantin's course of action had not been discussed in the many letters that passed back and forth between them from October until 23 Feburary, when Maistre arrived at Truaz.[42] He would have had with him the manuscript for his "Address to the National Convention." Although Constantin is, of course, not mentioned by name in the pamphlet, his situation is addressed clearly enough in a couple of passages:

what was, at that epoque so fatal for us [ie, the invasion], the duty of Savoyard servicemen? There could have been only one response: "They had to follow their colours" ... [and] obey the officers who called them to Piedmont, and that is what they did ...

The *post* of every citizen, and especially of a military man, is where the sovereign puts him. It is to the sovereign that he has sworn fidelity; he must follow him and only him ...

They [the nobles especially] have sworn by all that is most sacred to be his only, to employ for his defence all the means that nature has given them, to serve him against all his enemies at the peril of their fortunes and their lives, and to be crushed under the ruins of his throne if the throne must fall. – And they [ie, the French] would want his *faithful* to abandon him at the moment of danger! That, changed all of sudden into perjured cowards, into apostate *reasoners*, they remain in Savoy, not only to serve another power, but to wait and see, if by *chance*, another might be formed.[43]

These words were supposedly addressed to the National Convention; but in Turin they could be read as Maistre's disavowal of his brother-in-law's failure to fulfil his duties as a Savoyard officer and gentleman, and as a declaration of his own pure royalism.[44] As for Constantin, for whatever reasons, whether he was persuaded by his brother-in-law's written and verbal arguments or whether he had simply become disillusioned with the new regime, he now changed course, spoke out against the confiscation of the Church's property, was denounced for incivism, and arrested (on 23 March, while Joseph de Maistre happened to be away at Seyssel).

As Maistre described the episode in a letter to the Marquis de Sales a few days later, Constantin had just been on the point of leaving for Piedmont to rejoin the army when his arrest occurred.[45] Perhaps this detail was a bit of embellishment added to convince Maistre's correspondent (and the Sardinian government) of the loyalty of Constantin and of Maistre himself.[46] In any case, Constantin spent some months in prison in Carouge, was finally released on parole to Truaz (with the help, apparently, of Maistre's advice and influence), and then broke parole to flee to Lausanne. As a consequence of his flight, his wife (Maistre's sister) was twice arrested, before she too managed to get to Lausanne. Constantin rejoined the Sardinian army in August 1793, fought bravely (in the ranks) in that autumn's campaign in Savoy, and retreated with his unit after they were defeated by the French. But he failed to regain his commission and so retired to Switzerland to await better days.[47] Significantly, Maistre's later correspondence scarcely mentions Constantin's adventures, and of his brief collaboration with the new regime there is never a word.

With the arrest of his brother-in-law and the publication of his first pamphlet (which Mallet du Pan had arranged), Maistre concluded that he could no longer remain in Savoy. The pamphlet had been published anonymously, but the identity of the author was soon suspected. As Maistre wrote in a letter of 2 April: "I do not know by what miracle I have been left undisturbed up to now. However, it appears the moment has come to be worried; I have just come to make a tour of Geneva and I am wildly tempted to take a promenade in Switzerland … I have my freedom, it would cost me much to lose it."[48] The French representative in Geneva demanded that Maistre's pamphlet be seized; then Hérault de Séchelles, the deputy on mission in Savoy, prepared to demand the author's arrest.[49] It was time to take refuge a little farther afield than Geneva.

ESTABLISHMENT IN LAUSANNE

The choice of Lausanne as a place of refuge was not surprising. Close to Savoy and Geneva, yet as a dependency of Bern relatively independent of Geneva, Lausanne was also French-speaking. From Lausanne it was easy for Maistre to remain in close contact with his family and friends. Moreover, he expected Lausanne would be a good place to publish; in his February letter to Mallet du Pan he had requested the latter's assistance with the remark: "Would you do me the honour of having it [his pamphlet] published: I am assured that nothing is easier in Lausanne."[50] If he was going to try to make a reputation as a counter-revolutionary publicist, a little distance between himself and his government might be desirable; as Robert Triomphe puts it in a tone of not entirely misplaced cynicism, the project "would appear more easily realizable in Switzerland than in Turin, where his well-loved government would not have failed to bother him."[51]

Maistre also hoped for the assistance of his old acquaintance, Baron Vignet des Etoles, formerly intendant general of Savoy, who had just been named Sardinian ambassador to Bern. Vignet des Etoles had intervened on his behalf in Turin before, and Maistre apparently hoped that his friend might help him obtain a diplomatic appointment.[52]

Two days after Maistre's arrival in Lausanne, he met Mallet du Pan at the home of Baron d'Erlach, the *bailli* of Lausanne.[53] It must be presumed that Mallet du Pan encouraged his publicist ambitions, for a couple of days later Maistre noted in his diary that he had begun writing his *Lettres d'un Royaliste savoisien à ses compatriotes*. But he had arrived in Lausanne with only very limited funds, and he also needed some kind of position and salary.

On 20 April Maistre had a long dinner visit with Vignet des Etoles and an opportunity to discuss his prospects. He learned that in Turin he was accused of Jacobinism and of having been involved in a Masonic plot to prepare the way for the French invasion and to separate Savoy from her king. This was a serious allegation, and since many of the Savoyards who collaborated with the French after the invasion had in fact been active Freemasons, appearances seemed to give credence to the charge. Towards the end of 1790, the king had ordered all the lodges to suspend their activities; the government was now aware that some French-affiliated lodges had continued to meet. From Maistre's subsequent actions, we may conclude that Vignet des Etoles informed him that he would have to clear himself before he could expect an appointment.

Ten days later he gave Vignet des Etoles a substantial "Mémoire sur la Franc-Maçonnerie."[54] The memoir takes the form, not of a direct denial of Maistre's own involvement in any Masonic plot, but of a rather detached history and description of Savoyard Freemasonry. But beneath the cool tone of the document, one can sense Maistre's embarrassment. On the one hand, he does not gainsay his involvement in Masonry, and in fact makes a point of writing with the confident knowledge of an insider. But on the other hand, he appears to remain quite conscious of his Masonic oath of secrecy; except for the Bellegardes (father and son, founders of Savoyard Masonry), Brunswick (the now deceased former head of Scottish rite Masonry), and a Chambéry goldsmith (a notorious democrat who had welcomed the French with great enthusiasm), no individual Masons are named. Yet the memoir is carried off with aplomb. As Rebotton observes, Maistre proved a clever advocate of his own interests, "displaying the truth, but not the whole truth, voluntarily leaving in the shadow things that might do him a disservice with his questioner."[55]

In general terms, Maistre described the Savoyard lodges as "honest societies of pleasure, embellished by some acts of benevolence."[56] The "equality" of Masonry, which appears to have worried Vignet des Etoles, was dismissed as largely symbolic, restricted to expressions of brotherhood within the lodges (and between lodges as lodges), and having nothing to do with "the distinction of estates in society."[57]

On the political activities of Freemasons, Maistre tried to maintain a moderate balanced position. He could hardly deny the revolutionary activities of well-known Masons (up to and including Louis XVI's cousin, the Duke d'Orléans, who had headed the major branch of French Masonry on the eve of the Revolution). But he made the same distinction between the activities of individual Masons and Masonry as a movement that modern scholars make. He acknowledged that it was possible that French Freemasonry had served the Revolution, not as Freemasonry, but as an "association of clubs," since it was natural that with many Masons favouring the Revolution the lodges would be "converted into clubs."[58] As for Savoyard Masonry, Maistre acknowledged that a couple of the "bourgeois" lodges counted in their membership some "very bad" individuals and that it was possible the French had approached these people. But he denied that Savoyard Freemasonry and its principles had anything "in common with the French Revolution."[59] His own reformed lodge, Maistre assured his friend, had ceased meeting shortly after the troubles began in France, even before the king had ordered the suspension of activities. The denial of an explicit Masonic political goal was quite categorical: "What I can assure you is that even in the most suspect lodges in Savoy, there did not exist the least sign that announced a political goal in principle. And as to the Reform lodge, I can affirm this on all that is most sacred."[60] On this point the memoir departed from the truth. In his concern to deny the suspected "Masonic plot" (which in the sense of a real Masonic conspiracy to overthrow throne and altar never existed, of course), Maistre "neglected" to acknowledge that Masonry, his own lodge included, had encouraged discussion of political reforms. His own "Mémoire au Duc de Brunswick" of 1782, as we have seen, had proposed "the instruction of governments" as one of the goals of Freemasonry. Whatever mental reservations Maistre may have had in writing this memoir, it is hard to avoid the conclusion that he deliberately tried to mislead his friend on this issue.

Perhaps on the old principle that the best defence is a good offence, Maistre blamed the government itself for not being better informed sooner: "If the king had not been served by fools in this matter, as in everything else, it would have been easy to use the reformed lodge to inspect the others and discover lots of things; but the fatal system of fear and general distrust having prevailed, good subjects, paralyzed by suspicion, contented themselves with groaning; the wicked acted as they liked, and the king knew nothing."[61] One wonders if it was not Maistre's outspokenness as much as his Masonic past that kept him in disfavour in Turin!

We do not know what Vignet des Etoles did with Maistre's memoir – whether he simply used it for his own information or to plead Maistre's case with Turin or whether he forwarded the entire document. What we do know is that Maistre's involvement in Freemasonry continued to bedevil his reputation in Turin. In December 1793, some seven months after he submitted his memoir, and after the royalist forces had been thoroughly defeated in their attempt to reconquer Savoy (and scapegoats were being sought), Vignet des Etoles raised the matter again. This time Maistre responded, not with a careful memoir, but with an angry denial that Masonry had ever been of any importance:

> The one thing that makes me angry is to see you talking seriously about this nonsense of Freemasonry, a univeral childishness on this side of the Alps, and of which you would have been a part if you had lived among us, and in which I was so little involved after I became active in my profession that one day I received a delegation that wanted to know if I wished to be deleted from the list. But my good friends in Turin did not hesitate to call me *brother Joseph* while I tranquilly passed sentences in Chambéry. I am not surprised that in a country whose capital vice is to attach extreme importance to nothings, they have talked and talked too much about this trifle; but I am astonished that you have not sensed straightaway that this was only a pretext for making sport of my hopes for a position.[62]

Exasperated by the seeming impossibility of clearing himself by proving the inoffensive character of Savoyard Freemasonry, his vital interests at stake, his future and that of his children menaced, Maistre tried to bluff his way out by dismissing Masonry and his own involvement as unimportant silliness. Neither contention accords with what we know of Masonry or its place in Maistre's life and intellectual development.

From his interview with Vignet des Etoles, Maistre must have known that an immediate appointment from Turin was unlikely. He had already begun his *Lettres d'un Royaliste savoisien* and he did not allow the unforeseen difficulty over Masonry to distract him from this project. But even while writing the *Lettres*, he appears to have been preparing himself for other eventualities. On 7 May he began taking German lessons (which were to continue until 30 August), and in July he took a series of lessons in physics.[63] Maistre had concluded the memoir on Masonry with the suggestion that it would be useful to send an intelligent and trustworthy person to Germany to research "the different mysterious societies of that country,"[64] and it seems likely that this was intended as a not very subtle hint about an appropriate assignment for himself. Or he may already have been thinking of seeking a position as a tutor at one of the German courts, a possibility that received serious consideration in a later period of uncertainty. In the meantime, whatever his longer-term intentions or hopes may have been, he continued his initiative as a free-lance counter-revolutionary publicist.

Maistre's four *Lettres d'un Royaliste savoisien à ses compatriotes* were written between April and July 1793; the first appeared in mid-May, the second and third in June and July, and the last on 20 August. His ostensible and immediate purpose, as revealed in the *Lettres* themselves and in his efforts to ensure their distribution in French-occupied Savoy, was to revive royalist sentiment in the province and to help prepare the way for its reconquest by the monarchy and its Austrian ally. But the argument of the *Lettres* suggests that he also hoped to be read by influential people in his government. He was offering them an analysis of the Revolution and a counter-revolutionary strategy based on that analysis. A third purpose may have been to provide further evidence of his loyalty in the hope of bettering his chances for an appointment, but his correspondence with Vignet des Etoles over these months shows that he was aware that his project was risky on this score. He wrote without the express commission of his government, and although he sought and took into account solicited comments from Vignet des Etoles on his drafts, he deliberately avoided requesting Turin's permission to publish. In a letter written the day before the first letter appeared, Maistre acknowledged that Baron d'Erlach had expressly counselled him not to publish before consulting Turin, but realizing that if he consulted "they would say no,"[65] he went ahead and published anyway. In another letter a few days later he admitted that he had the printed brochure in front of him for four days before he "had the courage to sent it to M. the Count de Hauteville."[66] Before the fourth letter even appeared, Maistre was aware that sale of the *Lettres* had been forbidden in Turin, "apparently as anti-royalist."[67] He was also warned by Henry Costa, writing from Turin, that "anything that is too vigorously thought, anything that announces too much energy, sells poorly in this country."[68] As Maistre remarked to Vignet des Etoles, "I have not enhanced my fortune in fabricating these Letters."[69] In short, Maistre may have been ambitious for an appointment, but in his determination to publish he was willing to endanger his chances for a position.

Perhaps the most striking characteristic of the *Lettres d'un Royaliste savoisien* considered as counter-revolutionary propaganda designed for circulation in Savoy is the way Maistre tried to appeal to the reason and self-interest of his compatriots. For the most part the letters were a detailed and carefully argued apology for the wisdom and moderation of the Sardinian monarchy's rule in Savoy in the decades before the Revolution. The traditional roles of the nobility and the clergy were defended with a similar reasoned approach. The peace, order, and happiness of life under the old order were contrasted with the violence, disorder, and suffering introduced by the French invasion and the imposition of the "benefits" of the French Revolution. Although there were evocations of honour and sworn oaths to the old sovereign, the emphasis was on enlightened self-interest. Maistre entreated his readers to "learn how to be royalists; formerly this was an instinct, today it is a science." Recalling the fidelity of earlier generations, Maistre complained that loyalty had now become "a matter of calculation."

But what he was telling his fellow countrymen who had welcomed and supported the French was that they had miscalculated. Appealing to their reason, Maistre sought to persuade them that support for the traditional order was really in their own best interests. "Love your sovereign as you love *order*, with all the strength of your intelligence."[70] But this was appealing to the very rationalism that had repudiated the old order. Maistre's *Lettres* exemplify the dilemma of a purely political royalism in an age of democratic revolution.

Much of the strength of a traditional society lies in the fact that its structure and values are unquestioned – indeed unquestionable. It is only when the status quo has been attacked and disrupted that the need to defend it becomes imperative. The conservative theorist almost inevitably finds himself in a defensive posture, involved in a debate on the relative merits of the old order versus the new, and impelled to base his arguments on the assumptions of the innovators. And by engaging in the argument at all, he easily becomes suspect to members of the traditional élite who have always simply assumed the rightness of existing structures and values and their own privileged place in the traditional order.[71]

Maistre undertook the defence of the old order, but neither his strategy of appealing to reason and self-interest nor his own outlook (informed as it was by broad reading in the Enlightenment and his experiences in Freemasonry and the magistrature) inclined him to an uncritical defence. Moreover, his analysis of the nature of the Revolution and the reasons it was welcomed in Savoy led him to believe that winning back the province required a twofold strategy of propaganda to revive royalist sentiments and of reform of the monarchy to make it more effective and acceptable. The *Lettres d'un Royaliste savoisien* aimed openly at the first objective, but the second was hardly less apparent. Since Maistre opted for a reasoned appeal to his compatriots, frank discussions of the weaknesses of the old regime in France and elsewhere, and of the reasons for the Revolution's initial acceptance in France and in Savoy, served the two purposes of enhancing the credibility of his propaganda and of persuading influential people in the Sardinian government of the necessity of remedying abuses and implementing reforms. That the second audience and purpose was part of Maistre's intention seems evident both from the general tenure of the letters and from the explicit comment with which he concluded the third letter: "Such are the reflections that I have believed it my duty to present, not only to Savoy, but to my country in general."[72] Maistre himself, in the very next line, acknowledged "the extreme delicacy of the subject." Given the nature of his approach and the conservatism of the government, it is probably not surprising that his pamphlets were less than welcome in Turin.

While the *Lettres* enunciate many of the themes that will characterize Maistre's later writings (such as rejection of the "absurd" theory of popular sovereignty, Burkean apologies for the utility of prejudice, strictures on the limitations of reason, and startingly realistic description of the bloody punishments of the old regime), they also differ in one important respect. In contrast to the profoundly providential interpretation of the French Revolution that characterizes Maistre's *Considérations sur la France*, the analysis and the prescriptions offered in the *Lettres* are essentially political. There is, to be sure, one passage in which the Revolution is characterized as a "great judgment," with the suspension of "secondary causes" by an "inflexible Providence" used to explain the failure of most observers, including the king of Sardinia, to appreciate its nature.[73] But this evocation of Providence is little more than aside, and clearly incidental to the main thrust of the argument. It provides evidence that Maistre was beginning to meditate on a providential interpretation of the Revolution, but as we shall see it would be another year before he would think through and elaborate this approach.

In the interpretation offered in the *Lettres*, the French Revolution is portrayed as the consequence of the abuses and weaknesses of the old regime and the seduction of public opinion by the purveyors of a false philosophy that imagined and preached the possibility of a radical transformation of government and society. As Maistre described the situation on the eve of the Revolution, "the governments of Europe had aged and their decrepitude was only too well known to those who wanted to profit from the situation for the execution of their deadly projects." Abuses had accumulated, and the government of France, in particular, "had fallen into decay." With "no more unity, no more energy, no more public spirit, a revolution was inevitable."[74] Maistre assured his Savoyard readers that if they were initially mistaken as to the character of the French Revolution, they had simply shared a "universal error." At first, everyone had "believed in a possible regeneration." But with the meeting of the Estates-General, divisions had appeared as it became clear that the throne, the altar, and hereditary distinctions were all in danger. With the night of 4 August 1789, the Revolution was "left without a single wise supporter."[75]

Unfortunately, the people took longer to appreciate the disastrous character of the Revolution. The revolutionary slogans, "sovereignty of the people, the rights of man, liberty, equality," were terribly seductive. The innovators played on the most sensitive strings of the human heart and allied themselves with "ambition, interest, and vanity."[76]

Despite the benign and progressive character of the old order in Savoy, and the absence of the abuses that had characterized the old regime in France (such as venality of office, gross inequalities of taxation, and excessive Church wealth), the superficially attractive slogans of the Revolution had spread to Savoy. The response of the monarchy and its representatives in Savoy, Maistre acknowledged, had not been as measured or as wise as the occasion required. When these mistakes were added to old and inevitable ethnic tensions between Piedmontese and Savoyards, to resentment that had been aroused by the monarchy's unfortunate tendency to allow too much influence to the military, and to the impression of abandonment created by the hasty withdrawal of the Sardinian army at the time of the French invasion, the initial welcome accorded the French and their principles was not so surprising.

But now, as Maistre put it in the opening remarks of his first letter, "time has calmed this first effervescence and ... the sad and salutary instructions of experience" have opened "good minds and upright hearts" to persuasion.[77] In the preface that he added to a combined edition of the *Lettres* and the earlier "Address to the National Convention," Maistre spelled out the first part of his counter-revolutionary strategy with unequivocal clarity:

It is necessary to work on opinion, to undeceive peoples of the metaphysical theories with which they have been done so much harm, to teach them to appreciate the advantages of what they possess, to show them the danger of looking for an imaginary best without calculating the evils by which it must be purchased, to show them that, just as in religion there is a point where faith must be blind, so in politics there is a point where obedience must be the same, and that the mass of men is made to be led, that reason itself teaches distrust of reason, and that the masterpiece of reasoning is the discovery of the point where one must stop reasoning.[78]

All these themes were developed at some some length in the *Lettres*.

The second part of Maistre's counter-revolutionary strategy, regeneration of the monarchy, is implicit in his reference to the government's errors in dealing with the revolutionary crisis and his critical comments on its tendency to subordinate civil affairs to military authorities, and explicit in his specific references to reform. In one passage, for example, Maistre writes: "We are habituated to one kind of government; let us perfect it as much as possible; let us denounce the abuses of government with respect and moderation, but let us hold on to it."[79] In another place he says that "the act of reforming governments does not at all consist in overthrowing them to remake them according to idealistic theories, but in bringing them back to their internal and hidden principles."[80] In both cases advocacy of reform is carefully embedded in a conservative context, but the insistence on the necessity for change is nonetheless unmistakable. In another passage Maistre even seems to countenance concerted pressure by Savoyards in favour of certain reforms. Discussing a practice whereby military commanders have imposed punishment on civilians without trial (which he denounces as an abuse "outside the law"), Maistre concludes by remarking: "It is impossible that an entire people wisely asks for a reform without it being implemented."[81]

This early essay in counter-revolutionary propaganda failed to achieve either of the goals Maistre had envisaged. He lacked the financial and physical means to ensure distribution of any significant number of copies in French-occupied Savoy. His letters to Vignet des Etoles record some small successes,[82] but also reveal his frustration. Towards the end of July, for example, he writes: "An abbé who came from Piedmont to Geneva for religious matters filled a mule pack with royalist and Catholic pamphlets and passed them into Savoy. I was there for 25 copies, but that is a drop in the bucket."[83] The fourth letter did not even appear until after the military campaign it was designed to precede was well under way. By the end of September, the attempted reconquest had failed miserably, and so rendered superfluous pamphlets designed to assist military operations.[84] And as we have already seen, the *Lettres* succeeded no better in Turin, where the war minister banned their sale.

Despite his initial failure as a publicist, Maistre did manage to secure an official appointment. On 3 August he learned from Baron d'Erlach that he had been named the Sardinian "Correspondent" in Lausanne.[85] This position, which might be likened to that of a consul, provided a modest salary of 100 livres per month,[86] and involved him in a variety of activities. Working under the general supervision of Vignet des Etoles in his capacity as Sardinian ambassador to Bern, Maistre organized an intelligence net in occupied Savoy, kept Turin informed of everything he learned from this net and from his contacts in Lausanne, and provided assistance to Savoyard refugees. The responsibilities of this position kept Maistre very busily occupied from August 1793 until his departure from Lausanne at the end of February 1797. The correspondence especially must have been enormously time-consuming. He had some secretarial assistance from refugee priests, but he appears to have written most of his letters himself. He had no office, but worked out of cramped rented personal accommodations, often changed as he was joined in Lausanne by members of his family.

In May, his sister Anne had come from Chambéry with his son Rodolphe. At the end of August, it was his sister Thérèse who came from Truaz. Then in September, just when the military campaign was in full swing, Madame de Maistre herself came from Chambéry. Learning that Rodolphe was ill with smallpox, she had walked with Adèle to Annecy, where she left the little girl with a person of trust who promised to take her to Geneva when it was safe to do so (Adèle was finally delivered to Lausanne in early November). Then she disguised herself as a peasant, walked east through the lines, over the mountains, and around the far end of Lake Geneva to arrive at her husband's apartment at ten thirty in the evening on 10 September.[87] The other daughter, baby Constance, was left in the care of her grandmother, Madame de Morand. (Joseph de Maistre did not see Constance again until his wife and daughters finally joined him in St Petersburg in 1814.) Thérèse soon moved into her own apartment, but Jenny arrived in December (to remain until late February 1794 when she left for Turin to marry the Chevalier de Buttet). Finally, in March 1794, the household was again increased with the arrival of Maistre's other sister, Marthe, and his aunt, the Countess de Chavanne, and her daughter.

A few days after Maistre's nomination as Correspondent, the Austro-Sardinian campaign to regain Savoy got under way. At first hopes were very high. The timing appeared excellent; the French republic was distracted by the "federalist" revolt that had followed the expulsion of the Girondins from the Convention in early June. Troops were withdrawn from Savoy to deal with the rebellions at Marseille, Toulon, and Lyon. There were uprisings of armed bands in a number of centres in Savoy (which Maistre's propaganda may have helped inspire). In Paris, there was some talk in the Convention about abandoning the department of Mont-Blanc. But the Austro-Sardinian army did not begin its campaign until the night of 11–12 August, and moved too slowly to achieve surprise. The French reacted vigorously to the threat, arresting noble hostages in Chambéry, and transferring forces from the seige of Lyon. By the end of October, General Kellerman had completely suceeded in driving out the invading army.[88] Maistre had done all he could to assist the campaign, recruiting Savoyard and French émigrés to serve with the Sardinian forces, and sending a steady stream of intelligence to Turin and the local military commanders. But his correspondence had often been critical of the Austrian commanders for their caution. With the failure of the invasion, he in turn was blamed for having provided a misleading assessment of the strength of the French forces in the province and of the prospects of a mass uprising against the French.[89]

Maistre's letters to Vignet des Etoles during this period show that he was often in sharp disagreement with his superior and with official government policy and action. In early September, when prospects for the invasion had still appeared favourable, he had been offered a position as chief magistrate of a special court that the government proposed to establish to try Savoyards who had collaborated with the French. Maistre rejected the whole idea as "impolitic." He complained that "four full years of mistakes and misfortunes had taught nothing to those who lead us." Instead of inundating Savoy with encouraging and consoling writings, "they think only of planting gallows."[90] Vignet des Etoles responded to Maistre's criticisms of the government by asking him: "Do you like revolutions better?" Maistre's rejoinder shows him trying to maintain a moderate middle ground: "I recognize here one of the great evils of the French Revolution, which is that a very great number of good people have been led to believe that there is no longer a mean between the strangest political absurdities and the revolutions we have just seen. But between these two evils there is a middle way of a reasonable and tolerable government."[91]

Maistre's response to recriminations about the failure of the Savoyards to rise up en masse against the French is also interesting for what it reveals of his sense of the realities of the political situation in Savoy:

Every form of government has its advantages and disadvantages. Democracy must not hope for the wisdom, tranquility and duration of monarchy, which in turn has no right to require republican energy of its subjects. You perhaps believe that an armed gathering is something easy. Nothing is more difficult. The jealousy of the sovereign (a very reasonable and very legal jealousy) rejects every kind of assembly. The peasant, since infancy, has been nourished with the idea that assemblies, petitions, and other such practices of free governments are crimes: as a consequence the people understand nothing ... Accustomed to letting themselves be guided in everything by the will of another, they have no will of their own ... Today we need energetic people who know how to assemble and to arm themselves in an instant, to face cannon that they have never heard, and to risk death gaily. Very well, but the thing is impossible.[92]

The fall of 1793 was a terribly discouraging time for Joseph de Maistre. In addition to the disappointing failure of the attempted reconquest, he learned that his library in Chambéry had been pillaged. "My whole life work dispatched in the twinkling of an eye."[93] In financial difficulties, he was forced to borrow a substantial sum from Baron d'Erlach.[94] But when he was advised to submit a memoir to Turin explaining his embarrassed situation and asking for financial assistance, he rejected the idea: "That would be literally asking for alms; but I assure you that I would gaily mount the guillotine rather than send such a memoir." He felt he deserved employment not by "title of grace" but by strict justice, and told Vignet des Etoles that if he were a bachelor he would serve no more "either here or in Turin."[95]

Despite his precarious personal situation, Maistre refused to alter his political views to suit Vignet des Etoles. In early December, in the same letter in which he denied the significance of Freemasonry, he offered this confession of political belief:

To my way of thinking, the project of putting Lake Geneva in bottles is less foolish than that of restoring things on precisely the same footing as they were before the revolution ... Military government is something that I have always detested, that I detest now, and that I will detest all my life; however I prefer it to Jacobinism. It is better than the most execrable thing in the world, that is the unique commendation that one can give it ... If this fine government, which is the death of monarchy, is restored, I will say what I have always said, "Obey." I will excuse the most scandalous excesses with the most filial tone. But if, by chance, the monarchy is restored separated from *batonocracy*, I hope you will permit me to be content.[96]

In another letter in early January 1794, this political stance is placed in the broader context of Maistre's evolving views on the significance of the French Revolution:

You have known my way of thinking for a long time. I have long suspected and now I believe I am able to be sure that we are experiencing a great epoch, a general Revolution, and that we have to be patient. To speak plainly (but this is only between us) I firmly believe that Monarchy has been unalterably stricken (I mean absolute monarchy) and that there is only one way for it to save itself: that is for it to modify itself and win the minds of peoples. Unfortunately, that is just what it will not do. It thinks only of not retreating. You will see where that will lead us. The judgment fallen on monarchy is visible.[97]

Reviewing all the failures and disappointments of the anti-French coalition in 1793 (the failures of the "federalist" revolt, of the Vendée, and of the allied military campaigns in Savoy, on the Rhine, and in the Low Countries), Maistre concluded: "The princes must rid themselves of two equally foolish dreams: that of dismembering France and that of restoring the old regime. They must declare this publicly and frankly. If follows that they must bind their peoples to themselves by prudent concessions and act together not against France but against the Convention. Then *perhaps* they will be able to do something."[98] Maistre was upset about how he was being treated by Turin (Hauteville was not answering his letters), and he saw his own situation as demonstrating his pessimistic assessment:

If I had written for the Republic, it would surely have made much of me; the monarchy forbids my book and forgets me. This is a small proof of what I have just been telling you. It does not seek to recruit. It does not think of making partisans for itself. Anyway, I am speaking to you historically for I am not pouting. For the moment governments must be loved and served such as they are; for without that everything will go badly – perhaps even with that.[99]

Discontented and discouraged though he may have been, Maistre continued to try to serve the royalist cause.

Shortly after writing this letter, Maistre made a trip to Bern to visit Vignet des Etoles.[100] Following their discussions, Vignet des Etoles agreed to write to Hauteville and recommend him for a position in the foreign affairs department in Turin. This letter has survived and offers us an interesting glimpse of how Maistre was seen by others at this time:

It would appear to me to be valuable to have at your disposal a capable pen … Two words to him indicating your idea or your purpose would suffice for his mind to exhaust the matter with the touch that is appropriate to the subject. He is equally docile about redoing anything that you believe must be taken out of a first draft … As men do not have good qualities without a mixture of faults, friendship must not … hide those that could affect service. So I must warn you that M. Maistre displays too much wit and can make it felt inconsiderately in social occasions for which he has a great taste and from which, in consequence, he should be kept away. It is by this superiority that he has made for himself many enemies, for which I have reproached him for a long time. I also scold him for allowing himself to be easily disheartened.[101]

Hauteville's reply has also survived; it was a polite but categorical refusal: "I know his talents: he is as you say, Monsieur, a man of much wit. However, I do not believe that it is possible to draw from his pen, however good, such great advantages as you imagine."[102] So Maistre stayed on in Lausanne as the Correspondent of the monarchy.

CONSIDERING FRANCE

In the months immediately following completion of his *Lettres d'un Royaliste savoisien* and his appointment as Correspondent, Maistre had been too busy to undertake writing anything for publication. With the defeat of the Austro-Sardinian campaign, he was at first too disillusioned to try his hand again: "I have written nothing more since my 4th letter. Events so strongly vex prudence, that one trembles to write a line." But he admitted in the same letter that he had "three fine and fruitful subjects in mind: sovereignty of the people, hereditary aristocracy, and religion."[103] But it is not until towards the end of March 1794 that we find evidence of further literary production. In a letter to Vignet des Etoles, Maistre reveals that he has finished a work and that he is having it examined by a man he very much reveres.[104] Then on 24 March there is a diary entry showing that he has sent his "5th Savoyard letter" to Fribourg to a person identified as the bishop of Sisteron.[105] Maistre's reader, François de Bovet (an émigré French churchman who had been bishop of Sisteron before the Revolution and who would become the archbishop of Toulouse at the Restoration), returned the manuscript with a critique and a covering letter in mid-April.

As a consequence of Bovet's criticisms, Maistre rethought his project and abandoned the idea of publishing a "fifth letter." A couple of months later he mentioned the work again in another letter to Vignet des Etoles: "I do not know what to tell you about my work. It has gained infinitely, but the ideas spread out, and the infinite number of objections made by my bishop have produced a new work."[106] In particular, Maistre appears to have taken to heart Bovet's passing comment that "it will appear extraordinary that in treating *ex professo* the question of sovereignty of the people, the author has said nothing of J.J. Rousseau."[107] In any case, Maistre now undertook a systematic study of Rousseau's two famous works, the *Discours sur ...l'inégalité parmi les hommes* and the *Contrat social*, with a view to refuting the Genevan's ideas on social contract, popular sovereignty, and the state of nature. The manuscript "fifth letter" he had sent to Bovet was retitled "De la Souveraineté du Peuple. Discours Préliminaire," and then abandoned, but portions of it were incorporated into another much more substantial manuscript also carrying the title "De la Souveraineté du Peuple."[108] From the evidence of Maistre's letters to Vignet des Etoles and from contemporary references in the piece, it seems clear that Maistre worked on this manuscript from the beginning of 1794 through mid-1795.[109]

Maistre never completed or published "La Souveraineté du Peuple." Nor did he complete or publish a second manuscript on which he worked during this same period (or a bit later) and which he entitled "De l'état de nature."[110] Although left unfinished, these works remain important for what they tell us of Maistre's political theory. The positions he would defend in *Considérations sur la France* and *Du Pape* (see especially, the first four chapters of Book II) reflect the theoretical stance he had worked out in these manuscripts. We know from his correspondence with Vignet des Etoles that it was in part financial considerations that led Maistre to abandon these essays in political philosophy.[111] But the decision not to publish these pieces probably stems as well from Maistre's evolving interpretation of the Revolution and from his consequent reassessment of appropriate tactics for dealing with it.

With the defeat of the Austro-Sardinian invasion of Savoy in the early fall of 1793, with the continuing success of French armies in the winter and spring of 1794, and with the heightened violence of the Terror in France during this same period, Maistre was gradually coming to doubt his initial political analysis of the Revolution. Clues to the direction of his thinking may be found in the increasingly insistent references to providence in his letters during these same months. For example, in March 1794, after discussing the situation in Lyon after its reconquest by the revolutionaries, he remarks: "I am expecting only misfortunes until veritable miracles restore order."[112] A month later, reporting the French invasion of Piedmont: "The judgment of God goes its way." Later in the same letter, he tells Vignet des Etoles: "Do not be astonished by the general blindness, even on the part of priests and nobles: this blindness is necessary for the execution of the designs of Providence. We are suffering for it, but we must bow our heads."[113] In early May, reflecting again on the terrible news from Italy, Maistre put a more precise providential interpretation on these events:

Anyway, my dear friend, I am persuaded that all this will end, and what is more, I believe that all we are seeing will lead us to the good by unknown ways. This idea consoles me for everything; but when and how will we manage to get there? That is the secret of Providence. As far as I can judge, I believe we are still a fairly long way away.

What can still console us, is that the present order, as abominable as it is, is necessary so that justice be accomplished, and so that the chief scoundrels are punished.[114]

Finally, one last example from another letter written a few days later: "An order of things founded on atheism, immorality, theft, brigandage, murder, etc., cannot last. But when will it end? That is what we cannot know. We are seeing a veritable flogging. When the hand that flogs finds that there has been enough, we will all be surprised to see the scene ended by unexpected means."[115] As the months passed, the Revolution was seen more and more in terms of providential punishment that would somehow lead to something better.

Then at the end of May 1794, Maistre went through a wrenching personal experience that stimulated him to think through the implications of a providential interpretation of the Revolution. On 28 May he received news that young Eugène Costa, the son of his closest friend, Henry Costa, had died as a result of wounds received in fighting the French.[116] It fell to Maistre to go to nearby Nyon and break the news to Henry Costa's wife. He travelled there on the 29th, but could not bring himself to tell her until the 31st.[117] In the face of the mother's grief, and as a tribute to the young man for the sake of the father, Maistre set himself the task of writing a "discourse" on the life and death of their son. We can glimpse the seriousness of Maistre's involvement in this project from comments that Madame Costa made a few days later in a letter to her husband: "Maistre is working very hard. Alas, I fear that he is not up to his task and that he is not content with his work. I find him sad since he has been occupied with it. He has read me some of it; I find that he has not brought out the charms of his infancy enough. Politics is too much the base of his work. I do not believe Maistre is sensitive enough."[118] In effect, Maistre was trying to place Eugène's death in the context of many other innocent deaths brought about by the French Revolution.

As published in Lausanne in mid-August 1794, Maistre's discourse provides clear evidence that he had achieved a distinctive interpretation of the Revolution.[119] But the manuscript pages he chose not to publish are even more interesting; one finds in them an early statement of the main themes of his *Considérations sur la France*, as well as hints of other later works. Since these manuscript pages are of such great significance for establishing and dating this crucial turning point in Maistre's intellectual development, it seems essential to cite the suppressed passages at some length.[120]

The first omitted passage follows a section in the published discourse where Maistre has been praising the domestic education young Eugène had received from his parents.[121] The deleted material is a lengthly development of the thesis that "human reason reduced to its individual strengths is perfectly worthless not only for the creation but even for the preservation of any religious or political association, becauses it produces only disputes, and to conduct himself man needs not problems but beliefs." While the idea that "philosophy is … an essentially disruptive force" found expression in the *Considérations*,[122] almost the whole of this suppressed passage may be found in Maistre's unfinished "De la Souveraineté du Peuple."[123] The latter, however, does not include the portion of the passage that contains an early version of the famous portrait of Voltaire to be found in the fourth dialogue of the *Soirées de Saint-Pétersbourg*.[124] In the course of denouncing what he calls the sophists of the time, Maistre contrasted Fénelon and Voltaire – to the great disadvantage of the latter:

See especially their coryphaeus, the famous Voltaire. Certainly one cannot admire enough his so great and so varied talents. But how vile he was! How dominated he was by the basest and most miserable passions. I see him envious to the point of rage, proud to the point of madness, tirelessly casting down the statues of great men in order to lay hands on their pedestals, pitiless persecutor, wicked by taste and charitable by vanity, frenzied enemy of holy truths and all the more guilty because unpersuaded himself, writing with the same pen the role of Lusignan and the war of Geneva; I see him plunging immodestly into the most abject mire, prostituting his pen to immorality, rhyming at length to amuse Parisian turpitudes that would have scandalized Sodom. Seeing all this, suspended between admiration and horror, I would like to see a statue erected to him by the hand of the executioner.

The later version in the *Soirées* was much more powerful, of course, but it is interesting to observe how this early effort was later reworked into a literary tour de force.

The next suppressed passage is significant for what it reveals of the source of one of Maistre's characteristic themes: the notion that the Revolution was a providential punishment for the pride of the philosophes for wanting to construct a world without God. In the deleted passage in question, after citing a remark by Frederick ii of Prussia to the effect that "if he wanted to lose an empire he would have it governed by philosophers," Maistre continued:

So this is not a theological exaggeration, this is a very simple truth vigorously expressed in these words by a prelate we lost last year ... "In its pride Philosophy said: 'To me belongs wisdom, science, and domination, to me belongs the conduct of men since it is I who enlightens them.' To punish it, to cover it with opprobrium, God had to condemn it to reigning for a moment." (The Archbishop of Tarentaise to his people, 28 April 1793) In effect, it reigned, it will reign again no doubt, and it will never be more than *a moment for the master of moments*. During this moment it enjoyed human omnipotence, and in all the acts of the French Revolution one can hear the voice of divinity saying "I want to show you what you can do without me." Never has human pride attempted more, never has it been more ridiculous.

This image, which was more implicit that explicit in the *Considérations*, was expressed most forcefully in paragraph LXVI of Maistre's *Essai sur le principe générateur*.[125]

But the most significant suppressed passage occurs near the end of Maistre's manuscript. In the published version of the discourse, after having portrayed the infancy, childhood, military career, and death of Eugène, Maistre began his peroration with this characterization of the Revolution and its victims:

We must have the courage to admit it, Madame, for a long time we have not understood the Revolution of which we are the witnesses. For a long time we have taken it for an *occurrence* [*événement*]. We were in error; this is an *epoch*; and unhappy are generations that assist at epochs of the world! A thousand times happier are men who are called only to the contemplation of the history of great revolutions, the fevers of opinion, the furies of parties, the clash of empires, and the funerals of nations! Happy the men who are on earth in one of those moments of rest that serve as intervals to the convulsions of a condemned and suffering nature! Let us flee, Madame! But where to flee? Are we not bound by all the laws of love and duty? Let us suffer then, let us suffer with a reflective resignation. If we know how to unite our reason to eternal reason, instead of being only *patients*, we will at least be *victims*.[126]

It is just at this point that Maistre's manuscript has some very important pages that he decided to exclude from the printed version of the discourse. Following a slightly different version of the last few lines of the above paragraph, the manuscript continues as follows:

Above all, let us elevate ourselves to great thoughts and let us see in the French Revolution what must be seen in it: a terrible Judgment for the present moment and an infallible Regeneration for that which will follow. In truth, we do not know the length of these moments, but what does it matter, all durations are only instants.

Man is free, undoubtedly, but he is dependent, and the sphere of his faculties does not always have the same dimensions. He is bound to the throne of the universal Sovereign by a supple chain that retracts more or less. He is free enough in this movements to win or lose merit, and not enough to be able to derange the universal plans.

In ordinary times, this chain has all possible extension: man senses his dependence less because a greater number of acts are abandoned to his action, and in regulating his conduct by the decisions of his reason, he sees only that his action produces the results he expected. But in moments of Revolution, the sovereign power brusquely comes nearer to man and clasps him tightly. The hand that presses him makes itself palpable, so to say, and this is what we are experiencing at the present moment. The movement of the Revolution sweeps us away like light straw before a storm. All our projects are in vain, all our calculations are in error, all our wisdom is at fault, all our power is null; one senses, one touches, so to say, a hidden force that opposes itself to all our enterprises and turns them against us. In short, all the powers united against the French Revolution are like a gauze sail against a waterspout.[127]

Certainly, Madame, this shock will end, probably by very unexpected means. Perhaps one could even, without temerity, indicate some of the lines of the future plans that appear decreed. But what man can summon the moment of calm, and by how many misfortunes can the present generation buy the happiness it will perhaps never see? Instead of feeding on foolish hopes, let us fortify our souls, let us unite our reason to eternal reason. If only we have the strength to accept what we cannot avoid, instead of being only *patients*, we will be *victims*.

But there is a great spectacle that nothing can prevent us from contemplating with pleasure even now, provided that we do so without a spirit of vengeance and motivated only by a love of order, and that is the spectacle of the punishment of the leading culprits at the hands of their accomplices and at the hands of those who have been dependent on them. The authors of the Revolt, the founders of the Republic, the assassins of the Clergy, the assassins of the émigrés, the traitors, the solemn apostates, the mortal enemies of religion and the government, the generals who have best served the Revolution, in short, the veritable creators of all we have seen, have almost all fallen beneath the national ax; assassinations and enemy steel are purging the earth of a still greater number ... It is clear that human justice could never have reached all these culprits; would it not have lacked the time, the courage, the proofs, and the strength? Moreover, punishment would have resembled vengeance too much, justice would infallibly have dishonoured itself, and a great number would always have escaped.

TO HIM, THEN, THE VENGEANCE.

I sense that human reason shudders at the sight of these torrents of innocent blood mingled with the blood of the guilty. It is not without timidity, Madame, and even with a kind of religious terror, that I feel myself led to treat, or rather to touch, one of the most profound points of the divine metaphysic. The blind have said that all is good; the blind have refused to see in the universe a violent and forced state *absolutely against nature* in the full sense of the phrase. However, this is what universal conscience has never been able to deny, since it is infallible. Moreover, in the deplorable state of degradation and misfortune to which we are condemned, all men in every century have always believed that the sufferings of the innocent have the double effect of restraining the action of evil and of expiating it. From this belief comes the idea of abstinences and of voluntary privations that have always been believed agreeable to the divinity and useful for the human family. Even in the banter of Ovid, you can find traces of this universal dogma.

From this belief, among us in particular, come those [religious] orders of frightening austerity, isolated from the world to be *lightning rods*.

But the effusion of human blood, especially, has possessed eminently in the opinion of all men this mysterious force of which I have just spoken. From this comes the idea of sacrifices, an idea as old as the world; and take care to note that ferocious or stupid animals, strangers to man by their instinct, such as carnivorous animals, birds of prey, serpents, fish, etc., have never been immolated. Pythagoras cried out in vain:

INNOCENT EWES, WHAT HAVE YOU MERITED?

He was not believed, for no man has the power to uproot a natural idea. With a few minor exceptions that derive from another principle, the choice has always been for victims that are the most precious because of their utility, the most tender, the most innocent, the most in rapport with man because of their instincts and habits, in a word, the most human, if it may be put that way. The abuse of this idea has produced human sacrifices.

So it would be too much if the innocent blood flowing today was not useful to the world. Everything has its reason that we will one day know. The blood of the heavenly Elizabeth[128] was perhaps necessary to balance the Revolutionary Tribunal in the general plan, and that of Louis XVI will perhaps save France.[129]

The theme of a divine metaphysic whereby the suffering of the innocent redeems a guilty world is the leitmotif of nearly all Maistre's later writings. In *Considérations sur la France* it is the key to his interpretation of the French Revolution. It underlies the theodicy of the *Soirées de Saint-Pétersbourg*, and is the exclusive topic of the *Eclaircissement sur les sacrifices*. The same theme and the ideas that surround it (of ancient and natural beliefs) appear as well in the *Essai sur le principe générateur* and in *Du Pape*. These inspired pages ("I sense myself led to treat … one of the most profound points of the divine metaphysic") express clearly for the first time an "illumination" on "the metaphysical significance of the French Revolution."[130] With an interpretation that saw the Revolution both as a divine punishment and as a divinely ordained means for regeneration, the political dilemma of the Savoyard royalist found resolution in a religious vision of redemption.

But if these suppressed pages establish the crux in the development of Joseph de Maistre's understanding of the French Revolution and of mankind's suffering situation, there remain two other questions of great interest. Why did he delete these passages in 1794, only to rework them as the opening keynote paragraphs of the *Considérations* in 1796? And what were the sources of his "illumination"? Nowhere do the documents give explicit answers to these questions, so I am more or less reduced to conjecture.[131]

Although Maistre himself used the word "illumination" to characterize his insight, it seems clear that was involved was an evolution rather than a sudden "conversion." As we have seen, reference to providence had never been entirely absent from Maistre's habits of mind or from his writings. We have seen too, in his letters to Vignet des Etoles, how conventional references gradually became more deliberate and specific as he struggled to make sense of the repeated defeats of counter-revolutionary efforts. In addition to Maistre's reaction to the otherwise seemingly inexplicable course of the Revolution, we can identify at least two other possible influences on his evolving providentialism: his reading and the émigré milieu in which he lived in Lausanne.

Maistre's diary gave us some interesting indications of his reading in the months following his initial flight from Chambéry in September 1792.[132] But from the time he settled in Lausanne in April 1793, Maistre stopped the practice of using his diary to keep a record of the books he was reading. There are, however, a few references and comments in his letters to Vignet des Etoles that make it possible to identify and date some of his reading and to know something of his reactions to particular books.

It was in August 1793 that Jacques Mallet du Pan published his *Considérations sur la nature de la Révolution de France*.[133] Given Maistre's acquaintance with the author, it is not surprising that he read and approved the work:

I find Mallet du Pan's work very good; his general ideas are sane and luminous. He combats with reasons that seem trenchant to me the chimera of the *ancien régime*; but what is not known is that it is as chimerical for us as for the French. Have you noticed that M. Mallet has borrowed some ideas from me? For example, *corruption of corruption*! And the two English verses from Pope, which I indicated to him in a letter.[134]

We can identify a couple of themes in Mallet du Pan's work that can be found in Maistre's discourse as well. One example is the notion of a European as opposed to a specifically French revolution: "the Revolution being, if I may so call it, *a citizen of the World*; it is no longer the exclusive concern of Frenchmen," Mallet du Pan had written in his preface.[135] He had also noted how the Revolution seemed to be advanced by the efforts of its enemies and how it seemed to lead men rather than being led. But when Mallet du Pan spoke of the "force of things," it was not in providential terms but in terms of the complex political, economic, and diplomatic circumstances that so often seem to place events beyond the control of individual statesmen.

The next book mentioned in Maistre's correspondence is Tom Paine's *The Rights of Man*; he told Vignet des Etoles that he would like to have the work since "the refutation of the principles of this wretch enters into a plan that I have in mind."[136] Obviously no direct dependence here. Maistre also read Arthur Young's counter-revolutionary tract, *The Example of France, a Warning to Britain* (1793).[137] Letters written after August 1794 contain references to a few more works, but this short list exhausts the books on the Revolution that might have had some bearing on Maistre's thinking up to the time he wrote the suppressed pages of interest here.

One might hope to find a few more clues in Maistre's notebooks since the one entitled "Mélanges A" does have a few dated entries from 1794. But the dated entries for this period are sparse and diverse and for the most part have no possible bearing on providentialism. The one exception is a page of biblical quotations and references in which there is a reference to Isaiah 24, dated July 1794.[138] The twenty-fourth chapter of Isaiah is part of an apocalyptic poem; the verse Maistre cites reads: "That day, Yahweh will punish above, the armies of the sky, below, the kings of the earth." Other entries and references on this page, though not dated, include the fourteenth chapter of Isaiah, which is a satire on the death of a tyrant, and the thirty-second chapter of Ezekiel, which describes the descent of Eygpt into Sheol. These references are suggestive, but not much more. As Darcel remarks, the suppressed pages of Maistre's discourse "evoke the woeful tones of Job or Jeremiah, the prophetic and penitential lyricism of the Psalms, and the visionary and eschatological symbolism of the Apocalypse," but what is hard to know is if "the return to the Book of Books is a cause or an effect?"[139]

The possible influence of the émigré milieu in Lausanne on Maistre's providentialism is about as difficult to establish as that of his reading. There is no doubt that there was a heightening of religious sensibility in the refugee Catholic community in Lausanne, as in many other émigré centres.[140] As described by contemporary observers and later historians, this religiosity was a little slow to develop, but it grew progressively as hopes for the success of the counter-revolution diminished.[141] Confounded in their calculations, with no other resource than God, the émigré community tended to rally around émigré clergymen. The more the Protestants of Lausanne proved themselves hospitable to their Catholic guests, the more the Catholic community felt the need to safeguard its identity by "extreme professions of faith."[142] Joseph de Maistre was a full participant in this émigré Catholic community and he formed close friendships with a number of émigré churchmen. The Abbé Noiton served him as a personal secretary from August 1793 through 1795. Other names that recur in his diary and correspondence are those of the Abbés Thiollaz, Bigex, and Vuarin; we have already noted his correspondence with Bovet, the émigré French bishop whose advice he valued so highly. Years later on his return from Russia, he was to turn to the Abbé Vuarin for advice and assistance in the publication of *Du Pape*. But to what extent did Maistre owe his religious metaphysic to this milieu? According to Triomphe, "Maistre had the merit of systematizing it and putting it on paper with a certain skill, but it was not the original work of the Maistrian brain."[143] However, Triomphe is unable to offer any solid evidence for this contention; it may well be that Maistre contributed more than he received in his interaction with the émigré community. The favourable reception that the community accorded his 1794 discourse,[144] and later, his *Considérations sur la France*, demonstrates that Maistre's providentialism struck a responsive chord. But to deny his originality on the basis of such evidence does not appear justified.

On the other hand, the receptivity of members of the émigré community to his first tentative expressions of a providential interpretation of the Revolution may have been of considerable importance in encouraging Maistre to develop his ideas further and in his decision to use this interpretation as the basis of the *Considérations*. In deleting the most distinctive statement of this interpretation from the discourse on Eugène Costa, Maistre displayed an initial reticence about exposing these ideas publicly. He even seemed a bit embarrassed about sending the published version to his good friend Vignet des Etoles. In doing so he told him: "I am quite mindful in sending you my last little work, that it is not in your genre; however I would not want to be negligent in sending you whatever work comes from my pen."[145] Perhaps even more important than the favourable reception given his discourse, was Maistre's success in the Swiss salons.

Joseph de Maistre had always enjoyed good company and good conversation; I have noted how important his friendships with Salteur, Roze, and Costa had been to him in Chambéry. In Lausanne he found intellectual pleasure and stimulation in the émigré salons and in the homes of good Swiss Protestants. Both his diary and his later correspondence offer ample testimony to how much these occasions meant to him. It is clear too that he was in the habit of expounding his ideas to these salon audiences. Vignet des Etoles may have tried to discourage Maistre's sociability (recall his February 1794 letter to Hauteville), but without apparent success. He may have been correct when he told Hauteville that Maistre's volubility made some enemies, but others were pleased and impressed. One lady, not content with the memory of pleasant evenings in Lausanne, later wrote from Turin to ask that he put some of his ideas in writing for her: "I recall one of our charming Helvetian evenings when you dealt at length with the *utility of paradoxes*. You must know how you were supported! And really, it is necessary to be just to you; the general approbation so stimulated you, that for eight days at least you told us things of the other world."[146] In an early letter to Vignet des Etoles, Maistre confessed to his friend that there is "no man who has more need of a perpetual *Stimulus* than I."[147] The émigré milieu of Lausanne was probably more important to Maistre as a stimulus than as a source of ideas.

Maistre had arrived at the essentials of his providential interpretation of the French Revolution by mid-1794. As Darcel observes, "he could have written the *Considérations* at that date."[148] Yet almost two years passed before he undertook the work. Possible reasons for the delay have already been touched upon: his workload as the Sardinian Correspondent in Lausanne; the felt necessity to reread and refute Rousseau, which led him to devote a lot of time and energy to two manuscripts on political philosophy that he would eventually abandon; and finally, the initial hesitancy he felt about publishing a "religious" interpretation of the Revolution. It was only in mid-1796 that a particular combination of circumstances stimulated him to overcome these obstacles and produce the book that made his reputation. As written, of course, the book reflected Maistre's experience and reading in the intervening period.

While these years saw little apparent change in Maistre's position as Sardinian Correspondent in Lausanne, developments elsewhere did have repercussions on his situation and perspectives. By a curious irony, Maistre had arrived at his new interpretation of the French Revolution just at a time when it was changing direction. Robespierre's fall (28 July 1794) and the trend of French politics during the period of the Thermidorian reaction revived royalist hopes. Maistre followed these events with great interest, and was of course disappointed when those hopes were dashed in 1795 with the Quiberon disaster, the failure of the Vendémiaire uprising, and the inauguration of the Directory. During the first six months of its existence, the Directory leaned to the left, and it was only with the exposure of the Babeuf plot in May 1796 and the regime's subsequent swing to the right that royalist enterprises took on new life. The timing of the writing and publication of Maistre's *Considérations sur la France* will be directly related to the reviving prospects of French royalism in the summer and fall of 1796. Prior to this event, however, there were developments affecting Piedmont-Sardinia that had a more immediate impact on Maistre's fortunes.

Following the defeat of the Austro-Sardinian attempted reconquest of Savoy in the fall of 1793, Maistre had been in semi-disgrace in Turin. As we have seen, he had made no secret of his disdain for Austrian conduct in that campaign. Although there were internal divisions in the Sardinian government over the wisdom of the Austrian alliance, it was the pro-Austrian faction that remained dominant until the fall of 1794. Then in October that year King Victor-Amadeus III fell gravely ill, and as a consequence his heir, the Prince of Piedmont, was allowed more direct involvement in affairs in view of his seemingly imminent succession to the throne. Among other things he began to read the reports of Sardinian diplomatic representatives abroad. This prince was anti-Austrian and pro-French, and soon found Joseph de Maistre's correspondence from Lausanne much to his liking.[149] This development brought a substantial reversal of Maistre's standing in Turin. In December 1794 we find him writing to Vignet des Etoles to share the good news:

The Duke of Montferrat [the king's brother] has written to me *in his own hand* a most flattering, and I can tell you, a most amiable letter … And this is not all; you are too attached to me and I to you not to tell you (but this only between the two of us) that Count de Hauteville has just advised me confidentially that the Prince of Piedmont wants to read all my letters, and he has warned me that I should give them a turn such that he can read them in their entirety. All this was seasoned with very flattering remarks.[150]

This accession to favour in Turin also brought some improvement in Maistre's financial situation.[151] But Victor-Amadeus's illness lingered and it was only in October 1796 that he died and the Prince of Piedmont ascended the throne as Charles-Emmanuel IV. By this time, however, Maistre's situation had been adversely affected in another way by the fortunes of war.

The war between revolutionary France and the monarchical powers of Europe had not at first been much affected by the events of Thermidor. Holland was conquered in February 1795, and, partly as a consequence of continuing French victories, Prussia made its peace with the Republic in April, followed by Spain in July. By the fall of 1795, Maistre had good reason to fear that Piedmont-Sardinia was also tempted to withdraw from the alliance and attempt a separate peace with France. The price would almost certainly be the abandonment of all claims to Savoy and recognition of its permanent incorporation into France. But Joseph de Maistre thought he saw another possibility. In mid-November 1795 he submitted a memoir to Hauteville that proposed the neutralization of Savoy by incorporating it into the Swiss federation under the nominal sovereignty of a prince of the House of Savoy.[152] His memoir was a well-informed, intelligent, and nuanced discussion of the possibility, but nothing came of it.[153] Maistre also warned Turin of the likelihood of a French attack on Piedmont itself, but for whatever reasons (drift within the government under the sick old king, the incompetence of the Austrian ally), young General Bonaparte's quick victories in the spring of 1796 took Piedmont-Sardinia out of the war and imposed a settlement that confirmed French possession of Savoy. One provision of this Peace of Paris (5 May 1796) permitted the king to retain in his service Savoyard nobles who had positions in his army and administration, but he was obliged to recognize the appropriation and sale of their property in Savoy.[154] For Joseph de Maistre, of course, this meant the apparent loss of any hope of recovering his property in Chambéry.[155] However, he at first refused to acquiesce in this outcome, and prepared and published a "Mémoire sur les prétendus émigrés sovoisiens" in which he again protested against the equation of Savoyard refugees and French émigrés, and put forward a number of legal arguments in defence of the property rights of those affected by the original 1792 decree and the 1796 peace treaty.[156] In addition to the memoir, Maistre engaged a lawyer in Paris to act on his behalf, wrote to others in Paris he thought might help, and to the French ambassador in Basel.[157] But it does not appear that any of these initiatives had any effect whatsoever.

The fact that Piedmont-Sardinia was no longer at war with France meant a change in Maistre's situation as a counter-revolutionary publicist. It could no longer be a question of addressing a defence of the old order to his fellow Savoyards. His perspective had already been changing in mid-1794 when he abandoned the project of writing a fifth Savoyard letter in favour of refutation of revolutionary theory. But he was also tempted, from a relatively early date, to become more directly involved in French politics. In December 1794, following the appearance of a book defending the constitutional monarchy established by the Constitution of 1791, Maistre indicated to Vignet des Etoles that he was thinking of attempting a refutation: "You have no doubt seen the anonymous and constitutional work of Montesquiou entitled *Coup d'oeil sur la Révolution française*. I had been on the point of undertaking a strong and honest refutation of it. This work would have given me the occasion to develop the most admirable political principles. But I lack the time."[158] He made every effort to keep himself well-informed on developments in France, keeping a notebook in which he copied newspaper reports of speeches delivered in the National Convention and similar materials.[159] He was also reading other counter-revolutionary publicists. A letter of December 1794 mentions Count Ferrand's *Considérations sur la Révolution* and Count de Montgaillard's *L'Etat de la France au mois d'avril 1794*.[160] Another letter the same month praised the latest work of the Count d'Antraigues, but without mentioning a title.[161]

The one work that appeared in this period that some scholars have credited with considerable influence on Joseph de Maistre's providential interpretation of the Revolution is the one whose influence is the most problematic. It was in July 1795 that Louis-Claude de Saint-Martin published his *Lettre à un Ami ou Considérations politiques, philosophiques et religieuses sur la Révolution française* (Paris, An III). As we have seen, Maistre had read and admired Saint-Martin's earlier works. If he read *Lettre à un Ami*, he would have found there an explicitly providential interpretation of the French Revolution. But there is absolutely no documentary evidence to prove that he did read the work. Nowhere in Maistre's letters, notebooks, or published works do we find any reference to this particular work by Saint-Martin.

However, Jean-Louis Darcel thinks it probable that Maistre read and meditated on Saint-Martin's essay, and while he acknowledges that the two providential interpretations are quite different (for Saint-Martin the Revolution was liberating and divine, for Maistre it was satanic), he believes reading Saint-Martin's "religious" interpretation liberated Maistre to "abandon himself to his visionary imagination."[162] On the basis of this assumption, Darcel suggests as well that Maistre may also have felt a duty to refute Saint-Martin's reading of the divine will for France, and that this hypothesis may explain some apparent ambiguities in Maistre's *Considérations*. According to Darcel, the latter work is susceptible to two readings. At one level it is the work of a Catholic and monarchist thinker. But at another level, carefully veiled from profane eyes, it is the work of a mystic Mason seeking to persuade his erstwhile "brothers" of their errors.[163] An interesting hypothesis but, without more evidence, one that can neither be proved nor disproved.

Jean Rebotton also thinks it probable that Maistre read the *Lettre à un ami*, and points to analogies between the providential and redemptive themes in both Saint-Martin and Maistre.[164] In addition, Rebotton credits Saint-Martin with stimulating Maistre to develop his thesis on the divine origins of political constitutions. It may be true that Saint-Martin wrote of the social body as a natural assemblage of myriad elements whose particular form was willed by God and not men.[165] But it must be pointed out that Maistre had developed his thesis on the divine origins of constitutions prior to 1795; it appears already in the manuscript "fifth letter" he had sent to Bovet in March 1794 and in the unpublished "De la Souveraineté du Peuple" on which he had been working since early 1794. The fourth chapter of this work begins: "The same power that has decreed the social order and sovereignty has also decreed the different modifications of sovereignty following the different characters of nations."[166] The concept will be stated a bit more dramatically in the *Considérations* and developed at much greater length in the *Essai sur le principe générateur des constitutions politiques*, but there is no solid evidence to prove that Maistre's development of the idea owed anything to reading Saint-Martin's essay. It would seem just as plausible to link any similarities that can be found in the way the two men treated problems such as the Revolution and the structure of society to their common involvement in the milieu of Masonry and "illuminism."

It is well to remember, moreover, that Joseph de Maistre's fascination with esoteric currents of thought was a life-long affair, not something he abandoned when he fled Chambéry. We know from his diary and his letter registers that during his years in Switzerland he maintained contact with many men who had been and were still involved in Freemasonry and illuminism.[167] Lausanne was a notable centre of reformed Scottish rite Masonry, illuminism, and pietism, and Maistre was well-informed about what was going on in these circles.[168] He also retained an interest in the kind of books that were popular and influential in this milieu. In a diary entry for 26 July 1796, for example, he noted he had just completed reading "the English book entitled *The Spirit of Prayer* … by W. Law."[169] William Law was an important English disciple of Jacob Böhme, the great German mystic whose ideas also influenced Saint-Martin.[170] Maistre's meditations on the ways of providence seem to have been nourished by heterodox sources other than Saint-Martin as well as by pious émigré priests.

But it was the émigré priests who involved Maistre in the "retraction" of the former constitutional bishop of Mont-Blanc in early 1795. François-Thérèse Panisset had accepted election as bishop of Mont-Blanc following imposition of the Civil Constitution of the Clergy on Savoy in the spring of 1793. By 1795, he appears to have been aware that his position was becoming a bit ridiculous but lacked the will to resolve the situation. In this circumstance, three Savoyard priests took the initiative, formed a pious plot, took him in hand, and delivered him to some émigré clergymen in Lausanne.[171] At this point Maistre became involved in editing the retraction Panisset was pressured to sign. This document, which included a repudiation of the constitutional church and an eloquent declaration of loyalty to the pope as the centre of Catholic unity, was subsequently printed and widely distributed.[172] It was the first such retraction by a constitutional bishop, and Pope Pius VI acknowledged its significance with a letter of appreciation and praise.[173] Panisset himself appears to have been a weak nonentity; at the time Maistre had doubts about his sanity, and he later characterized him as a wretch.[174] But Maistre's role in this retraction shows that by this date he had moved from the Gallican stance of his youth to the strongly ultramontane position of his later years.

Many of the émigré clergymen who had gathered in Lausanne were badly shaken by the catastrophe that had befallen the Church in France and were ready to rally to the papacy as a visible symbol of survival. Some scholars have credited Maistre's "conversion" to ultramontanism to his involvement in this milieu.[175] But as with his developing providentialism, it is a nice question as to who was influencing whom. Years later, after Maistre had published *Du Pape*, it turned out that the priest who had drafted the first version of Panisset's retraction, the Abbé de Thiollaz, had serious reservations about Maistre's high papalism.[176] In any case, Maistre would not give public expression to his ultramontane views until much later; nothing is said about the papacy in *Considérations sur la France*, and in the *Essai sur le principe générateur* of 1809 there is only a passing reference to the historical growth of papal authority. It was only in 1819, with the publication of *Du Pape*, that Maistre took a strong public stand for ultramontanism.

Also dating from 1795 was another essay in counter-revolutionary propaganda written to influence events in French-occupied Savoy. According to Maistre's own account, he had been asked by Savoyard priests for a popular pamphlet to profit from the occasion offered by the convocation of "primary assemblies" in Savoy.[177] (These assemblies were called to approve the Constitution of the Year III and to elect representatives under the new constitution.) What Maistre provided was an "Address by the mayor of Montagnole to his fellow citizens."[178] (Montagnole was a small mountain village near Chambéry whose very name, according to Maistre, was something of a joke.) His mayor, "Jean-Claude Têtu," rehearsed all the broken promises of the French, stressed their shameful treatment of the Church, and urged his listeners to refuse participation in the assemblies on the grounds that taking part would be taken by the French as evidence of their acceptance of the permanent union of Savoy to France. Large quantities of the pamphlet were printed in Geneva; Maistre claimed that "it had an extraordinary popularity in Savoy and in Switzerland."[179] We have no way of knowing what influence it may have had, but the apparent success of this project may have encouraged Maistre to undertake his more ambitious incursion into French politics the following year.

The specific impetus that led Joseph de Maistre to begin his *Considérations* was the appearance in May 1796 of Benjamin Constant's *De la force du gouvernement actuel de la France et de la nécessité de s'y rallier.* The explanation of why Maistre was particularly provoked by Constant's little work involves intertwined personal and political circumstances. Constant was linked personally and politically with Madame de Staël, the daughter of Jacques Necker, and the party of constitutional royalists with which her father's name was still associated. From early 1795 this party had been moving away from support of counter-revolutionary plots towards working within the framework of the Republic.

Madame de Staël herself had published a couple of pamphlets advising constitutional monarchists to rally to the Republic and the Constitution of 1795 as the best way to defend liberty in France against extremists of the right and the left.[180] Joseph de Maistre had been an admirer of Jacques Necker before the Revolution, and he had continued to respect the Genevan even though many émigrés now condemned him for his role in the early phases of the Revolution. Madame de Staël and Benjamin Constant had been living at Coppet, the Necker estate near Geneva, and Maistre had encountered both of them on social occasions. He seems to have gotten on rather well with Madame de Staël, but to have taken an intense dislike to Constant.[181] When Madame de Staël's pamphlets appeared in the spring of 1795, Maistre recommended them to Vignet des Etoles as "prudent and profound."[182] He reported the news of her arrival in Paris in mid-May with the comment that "she is going to do an excellent job."[183] Darcel explains these remarks with the hypothesis that Maistre was under the impression at this point (perhaps from his salon conversations with her) that Madame de Staël remained a secret royalist and that she feigned support for the Republic in order to obtain authorization to return to Paris and solicit support for the royalist cause.[184] The appearance of Constant's work in Paris in May 1796 and the printing of extracts from it in the *Moniteur* would have disabused Maistre of any illusions about the political position of Madame de Staël and her lover. Constant's arguments for supporting the Directory were essentially the same as those she had offered the year before. But Maistre found Constant's work an "ugly pamphlet"[185] and he took care to answer those argments point by point in Chapter IV of his *Considérations.*

Constant's pamphlet was important in stimulating Maistre to begin his *Considérations,* but other circumstances seem to have affected the timing and form of its publication. As a consequence of the conservative trend in

French politics following the exposure of the Babeuf plot in May 1796, royalist hopes were again rising in the summer and fall of that year. Some royalists hoped for victory at the polls in the elections that were to occur in March 1797, others plotted a coup d'état to assist the election results if necessary. Among those involved in such plans were Mallet du Pan (resident in Bern), William Wickham, the British ambassador to Bern, and Louis Fauche-Borel, a printer from Neuchâtel. These people were being funded to produce royalist propaganda and were in secret contact with General Pichegru (future deputy and future president of the Council of Five Hundred). We know from Maistre's letter registers that he was in regular correspondence with Wickham (five letters between 26 April and 26 October 1796) and with Mallet du Pan. It was Mallet du Pan who made the arrangements to have Maistre's *Considérations* printed by Fauche-Borel at Neuchâtel. Given these relationships, it seems reasonable to conclude the Maistre's work was intended to support the royalist cause on the eve of the March 1797 elections.[186]

This hypothesis goes far towards explaining some peculiarities of the work. We know from Mallet du Pan's "Editor's Notice" at the head of the first edition that the printer had to work from a hastily completed manuscript marred by deletions and additions; it appears that Maistre had sent it off in this faulty form because of pressure to get the work published before the elections.[187] (The effort was to no avail; the book did not come off the presses until the end of April 1797, too late to influence the elections.) It seems clear too that the tone of Maistre's work, which is that of a manifesto as much as that of a refutation, reflects his intention of strengthening royalist sentiment in France on the eve of elections that might pave the way for a restoration.

Viewed in this context, *Considérations sur la France* may be seen as a shrewdly written tract for the times. By 1797 many Frenchmen were thoroughly disillusioned with the French Revolution. The high hopes of 1789 had been shattered by the violence of the Terror and the hardships of war. The Republic had been consolidated by the Constitution of 1795, but the Directory lacked popular support. At the time Maistre was writing, it was becoming increasingly clear that the majority of French voters might opt for royalist candidates and the restoration of throne and altar. Maistre played on growing disenchantment with the Revolution by highlighting its goriest incidents. Publicizing the most glaring weaknesses of the Directory, he emphasized the regime's declining popularity and sought to strengthen the trend of public opinion towards the possibility and desirability of a Bourbon restoration. The crimes of the Revolution and the failures of the Directory were contrasted with the stability and peace that would attend the restoration of France's legitimate government.

But *Considérations sur la France* was much more than a timely piece of royalist propaganda. Maistre's powerful prose crystallized an interpretation of the Revolution that would eventually be adopted by a great many Frenchmen. He was not the first to publish a providential explanation of events in France. There was, after all, ample precedent in the Christian tradition for regarding such a catastrophe as the work of Providence, and there were other writers who advanced providential interpretations of the Revolution. But Maistre was distinctive in the sophistication, force, and clarity with which he presented the theory. An interpretation that portrayed the Revolution both as a divine punishment and as a divinely ordained means for the regeneration of France enabled him to condemn the Revolution and the ideas it embodied, and, at the same time, to treat it as a necessary prelude to the confidently prophesied resurrection of the monarchy. What Maistre offered that was new and attractive was an essentially "religious" vision of redemption.[188] Presenting his ideas in broad historical and philosophical perspective, Maistre challenged the whole ethos of the Enlightenment as well as the political ideology of the Revolution. With *Considérations sur la France* we have Joseph de Maistre whole and entire. With his wit and verve, his prophetic tone and at times apocalyptic lyricism, his distinctively mordant and eminently readable literary style, and his sharp critique of the naïve and optimistic assumptions of his contemporaries, he steps forth as a brilliant spokesman for the conservative cause.

Given its importance, its influence, and its decisive position in Maistre's intellectual biography, *Considérations sur la France* deserves to be read in its entirety.[189] Nevertheless, a brief review is required to demonstrate the extent to which this book exemplifies the mature Maistre's doctrine. There is a sense in which all his later writings do little more than develop the fundamental insights that were enunciated here. Maistre would continue to observe, to read broadly, and to meditate, and his later works would be enriched by these continuing activities, but his basic intellectual decisions had all been taken by the time he published his *Considérations*. The "making" of Joseph de Maistre was essentially complete by 1797.

The book opens with a ringing statement of its theme: "We are all attached to the throne of the Supreme Being by a supple chain that restrains us without enslaving us."[190] This line should be compared to the opening sentence of the *Contrat social*, where Rousseau proclaimed that "man is born free, and everywhere he is in chains." To Rousseau's concern about man's dependence on other men, Maistre responded that it was more important for man to recognize his dependence on God. This dependence, Maistre announced, is miraculously apparent in the events of the French Revolution. Just as Augustine had affirmed the providential governance of history amid the ruins of the Roman world, so Maistre proclaimed that never had the role of providence been more palpable than in the bewildering course of the Revolution. Its "apparently most active personages" were no more than "passive and mechanical" instruments employed by the divinity for the punishment and regeneration of France (p 30).

But Maistre combined his providential interpretation of the Revolution with a flattering appeal to French pride. Belief in a divinely assigned French mission goes back at least to the Crusades, and the· nationalism of the Revolution was in some ways a secularization of this old idea. The French were proud of their army and its magnificent victories against the First Coalition. Maistre astutely acknowledged these glorious achievements, including the energy of the Jacobins in mobilizing French resources to meet all threats to the integrity of the nation. He called, not for repudiation of past accomplishments, but for recognition of a higher mission that included the religious dimension so important in French tradition. A purified France could lead a "moral revolution" in Europe (p 48).

In suggesting that those who favoured the Revolution did so for morally reprehensible reasons, Maistre played on the guilt feelings of all those who were appalled by the violence unleashed by the upheaval. Similarly, his dramatic portrayal of the punishment the French had brought upon themselves by regicide made the most of Louis xvi's "innocence." Maistre himself had been scandalized by the crimes associated with the Revolution and with the great crime of regicide in particular. Arguing that "all great crimes against sovereignty are punished without delay and in a terrible manner," Maistre predicted that "perhaps four million Frenchmen will pay with their heads for this great national crime of an anti-religious and antisocial insurrection crowned by a regicide" (pp 35–6). In a surprising combination of exalted religious perspectives and worldly political realism, he interspersed imagery of punishment and rebirth with acid and perceptive observations on the goals of the anti-French coalition and the blindness of certain counter-revolutionaries.

If the Revolution was willed by providence, "the horrible effusion of human blood" (p 50) it occasioned must be interpreted as an appropriate means for the redemption of France. Maistre's reflections "On the Violent Destruction of the Human Species" (Chapter III) may be more comprehensible to us than they were to his nineteenth-century liberal critics. We can add the catastrophes of the twentieth century to Maistre's "frightful catalogue" (p 57) of bloodletting; we have had plenty of time and ample reason to dismiss "the dreams of Condorcet" (p 60). But for Maistre's contemporaries his meditations on the shedding of human blood must have seemed a shocking repudiation of faith in reason and progress. And Maistre dared justify all this suffering in terms of religious sacrifice, arguing that Christianity "rests entirely on an enlargement of this same dogma of innocence paying for crime" (p 62). But this theme was central to Maistre's thought. His notorious speculations on the divinity of war in the *Soirées de*

Saint-Pétersbourg, as well as the *Eclaircissement sur les sacrifices* appended to the first edition of the *Soirées*, were developments of this same idea of the "reversibility of merits." In the "ninth conversation" of the *Soirées* Maistre makes this doctrine the ultimate key to understanding the condition of fallen humanity:

the great victim, *lifted up to attract all things to himself*, cried out on Calvary: ALL IS CONSUMMATED! Then, the veil of the Temple being torn, the great secret of the sanctuary became known, insofar as it can be in this order of things of which we are a part. We understand why man has always believed that one soul can be saved by another, and why he has always looked for his regeneration in blood.[191]

In fact, Maistre pushed this doctrine a little beyond the bounds of orthodoxy. In traditional Christian theology, passive suffering and bloodshed are not in themselves of supernatural value. It is only when the victim consents, when the victim freely unites his suffering to the free sacrifice of Christ, that "reversibility of merits" is possible thanks to the "communion of saints."[192] Some of Maistre's speculations tend to ignore this distinction.

The rhetorical question "Can the French Republic last?" (Chapter IV) focused attention on the precariousness of the Directory. Maistre sought to prove the theoretical impossibility of a permanent republican government for France.[193] His attempt to use the laws of probablity to provide an "arithmetical" demonstration of his case (p 66) will strike the modern reader as curious, but his discussion of English history is more interesting. Maistre was essentially correct in stressing the feudal origins of representative government and the role of royal initiative in the development of the English Parliament. It should be noted that he had no quarrel with the existing English system; he simply denied that it exemplified popular sovereignty or a system of "*perfected* representation" (p 70). The representative system prescribed by the Constitution of 1795 was subjected to sharper criticism. By calculating "the prodigious number of sovereigns condemned to die without having reigned" (p 71), Maistre satirized the whole idea of sovereignty of the people. Since the people are excluded from the effective exercise of sovereignty by the French system, the question is reduced to a comparative assessment of the rule of the Directory versus monarchical rule. To this question, "the French know the answer well enough!" But Maistre also stressed the Directory's criminal origins in the Revolution. Arguing that "what distinguishes the French Revolution and makes it an *event* unique in history is that it is radically *bad*," he asked "how anyone can believe in the permanence of a liberty that springs from gangrene?" (p 73). He contended that it was impossible for any durable government (let alone a republic, "that form of government which less than any other may dispense with virtue") to emerge from immorality and corruption (p 74).

But "the great anathema that burdens the Republic" (p 77) is irreligion, and Maistre devoted an entire chapter to the anti-religious character of the French Revolution. In this "Digression on Christianity" (as Chapter v is subtitled), Maistre maintained that religion must be recognized as "the unique basis of all durable institutions" (p 80). Most historians would probably agree that the revolutionaries blundered into political disaster in attacking the Church since the Civil Constitution of the Clergy provoked massive resistance, which in turn contributed to the Terror. But Maistre was more concerned about the metaphysical and sociological implications of the repudiation of Christianity.

On the metaphysical level, Maistre argued that man cannot be truly creative unless he puts himself in conscious harmony with the Creator and acts in His name. Only in this way can man share in the divinity's creative power. But Maistre addressed his reflections to everyone, "to the believer as well as to the sceptic" (p 80), and his idea was also advanced as a sociological principle. Human reason, philosophy, is essentially disruptive; it you want to render an institution strong and durable, *deify* it (ibid.) Significantly, Maistre's historical illustrations were drawn from pagan antiquity and Islam as well as from Judaism and Christianity. Maistre's later religious apologetic (*Du Pape* in particular) would be based on similar arguments.

Reflecting further on the political implications of these metaphysical and sociological principles, Maistre suggested that it would be "curious to examine our European institutions one by one and to show how they are all *Christianized*, how religion mingles in everything, animates and sustains everything."[194] In his later works, Maistre developed this argument into a political indictment of Protestantism for having undermined the political and spiritual unity of European governments.[195]

When Europe's problems are viewed in the perspective of these "truths," Maistre argued, "true philosophy must opt between" two hypotheses: the appearance of a new religion or the rejuvenation of Christianity (pp 84–5). Now the idea of a new religion to replace Christianity was becoming a commonplace in Maistre's time. Robespierre's Cult of the Supreme Being (which was based on Rousseau's proposal for a purely civic religion) was only the best-known attempt to combine rejection of what many regarded as an outworn creed with the social benefits of religion. Maistre was original in boldly agreeing with the new prophets in their diagnosis of the situation and then paradoxically using their prescription as an apologia for traditional Christianity. He agreed that men were witnessing a "fight to the death between Christianity and philosophism" (p 85), but he expressed confidence that Christianity would emerge from the ordeal of the Revolution "purer and more vigorous" than ever (p 89). However, Maistre, like many French Catholic royalists in the nineteenth century, tended to identify the survival of the Catholic Church with the restoration of the Bourbon monarchy. In his vision, the royal coinage again carries the triumphant device: "Christ commands, He reigns, He is the Victor."[196]

Maistre's chapter "On the Divine Influence in Political Constitutions" (Chapter VI) is a summary statement of the ideas that he would develop more fully in his *Essai sur le principe générateur*. In fact in the preface to the 1814 edition of the later work, Maistre reproduced his points about God's "rights" in the formation of governments with the following comment: "Since 1796, the date of the first edition of the work we quote, it does not appear that anything has happened in the world that might have induced the author to abandon his theory."[197] At one level Maistre was arguing that written constitutional documents are relatively unimportant for the operation of any political system compared to the effects of historical, cultural, and political circumstances. To the political universalism of Jacobinism, he opposed the principle of differentiation of political cultures: "The Constitution of 1795, like its predecessors, was made for *man*. But there is no such thing as *man* in the world. In my lifetime I have seen Frenchmen, Italians, Russians, etc.; thanks to Montesquieu, I even know that *one can be Persian*. But as for *man*, I declare that I have never in my life met him; if he exists, he is unknown to me" (p 97).

But at a more profound level Maistre was arguing that since the making of a constitution was the work of history, it was really a divine work. From this perspective, as he would put it in the 1814 preface to the *Essai*, "God literally makes kings."[198] And in this same preface he would be happy to adopt as his own the term "metapolitics," said to have been invented by the German philosophers "to be to politics what metaphysics is to physics."[199] Maistre's search for the "hidden foundations of the social edifice,"[200] had led him to a theory that was strikingly analogous to that of Hegel. As Stéphane Rials has pointed out, "if one replaces *Reason* by *Providence* and *Rational* by *Providential*," their systems are quite comparable.[201] Like Maistre's providence, Hegel's Reason governs history, using all its events as means to its own ends. Since there is no evidence of direct influence in either direction, one should perhaps think in terms of a parallelism of inspiration and of reaction to momentous historical events.

In the light of his theory of the divine origin of political constitutions, Maistre dismisses the French Constitution of 1795 as a mere "school composition" (p 97). Maistre has great fun ridiculing the "prodigious number of laws" (some 15,479) passed by French assemblies since 1789 (pp 99–100). Despite all the experiments in the "trade of constitution-making" (p 103), the government of the Directory is "a highly advanced despotism" whose "constitution exists only on paper" (p 104). Maistre concluded that he could "see nothing favouring this chimerical system of deliberation and political construction by abstract reasoning" (p 108). At most, one could mention America. But colonial America possessed the democratic elements inherited from the constitution of the mother country and was populated by democratic elements carried there by its early colonists. "The Americans built with these elements and on the plan of the three powers that they received from their ancestors, and not at all *tabula rasa*, as the French did" (p 108). Maistre was unusual for his time in recognizing the democratic character of the colonial pre-revolutionary experience. Even so, he had little confidence in the stability of the American government. Citing the quarrels then going on over the location of a national capital, he concluded that "one could bet a thousand to one that the city will not be built, that it will not be called *Washington*, and that the Congress will not meet there" (p 109). If Maistre's wager seems a typical bit of reactionary folly, it is well to remember that there is a sense in which his prediction was not far off. Washington did become the political capital, but unlike London or Paris it never became the financial or cultural capital of the new nation.

Maistre's judicial background is quite apparent in his long digression on the "old French constitution" (Chapter VIII). His portrayal of the roles of the monarch, the parlements, and the Estates-General is essentially that held by most eighteenth-century *parlementaires*. In fact much of his evidence for the character of the pre-revolutionary French "constitution" was borrowed from a book written by ex-magistrates of the parlements. Maistre had mistakenly assumed that the book had the approval of the émigré Louis XVIII. Upon receipt of a letter disabusing him of this assumption, he added a postscript to the second and subsequent editions of his book. But significantly enough, Maistre's postscript did not really repudiate the parlementary position. If the magistrate's book "contains errors which I overlooked, I sincerely disavow them" (p 194), he wrote, but he never admitted that there were any errors in the book in question. Maistre may have adopted a providential interpretation of the Revolution, but he had not abandoned his opposition to absolutism. He still took his stand with the French magistrates as an apologist of limited monarchy.

Maistre's prophetic description of the coming counter-revolution (Chapter IX) attracted considerable attention when the event belatedly came to pass some seventeen years later. Maistre boasted of its accuracy, claiming that he had predicted everything down to the first cities to declare for the king.[202] Perhaps it was not too difficult to single out cities like Bordeaux and Lyon since the first was a port city whose commerce had suffered from the blockades of the revolutionary war, and Lyon had endured a terrible punishment under the Terror. But was it clever rhetoric or gentle irony that led Maistre to introduce his prophecy with the line: "Let us leave theory and take a look at the facts" (p 133)?

The "supposed dangers of counter-revolution" (Chapter X) was a topic less susceptible to clever phrase-making, and here Maistre was forced to deal with such difficult questions as the disposition of confiscated property and possible royalist vengeance against the revolutionaries. He argued valiantly (and well on many points) that none of these considerations should prevent the French from enjoying the blessings of a restoration of the monarchy. But one suspects that his concluding bon mot carried as much weight as his argumentation: "the restoration of the monarchy, what they call the counter-revolution, will be not a *contrary revolution*, but the *contrary of revolution*" (p 169).

The last chapter of the *Considérations* is a curious piece of work in which Maistre used David Hume's account of the seventeenth-century English revolution as a "lesson from history" to demonstrate his own interpretation of the French Revolution.[203] The modern reader will scarcely be impressed by this pastiche of sentences from Hume, but can still admire Maistre's audacity in thus utilizing the writer he elsewhere judged to be the philosophe "who employed the most talent in the most cold-blooded way to do the most harm."[204]

Since the Directory forbade its sale in France, the immediate impact of Maistre's *Considérations* was largely limited to émigré circles. But it won an immediate popularity, and in addition to a second edition corrected by the author, there were also four pirated editions in the first eight months following its initial publication.[205] The book was published anonymously of course (Maistre's position as a representative of a government at peace with the French Republic precluded any other course), but the author's identity appears to have been something of an open secret. As Maistre himself acknowledged, his distinctive literary style was practically impossible to mistake. The ironic consequences the book had for his personal fortunes is a story that belongs to the next chapter.

CHAPTER FIVE

Italian Interlude

By the time *Considérations sur la France* came off the presses in Neuchâtel in the spring of 1797, the author was no longer in Switzerland, but in Turin. Following the death of Victor-Amadeus III and the accession of Charles-Emmanuel IV in late October 1796, it appeared at first that Maistre would be offered a ministerial position. In late January 1797 he was granted a modest pension and invited to come to the capital. But no position followed, and he remained unemployed until late 1799 when he was appointed to the top judicial post on the island of Sardinia, where he served until he was sent to St Petersburg three years later. The first three years in Italy were a time of disappointed hopes and financial problems. In the second three years, Maistre's financial situation was greatly alleviated, but his judicial assignment proved to be extremely difficult and frustrating. During these years Maistre wrote very little and published practically nothing (except the second edition of the *Considérations*, which appeared in September 1797). While these were not productive years from the perspective of Maistre's intellectual biography, they are not without interest. Very little of Maistre's correspondence for this period has survived,[1] but dated entries in his notebooks make it possible to know something of his reading. And even though he was not publishing, there are a few items from his pen to be examined. Moreover, Maistre's adventures during these years bear on his later relationship with the Sardinian government.

TURIN

It was on 28 January 1797 that Maistre received a letter from Turin announcing his recall to Piedmont with a pension of 2,000 livres.[2] He left Lausanne on 28 February (leaving behind his wife and two children) and arrived in Turin on 7 March. The king received him "kindly" on 10 March, but Maistre's diary entry notes: "nothing certain on my fate, which remains very problematic."[3] There appear to have been two major obstacles to an appointment. The new king may have been personally favourable, but he was a weak, indecisive man, presiding over a faction-ridden court.[4] This was a very difficult period for the monarchy; under great pressure from the Directory, Piedmont-Sardinia had agreed to a French alliance in February, which was modified by a second treaty on 5 April 1797.[5] Threats to the state's independence increased in the months that followed, and in December 1798, the king would be forced to abdicate and flee to Sardinia. The second obstacle was Maistre's personality. His old friend Henry Costa describes what happened when Maistre arrived in Turin:

Maistre has seen the powerful, and they have already found out that he speaks too loudly and that he is too cutting … he will always be the same, abounding in good qualities and all the sciences, and with that inflexible and dogmatic, that is to say, little likely to succeed here where they know nothing, but where, on the other hand, backbones have the suppleness of willows. For the moment, he is living in a garret where he has shut himself up to work on I do not know what; he thus spares himself from listening to a lot of foolishness and saying those beautiful truths he says so bluntly and that do not succeed.[6]

So Maistre spent the following months waiting for a change of fortune.

Maistre's mood during this time of personal uncertainty is hard to characterize; his diary entries for this period appear unusually ambigious. On 1 April 1797, his forty-fourth birthday, he wrote: "I have breathed a lot but not lived at all; and for me everything has been said in this world. To you Monsieur Rodolphe!"[7] A few days later he wrote of retiring and devoting himself uniquely to the education of his children. But in mid-May he received copies of his *Considérations* and was soon busy sending copies off to Paris.[8] By 9 June he had composed a memoir in Italian on paper money in Piedmont and sent it to his old friend, the Marquis de Barol.[9] Nothing is known of either the purpose or the effect of this memoir.

In early May, Maistre enjoyed a dinner with three of his brothers, André (the priest), and Nicolas and Xavier (both serving as officers in the army). Shortly after this he went to lodge at the Arsenal with his brother-in-law, Buttet, who was its director. But Buttet was already suffering from a serious illness and he died on 22 June in Aosta, where he had gone for a change of air. Maistre saw the king again on 28 June to report Buttet's death. The king's only comment was, "I have lost a good officer." After recording the king's remark, Maistre added: "That gave me much to reflect on."[10] We know too, from his diary entries, that during this period his wife made a trip from Lausanne to Chambéry (13 June–19 July). For whatever reason, daughter Constance was left with grandmother Morand when Madame de Maistre returned to Lausanne. In early September Maistre had to give up his accommodation at the Arsenal and find another place, since following her husband's death his sister moved to Aosta.

Shortly after this, Maistre made this startling entry in his diary: "I have experienced an extraordinary change; old tastes are being strengthened, vague ideas are becoming settled; conjectures are turning into certitudes. Today, 18 September, I am beginning a work whose title I do not yet know. It seems to me that I am beginning to catch sight of my vocation – at forty-four years of age!"[11] Unfortunately, we are reduced to speculation when it comes to knowing what work Maistre referred to in this entry. Some scholars believe that it was his "Réflexions sur le Protestantisme dans ses rapports avec la Souveraineté."[12] Another suggests that Maistre's diary entry reflects the flattering success of his *Considérations*.[13] By this date he had received a letter from the Count d'Avaray informing him that the French pretender, Louis XVIII, was extremely pleased with the work and ready to subsidize a second edition with a view to ensuring its wide distribution in France.[14] Maistre's reply to Avaray included an unequivocal statement of belief in the French pretender's cause and the hint that he was ready to write more on his behalf:

I have for his person [Louis XVIII] a rational attachment that has never varied; I love him as one loves symmetry, order, and health! No effort would cost me too much if it could gain a friend for him. I believe his happiness necessary for Europe; I detest his enemies with a philosophic hate that has nothing in common with passion except heat and energy. I abominate the Revolution that has dethroned his family; I have spared no effort to uncover its hideous and fetid root ...

I sense myself disposed, called, and drawn to defend his cause, which seems to me to be that of the social order.[15]

In Maistre's letters to Avaray prior to 18 September, however, there was no mention of any new work, but only of a postscript to the second edition of *Considérations*. But in the above letter, Maistre indicated that he had "no hope of being employed" in Piedmont, and went on to hint that he would be willing to transfer his allegiance: "However, I must choose a party, and, if it is impossible for me to remain a subject of the king of Sardinia, my ambition is to become French and serve the cause of the king of France."[16] Maistre also solicited the French pretender's assistance in recovering his confiscated property in Savoy. This letter was written just prior to the coup d'état of Fructidor (4 September 1797), which dashed any hopes of an immediate Bourbon restoration in France and which removed from the chambers in Paris royalists who might have helped Maistre's cause in Savoy. His next letter to Avaray, of 6 September, however, would have been written before news of Fructidor could have reached Turin, and in it Maistre wrote of the importance of distributing royalist propaganda: "It is necessary to provoke our enemies and to circulate religious ideas and royalism, as they make and circulate their poisons, by all possible means."[17] These letters to Avaray seem to leave open the possibility that the work Maistre had in mind in his 18 September diary entry was another propaganda piece along the lines of his *Considérations*.

Maistre's personal fate remained very much up in the air in September 1797. In his 30 August letter to Avaray, he had also indicated that an English ambassador (this would have been John Hampden-Trévor, the English ambassador to Turin, who Maistre had met in Lausanne) was trying to find him a place as the companion of some young Englishman doing his tour of the continent, and he had raised as well the possibility of finding a position as a tutor with some young German prince.[18] Presumably, it was the latter prospect that led Maistre, on 12 October, to take a German master to help him improve his "pronunciation and writing."[19]

Then dramatically, towards the end of the same month, it suddenly appeared that his fortune was made. On 26 October he learned that his family and that of his wife had been "admitted" to the court, and on the 27th Hauteville told him that it appeared that the king was disposed to accord him "the title of Councilor of State and the order of St Maurice."[20] Just why Maistre was now to be favoured is not known. It has been suggested that it was the success of *Considérations sur la France* that led the government to wonder if it had not "welcomed too lightly such a remarkable personality."[21] In any case, the favour was short-lived.

On 28 October, the day after he had learned of his possible good fortune, Maistre made this diary entry: "I learn that a letter, intercepted at Milan, overturns all my hopes in this country and that I will perhaps be obliged to look for a country elsewhere. From appearances, this event changes my future destiny."[22] The letter in question was from Avaray explaining that the events of Fructidor now made it impossible for Louis XVIII to assist Maistre in regaining his property in Savoy and rather pointless to subsidize distribution of a second edition of *Considérations*.[23] The letter had been intercepted by General Bonaparte's staff, forwarded to Paris, and published by the Directory as part of its strategy of exposing royalist intrigues in order to justify its recent coup d'état. The interception of this letter exposed Maistre publicly as the author of the *Considérations* and made it impossible for his king, who was bound by a close alliance with the Directory, to favour him in any way. In a letter written to Avaray on the same day that he learned the bad news, Maistre wrote that "it seems certain to me that I will be forced to quit the king's service" and announced his immediate departure for Aosta and "from there to I do not know where."[24] But a few days later he wrote again to Avaray to say that the unhappy adventure of the letter had not yet forced him to leave. He had since learned the contents of the intercepted letter and now declined Avaray's suggestion in that letter that he write something on the

coup d'état of Fructidor: "Your letter is known and my style is s
in this country that if the piece appeared they would recognize ι.
would be buried alive."[25] Maistre still wrote of leaving Turin, peι.
Switzerland, and this time made a direct appeal for Louis xviii's assistanc
finding a place as a tutor at some northern court.[26] In the upshot he was left
without a position in the Sardinian government (and in fact, in some disgrace
for having attracted the disfavour of the Directory and for alleged disloyalty
because of his relations with the French pretender), and with no offers of
employment elsewhere.

In these circumstances, Maistre had nothing to do but devote himself to his
studies. A diary entry for 4 December 1797, reads: "At nine o'clock this
morning, I finished copying three discourses in use in a French society of
illuminés. I began this task on 17 July, and taking note of the time I have
devoted to it, I see that I took 38 hours and 13 minutes. This piece is curious
and shows very well the doctrine of these gentlemen."[27] But Maistre's studies
during this period were not limited to illuminist literature. An analysis of
dated references and entries in his notebooks shows that both the number of
works cited and the number of pages of notes that he took were four or five
times greater for 1797 and 1798 than those for the years immediately
preceding and immediately following.[28] Some of the authors and works read
in 1797 include: Cicero (various works), St Augustine's *City of God*, Pierre
Charron's *De la Sagesse*, Johann August Ernesti's *Opuscula Theologica*
(1773), Lucian, Origen's *Contra Celsus*, Ovid, and Saint-Martin's *L'Homme
de désir*. Judging from the number of references and notes, these are works
Maistre read more or less systematically; there are many other scattered
references to other works and authors. For 1798, the equivalent list of
systematically studied authors and works include the following:
Demosthenes, Luigi Antonio Lanzi's *Saggio di lingua etrusca et di altre
antiche d'Italia* (3 volumes, 1789), the works of Justus Lipsius (the sixteenth-
century Catholic Stoic), Robert Lowth's *De sacra poesi hebraeorum
praelectiones academicae* (1753), George Macartney's *Voyage dans
l'intérieur de la Chine* … (4 volumes, 1798), John Milton's *Paradise Lost,
La perpétuité de la foy de l'Eglise Catholique touchant l'Eucharistie* by
Pierre Nicole and Antoine Arnauld (1664), *Histoire de l'Amérique* (4
volumes, 1778) and *An Historical Disquisition Concerning the Knowledge
Which the Ancients Had of India* (1792) by the Scottish historian William
Robertson, Seneca's letters, Voltaire (in the Kehl edition of his works),
Xenophon, and Edward Young's *Night Thoughts on Life, Death and
Immortality* (1779).[29] One is always struck by the breadth and variety of
Maistre's interests.

It was in 1798 too that he began a new notebook carrying the following
statement on the title-page: "Fragments on religion, or Collection of extracts
and reflections relative to a work where the Catholic system will be
envisaged from a new point of view."[30] This huge folio notebook eventually

contained over 800 pages of extracts and draft pages that would be mined for *Du Pape* and *Les Soirées de Saint-Pétersbourg*. It is just possible that a work on the "Catholic system" was what Maistre was thinking about when he made the 18 September 1797 diary entry about beginning a new work.[31]

Whatever literary projects Maistre may have had in mind, he used this period of forced leisure for serious reading and reflection rather than authorship. Only one small piece, a letter "A une dame protestante sur la maxime qu'un honnête homme ne change jamais de religion," survives from 1797.[32] A copy of this letter may have gone to some Swiss acquaintance, but Maistre seems to have done nothing else with it until many years later when it was circulated in manuscript in St Petersburg.

The only dated composition we have from Maistre's pen from 1798 is the already mentioned "Réflexions sur le Protestantisme dans ses rapports avec la Souveraineté."[33] This work is an impassioned attack on Protestantism for undermining the spiritual and political unity of Europe. The argument is a relatively straightforward development of Maistre's contention that Christianity is the religion of Europe and that Protestantism was not only a religious heresy "but a civil heresy, because in freeing the people from the yoke of obedience and according them religious sovereignty, it unchained general pride against authority and put discussion in place of obedience."[34] Perhaps more interesting than Maistre's arguments are the authors and sources he cited in support of his position. These included, in pride of place, Edmund Burke, who is described as "this grand patriot, this great writer who discerned the French Revolution."[35] Montesquieu, Montaigne, Madame de Sévigné, the Thirty-Nine Articles of the Anglican Church, and various items from English newspapers. The piece provides a good example of how Maistre used his reading and his notebooks to stockpile ammunition for his polemics. It is not clear why he decided against publishing this essay, but some of the arguments and citations found their way into later works.

The external circumstances of Maistre's life changed little in the thirteen months between late October 1797, when Avaray's intercepted letter cost him the possibility of employment, and late December 1798, when changed political circumstances led to a flight down the Po to Venice. He attempted to see Hauteville, the minister of foreign affairs, on 15 January 1798, but was refused admittance.[36] A few days later he received word that his wife and children had arrived in Aosta from Lausanne, and on 5 February, he left Turin to join them there. It was at this juncture, just before leaving Turin, that he burned the manuscript of his Savoyard letters.[37] Maistre remained in Aosta until 16 May. In mid-March, he noted in his diary the names of members of his family that "the wind of Revolution had assembled in the City of Aosta": his sister Anne and her husband Saint-Réal; his aunt, Madame de la Chavanne, her daughter and two grandsons; his brother André; his brother Xavier; and finally, his wife and two children.[38] But by late April, Maistre was informed that the presence of a number of Savoyards in the city was upsetting local "democrats," the French, and his own government, and that it would be convenient for him to depart. So leaving his wife and children behind, Maistre returned to Turin.[39]

From Maistre's perspective, the political situation in Italy had continued to deteriorate during these months. His diary records the successive encroachments of the French: General Berthier's conquest of Rome and the expulsion of Pope Pius VI in mid-March, the French takeover of Genoa at about the same time, and the French occupation of the citadel in Turin on 28 June 1798.[40] Understanding that this last maneuvre, in effect, "dethroned the sovereign," Maistre went to Aosta in the first days of July and brought his wife and children back with him to Turin.[41] But the crisis did not come until 6 December, when the French finally took over open control of Piedmont. King Charles-Emmanuel then abdicated and departed for Sardinia.

On 26 December 1798, noting in his diary that he had "nothing more to do in Turin since the arrival of the French," Joseph de Maistre embarked on the Po with his wife and children.[42] He had provided himself with a false Prussian passport that identified him as a merchant from Neuchâtel, but it was still a long difficult journey. The weather was very cold, and the family suffered from inadequate accommodations the whole way. Rodolphe, who would have been ten years old at the time, later recounted details of their journey in his biographical notice on his father.[43] At Casal they transferred from their small boat to a larger vessel transporting salt to Venice. This boat was filled with French refugees of every sort, including noble ladies, officers, priests, monks, and even the ex-bishop of Nancy. All were camped on the open deck, unprotected from the cold and the heavy snow. More than once the boat was halted by ice on the river. For part of the way, the left bank was occupied by the Austrians, the right bank by the French, and the vessel was challenged by both. At one customs station, Maistre was robbed by French soldiers.[44] It was only on 22 January 1799 that they finally arrived safely in Venice, where they would remain until 26 August.

VENICE

The seven months Maistre spent in Venice were of considerable importance for his intellectual biography. Like Lausanne, Venice was an important émigré centre at this time, and Maistre again had the opportunity to meet and converse with a number of interesting personalities. Perhaps the most unusual was Cardinal Maury, a French prelate who had made a name for himself defending the clergy and nobility in the Constituent Assembly in the early days of the Revolution. Apparently Maistre went to see Maury shortly after his arrival, and found the churchman most sympathetic to his "embarrassing position" as an unemployed refugee. Maury told him that "We will arrange all that."[45] A few days later, when Maistre met Maury again at a social occasion, Maury drew him aside. Maistre thought he would be told about something that would rescue him from "the abyss" into which he had fallen, but Maury simply took three apples from his pocket and gave them to Maistre for his children.[46] Nevertheless the two men seem to have gotten on well; a few days later Maury came and spent an entire morning with Maistre, who subsequently recorded the gist of their conversation.[47] Maistre was also present when Maury conferred minor orders on a man by the name of Nicolò Paccanari, whose ambition it was to restore the Jesuits.[48]

The Maistre family's financial situation during this period was difficult, but not desperate. Most worrisome was the fact that they were eating up their capital, selling their silver serving pieces to survive. They lived in various rented quarters, finally settling in a hall in the residence of Count de Kevenhüller, an Austrian gentleman whose acquaintance Maistre had made in Turin.[49]

Joseph de Maistre found many things to interest him in Venice. He attended an Oriental rite mass (the liturgy of St John Chrysostom) and declared the Greek formula of consecration "more satisfactory than our own."[50] There were at least two trips to the Lido, one to dine with priests he had known in Lausanne and his brother André. After dining, they went together to see the dike of Palestrine, "a work worthy of the most powerful empire."[51] Maistre also witnessed an annual event that involved the establishment of a bridge of boats from a quai across to the Church of the Redeemer; he paced off the bridge and noted that it was 120 feet long.[52]

These months in Venice were one of the few periods of his life when Maistre had problems with his health. He was struck down with malaria in early July and again in early August, but even this experience was grist for his philosophizing: "It is remarkable that I was taken with the fever on the 2nd of July and on the 2nd of August and that it lasted 4 days in each case; order is everywhere."[53]

This was another period of forced leisure, and he used the time for more reading, reflection, and a bit of writing. The notebook entries for these months suggest a scattering of interest; the one work which he appears to have studied systmatically was Pierre-Daniel Huet's *Demonstratio evangelica* (1679).[54] Maistre's published works contain one piece dated Venice 1799, a burlesque "Discours du citoyen Cherchemot." This piece was apparently found among Maistre's papers; it was printed in his *Oeuvres* with his own explanatory comment: "Having made a great collection of revolutionary phrases without any particular end in mind, I then thought of casting them together in an imaginary discourse of citizen *Cherchemot*, which would be extremely funny if it were printed very exactly, which would be essential because of the numerous and accurate citations."[55] The modern reader might not appreciate the humour, but what Maistre did was put all the cant phrases of the Revolution into the mouth of an honest citizen trying manfully to celebrate the glories of the sovereignty of the people.

Much more interesting in the light of the religious, metaphysical, and epistemological speculations that will characterize Maistre's later works, *Les Soirées de Saint-Pétersbourg* in particular, is an unedited "Essai sur les Planètes" to be found in one of his notebooks and which is dated "Venice, 1799."[56] This little essay is not particularly well organized or developed, but it nevertheless reveals Maistre's fascination with certain problems that will continue to intrigue him for the rest of his life. Consequently, it is worthwhile to look at it a little more closely.

Although Maistre entitled his manuscript an "essay on the planets," its focus is not astronomical but philosophical and religious. His particular concern was the way the philosophes had used astronomy "to diminish man." He began by pointing to their "ridiculous" contradictions with respect to the dignity of man. "When it is a question of arming pride against primitive truths," modern philosophy goes on about "man's greatness," about man being "made for truth," about "no power having the right to impede his thought." But if it is a question of drawing arguments from the "veritable greatness of man" to discuss his future state, modern philosophy changes its tune and speaks only of human ignorance. Exploiting modern astronomy, the philosophes have said that man is nothing compared to the immense distances of space, and have done their best to ridicule the claim that the whole universe was made for man.[57]

It was precisely Maistre's intention to argue that this claim is not "ridiculous." The argument proceeds from a statement he put forward as an incontestable metaphysical axiom: "everything has been created *by* and *for* intelligence."[58] For Maistre, this implied that there would be no point for God to create material things that would never have any relationship to created intelligence. Therefore "the planets are only, and can only be, dwellings or prisons of intelligence in general as the individual body of a man is only that of his individual intelligence."

Maistre's second axiom was that the universe is only "a system of invisible things manifested visibly."[59] This maxim of St Paul "contains absolutely all speculative philosophy and accords perfectly with the first principle." Maistre also quoted from the Swiss naturalist, Charles Bonnet: "All nature is therefore for you only a great and magnificent spectacle of appearances."[60] These principles were then used in various ways to try to show how the whole universe may be related to created intelligence and to man in particular. The argument led Maistre to some quite adventuresome speculation.

Similarities between the earth and the other planets (with all circling around a common centre of light and warmth, exhibiting similar phenomena such as poles, equators, seasons, and days and nights) suggested to Maistre that the other planets must also be inhabited. He acknowledged that there are

Christian scholars who "are alarmed by this multitude of worlds," but replied "that if the men of these other planets are guilty and degraded like us, God has provided for them or will provide for them by means of which we need know nothing."[61]

Similar considerations led Maistre to reflect on astrology and to suggest that modern men "pass over it too quickly." He acknowledged that "a lot of extravagances" have been produced in its name, but went on to say that he would find it very difficult to believe "that a great error profoundly rooted in the minds of all men in every century is not attached in some way to some true root." He charged that modern philosophy, "in completely materializing everything, has prodigiously constricted the circle of knowledge."[62]

The themes of human dignity and creation by and for intelligence involved Maistre in speculation about the very nature of intelligence. One passage in particular foreshadows some of his later epistemological theorizing:

It is sometimes said that angels are beings of a different nature than ourselves; I do not believe it. There is between all intelligences a relationship that stems from the very nature of things. Intelligence is something absolute: undoubtedly one may understand more or less, but one understands or one does not. Intelligences can only differ in extent, not in nature. One can imagine, in effect, some truth conceived by man and one can understand that an angel can conceive the same truth better or more fully; but what is true for us is true for an angel. No intelligence can know otherwise or better than I that the three angles of a triangle add up to two right angles.[63]

Human reason, when freed from prejudice and not blinded by passion, Maistre believes, can come to recognize its need for revelation, with "the conjectures of the first reinforcing the oracles of the second."[64]

Turning to Revelation, Maistre suggests that "the first and the greatest oracle we have on our nature" is the statement in Genesis: "Let us make man in our image." He goes on to argue that "the least resemblance to God gives an idea of a greatness that no language can express or mind comprehend." Citations from the Old and New Testaments, Homer, Origen, and Milton are marshalled to support Maistre's contention that on the question of the dignity of human nature, "Revelation has confirmed the calculations of reason."[65] Even the fact that man can thwart the plans of the Creator, that man can offend God by sin and thus require the Incarnation for his redemption, testifies to the greatness of man.

In opposition to modern philosophy, which considers "the celestial bodies as brute masses absolutely foreign to life," Maistre cited the ancient belief that supposed them and the earth itself to be somehow alive. This line of argument leads him to introduce a flood of quotations to illustrate the idea that "blood is the vehicle of life," and that the earth thirsts for blood.[66] Maistre acknowledges that this tradition pertains less to ancient philosophy properly speaking than to ancient "mystical theology." Nevertheless, he feels, the point shows "how antiquity loathed that *dead* philosophy so beloved of modern taste."[67]

Maistre's essay closes with a discussion of the Platonic belief that the stars are divinities of some kind. He concludes that far from rejecting these ideas, "Christianity judged them conformable with its dogmas, appropriated them, and corrected them in a way to make them conform to its doctrine."[68] He then introduced a long quotation from Origen to support a suggestion that "this theory was one of the objects of the Christian initiation," and concludes that "we can see that these primitive Christians would have found no metaphor in this passage from one of the prophets, 'the stars shine joyfully at their set times: when he calls them, they answer, here we are; they gladly shine for their creator'."[69] In short, this little unedited essay displays the imagination and speculative verve that will typify Maistre's *Soirées de Saint-Pétersbourg*.[70]

The first three months of Joseph de Maistre's sojourn in Venice were probably the most difficult from the point of view of the general political situation in northern Italy and his perception of his own future. By late April 1799, he noted French defeats by the Austrian forces, and on 25 June recorded the news of the capitulation of Turin to an Austro-Russian army with the comment that "it appears that the time of my departure is approaching."[71] Shortly after this, he made a brief outing with friends to Padua to see the sights; his diary entries for this little pleasure trip contain detailed descriptions of the countryside, the architecture, and the library of St Justine in Padua. But Maistre noted that his principal reason for going to Padua was "the desire to see there the Russians and Cossacks that Emperor Paul I has marched to Italy against the French."[72] He talked to some of the Russian officers, heard the Russian troops singing tunes of which his ear "understood nothing," found that the Cossacks appeared to him "more as *killers* than as soldiers," and noted the absence of any common physical type among the Russian and Cossack soldiery. "What reflections seeing them inspired in me." Maistre also noted the cost of his outing – approximately as much as a month's rent for his family in Venice.[73]

In late July, Maistre wrote to his government offering his services (even in Sardinia).[74] The family left Venice on 26 August and arrived in Turin on 4 September. On 19 September Maistre learned that he had been named to the post of Regent of the island of Sardinia with a salary "of at least 12,000 livres."[75] The appointment and the salary were a great boost to Maistre's morale and to his financial situation.

The newly named Regent left Turin almost immediately on his way to his new posting, but proceeded by way of Florence to see the king. By this date, Charles-Emmanuel IV had returned to the mainland from Sardinia (where he had fled the previous December), but the Austrians, who were in control in

Turin, were preventing the unfortunate monarch from returning to his capital. Maistre was received by the king and queen on 18 October, and immediately used his new position to improve the situations of other members of his family. His brother Xavier had gone off without proper authorization to join General Suvorov earlier in the month, and Joseph was now able to regularize his position.[76] He also made arrangements for his other brother, Nicolas, who was serving in Aosta, to be assigned to Sardinia as well.[77] (Maistre's brother-in-law, Alexis de Saint-Réal, had been appointed general intendant of Sardinia at the same time as Joseph had been named Regent.)[78] Maistre was also awarded a decoration in the form of the Cross of the Order of St Maurice and St Lazare.[79] His high spirits as a consequence of all this good fortune found expression in enthusiastic diary entries describing the sights of Florence. He visited the famous gallery in the company of its director and recorded his joy at seeing that "there existed in Italy a happy corner of earth that the sacrilegious hand of the Parisian Vandals had not ravaged and profaned."[80] He visited as well the Church and Library of St Lawrence and viewed "with inexpressible pleasure the autograph manuscripts of Sannazar and Machiavelli."[81]

While in Florence in October 1799, Maistre was consulted on a sensitive question of public law and criminal jurisprudence; he was asked to comment on the question of how the restored monarchy "should view and treat persons who had manifested republican sentiments or served the Republic during the Republican period."[82] (With the Austro-Russian victories it was assumed that the king would soon regain Turin.) Maistre's reply, which took the form of a six-page letter, reveals that the supposedly rigid theorist of the authority of sovereigns could be realistic, flexible, and humane in judicial practice.

Even before he took up the question at issue, Maistre began his letter by pointing out that Piedmontese hostages were being held at Dijon, and since even the rumour of chastising partisans of the republic in Turin would endanger the safety of the hostages, it would be "completely impolitic" to begin proceedings against suspects for the moment. But Maistre also advised against holding suspects indefinitely, because imprisonment is also a punishment, which is aggravated if prolonged without term.

As for those who have manifested republican sentiments, Maistre's advice was categorical:

To love republican government is not a crime, since we are not responsible for our sentiments. The supreme truth and the supreme justice itself does not say "love," but only "honour your parents," since love cannot be commanded. Likewise, everyone is obliged to honour but not to like the government under which he is born; he owes it obedience and fidelity to death … if we find in a monarchy a man who does not like this form of government, provided he obeys it and supports it with all his strength, he is within the rules.

Maistre also stressed how difficult it would be to discover the real sentiments of those who had to live under the republic: Moreover, among those men who rendered more or less open hommage to the republic, how many did so out of fear? This sentiment dictated a thousand reactions which have been denounced as offences, although as always happens, the most guilty were those who revealed themselves the least, knowing how to keep in the shadows and get others to act." Many of those who had served the republic, Maistre pointed out, having lost hope in the restoration of the monarchy, "submitted to circumstances, served the republic without liking it, and tried to render the regime less insupportable by involving in it the most honest men possible."

Joseph de Maistre was particularly upset about the idea of punishing former officials of the monarchy for continuing in their posts under the republic:

With respect to those formerly employed in the king's service, removed for having occupied positions under the republic, I must tell you, Monsieur, that I see not a single reason that can justify anything like such severity. You, Monsieur, undoubtedly have a head as well made as anyone else: permit me to ask you. On 8 December 1798 [the date of the king's abdication] could you have guessed 26 May 1799 [the date of reconquest]? Be frank and admit that such a hope would have passed for a fool's dream ... I would ask if someone should be punished for not being a prophet? Some men of character and independent fortune could separate themselves entirely from affairs; the greatest number could only do what they did. Especially, persons for whom their appointments were their only or principal means of subsistence had necessarily to seek employment: the imperious need to live permitting everything except crime, how, in good faith, can one seriously maintain, nobody being able to foresee the end of the order of things then in place, that all honest men were bound to retire from affairs and leave all positions without exception in the hand of rascals? I will never understand how such a system can enter into a sane head.

Although Maistre himself had fled rather than serve the French Republic, he was certainly most sympathetic to those prevented by circumstances from doing the same.

Maistre concluded his letter with a caution against abuse, and pleas for better public relations and amnesty:

More than ever monarchy needs friends. We will never win them by provocative severity. His Majesty must not be left ignorant that intrigue can often adopt a mask of zeal, and that a certain severity against the best names may be no more than a way to impose on the government, and in hands more clever than pure a means of displacing certain men to replace them with others ... Far from trying to augment the already large number of unfortunates, it is important that the government draw a veil over the greatest number of these forced irregularities.

When monarchies were finally restored in Europe in 1814, rulers such as Louis XVI, by force of necessity, had to act more or less as Maistre had recommended to his government in 1799.

Maistre left Florence for Livorno on 19 November 1799. It was while there waiting for a vessel to take him to Sardinia, that he received news of "the Revolution that had occured in Paris 8 November (18 Brumaire.)"[83] Maistre's advice on how to handle republican suspects would be rendered academic by the new First Consul's reconquest of northern Italy. But the repercussions of these events on Maistre's personal life would not be felt for a couple of years. For the moment his interest was Sardinia. He had left his wife and family in Turin, but he was joined in Livorno by the Saint-Réal family, who brought with them his son Rodolphe. The party embarked for Cagliari on a small Sicilian boat on 18 December 1799. Adverse winds kept the vessel at anchor in the Bay of Tortoly until 11 January however, and they did not arrive at their destination in Sardinia until 12 January 1800.[84]

CAGLIARI

Joseph de Maistre's tenure of office as Regent in Sardinia was beset by all kinds of difficulties and has been the subject of considerable disagreement. After leaving the island, Maistre himself always looked back on his experience there with exasperation and bitterness.[85] Without entering into the details, which are scarcely relevant to his intellectual biography, something should nevertheless be said about the nature of Maistre's problems in this period.

A couple of days after arriving in Cagliari, the Regent dined with the Viceroy, Charles-Felix, and noted in his diary how his fortunes had changed since the previous year: "during the meal, I amused myself by thinking of where I was last year on the same day ... stuck in the ice, without servants, without furniture, and almost without hope."[86] But his euphoria was short-lived. Part of the problem, undoubtedly, was sheer boredom at being again immersed in legal minutiae. The next diary entry but one reads: "1 February, 1 March. I get up, I go to bed, I work. Uninterrupted platitudes."[87] Maistre evidently missed the intellectual stimulation of good conversation with well-informed and intelligent people. Cagliari was a very restricted and provincial place after Lausanne, Turin, Venice, and Florence. Even more serious were difficulties inherent in Maistre's official position.

Sardinia at this time was in a state of near anarchy; there had been a revolt in Cagliari in 1794, and further trouble in 1799, a few months before Maistre's arrival.[88] Violence was endemic between various quasi-feudal factions, and it appears that the appointment of a new Regent was part of an attempt to restore the administration of justice. The *Régent de la grand Chancellerie*, to give his full title, was responsible for all judicial services on the island, including civil, criminal, and maritime law. Since the British navy controlled the Mediterranean at this time and used this control to seize foreign vessels in Sardinian ports, to introduce contraband goods, and to requisition supplies, it was no easy task to maintain Sardinian sovereignty. Maistre's original letter of appointment, which had been addressed to him in Venice from Cagliari and dated 15 August 1799 (ie, before Charles-Emmanuel had returned to the mainland), had informed him that the king's brother, Charles-Felix, was being appointed Viceroy at the same time and that it was hoped that Maistre would arrive in Cagliari before the king's departure so that "preventative arrangements" could be made in concert with the new Viceroy "following such dispositions as your experience in affairs and your enlightenment will suggest to you."[89] The letter implied that Maistre's position vis-à-vis the Viceroy would be one of association rather than one of subjection.

As it turned out, the Viceroy and the Regent did not work well together. The differences appear to have been both personal and ideological. In part, it was a clash between a Piedmontese military officer and a Savoyard magistrate, but it was also a conflict between two different conceptions of monarchical government. Charles-Felix was ready to use vigorous military methods to govern the unruly islanders; Maistre tried to insist on correct civilian legal procedures. One historian, who has examined the records of Maistre's activities as Regent, speaks of "the minute care he employed in the inspection of dossiers, the visiting of prisons, the interrogation of the imprisoned, and the offering of measures of clemency whenever they were merited by repentance or good conduct."[90] However, the Viceroy judged Maistre insubordinate and unco-operative, and was soon demanding that he be replaced.[91]

Charles-Emmanuel, weak and irresolute as ever, was reluctant to decide whether he should support the Viceroy or the Regent. But in October 1801, he finally chose to have an official letter of reprimand sent to Joseph de Maistre decrying faults in the administration of justice on the island and calling for more effective efforts.[92] But on the same date as this official letter, which was routed through the Viceroy, two other private letters were sent to Maistre explaining why the first had been sent, asking him to carry on, and suggesting how he might use the official letter to make his authority felt more effectively.[93] For the period from August 1801 through his departure from Sardinia in February 1803, Maistre was engaged in a confidential correspondence with the Count de Challembert, the king's first minister.[94] But Maistre's political position with respect to the Viceroy was weakened by the death of Queen Clotilde, a sister of Louis XVI, in March 1803,[95] and the abdication of Charles-Emmanuel in June of the same year. The new king, Victor-Emmanuel I, seems to have been confident enough in Maistre's abilities as a magistrate,[96] but Charles-Felix again requested Maistre's recall. It is unclear whether it was the Viceroy's letter or other circumstances that led to the decision to send Maistre to St Petersburg as the Sardinian ambassador.[97]

But before taking up the story of Maistre's Russian assignment, a few words should be said about other aspects of his life in Sardinia. He was accompanied to the island by his son and the Saint-Réal family. Rodolphe was placed with an Abbé Morena, an ex-Jesuit, shortly after their arrival.[98] His wife, his daughter Adèle, and his brother Nicolas arrived in Cagliari in June 1800, but the family's joy at being reunited was marred in October by the death of the Saint-Réal's year-old son.[99] Moreover, political developments elsewhere continued to have repercussions on Maistre's private life. The Peace of Amiens and the Consultate's decision to reduce the list of proscribed émigrés made it possible for Nicolas to return to Savoy in early 1802.[100] Maistre tried to make arrangements to have Nicoas send out his other daughter, Constance, but the chosen courier arrived in Cagliari in May 1802 without the girl; the grandmother "had not the strength to separate herself from her."[101] In any case, his wife's name had also been removed from the émigré list, and following the abdication of Charles-Emmanuel (which he realized put his own position as Regent in doubt), Maistre made the decision to send her, Adèle, and Rodolphe back to Savoy.[102]

In the same month that his family left Cagliari, Maistre sent a letter and a memoir to the French ambassador in Naples requesting exemption from the French law of 6 Floréal (26 April 1802) requiring all French émigrés (including Savoyards) to return under penalty of loss of their property.[103] He explained his case (which was essentially the one he had argued in 1793 and 1796 – ie, that he did not regard himself as an émigré), indicated that he intended to continue to serve the king of Sardinia, and asked that his name be deleted from the list of émigrés. Maistre left Sardinia before a response was forthcoming, but a year later his government was surprised to get a note from the French government saying that Maistre's name had been struck from the list of émigrés, that he was free to continue to serve his king, and that he would continue to keep his rights as a French citizen.[104]

Maistre's heavy professional responsibilites as Regent meant little leisure for the pleasures of intellectual life, but he did find or take time to continue his studies. We know that he arranged to have a Lithuanian Dominican teaching oriental languages at the local college, a man named Jacques Hintz, to come to visit him in the afternoons.[105] Dated entries for these years in his notebooks and papers suggest systematic study of a few works. In August and September 1801 he made notes on Augustin Barruel's *Mémoires pour servir à l'histoire du Jacobinism* (5 volumes, 1798–9). The notes indicate that

Maistre refused to accept Barruel's general thesis, which blamed the French Revolution on a Masonic plot. Citing Barruel's admission that "the number of honest Masons has been and is still great," Maistre argued that by Barruel's own admission, "Freemasonry is not essentially bad." The association as such is quite innocent, "but there are a very small number of scoundrels among the immense number of its associates."[106] Maistre was particularly upset by the way Barruel confused Bavarian illuminism with the French disciples of Saint-Martin: "Everything the author has to say on the subject of M. de Saint-Martin is so false, so calumnious, that one has a right to be astonished. As for the accusation of Manicheism made against this writer, it ceases to be calumnious because it becomes ridiculous."[107]

Other works that Maistre appears to have studied during these years in Sardinia include: Gian Battista Bianconi's *Letteris Hebraeorum et Graecorum* (1748), read in July 1802; Antoine de Solis y Ribadeneyra's *Histoire de la conquête du Mexique* (1794), read in November 1802; and Alexander Pope's *Essay on Criticism* (1794), read in the same month. Maistre was also reading Voltaire; in January 1803, he copied part of the latter's *Poème sur le désastre de Lisbonne* and followed the citation with the following reflection:

Never have better arguments in favour of the necessity of a Revelation been provided. Observe the singular contradictions of this man. He wrote an entire work (*Poème sur la loi naturelle*) to prove to us that natural reason is everything and Revelation nothing, that Nature says everything to man, *and that by it finally God speaks to the world* (See especially the First Part). Then, in another work, he lets this great truth escape:

Nature is mute, we question it in vain; We need a God who speaks to mankind.[108]

We have no compositions from Maistre's pen from these years, but we know that in March 1802 he wrote and published a "harangue" in Italian on the death of Queen Clotilde.[109]

Maistre's departure from Sardinia, like so many other events in his life since 1789, was the consequence of changing circumstances in France and the impact of these developments on her neighbours. in this case, one repercussion of the French annexation of Piedmont and the subsequent decree of 10 Messidor (29 June 1802), which obliged all absent Piedmontese to return immediately to their country under pain of confiscation of their property and to renounce the service of their old sovereign, was to leave the new king, Victor-Emmanuel I, without representation in the Russian capital.[110] The Count de Vallaise, who had been serving as ambassador in St Petersburg, was one of those who returned to Piedmont, leaving vacant one of the two diplomatic posts that were essential for the survival of the monarchy. (Since Sardinia barely produced enough revenue to pay for its own administration, the Sardinian kings were heavily dependent on subsidies from England and Russia during the whole period from 1800 to 1814.) These were the circumstances that led to the decision to send Joseph de Maistre to the Russian court.

When the letter informing him of his new appointment reached Maistre in Cagliari on 23 October 1802, his immediate reaction was to rejoice in his good fortune:

I learn that the king has destined me for the Mission in St Petersburg: great and un-expected event, which, from appearances, removes me from the magistrature forever, and which must change my destiny absolutely. If the pitiless French law against the Piedmontese had not forced the Count de Vallaise to leave his post, I would not have had this good fortune. This is always my device: *inimicis juvantibus*.[111]

However, Maistre did not leave Sardinia immediately, since he was not satisfied with the original conditions of his appointment – which were for a provisional appointment with only his title as Regent. He negotiated to obtain titles and conditions that would be more appropriate for the posting, and negotiations were slow since it took over six weeks for Maistre to get a response from the court in Rome.[112] His requests for the "Great Cross" of St Maurice and for a Sardinian title were refused, but in the end he was granted the title Envoyé extraordinaire et Ministre plénipotentiaire.[113] It was only on 11 February 1803 that he finally sailed from Cagliari on the first stage of a long journey to an entirely new adventure.

Officially at least, Joseph de Maistre was the Envoyé extraordinaire from the moment he left Cagliari. But his adventures until 8 April, when he passed through Venice on his way to Russia, may be counted as part of his Italian interlude. Taking advantage of the opportunities offered by his travels, Maistre took time to view the celebrated sights of Naples and Rome, and a number of pages of his diary are devoted to describing what he saw and recording his reflections.[114] Disembarking in Naples on 17 February, he managed to visit many renowned attractions before he set out for Rome. Architecture, sculpture, inscriptions, museums, libraries, and Roman ruins are all mentioned. He was particularly impressed by the manuscript collection at the university library: "So I have made the acquaintance of the handwriting of Petrarch, Machiavelli, Sannazar, and Tasso."[115] He visited Pompeii and Herculaneum, and was scandalized by the singular sign to be found on one of the houses of Pompeii: "one wonders if the honest women of that time did not pass by in that street? It has been said that men are always the same, but this is true in only a very general sense. All our modern corruption would never tolerate this sign."[116] Maistre was sentitive to the importance of the literary remains unearthed at Herculaneum. He thought they were "incontestably the most ancient in the world," since the next most ancient that he was aware of dated from the fourth century A.D., and he was pleased to find that he could read the Greek of a fragment displayed under glass.[117]

Before leaving Naples, Maistre paid a visit to the French Ambassador, Charles Alquier, to ask what had happened to his request of the previous August to be deleted from the list of French émigrés. As he later described the meeting, he had a lively conversation with the Frenchman:

The French minister was most polite to me, praised the sentiments, the reasoning, and the style of my memoir, and excused himself rather poorly for not having responded, saying that he had not done so because he himself knew nothing of its success ... His conversation having turned to politics, I said to him ... "You have done perfectly well, Monsieur, in abolishing the word *monarchy* to substitute for it *government by one*; our language is rich enough, why borrow from the Greek?" He burst out laughing. I have always observed that you can say anything to the French; the manner is everything. Time and strength are lacking for me to report to you on the details of our conversation. I will say only that after I had shaken him up in my way, he exclaimed two or three times: "Monsieur, what are you going to do in St Petersburg? Go tell your ideas to the First Consul; never has he been told such things, and never have they been said like you say them." I was greatly amused by this scene and attached no importance to the thing, persuaded that there was no hope.[118]

We also have Alquier's impressions of Joseph de Maistre; in a letter to Talleyrand he described Maistre as "a man full of wit and talent, very likable, and of facile elocution," and suggested that they should try to recruit the Savoyard: "this would be, I believe, a good acquisition to make, and I am convinced that it would not be difficult."[119] A few years later, in 1807, Maistre would try to seek an interview with Napoleon, and one suspects that the idea came from this encounter with Alquier.[120]

Maistre left Naples on 27 February, taking the land route to Rome, where he arrived on 2 March 1803. His stay in Rome lasted until the 22nd of the month, but he despaired of recording his impressions in his diary.[121] However we know from his later correspondence that he visited such sights as the Villa Borghese.[122] On 7 March he was presented to Pope Pius VII, and a couple of days later described the experience in a letter to his daughter:

The day before yesterday I saw the pope, whose goodness and simplicity greatly astonished me. He came to meet me, scarcely let me bend a knee, and made me sit beside him. We gossiped pleasantly for half an hour, after which he accompanied us (I was with the king's minister), and he put his own hand on the doorhandle to open the door. I must tell you I was struck stiff by such unregal manners; I believed I had seen St Peter instead of his successor.[123]

From what he had to say in later correspondence, it appears that he was less impressed with the situation at the court of Victor-Emmanuel.

On 22 March 1803 Joseph de Maistre left Rome in am old carriage provided by the king and accompanied by two servants. Stopping only to repair the carriage (which kept breaking down), and for short visits in Florence, Venice, and Vienna (where he was presented to the Austrian emperor), he arrived in St Petersburg on 13 May. A month later, after he had been presented to the Russian emperor and other members of the imperial family, Maistre made this entry in his diary: "In less than three months I have been presented to the Pope, the Emperor of Germany, and the Emperor of Russia. That is a great deal for an Allobroge who was supposed to die, attached to his rock, like an oyster."[124] With this journey, Joseph de Maistre left behind the restricted stages of Chambéry, Lausanne, and Cagliari to play a role in one of the great capitals of the world. Though he represented only a third-rate king in exile from his own capital, the Savoyard magistrate become diplomat found in St Petersburg the milieu, the stimulation, and the time to produce the great literary works that ensured his reputation and influence.

CHAPTER SIX

St Petersburg

The fourteen years Joseph de Maistre spent in St Petersburg were the fullest and most productive years of his life. Curiously enough, his role as representative of Victor-Emmanuel I, though enormously time-consuming, was in some ways the least significant of the many parts he played there. None of his literary works from this period were related to his official role, but most of them are best understood in the context of other aspects of his life in the Russian capital.[1]

It was his official position as Envoyé extraordinaire of the Sardinian monarchy to the court of the tsar that kept Joseph de Maistre in St Petersburg and that gave him opportunities to play other roles. Without entering into the details of Maistre's diplomatic efforts on behalf of his sovereign, enough must be said about his ambassadorial role to understand the context of his other activities. In addition to representing Sardinia, Maistre was consulted as an adviser by the exiled Louis XVIII of France, involved in Russian politics (becoming at one point an adviser to Tsar Alexander I), and became a familiar figure in the salons of St Petersburg, where he won friends and influenced people in the French émigré community, the diplomatic community, and elite Russian families. He was also a close associate of the Jesuit community, using his influence at the Russian court on their behalf, and with them proselytising for Catholicism. And finally, he found time amid all these other activities to continue serious studies and to write his most important works. The emphasis here will be on the circumstances surrounding his activies as a writer. Given the multifaceted nature of Maistre's activities during these years, the approach will be topical rather than primarily chronological.

THE SARDINIAN AMBASSADOR

At the time Joseph de Maistre accepted his new diplomatic assignment, the prospects for the Sardinian monarchy were about as bleak as could be imagined. Since Bonaparte's victory at Marengo in June 1800 and subsequent annexation of Piedmont to France, the island of Sardinia remained the monarchy's only possession. Driven from Florence, where Maistre had visited the royal family in late 1799, the little Sardinian court had settled in Rome under the protection of the pope. The decree of 10 Messidor (29 June 1802), which had required all Piedmontese to return to their native province, had left the new monarch, Victor-Emmanuel I, with only a handful of officials around him. The personal qualities of the king included affability, benevolence, love of justice, and bravery, but he has also been described as lacking in intelligence and knowledge and as easily influenced by his immediate entourage. He had a stubborn faith in the political traditions of his house and in an eventual restoration, but proved inflexible and unimaginative in dealing with the exigencies of European politics during the years of Napoleonic domination.[2] The Messidor decree had left the new king without any really able advisers and those that remained were divided by jealousies and intrigues. Queen Marie-Thérèse, daughter of the Austrian Habsburg empress Maria-Theresa, was a haughty personality who resented any other influence over her husband than her own. The three most influential personalities at court were the queen, the king's confessor, and Count de Roburent, the king's military chief [premier écuyer]. Joseph de Maistre was under no illusions about this situation; he had observed the court at first hand while passing through Rome in March 1803. In an unofficial letter to Chevalier de Rossi in October 1803, he remarked: "What worries me and torments me is that I see no heads around the king capable of directing our boat in this squall."[3]

The little court lived in Rome until June 1804 when French pressure on the pope forced a withdrawal to Gaeta, but with the French takeover of the Kingdom of Naples even that refuge became untenable, and in February 1806 Victor-Emmanuel fled to Cagliari, where he remained until 1814. With the court at Cagliari, internal divisions were worse than ever, since the Viceroy, Charles-Felix, resented any diminution of his own authority, and there was rivalry between the entourage of the king and that of his brother. Victor-Emmanuel took no interest in the details of the administration of the island, occupying himself with drilling his little army of 500 men and supervising the traditionally strict etiquette of his court. The nine years he spent on the island accomplished nothing for its inhabitants.[4] The monarchy's financial situation remained extremely precarious; since Sardinian revenues hardly supported the administration of the island, the king was heavily dependent on the sale of titles of nobility and subsidies from England and Russia.[5]

It was this strange little court, with a mediocre, impoverished king surrounded by second-rate advisers barely surviving on the poor restive isolated island of Sardinia that Joseph de Maistre represented in St Petersburg. He was there to beg subsidies and to keep reminding Russian statesmen of Victor-Emmanuel's claims to his lost mainland possessions. Maistre accomplished these two basic tasks quite successfully, but the relationship between the court and its brilliant ambassador was never easy. Sources of tension included old suspicions of Maistre because of his Savoyard origins, his reputation as a Freemason and Francophile, jealousy of his abilities, personal dislike on the part of some (such as Charles-Felix), Maistre's personality and style, and his continuing complaints about being mistreated and unappreciated.

The vivacity, verve, and ardour of Maistre's epistolary style was not what was expected of a Sardinian diplomat, and it seems that neither the king nor his ministers knew quite what to make of his dispatches. With the arrival of Maistre's first letters from St Petersburg, Gabet tried to caution him on the matter:

[The king] has spoken of you in very flattering terms, has given evidence of how much he counts on your zeal, your talents, and your knowledge; but he has laughingly had the goodness to tell me that your pen is a lightning bolt, that its velocity can sometimes outdistance reflection, and that a turn of phrase may appear to be a bon mot to the one who writes it, although a different interpretation can make it appear an injury to the one who is its object. In short, a man warned is worth two.[6]

Maistre thanked Gabet for the advice and promised to try "to conform more perfectly to His Majesty's taste," but pointed out that "one cannot have my style without the faults of my style." He then went on to explain his use of irony: "Another word on a certain Parisian irony for which I have a talent I can sometimes abuse. When irony is practised on nothings and employed uselessly it is a very foolish superfluity. It is not the same when it sharpens reasoning, and when it makes a hole through which reasoning passes like a needle passes the thread."[7] Maistre's style apparently led to fears that he would act recklessly and exceed his instructions. He tried to reassure his superiors that the style of his dispatches was one thing and his diplomacy another:

I have received from nature the talent (which has its drawbacks like every other human thing) to express my ideas in a lively and picturesque way. Certainly nothing is more foreign to the style of our old offices; but one cannot be remade. Each is what he is. What is sure is that all this exterior fire has no influence on my conduct and that when it must come to action, I know how to put one foot before the other.[8]

The concerns about style seems to have declined with the years and Victor-Emmanuel apparently came to appreciate his ambassador's talent for political journalism. But the issue of supervision remained touchy. Pointing out the distance and time it took to get a reply from the Sardinian court (which was usually at least a month – and at some periods up to a year), Maistre insisted that he had to be trusted to use his own initiative and judgment. Since he was often in disagreement with the policies of his government and seldom bothered to disguise the fact in his letters, and since he was fertile in proposing all kinds of imaginative possibilities to the king and his ministers, it is understandable that a certain amount of distrust continued to characterize the relationship.[9] Part of the problem was that Maistre remained a good deal more "liberal" than the tradition-bound little court he served. In a personal note to Rossi, Maistre once burst out: "*one must never innovate*: this is what I sometimes laughingly call *Turinism*, and this in great part is what has gotten us where we are. When we dare no innovations and our enemies innovate without fear and without measure, we are soon brought to earth."[10] The ambassador's perceptions of the world differed significantly from that of his court.

The issues of status and pay were also sources of continuing bitterness. Whether the bitterness was warranted is a matter of perspective; Maistre's own perception (which has been accepted by many of his biographers) was that his talents were unappreciated and insufficiently rewarded, but critics have blamed him for pride, hypocrisy, and avarice.[11] The question is not easy to resolve. On the one side, Maistre was an able, intelligent, and effective diplomat; he was also well aware of his own talents and ambitious for advancement for himself and his family. On the other side his expectations clashed with the traditions of the monarchy and its financial situation. Almost from the moment of his arrival in St Petersburg, Maistre's letters to his superiors and to the king were replete with lengthy complaints about his treatment.

The ambassador's salary was set at 20,000 livres per year, the same amount Maistre had received as Regent. In Sardinia, that amount had enabled the Regent to pay off his debts and to accumulate some savings. But no sooner had Maistre arrived in St Petersburg than he began complaining that this amount was insufficient for an ambassador at the Russian court.[12] Despite repeated demands on Maistre's part, the salary remained the same; there were also difficulties about paying an allowance to his wife in Turin. Maistre was annoyed, too, by his government's refusal to pay anything towards the cost of establishing himself in St Petersburg.

The question of titles and decorations remained another sore point. In his very first letter to the king from Russia, Maistre let it be known that he had been questioned by another diplomat as to why he did not wear the attire of a chamberlain, which should have gone with his title, and if his cross of St Maurice was the "great cross." In the same letter he went on to tell the king: "You are the sixth sovereign, Sire, that my family has served in a century. At this point Your Majesty can easily raise me; but I cannot remain stationary. It is necessary to ascend or descend ... I in no way hide a very legitimate desire to rise by handling Your Majesty's affairs well (and why should I hide it, Sire)."[13] Since this brought no change in his status, Maistre continued to complain, and in March 1804 forwarded a long memoir to the king which repeated all his grievances and requested that his resignation be accepted.[14] The resignation was not accepted, but Maistre was granted the Great Cross of St Maurice, which mollified him for a time.

Another source of grievance arose when he finally persuaded the court that his son, Rodolphe, should come to St Petersburg as secretary of the legation. In this case, the king refused to grant the lad a military rank (which Maistre deemed indispensable for presentation at the Russian court). After bitter complaints, Rodolphe was finally granted the Cross of St Maurice and a small salary. The boy joined his father in August 1805, but when the opportunity arose in January 1807, Maistre took advantage of an offer from Tsar Alexander and placed him in the Russian Imperial Guard. Maistre remained extremely sensitive to the slightest criticism; in early 1806 he sent off another long letter of complaint to the king, again offering his resignation.[15] But his offers of resignation always contained the proviso that he would stay on if this was really the king's wish. And so despite the tempests, he continued in his position.

It has been suggested that these temper tantrums were for effect and designed to elicit new favours.[16] While it is true that Maistre certainly knew how to dramatize his "martyrdom" (the inadequacy of his salary, the separation from his family, the humiliations of his position), there is also good evidence that his bitterness was not feigned. Only one complete letter from Maistre to his wife has survived (in his letterbook copy), but it is quite significant in this regard.[17] This was a confidential letter, entrusted to a private courier,[18] which he indicated was the first he had been able to send her since his arrival in St Petersburg in which he could speak freely (he was quite aware that all his regular mail was read by the Russians). Explaining his situation at considerable length, he wrote of his financial problems, of his humiliation at being refused titles and honours, of his offers to resign, of the grievance about a rank for Rodolphe, and why he had made the decision to accept the offer to place their son in the Imperial Guard. In trying to explain why he had been treated so poorly, Maistre put most of the blame on the king himself:

If the king wished, at the moment I am writing to you, the destiny of my family could be changed without it costing His Majesty anything but willing it. But I can you assure that during the last six years I have never conceived the least project for my advantage or that of my family without finding in my way the inflexible will of the king, who has opposed everything. Oh, the harm he has done me, my dear friend! It is impossible to express it. You are undoubtedly asking: but why, but why? – In general, my dear child, I believe that the king does not like me very much. He used my services because he believed me useful; and he continues to do so because he sees that I succeed, but actually I strongly doubt that I am his man. It suffices that I belong to the magistrature, which he cannot suffer as you know. There are other reasons, from antipathy arising from intrigue and jealousy; there is more of this in small states than in large. Certain persons are very seriously worried about what I might be at the Restoration, and that I might be greater than they. I have also been warned by a friend that the queen is against me because she believes me an extreme enemy of her family.[19] But taking account of these motives, which have their weight, one must also agree that there is much absurdity. The king, my dear friend, still has the same ideas he had in Turin twenty years ago, and he still conducts himself by the same rules. One of those sacred rules was that to be an Envoyé extraordinaire it was necessary to be a *gentilhomme de la chambre*, and I was not. I am persuaded that he is still not reconciled to the violence that made him violate that sacred maxim.[20]

A few pages later, Maistre returned to the theme, urged his wife not to be too upset, and admitted he had not suffered it all in silence:

You must not be angry beyond measure at what you have just learned about the court; our princes are made so. Never can you get into one of their heads an idea that was not there. They hold unmercifully to their old systems; and when the whole world is laughing around them have no doubts about being wrong. The king has it in his head to do something for me *when he is again on the throne:* and he also has it in his head that there would be terrible disadvantages to do *now* anything that would be agreeable to me. No human reasoning can get him to believe that I will not be anything when I am dead and it is impossible to serve him. If he recalls me I will be completely consoled; you see that there is nothing great to regret. If he keeps me here I will continue to serve him tranquilly, and I will even console myself with the thought that there are always disadvantages is quitting the part one has chosen, and I will count on the same Providence that has led me and sustained me until now. Moreover, I must do justice to myself and believe that all the wrongs are not on one side. If they have treated me in a manner I believe inexcusable, from my side I have sent them phrases that were not made of honey. There have been times when I was literally enraged and completely out of character.[21]

Writing of his offers to resign, Maistre explained that in making the offers he had declared that if his services could still be useful and agreeable, he would continue. But, he told his wife, "affection is dead."

Despite his perceived lack of personal success with his own court, Maistre had won great respect in St Petersburg, and many of his Russian friends had urged him to abandon Sardinia and seek his fortune in Russia. Although he never admitted as much in his letters to his court, this letter to his wife shows that he gave this possibility serious consideration. In the course of explaining how difficult it was to live in St Petersburg on his salary, he remarked:

"Passage to Russian service likewise has its painful aspects. We are in a terrible crisis here because of the rapid fall in the banknotes, so this is not the time to make a decision."[22] In short, this confidential letter to his wife shows that Maistre was genuinely grieved by the treatment he received from his court, and that he was terribly torn between his sworn loyalty to the Sardinian monarchy and his resentment over what he perceived as shabby treatment. Given his sense of grievance, it is not surprising that he should have been tempted to seek service elsewhere. As things worked out, the time and opportunities were never quite right for making a switch, so Maistre retained an unblemished reputation for steadfast loyalty – at least during his lifetime.

Maistre's official mission in St Petersburg, of course, was to represent the interests of Victor-Emmanuel I, and in particular, to win Russian subsidies and diplomatic support for his little state. But from the beginning the Sardinian ambassador took a broad view of his responsibilities. The restoration of Victor-Emmanuel to his mainland possessions, he believed, was possible only in the context of a Bourbon restoration in France and the restoration of something like a traditional balance of power in Europe. So long as the revolutionary spirit reigned, so long as Napoleonic France dominated the European continent, so long as there was no return to traditional monarchical institutions and traditional religion, substantial amelioration of the situation of his own country seemed unlikely. The two great powers that might be expected to lead an anti-French, counter-revolutionary coalition, in Maistre's view, were England and Russia. The other possible contender, Austria, was always the subject of Maistre's intense suspicion and dislike, and from 1793 to his death he never ceased to denounce Austrian ambitions in Italy.[23] Despite Maistre's general admiration for things English and his recognition of the necessity of English participation in any viable anti-French coalition, he always had serious reservations about British foreign policy.[24] Russia and Tsar Alexander were, almost inevitably, Maistre's leading candidates for starring roles in the salvation of Piedmont-Sardinia and Europe.

The ambiguities, uncertainties, and reversals of Russian foreign and domestic policies during the reign of the "enigmatic tsar" are well known.[25] Maistre's hopes and expectations for Russia fluctuated with these vacillations and his growing understanding of the circumstances and pressures influencing the tsar's decisions. His first concern, of course, was with the direction of Russian foreign policy, but with time and as his own circumstances and those of Russian politics evolved, his attention gradually shifted to the domestic scene. Especially after Tilsit, with the apparent ascendancy of French reform ideas in internal policy a seeming counterpart of the French alliance, Maistre's personal ties with conservative Russian opponents of these "progressive" trends led to his more or less direct involvement in opposition to these developments.

Perhaps it would not be too fanciful to liken the way Joseph de Maistre went about both his official and self-imposed tasks in St Petersburg with the methods used by Benjamin Franklin in Paris as the representative of the rebellious American colonies.[26] Just as Franklin had not hesitated to capitalize on his literary reputation and skills to influence French opinion or to exploit his own personality for the cause of independence and freedom, so did Maistre deliberately deploy all his literary and personal talents to advance his own chosen causes. The main avenue of approach open to the impecunious representative of a powerless monarch was to win the friendship and trust of experienced and influential people in the diplomatic community and court circles. Maistre saw the "conquest" of important friends (to use the metaphor that constantly recurs in his correspondence) as an integral part of his mission.

In his campaign to win friends and influence people, Maistre quite consciously made the most of his gifts of intelligence, memory, and repartee. He also knew how to exploit his growing reputation as a spokesman for conservatism. Abundant evidence testifying to his methods and to his success may be found in both his own correspondence and in the letters and memoirs of those who observed him in the salons of the Russian capital. From his own perspective first, let us see how he "played" the role of witty philosopher of reaction. Responding to a letter in which his superior had cautioned the loquacious ambassador about inappropriate friendships and indulgence in sallies and pleasantries that might be reported to Russian ministers, and urged him to be reserved, circumspect, and prudent,[27] Maistre described and defended his techniques at some length:

Do not fear for my secrets, for I have none. I am sure there is little doubt in Europe about the reason I am here. As for my opinions, God keep me from hiding them. On the contrary, they are the key I use to gain entrance everywhere. I found myself one day sitting in company beside the secretary of the French legation (M. de Removal) and some other people. The conversation turned to the French Revolution and all the evils it had produced. I said to him: "What can you complain about, I ask you? Have you not formally said to God, 'We do not want you any more, get out of our laws, our institutions, even our education, etc.' What did he do? He retired, and said to you, 'Let it be done,' and the result was what you have seen, the lovable reign of Robespierre. Your revolution, Monsieur, is only a great and terrible sermon that Providence has preached to men. There are two points to it. *It is abuses that make revolutions:* this is the first point, and it is addressed to sovereigns. *But abuses cost infinitely less than revolutions,* this is the second point, which is addressed to peoples. You see that all the world has its portion." My faith, Monsieur, he said to me, you are really a philosopher. Moreover, he added, we are of no nation here, we are cosmopolitans. – And he immediately took to talking of Bonaparte, his projects, his tics, his faults, as if he had been speaking of some personage from ancient history.

Do you perhaps believe … that I would have done better to purse my lips and let him talk to the others. – No, I can only believe that you must be mistaken on this point.

There is not a man who cannot be won by moderate opinions. Truth and moderation never offend. I have observed this a thousand times. It is the passions that clash like stones and make fire.

Besides, I do not employ *prudence* in my affairs. I understand nothing of it, I assure you. I only use *my* prudence, an infinitely weaker instrument no doubt, but one with which I will perhaps not make false moves because I am habituated to it. Every man must know himself and act as he is able with his own character. With that of another he will only make gaffes.[28]

Further on in this same letter, after acknowledging his government's fears about methods so out of conformity with the ordinary rules, Maistre requested continuing support in his attempts to win opinion, characterizing it as "the unique thing that I need."[29]

Although some who were opponents of Maistre's views spoke slightingly of him, characterizing him as a "salon orator," he nevertheless won genuine renown in the drawing rooms of St Petersburg. Since Maistre's self-portrait was taken from one of his early letters from Russia, perhaps it would be appropriate to show how he was perceived by others by citing someone who observed him in his later years there. Alexander Stourdza had been an opponent of Maistre's religious position,[30] but when writing about him many years later still remembered the Sardinian ambassador with awe and affection:

I believe I can still see before me that noble old man, always walking with his head high, crowned by hair whitened by both nature and the caprice of fashion. His large forehead, his pale face stamped with features as striking as his thoughts, marked too by the misfortunes of his life, his blue eyes half dimmed by deep and laborious studies; and finally the accomplished elegance of his costume, the urbanity of his language and manners – all that forms in my mind a certain original and suave whole …

Monsieur de Maistre was, without contradiction, the outstanding personage of the time and place where we lived, I mean to say the court of the Emperor Alexander and the time between 1807 and 1820 …

We were all ears when, seated in an armchair, his head high, with a large green ribbon suspending across his chest the more religious than secular cross of Saints Maurice and Lazare, Count de Maistre abandoned himself to the limpid course of his eloquence, laughing whole-heartedly, arguing with grace, animating and governing the conversation.[31]

That such an original personality evoked diverse reactions is not surprising. Maistre himself knew quite well that he displayed traits that were offensive to some:

Every disposition has its disadvantages. Do you suppose me not to be aware that I yawn when I am bored; that a sort of mechanical smile sometimes says, "You talk like a fool," that in my way of speaking there is something original, something *vibrante*, as the Italians say, something trenchant, which seems, particularly in moments of heat or inadvertence, to announce a certain imperiousness of opinion to which I have no more right than any other man? I know it perfectly well, Madame: nature driven out by the door comes back by the window.[32]

With remarkable insight into his own strengths and weaknesses, Joseph de Maistre utilized the only weapons at his command, his own personality and his way with words, both spoken and written, in a sustained campaign to win Russian support for his king and his ideology.

His initial tactic was to win the friendship of two of the most experienced and sympathetic members of the diplomatic community, Duke de Serra-Capriola, the representative of the Bourbons of Naples, and Baron (later Marshal) Kurt de Stedingk, the Swedish ambassador. Maistre could scarcely have avoided meeting the Neapolitan ambassador since the latter had been asked to look after Sardinian affairs in the interim between the departure of Maistre's predecessor, Count de Vallaise, and his own arrival. Serra-Capriola, who had spent his own fortune representing his country in the Russian capital since 1782, was the dean of the diplomatic colony. He had married a Russian princess in a second marriage, and was well placed to advise the new Sardinian ambassador about how to proceed and to introduce him to the right Russian families. His Russian mother-in-law, who had married another daughter to the Danish ambassador, adored foreigners.[33] Her salon was such a popular gathering place for diplomats that she was jokingly called the "mother-in-law of the diplomatic corps."[34] By his own account, Maistre was "one of the most assiduous" of her guests until 1808, when her salon's popularity with the French ambassador led Serra-Capriola, who was a staunch opponent of Napoleon, to open his own home to his ambassadorial friends.[35] Maistre then transferred his allegiance to his friend's soirées.

The relations between Joseph de Maistre and Serra-Capriola became extremely close, with the Duke one of the most frequently mentioned persons in Maistre's diplomatic correspondence. Some of Maistre's letters (occasionally in Italian) to the Neapolitan address him as "dear papa."[36] In 1808 Maistre told his wife that he was more closely linked to the Serra-Capriola family than any other in St Petersburg, and that their son Rodolphe was also a constant guest at their household where he was welcomed by their children, a seventeen-year-old son and a fifteen-year-old daughter.[37] This relationship was approved and encouraged by the Sardinian court, but Maistre's friendship with the Swedish ambassador, Baron de Stedingk, was at first discouraged.

Maistre made Stedingk's acquaintance shortly after his arrival in St Petersburg, and the Swedish ambassador almost immediately offered him helpful advice on how to deal with the Russian foreign minister, Count Vorontzov.[38] On 8 July 1803 Maistre noted in his diary that he had dined with Stedingk and had with him "an interesting conversation on the affairs of the king and my own position."[39] The friendship blossomed quickly and endured until Stedingk returned to his homeland in 1811.

Baron de Stedingk, who had been serving as the Swedish ambassador to the Russian court since 1790, had quite an interesting background.[40] Born in 1746 (which means he was seven years Maistre's senior), he had studied at the University of Upsala before embarking on a military career. With his friend, Count Axel de Fersen (Queen Marie-Antoinette's devoted admirer), he had taken service in the Swedish regiment of the French army and become a familiar at the French court. He served under the Count d'Estaing in the American War of Independence, where he was wounded in the siege of Savannah (1779). On his return to France he served as one of the senior officers in the French Alsace regiment until he was recalled to Sweden in 1787, where he won distinction in a campaign against the Russians. Stedingk spoke and wrote a pure, even elegant French; he was modest, well-informed, and extremely affable. Maistre and Stedingk had in common their love of French language and culture, their devotion to the French royal family, and their interest in Scottish rite Freemasonry.[41] Stedingk's Lutheranism appears to have been no impediment to the intimacy that developed between the two diplomats. When Maistre's superior cautioned him against friendship with Stedingk on the grounds that he was rumoured to be a Jacobin,[42] Maistre responded with derision that one could just as well speak of the "Jacobin principles of this ambassador as of the Calvinist principles of Pius VII."[43] Apart from the obvious mutual personal satisfaction each derived from their relationship, Stedingk also proved invaluable to Maistre because of his expert knowledge of the diplomatic corps and the Russian bureaucracy, and because of the personal favour he enjoyed at the Russian court. He introduced Maistre to other diplomats and to useful Russian officials.

When the new Sardinian ambassador had first presented his credentials to the Russian foreign minister, Vorontzov, and to his assistant, Prince Adam Czartoryski, he had received a rather frosty welcome.[44] The dinner with Stedingk appears to have marked an important turning point. By mid-August Czartoryski had invited Maistre to come and spend an afternoon at his place in the country.[45] Maistre also won over Vorontzov, for the latter told him one day that "the king of Sardinia was fortunate to have a man like you here."[46] In April 1804, Tsar Alexander himself honoured Maistre by stopping to speak to him on one of the principal streets of the capital.[47] By the beginning of the next year, 1805, he was reporting other conversations with the empress and with Alexander.[48] Shortly after, thanks to Maistre's friendship with Admiral Chichagov, minister of the navy, his brother Xavier was granted a post of some importance as director of the scientific department of the Admirality. With the initial assistance of Serra-Capriola and Stedingk, Maistre made his way quite successfully.[49]

The rhythm of Joseph de Maistre's diplomatic activity in Russia was dictated by the state of relations between Russia and France. When he arrived in 1803, Russia appeared Sardinia's best hope for support against France. As long as Russia remained hostile to France, there remained the possibility that France might be pressured towards an Italian settlement more favourable to Sardinia. Periods of active warfare between Russia and France were periods of hope and activity for the Sardinian ambassador. But with Russia's defeat and the Treaty of Tilsit in 1807, these hopes were all dashed. From 1807 to 1812, with Russia an official ally of France, there was little Maistre could do for Sardinia except keep the subsidies coming and look after the interests of his fellow countrymen who, like his brother Xavier, had come to Russia with General Suvorov in 1799. Even his personal position became precarious, since from the viewpoint of the French government he remained a French citizen, and if the French had insisted, the Russians would have had no choice but to hand him over. In these circumstances, Maistre took the precaution of having himself naturalized as a Russian subject.[50]

It was in the months following the Peace of Tilsit that Joseph de Maistre attempted to secure a personal interview with Napoleon. This whole episode remains clouded in controversy and since our only evidence for the affair is Maistre's correspondence with his own court (in which he sought to portray his initiative as an action undertaken solely to advance the cause of Piedmont-Sardinia) and a few diary entries, it is hard to arrive at a balanced assessment of his intentions. He refused to tell the French representative in St Petersburg (through whom the request for an interview was routed) or his own government just what he planned to say to Emperor Napoleon, but somehow the idea of this interview seems to have become something of an obsession. From comments elsewhere in his correspondence, Maistre seems to have believed that others had not known how to deal with the French emperor – and it is possible he saw himself as chosen by providence "to confront" Napoleon on Europe's behalf.[51]

Following Tilsit, Napoleon had at first spoken of a congress to complete the peace negotiated there, and Maistre hoped to represent Sardinia at such a meeting and thus "confront" the Corsican.[52] (Maistre's hopes for Russian support for his sovereign's claims were sorely disappointed by the Treaty of Tilsit, which altogether ignored Sardinia.) But Alexander was opposed to the idea of a conference, and so Maistre had to try another approach. After discussions of the matter with his close friend, the Duke de Serra-Capriola, and with friends in the Russian ministry of foreign affairs, he managed to secure a long interview with General Savary, Napoleon's representative in the Russian capital.[53] According to Maistre, Savary agreed to forward a memoir to Paris on his behalf. In his memoir, Maistre proposed that he come to Paris as a private citizen (without the foreknowledge or approval of his king) for the purpose of having a private interview with Napoleon in which Sardinian affairs would be discussed.[54] While the memoir remained extremely vague with respect to the purpose of the proposed interview, there is one passage which perhaps hints that Maistre had more in mind than Sardinian affairs: "Five hundred leagues separate me from His Majesty, the Emperor of the French: I will travel this distance without the least personal prospect, and without any other hope than that of acquainting him with some ideas that I believe essential for an object much beyond the well-being of a simple individual."[55]

In any case, nothing came of Maistre's initiative. It is not even known whether Savary ever forwarded the memoir.[56] When Maistre's dispatch describing his project finally arrived in Sardinia, Rossi responded by saying that "His Majesty has ordered me to write to you that, without putting a sinister interpretation on your actions, he thoroughly disapproves of them."[57] So all Maistre accomplished was to alarm his own government and to increase the distrust with which he was viewed by the court in Cagliari.

With Napoleon's defeat in Russia in 1812 and the leading place taken by Russia in the coalition that led to his final defeat and deposition in 1814, Joseph de Maistre at first hoped that his excellent personal relations with Tsar Alexander would allow him to play an important role in negotiating a peace settlement that would restore Victor-Emmanuel to an enlarged Italian kingdom. His expectations were bitterly disappointed. For reasons that remain somewhat unclear, he was left in St Petersburg while his king sent other representatives to follow Alexander's camp in 1813 and to the Congress of Vienna in 1814. As this scenario developed, Maistre was almost beside himself with chagrin and humiliation.

When Maistre learned, in the summer of 1813, that the Chevalier Gaëtano Balbo had been sent to join Tsar Alexander's headquarters in Germany to represent Victor-Emmanuel's interests there, he questioned the arrangement.[58] He received the explanation that it was simply a matter of timing, that it would have taken too long to make the necessary arrangements for him to come from St Petersburg, and that the Balbo mission did not mean any loss of confidence in Maistre himself.[59] But Maistre remained unconvinced on the last point. His letters to his son Rodolphe make it clear that he regarded Balbo as a fool and the decision to use him a mistake and an insult to himself.[60] When he learned that Rodolphe might have the opportunity to visit the Sardinian court, Maistre sent him a long letter explaining these concerns, and giving him detailed advice as to who to see, what to say, what to avoid, and how, generally, to advance the family's cause.[61]

When Rodolphe finally arrived in Turin in May 1814, he was received at court and had a long conversation with the king about his father's position. (Rodolphe neglects to mention the exact date of this meeting, but from the context we may conclude that it took place before news of the first Peace of Paris had reached Turin. Both the king and Rodolphe appear to assume that all of Savoy would be returned to Piedmont-Sardinia.) As Rodolphe reports the conversation, Victor-Emmanuel expressed surprise that Joseph de Maistre would have interpreted Balbo's mission as implying a loss of confidence in his ambassador in St Petersburg. When Rodolphe pressed the point and raised the issue of representation at the coming peace conference, the king replied: "I would like nothing better than to have your father represent my interests at the Congress; he knows best what must be said and those to whom he is speaking."[62] When Rodolphe pointed out that another Sardinian representative had already been named to attend the conference, the king replied that he would write to Alexander saying that the other was being sent conditionally, and that when Count de Maistre arrived the other's functions would end. At the close of the conversation Rodolphe was told: "Write to your father what I have just told you and assure him that there is no one I would rather employ here or elsewhere and that I have a perfect confidence in him."[63] However, nothing came of this fine talk. Perhaps the king was persuaded to change his mind by his advisers; Maistre's known hostility to Austria may have made the Sardinian court wary about sending him to the Congress of Vienna, since Piedmont-Sardinia felt more dependent on Austria than on Russia at this point.

In any case, by early June 1814, Rodolphe was writing to his father again to report that the Treaty of Paris (which left part of Savoy, including Chambéry, in French hands) had left him without a country and assuring him that he should be thankful "his name would not be found on that treaty of spoliation."[64] After describing the political situation in northern Italy and the movement for Italian unity and independence, Rodolphe gave it as his opinion that if Victor-Emmanuel put himself and his army at the head of the movement he would succeed and that if not he would be overturned in three or four years at most. Following his analysis of political prospects, Rodolphe gave his father some pointed advice on safeguarding the family's future:

Therefore, do everything you can not only not to come here yourself, but to get mama and my sisters out of here as soon as possible. We must reflect that we have become foreigners to the House of Savoy, that it would be easier for you to obtain from Louis XVIII the ambassadorship to Russia than to obtain from Victor-Emmanuel a suitable position here. If you remain in the king's service, it can only be in St Petersburg, and even then with a salary increase that you will have to quibble over.[65]

The advice was followed, and Maistre arranged to have Rodolphe bring his wife and daughters to Russia later that year. He also managed to get the salary increase – but only after more long letters and memoirs complaining of his treatment. The bickering over financial matters continued all the time he was in St Petersburg, and even after his return.

Despite these squabbles, Joseph de Maistre would have been content to serve as Sardinian ambassador to Russia until death or retirement. His return to Turin in 1817 has less to do with his relationship with the House of Savoy than with the unexpected consequences of some of his unofficial activities in St Petersburg, and so the story of the circumstances that led to his recall belongs to another part of our account.

Although the literary works Maistre wrote during these years are unrelated to his ambassadorial role, it should be pointed out that his voluminous diplomatic correspondence has its own historical and literary importance. Maistre was a keen, intelligent, and well-placed observer of contemporary events, and his long letters to his superiors and to Victor-Emmanuel I provide valuable perspectives on life in the Russian capital, Russian politics, international relations, and the Napoleonic wars.[66] However, anyone reading this correspondence should be aware that much of it was written with more than one audience in mind. Maistre knew that any letters not carried by safe private couriers were being read by the Russians, and much of what he wrote was deliberately calculated to influence Russian ministers and Tsar Alexander. Shortly after Tilsit, when he was desperate for the Russians to be aware of his views, he explained his technique in a confidential letter to Rossi:

Knowing no other way of making myself heard, I took the singular decision to write supposedly confidential letters to my absent Russian friends, in which I expressed the sentiments I believed most appropriate for turning favour towards me and the cause I am defending. All our letters are read here; it is as though I had spoken to those I cannot confront, with the indispensable appearance of extreme freedom. Every word is weighed, and sometimes I have redone the same page three or four times ... I believe I have succeeded; I have since been told: "I believe you are in favour."[67]

He was also aware that the Russians had broken his cipher, and took advantage of this knowledge in the same way.[68] Since Maistre was battling for the general cause of royalty and religion as much as for the specific interests of the House of Savoy, his diplomatic correspondence should be read with all these biases and distortions taken into account.

ADVISOR TO LOUIS XVIII

Joseph de Maistre had been involved with the French royalist cause from the time he had written his *Considérations sur la France* in 1796. We saw how that work, written to influence opinion in France, had won the approval of the French pretender, and how subsequent correspondence with the king's favourite, Avaray, had cost Maistre a position in Turin in 1797. Despite the unhappy consequences of this first involvement, Maistre had not abandoned his faith in a Bourbon restoration, and when the opportunity presented itself, involved himself again in French royalist politics.

We know that Maistre wrote to Avaray in January 1799,[69] but then there seems to have been no further contact until he happened to meet the Frenchman in Rome in the spring of 1803. It was in Florence that same spring that he also met Avaray's close friend, Count (later Duke) Pierre-Louis de Blacas, who eventually replaced Avaray as Louis xviii's favourite.[70] Despite the difference in their ages (Maistre was fifty and Blacas thirty-three in 1803), the two men appear to have taken an immediate liking to each other. Blacas would be Maistre's next-door neighbour in St Petersburg from 1804 to 1808 and an intimate friendship developed that ended only with Maistre's death.

The initiative for Maistre's renewed involvement in French politics came from the French pretender himself in the summer of 1804.[71] Two letters from Warsaw, one from the king himself and one from Avaray, requested Maistre's assistance in drafting a royal declaration of protest against Napoleon's assumption of the imperial title (in May 1804).[72] Maistre's response to this overture reveals a very interesting mixture of canny wariness, royalist sentiment, and political realism.

Even before the royal invitation reached him in mid-July 1804, Joseph de Maistre had been reflecting about the meaning of Napoleon's move to establish a more monarchical form of government in France. In March 1804, the Savoyard's faith in a Bourbon restoration had remained unshaken and he had still written of the return of Louis xviii to his throne as an event "which, no matter what can be said, I will never cease to believe possible and even probable."[73] But news of the proclamation of the Empire caused him to reassess his belief. In a long letter to Rossi (written just a month before he received Louis xviii's letter), Maistre meditated on the meaning of what he characterized as this "great event ... unique in history," and which he found "fortunate in all possible suppositions."[74] In giving his reasons for this view, Maistre unconsciously revealed the difficulties inherent in his political providentialism:

Everyone knows there are fortunate revolutions and usurpations very criminal in their principles, to which, however, Providence has been pleased to affix the seal of legitimacy by long possession. Who can doubt that William of Orange was a very culpable usurper? And yet who can doubt that George iii is a very legitimate sovereign?

If the house of Bourbon is decisively proscribed (*quod abominor*),[75] it is good that government is consolidated in France. I like Bonaparte better as king than as simple conqueror. This imperial farce adds nothing at all to his power, and irreversibly kills what is properly called the *French Revolution*, that is to say the *revolutionary* spirit, since the most powerful sovereign in Europe will have as much interest in smothering this spirit as he had in supporting it and exalting it when he needed it to attain his goal ... Has the House of Bourbon arrived at the point of repeating the inevitable fall of the Carolingians? That is what the partisans of the *new* man are saying in Paris, but I have good reasons for believing the contrary, and I am delighted to think this way since this is the House to which I am most attached after that to which I owe everything. However, there is something in all these declamations from Paris. The Bourbons are certainly not inferior to any ruling dynasty; they have a great deal of intelligence and goodness; moreover, they have the kind of *consideration* that is born of ancient greatness, and finally, the necessary instruction given by misfortune; but although I believe them very capable of *enjoying* royalty, I believe them in no way capable of *re-establishing* it. Certainly only a usurper of genius has the hand firm enough and even hard enough for the execution of this work ... I return to my terrible dilemma: – either the House of Bourbon is used up and condemned by one of those judgments of Providence which it is impossible to understand, and, in this case, it is good that a new dynasty begins a legitimate succession (which one does not matter); – or this august family must regain its place, and nothing can be more useful for it than the transient accession of Bonaparte, who will hasten his own downfall, and who will re-establish all the bases of monarchy without it costing the least disfavour to the legitimate prince.[76]

It was while entertaining such disquieting reflections that Maistre received the invitation to exercise his literary talents in the cause of the old dynasty.

This time he sought to avoid the problems that had gotten him into trouble in 1797; he immediately informed his own government of his correspondence with the exiled French court, and even sent Rossi an exact copy (made on an "English press" – some kind of spirit duplicator apparently) of his carefully worded reply to Avaray.[77] In his reply to Avaray, Maistre began by recalling his earlier misfortunes and emphasizing the delicacy of his official position as Sardinian ambassador: "When I exposed myself, some years ago, for the great cause we so cherish, I had the right to do so, since I only exposed myself. Today, if I were even suspected of the same offense, I would first of all expose my status as minister, which is not my right, and moreover, the person of His Majesty whose tranquility and security must be for me ahead of all other imaginable considerations."[78]

However, after saying that his official position and his too easily recognizable style made it impossible for him to undertake drafting the requested declaration, Maistre did offer advice on the form it should take.[79] He then went on to suggest that the king's manifesto should be followed immediately by the publication of an "Address to the French ... in which the author would exhaust all the resources of logic and even of sentiment to bring about the triumph of a cause that has against it only an inexplicable fate."[80] In the course of describing the contents of the proposed work, Maistre made it quite plain that he opposed the intransigence and inflexibility of many in the French royalist camp:

The author will have to be in agreement with His Majesty on all the points of this piece, for it will be necessary to touch some delicate strings. Actually, Monsieur, I believe that the most useful book to consult before undertaking this work is the almanac; for if one forgets for a moment that we are in 1804 the work will fail.

I am completely of Cicero's opinion. The first quality of a statesman is to know how to change one's mind. A given idea absurd ten years ago has ceased to be so today. It is not that the king must please fools by abandoning his principles; he has an infinite need of them. But the social fabric is not composed of hard and inflexible threads: on the contrary, they stretch and break only under excessive tension. This is how it must be in a system of free and ignorant beings who never cease to err. It seems to me I posed a true principle in a work that had the good fortune of not displeasing His Majesty (P 142 of the first edition)[81] when I wrote "that with the same constitution the King can give the French a totally different regime." One could make a great deal of this principle in the work I have suggested if it were developed in a certain way.[82]

Maistre also seemed to indicate that he was now less confident in his judgment of the French Revolution than he had been in 1796: "In the beginning I fought the campaign like all the others, but I was perhaps less foolish that the others in that I came sooner to doubt what I was; since I have begun to understand what is involved, I have become timid and learned to distrust our petty calculations."[83]

At the same time, Maistre seemed strangely stimulated by the idea of another work defending the Bourbon cause: "You would not believe, Count, how many strong, vivid, penetrating, memorable ideas come to my mind." Then he retreated: "Unfortunately, I can do nothing in this genre; a single line from me could have deadly consequences for the king my master."[84] But by describing the proposed work in such detail, and then sending a copy of his letter to his own government, Maistre may have been hoping for an express commission from Louis xviii and a word of approval and encouragement from Victor-Emmanuel i. If so, neither monarch took the hint.

However, the French pretender did take advantage of Maistre's willingness to offer advice on the proposed declaration. In September 1804, the Count de Blacas was sent to St Petersburg with a draft declaration that had been prepared by Avaray and the king, and Maistre was invited to edit the document. Keeping his involvement secret from even his good friend Serra-Capriola, he worked with Blacas at night to "sharpen" the draft.[85] Maistre's emendations were mostly stylistic; the major substantive disagreement was over his advice to include a clear statement of the royal intentions with respect to the confiscated property of the church and the émigrés.[86] In the end, almost none of Maistre's suggestions appeared in the declaration as finally published – and which had little success in any case.

But Maistre's relations with the pretender's court remained cordial, and his friendship with Blacas deepened as the latter stayed on in St Petersburg as Louis XVIII's unofficial representative to the Russian court. Maistre appears to have seconded his friend's efforts to win Russian support for the French royalist cause, and when a meeting was finally arranged between Louis XVIII and Tsar Alexander at Mittau in March 1807 (in the interval between Eylau and Friedland), he reported the event to his own government as a kind of personal triumph.[87] But with the Russian defeat at Friedland and the subsequent Peace of Tilsit, Louis XVIII's little court was obliged to withdraw to England, and in June 1808, Blacas also left to join the émigré king at Hartwell.

Whenever circumstances permitted (ie, whenever the travels of a trusted person made it possible), Maistre and Blacas continued to correspond, encouraging each other in their faith in an eventual Bourbon restoration in France.[88] In one of his long disquisitions to his friend on what he himself characterized as his "theological philosophy," Maistre chanced to write at some length of his views on the relationship between the Church and the Bourbon monarchy. Blaming the monarchy for destroying the "European religious system" (ie, Catholicism) by its support of Gallicanism, he was particularly critical of Louis XIV for permitting the establishment in France of "the four propositions of 1682, the most miserable rag in ecclesiastical history."[89] Maistre argued that "despite the repentance and formal disavowal of Louis XIV," French adherence to Gallican doctrines had resulted in the complete destruction of "religious sovereignty and political religion."[90] These remarks scandalized Blacas, who wrote to say:

I have hidden your letter from the gaze of Bossuet whose portrait hangs in my room; but for pity's sake, where have you seen the repentance and disavowal of Louis XIV? If it was innovators who sought to hide it [as Maistre had claimed], it must be said that they succeeded perfectly, since the descendants of the great king know nothing of his repentance and disavowal, which they believe an invention of ultramontane innovators.[91]

Maistre in turn was very upset to learn that the Bourbons still adhered to Gallican doctrines.[92]

There followed a lengthy exchange of letters in which Maistre sought to convince Blacas, and through him Louis XVIII, that Gallicanism had been "a monstrous solecism against logic, against politics, against Catholicism."[93] He argued that the French monarchy, by encouraging French churchmen to insist on their Gallican "liberties," by tolerating the encroachments of the parlements on the jurisdiction of the French Church, and by insisting on its own rights over the ecclesiastical establishment, had weakened French Catholicism and in this way prepared the way for the French Revolution. Blacas proved difficult to convince, and it was in responding to his friend's objections that Maistre hammered out many of the arguments he later incorporated into *Du Pape*. The discussion was broken off in 1814 with Blacas still attached to his Gallican opinions, but the exchange strengthened Maistre's conviction that Gallicanism must be discredited, and was undoubtedly of crucial importance in inspiring him to undertake the composition of a major work on the papacy.[94] From brief references in Maistre's correspondence, it appears that most of the writing took place in 1815 and 1816; by the time he left St Petersburg in 1817, he had a complete manuscript in his portfolio. The story of the work's eventual publication in 1819 belongs to the next chapter.

Maistre's relationship with Blacas, and through Blacas, with the émigré pretender's court, was thus of great importance in the genesis of *Du Pape*. The relationship seems also to have led Maistre to hope for some kind of position under the restored French monarchy in 1814. In one of the early letters in their exchange of views on Gallicanism, Blacas had written in terms Maistre may have interpreted as a promise:

You may be very certain, my dear Count, that if things were to change in France, and if I were, to my misfortune, to be what you call the Master, instead of creating a schism, my first care would be to render to God what belongs to God and to Caesar what belongs to Caesar; and then to entreat the author of the *Considérations* to come to my aid, since I regard him as the only one who has said and demonstrated the truth; and informed by his enlightenment and strengthened by his counsels, we will have all the means to reconstruct, or better, to re-establish the great edifice.[95]

In another letter written in December 1812, Blacas had invited Maistre's involvement in preparing a new royal declaration.[96] Maistre was at first disinclined to get involved in such a project again,[97] but he eventually forwarded a draft he himself judged unsatisfactory.[98] Although nothing came of this second declaration project, it probably encouraged Maistre to believe that his talents were still valued by the pretender.

As the Napoleonic epoch drew to a close, and prospects for a Bourbon restoration in France grew brighter, Maistre dropped broad hints of his availability for a suitable position. In August 1813, he offered to use his good relations with Tsar Alexander on behalf of Louis XVIII, even "outside the country" (ie, Russia).[99] Blacas may have unwittingly fired Maistre's hopes; writing in February 1814, he closed his letter with these comments: "I do not know where your reply will find me; I wish that you could bring it to me yourself to Paris and that we would have to part no more."[100] In any case, in Maistre's last letter in his campaign to persuade the Bourbon court of the necessity of abandoning its traditional Gallicanism, there is a passage that may perhaps be interpreted as a suggestion of an appropriate role for himself. In the course of reviewing past disputes between Rome and Paris, he suggested that with the right man these problems would be easy to solve: "If only the King of France sent to Rome one of those pure hearts, foreign to all hate and duplicity, one of those serene brows that call forth confidence, questions that would evoke reams of scribbling in Paris would be settled with the Pope on a sheet of paper."[101] It seems likely Maistre pictured himself as the French ambassador in Rome, negotiating a replacement for the Napoleonic Concordat.

In the event, Blacas did have an important role in the First Restoration. He had been the king's "favourite" since the departure of Avaray in 1810, and now, in addition to his position as grand master of the wardrobe, he was named Minister of the Royal Household.[102] But for whatever reasons, there was no invitation for Joseph de Maistre to come to Paris. Blacas dropped his friend a note in August 1814, saying how happy he would have been to have found him in Paris.[103] Another letter in November jokingly chided Maistre for his lack of faith, hope, and charity, and spoke of doing something for Rodolphe.[104] Maistre's own letters to Blacas from May to December 1814 appear to have been lost,[105] but in a letter written in early January 1815, his disappointment seems quite evident:

In 1797, the favours of your master came and sought me out in my solitude because of a work dictated by the most disinterested zeal since I had never had the honour of being known to him. Today, now that this work has become prophetic, now that the French are paying it great attention and giving me many proofs of this, I tell myself, especially being a little better known, *who knows!* You know that self-esteem is by nature foolish. Mine could well have made me blunder in this circumstance. In any case, my dear Count, it seems to me that I am within the rules in asking you to regard as not said anything that does not conform to the rules; and that it is not really important for me to obtain a public mark of approbation from him, that it is only important for me to know that I have his approval, which I prefer to that of all the world.[106]

Then in February 1815, Maistre learned that a publishing event in France had destroyed any hopes he may still have had for obtaining favour from the restored Bourbon monarchy.

As the above letter indicates, Maistre was quite aware of the popularity of his *Considérations sur la France* in 1814. He not only authorized his friends to arrange publication of a new edition, he sent along a copy of the *Essai sur le principe générateur*, which he had just published privately (and anonymously) in St Petersburg.[107] Copies had gone to Blacas and to Louis de Bonald (the other great counter-revolutionary theorist) and Maistre had told Bonald to use his judgment about reprinting the second work.[108] To Maistre's astonishment, the Paris edition of the *Essai* that reached him in February 1815 carried his name on the title-page. He knew immediately that the work would be interpreted as an attack on the constitutional charter Louis XVIII had issued (in reality, been forced to accept) on his restoration, and he sent off furious letters to both Bonald and Blacas.[109]

Maistre was quite upset by the role Blacas appeared to have played in the affair. In his letter to Blacas, he noted receiving "on a separate sheet a note of advice from your censor, which while all the while permitting the printing of the work, speaks of it in the most contemptible and the most bilious way, and represents it mainly as an attack directed against the French Constitution."[110] He also wanted to know how one of Avaray's letters to him of 1796 or 1797 could have been included in the preface of the new edition of the *Considérations*; he surmised that it could only have come from a copy in the possession of Blacas.[111] Maistre insisted that the last thing he would have wanted to do was to give the appearance of opposing the king,[112] and he blamed Blacas for allowing the *Essai* to be published instead of quietly suppressing it when he knew it would be offensive to Louis XVIII.

For about a year there was no further correspondence between the two men. Following the Hundred Days, Louis XVIII was forced to give up his favourite, and Blacas was named French ambassador to Naples. It was from there, in December 1815, that he sent off a conciliatory letter to his old friend in St Petersburg.[113] In his reply, Maistre indicated his grievances plainly enough (the "silence" of Blacas after ascending "his pedestal," and his role in the publication of the offending editions of Maistre's two works), and he also described and acknowledged the disappointment of his hopes in the spring of 1814:

When you arrived in France, there was a feast in the middle of my heart ... Then it entered my head, I do not know how, that in one way or another it depended on you to get me to Paris. It seemed to me that some glance, coming from where you were, would not have exceeded the legitimate hopes of a heart exalted without being presumptious. But every man being naturally disposed to estimate himself too highly, I do not refuse to learn my lesson on this point.[114]

With this letter the relationship appears to have resumed its old intimacy; on Maistre's return to Italy in 1817, Blacas did his best to assist his old friend in various ways.

But Maistre was right in assuming that Louis XVIII had been offended by the *Essai sur le principe générateur;* when he was presented to the king in

Paris in 1817, he was more or less snubbed, an outcome he blamed on his "anti-constitutional confession of faith."[115]

Joseph de Maistre's involvement in Russian politics is one of the most extraordinary aspects of his career. Arriving in St Petersburg in 1803 as the unknown representative of one of the least important European states, Maistre gradually won favour with influential Russian statesmen and with the tsar himself. Using his social skills and his pen, Maistre did his best to influence Russian foreign policy, and domestic policies as well, in directions that would favour Piedmont-Sardinia and the cause of counter-revolution in Europe generally. His personal ascendancy with the tsar and certain Russian ministers won favours for his brother Xavier, his son Rodolphe, and the Jesuits. At the high point of his influence, in the winter and spring of 1812, he was consulted by Tsar Alexander on questions of high state policy, and it appeared for a time (at least to Maistre himself) that he was on the point of becoming a Russian minister of state. Although he later lost favour for various reasons, including a shift in Russian policy towards the Jesuits and Catholicism, it was probably in this role of self-appointed adviser to Russian statesmen that Joseph de Maistre achieved his most significant immediate influence on the course of European politics. Moreover, it was the stimulus of passionate involvement in Russian affairs that inspired a number of his writings from this period.

Maistre's first attempts to influence Russian politics were limited to the sphere of foreign policy. In January 1804 he had prepared a "memoir on the present state of Europe with some particular reflections on Italy,"[116] and a year later he noted in his diary that his memoir had been communicated (to important Russian officials presumably) "by a friend's hand, outside official channels."[117] By the spring of 1805, relations between Russia and France were worsening, and Russia allied with Britain in April. When Austria joined the Third Coalition in August, there appeared some hope of defeating Napoleon. These hopes were, of course, dashed by Alexander's humiliating defeat at the Battle of Austerlitz in December 1805. Presuming that Maistre's correspondence during this period was designed for Russian eyes, it is interesting to note that in September he was describing Alexander as "the Godfrey of a new Crusade."[118] Following Austerlitz, Maistre was privately despondent,[119] but in a memoir written at the request of Serra-Capriola (to be used with a Russian minister) and in letters to his own court, which appear to have been written for the benefit of the Russian leaders as well, Maistre excused Alexander on the grounds of youth and bad advisers, and offered advice for continuing the struggle against France.[120] As was consonant with his commitment to the Bourbon cause, Maistre's counsels put great emphasis on the importance of continued support of the French royalist cause as a way of harassing Napoleon. The Russian defeat at Friedland and the subsequent Peace of Tilsit in 1807 were deeply discouraging for Joseph de Maistre, not only because of Napoleon's military and diplomatic triumphs, but also because those victories appeared to strengthen the ascendancy of Enlightenment ideas in Russian domestic politics.

Maistre's effective representation of Sardinia's interests helped ensure that Russian subsidies continued, but beyond this his efforts appear to have had no influence on Russian foreign policy. Following Tilsit, however, he shifted his attention to Russian domestic politics, and here his influence was of more consequence. By 1807, Maistre had connections with select, influential, and overlapping court, government, and intellectual circles.[121] He was particularly close to the leaders of a movement that has been described as "old Russian, anti-French," or, perhaps more precisely in this period, as anti-Napoleon. To understand how Maistre used and was used by this party, something must be said of the context of his involvement in the domestic politics of Russia.

Maistre's conservative Russian friends were reacting to reform ideas and activities that had been affecting Russia for some time. The movement to modernize and Europeanize Russia dates from the time of Peter the Great, but during the reign of Catherine the Great the inspiration for reform came increasingly to be drawn from the French Enlightenment. There were setbacks during the reign of the erratic Paul I, but with the accession of Alexander (who had been introduced to Enlightenment ideas by his Swiss tutor, Frédéric de la Harpe), the enlightened reform party could again hope for fundamental changes in Russian social and political structures. Two areas of crucial concern for the reformers were the Russian educational system and modernization of governmental structures (ie, "constitutional" questions). These were the two issues that attracted Maistre's involvement.

To speak of conservative and reform parties in Russia at this time is somewhat misleading. Russia was an autocracy, and the "politics" of Russian reformers and conservatives tended to be limited in practice to little more than attempts to persuade the tsar to adopt or reject a particular policy. It was a situation in which both groups had embarrassingly little freedom of action. Conservatives, as conservatives, were hard put "to defend the traditional order by resisting the autocrat, for the autocracy was the heart of the traditional order."[122] At the same time, those working for change "could not attempt to limit the competence of the autocracy, for without the power of the autocrat on their side, liberals would be unable to affect change."[123] It was a situation in which personal and intellectual influence on a very restricted number of highly placed people could make a significant difference. Maistre's importance was that of an articulate personality and persuasive writer able to offer a coherent theory of conservatism to those who felt threatened by change.

Although Maistre did not become involved in the issue until 1810, one of the first reforms of Alexander's reign was the implementation of a policy aiming at a complete restructuring of Russia's system of education. Starting from the top, a ministry of public instruction was established in September 1802. Over the next two years there were decrees calling for a restructuring of the secular educational system from the primary grades through to the universities. The new system was to be modern and utilitarian in emphasis and was intended to train prospective state employees and thus to provide a more competent bureaucracy. Access and advancement were to be based on merit, not birth. The egalitarian and utilitarian features of the reform evoked the hostility of many nobles who feared that the proposed system would break their practical monopoly in the state service. Allowing talented commoners to compete on an equal basis and requiring young noblemen to meet educational requirements and to pass examinations were perceived by conservative nobles as dire threats to their social status and financial security.[124]

These reforms were making their way through the governmental machinery during Maistre's first years in Russia, but he did not begin to think seriously about these problems until a second phase of educational reform, this one dealing with ecclesiastical education, began to be implemented in the years following 1808. Opponents of the new system launched in 1802 had tried to minimize its impact by having specific schools and types of schools exempted from the system. The Russian Church and the Jesuits, who also feared the consequences of having their schools included in the new "Enlightened" system, now joined the nobility in opposition to the government's educational reform program.[125] As a friend of the Jesuits and of many of the more conservative noble families in St Petersburg, and as a known opponent of the Enlightenment, the French Revolution, and Napoleon, Joseph de Maistre was a natural ally of those who opposed this latest round of reforms.

Maistre's first direct involvement in Russian internal politics was on broader "constitutional" issues rather than the specific issue of education. Following Tilsit, the man who became Alexander's most trusted adviser on domestic matters, including educational reform, was Michael Speransky, himself a striking example of the bright commoner who owed his success to ability and hard work rather than to birth. Speransky was hated and feared by many of Maistre's aristocratic Russian friends, but in the period from the fall of 1808 to the spring of 1812, he "remained Alexander's most trusted political confidant."[126] He was involved in a number of projects designed to strengthen and modernize the practices of the Russian government; in particular, he appears to have aimed at transforming the existing autocratic oligarchical regime into something like the new Napoleonic structure in France.[127] He wished to define the precise limits of the various functions of government, to codify the laws, and to improve the systems of tax assessment and collection. Speransky was no democrat, or even very "liberal," but his program involved the drawing up and promulgation of various "constitutional" decrees. From Maistre's perspective, these schemes appeared as foolish and revolutionary as the constitution making of the French Revolution.[128] Convinced that Alexander "was attempting a very dangerous experiment,"[129] Maistre was stimulated by Speransky's projects to write what has proved to be one of his most important works, his *Essai sur le principe générateur des constitutions politiques et des autres institutions humaines.*

Completed in May 1809,[130] the *Essai* was an eloquent amplification of the constitutional theses of the *Considérations sur la France.* Describing the work to Victor-Emmanuel, Maistre summarized it in these terms: "This past year I amused myself by writing a dissertation to establish that man cannot create what they call constitutional or fundamental laws, and that by the very fact that such laws are written they are worthless. I gathered together a host of philosophical, religious, and experimental or historical reasons."[131] Maistre would not publish this work until 1814, but he circulated it in manuscript, and as he told the king, the *Essai* "singularly impressed the small number of good minds that I have had judge it."[132] Even with this limited circulation, it appears to have enhanced Maistre's reputation among his Russian friends as a man able to give intellectual respectability to their opposition to change.[133]

The Sardinian ambassador's opportunity to intervene more directly on the side of the Russian conservatives came in 1810 when the new minister of public instruction, Count Alexis K. Razumovsky, solicited his views on educational reform.[134] In particular, Razumovsky wanted advice on the curriculum proposed for the Tsarskoe Selo Lycée that Alexander was establishing for the education of his young brothers, Nicholas and Michael.[135] Maistre responded with a series of letters in which the proposed curriculum was treated in the broader context of public education in Russia.[136] He criticized the planned program for being far too ambitious, for putting too much emphasis on natural science and for neglecting moral education. In its place he recommended the traditional curriculum of pre-Enlightenment classical education with its emphasis on mastery of Latin and logic. Warning against the influence of foreign teachers imbued with all the errors of the Enlightenment, Maistre praised the Jesuit schools as an effective antidote to these dangerous influences. Razumovsky took Maistre's advice seriously and submitted a report to Alexander questioning the proposed curriculum. As a consequence a new curriculum was drawn up that was somewhat less ambitious (excluding Greek, natural history, archeology, astronomy, and chemistry). The Lycée was then approved by the tsar in August 1810.[137] Maistre's first direct involvement in Russian politics was thus a qualified success.

A few months later, Razumovsky asked Joseph de Maistre's opinion on another educational prospectus.[138] This one was not an official proposal, but the product of an ambitious adventurer promoting his own candidacy for the chair of Hebrew language and ecclesiastical antiquities at the Alexander Nevsky Seminary in St Petersburg. Ignatius Aurelius Fessler had a curious background; born Hungarian and Catholic and educated by the Jesuits, he had subsequently become a Capuchin and a Freemason in the Vienna of Joseph II.[139] He gained Joseph's favour (apparently by passing on to him the "secrets" of the Masons) and was named professor of exegesis and Hebrew at Lemberg. Following Joseph's death, Fessler fled to Silesia, became a Lutheran, and married. In 1809 he turned up in St Petersburg, where he became a protégé of Speransky. The Latin prospectus of lessons he proposed to give at the seminary inspired Maistre to compose a substantial critique.[140] Maistre's "Observations" have been credited with blocking Fessler's appointment to the seminary,[141] but this seems unlikely since the piece is dated 9 March 1811, and by Maistre's own account Fessler was "discarded" in December 1810, and not for the reasons advanced in Maistre's critique, but because he was reputed to be a Catholic, having had his child baptised in the Catholic Church. Moreover, the chair was finally awarded to a German Protestant professor named Horn whose qualifications, from Maistre's perspective, were just as suspect as Fessler's.[142]

Maistre's major substantive criticism of Fessler's prospectus (apart from its over-ambitious nature) was that it was "the venom of Kant concentrated and sublimated."[143] Maistre does not appear to have had a very thorough understanding of Kant's philosophical system, but he was familiar enough with it to argue forcefully against its adoption as the basic course in philosophy in an Orthodox seminary. In particular, he was scandalized by Kant's view that the existence of God was an a priori truth impossible to prove by reason, a position Maistre judged equivalent to atheism.[144] While he seems to have viewed Kant's position on "pure reason" as embodying a defence of innate ideas (which was the epistemological theory Maistre himself defended),[145] he could not accept the distinction Kant made between "truths of intuition that exist in the mind of man anterior to all experience, and that Kant calls *objective*; and the truths of reasoning that we hold from experience and that he calls *subjective*."[146] According to Maistre, Kant "could certainly has said the contrary with equal justice."[147] Whatever was involved in the final outcome of the seminary appointment, Maistre's "Observations" on Fessler's prospectus remains a document of interest for his own intellectual history since it provides our best evidence of his attitudes towards Kant. Although there are a couple of references to Kant and his philosophy elsewhere in Maistre's works, it is in this critique of Fessler's proposal that one finds his most detailed published comments on the Königsberg philosopher.[148]

When Joseph de Maistre recommended the Jesuits to Count Razumovsky in his letters on public education in July 1810, he had done so in rather general and abstract terms. But in the fall of 1811 he had the opportunity to become involved in their cause in a more immediate way. To understand the significance of Maistre's intervention on their behalf, a brief review of the situation of the Jesuits in the Russian empire may be helpful.

A significant Jesuit presence in Russia goes back to the First Partition of Poland in 1772, when a sizable Roman Catholic population and several Jesuit educational institutions were incorporated into the empire.[149] When the papacy suppressed the order in 1773, the year after the partition, Catherine II refused to allow publication of the papal brief in her dominions. Her reasons for protecting the Jesuits included appreciation of their effectiveness as educators, desire to assure the transfer of loyalty to the Russian state of the Catholic populations (especially the nobility) of her newly acquired territories, and calculation that Jesuit gratitude for protection from papal action would ensure their loyalty and enable her to use them as an instrument against papal opposition to her role in the partition.[150] During Catherine's reign, Jesuit activities were for the most part confined to the area that had once been Polish (ie, what was now called White Russia or Belorussia), but they did more than survive since they were allowed to open a noviciate in 1780. They concentrated on building up their base at Polotsk and other centres in the region. Understanding what the empress expected of them, they worked to persuade the local population to co-operate with their new rulers. By the time of her death in 1796, the French Revolution had begun something of a reversal of opinion among European monarchs and their supporters as to the value of the Jesuits. Catherine had welcomed French émigrés, including members of the clergy (among them ex-Jesuits) to St Petersburg, and by 1795 the number of Jesuit priests in Russia had increased from 97 (in 1772) to 202.[151]

During the reign of Paul I the Jesuits succeeded in extending their activities from their Belorussian base to St Petersburg and other areas. Perhaps the crucial turning point in their advance occurred when Father Gabriel Gruber, an extremely talented Jesuit of Austrian origin, won the tsar's personal favour in 1799. The position he acquired at court has been compared to that of Adam Schall at the Chinese court a century earlier.[152] Largely as a consequence of Gruber's influence with the tsar, the Jesuits were given a church and allowed to open a college in the capital. This college and an attached boarding school soon became popular with the nobility. Other favours followed, and Paul was persuaded to request papal authorization for the continued existence of the Jesuits in Russia (in effect, to sanction their "re-establishment"); the pope consented, although his brief did not arrive in

Russia until after Paul's death. Father Gruber's highest ambition was to achieve the reunion of the Orthodox and Roman Catholic churches. He may have been on the point of winning Paul's support for this project when the tsar was assassinated.[153]

Despite some fears that Alexander's accession would bring loss of the favour they had enjoyed under his father, the Jesuits continued to flourish in the early years of the new reign. Gruber was elected general of the order in October 1802, and until his accidental death in March 1805 guided the society with skill and prudence.[154] Their college in St Petersburg prospered, as did the schools at Polotsk and other centres in the former Polish area, and they were allowed to establish missions in such diverse places as the German colonies on the Volga, in the Crimea, and in the Caucasus.[155] The Jesuits felt threatened, of course, by the government's program of educational restructuring and reform, but by constant maneuvring at court, and with the sympathy of conservative officials who approved their work, they managed to keep their schools out of the effective reach of the new University of Vilna, which was supposed to be responsible for supervising their establishments.[156]

By the fall of 1811, changing circumstances (the death or departure from the scene of some of the early champions of educational reform, the tsar's increasing preoccupation with the struggle with France, and the growing strength of conservative opinion adverse to reforms based on Enlightenment ideals) led the Jesuits to try to secure a more formal recognition of the autonomy of their educational establishments. In October, their new general, Father Tadeusz Brzozowski, sent letters to Count Razumovsky, the minister of education, and to Prince Alexander N. Golitsyn, the over-procurator of the Holy Synod, requesting that the school at Polotsk be raised to the status of an autonomous "university" or academy and that it become the administrative centre of all Jesuit schools. (The new Russian universities, like the Napoleonic university in France, were responsible for supervision of lesser schools in their regions.) Among the reasons Brzozowski advanced for regularizing the independence of the Jesuit system were their success as educators, their loyalty to the government, and the fact that their schools were self-supporting. The Jesuits' bid for independence had the support of the Belorussian nobility; two leading landowners, one a senator, one a provincial governor, argued that unbelief, immorality, and a spirit of revolution were being spread by the new system supervised by the University of Vilna, and that, for the good of society, the Jesuit schools should be exempt from its control.[157]

It was in support of this campaign for Jesuit autonomy that Joseph de Maistre wrote his "Mémoire sur la liberté de l'enseignement public." The document is dated 28 September 1811, and he presented it to Golitsyn on 19 October.[158] The memoir was a brief resumé of the argument of his earlier letters to Razumovsky; the Jesuits could be counted on to oppose all those who sought to overthrow thrones and Christianity. The government's new system of education would constitute a monopoly and make of the ministry of education and its universities a state within the state. Maistre argued that monopolies were always dangerous to the state and that in its own interest the government should grant the Jesuits liberty to compete with the state system.

When the Council of Ministers considered the Jesuit request on 13 November 1811, it had before it a report prepared by Golitsyn, which repeated most of Brzozowski's arguments. Golitsyn stressed the fact that the Jesuit schools would not be an expense to the government (which was then burdened with war costs as well as the costs of the new universities), and that the request had the support of the local nobility. The recommendation was approved by the Council and Razumovsky was delegated to inform the tsar of the decision.[159] What is most surprising is that Alexander approved the recommendation. Many other similar requests justified by similar complaints against the new state system of education had been put forward by noble groups. The tsar rejected all these requests and allowed no other significant changes in the original plan for educational reform.[160] But in January 1812, he granted the Jesuit request; the college at Polotsk was made an "Academy awarded the privileges given to universities."[161]

Alexander's reasons for acceding to the Jesuit request are not altogether clear. It has been suggested that yielding on the Jesuit schools was a relatively unimportant and minor concession to conservative opinion on the eve of the French invasion since the Jesuit schools did not constitute a significant part of the Russian system of education. Most of their schools were located in the western provinces, and Alexander may well have thought of the concession as a way to retain the loyalty of his Polish subjects.[162] But he may also have been influenced by Joseph de Maistre's arguments about the dangers of revolutionary ideas and his recommendation of the Jesuits as defenders of religion and traditional values. We know that Golitsyn read Maistre's "Mémoire sur la liberté de l'enseignement public" to Alexander on 15 November 1811 (ie, two days after the Council of Ministers had recommended approval of the Jesuit request).[163] In his memoir Maistre had hinted that he had more to say on Russia's domestic situation, and Alexander asked Golitsyn to let Maistre know that he would be pleased to see the work. Maistre complied by completing his "Quatre chapitres sur la Russie," a work of some eighty pages dated 28 December 1811.[164] Alexander seems to have been impressed, since he later told Maistre: "You have caused me to read several things that have given me much pleasure."[165]

Briefly, Maistre's "Quatre chapitres" dealt with liberty (ie , the dangers of freeing the serfs in Russia where the alternate curb of religion was so weak), with science (ie, with the dangers of exalting scientific education at the expense of religious and moral education), with religion (ie, with the risks of allowing the spread of Protestantism), and with "illuminism" (in this case with a distinction between relatively harmless groups such as the Martinists and extremely dangerous groups such as the Bavarian illuminées). In a separate conclusion, this advice was reduced to ten "conservative maxims" for Russia. These maxims advised restraint in freeing the serfs (but with curbs on abuses), caution in ennobling new men (with favour to landed wealth and merit as opposed to commerce), restraint with respect to scientific education (which should not be made a general requirement for civilian or military office, nor encouraged for the lower classes of the population), encouragement of good relations between the Greek and Roman churches, protection for Catholicism as an ally of the state, restraint on the spread of Protestant teachings, employment of teachers of Russian origin (but with a preference for Catholics over Protestants if foreigners must be used), and surveillance of foreign teachers (especially of Germans and Protestants).

Whatever importance these works may have had in Alexander's decision to favour the Jesuit schools,[166] they certainly succeeded in bringing the Sardinian ambassador's ideas and literary talents to his attention. In the following months Joseph de Maistre appears to have come close to becoming one of Alexander's intimate advisers. One must say "appears" because all evidence for this relationship comes from Maistre's own diary and letters, and he may have been misled by Alexander or may have deceived himself as to just what role he had been invited to play.[167]

The timing and nature of Maistre's role as the tsar's adviser must be reconstructed from the entries in his diary and letter register, and from his letters to the Sardinian court. According to the diary, Maistre received "an important overture on the part of His Imperial Majesty" from Count Nicholas Tolstoy, grand marshal of the court, on 25 February 1812. In a second conversation the next day, he was told that all his ideas had been approved.[168] In a subsequent letter to Rossi, Maistre said that what Tolstoy proposed was that during the coming war he should become "the editor [ré-dacteur] of all official writings (published or private)" emanating directly from the tsar, and that for this purpose he would report directly to the tsar or the chancellor (Count Nicholas Rumiantsev, who was also the Russian foreign minister). Maistre's answer, or so he told Rossi, was that he could accept only on the understanding that he inform Victor-Emmanuel immediately, that nevertheless, since it was a question of a friendly prince acting against a common enemy, he believed he could begin without scruple, and that since his style was so well known, he could not leave his family exposed (ie, that arrangements would have to be made to bring his wife and daughters from Turin to Russia).[169] According to Maistre's account, agreement was reached on this basis, and "carriages, money, passports, recommendations" were all put at his disposal. Since Alexander would want him in close proximity during the coming campaign, it was also agreed that Maistre should go to Polotsk, using as a cover for this purpose a trip he had already been planning.[170] A few days after this conversation, Tolstoy sent Maistre 20,000 rubles for him to prepare to fulfil the tsar's views.[171]

All this may seem straightforward enough, but ambiguities remained. What Maistre seems to have had in mind was service to the Russian tsar while still retaining his status as Sardinian ambassador. On 17 March he had a long interview with Alexander at Tolstoy's apartment, and after discussion of substantive policy questions relating to the coming campaign, Maistre told the tsar that he would not be able to withhold secrets from the Sardinian king.[172] According to Maistre's account, Alexander agreed to this condition. But on Maistre's own evidence, it appears the Russians had something else in mind. In a subsequent conversation with Rumiantsev, the chancellor told Maistre that he had often talked with the tsar about "acquiring" Maistre, but that Alexander had always said Maistre would never consent. Maistre replied that the tsar "had expressed my true sentiments, and that as long as the House of Savoy existed and wanted to use me, I would never renounce its service."[173] But then Rumiantsev went on to tell Maistre that the matter could be arranged by a formal request for his services to the king of Sardinia. Maistre told his own court that he protested at great length that this was not his wish.[174] The Russians appear to have been content to leave Maistre's status ambiguous, since in this same letter he reported that they had made arrangements for a disguised officer to go to Vienna to meet his wife and daughters, and that he himself expected to be in Polotsk in early May.[175]

Maistre's advice was sought almost immediately. A Baron d'Arenfeldt, a Swedish-Finn in Russian service, was sent to get Maistre's opinion of Marquis Paulucci, a Piedmontese general who had been serving in Georgia, and who had just been named to the tsar's general staff. Maistre replied with an autograph memoir on 26 March.[176] Then on 20 April 1812 (on the eve of the tsar's departure from St Petersburg and a month after their first discussion), Maistre had a second long interview with Alexander.[177] According to Maistre's account, they talked of the Jesuits (with Maistre assuring the tsar that they could be counted on to work on opinion in Poland), and of the likely outcome of the war (with Maistre warning the tsar about the dangers of trying to act as his own commander-in-chief, but predicting victory for the legitimate sovereign who would be rewarded for protecting the Jesuits and Catholicism). From the note in Maistre's diary, they would also appear to have discussed Maistre's recommendation of General Paulucci. In his letter to Rossi written the morning after this interview, Maistre described how the tsar, in dismissing him, had embraced him affectionately.[178] A few days later he sent the tsar a "project for the erection of Poland as a separate realm."[179] But this appears to have been the last time Alexander requested Maistre's advice or collaboration.

The sequel to the story of Maistre's role as the tsar's adviser can be told quickly enough. He went off to Polotsk in good faith, departing the capital on

11 May and arriving at his destination on 17 May 1812. And there he remained, practically ignored by Alexander until 7 July, when he received a short note advising him to return to St Petersburg.[180] What had happened? Maistre himself believed that he had lost Alexander's confidence by his insistence that he could not withhold secrets from his own king.[181] It seems likely, however, that there were other reasons for Alexander's failure to follow up his initiative with the Sardinian ambassador. During the weeks Maistre spent at Polotsk, the tsar was at Vilna, undecided between a number of possible diplomatic and military policies.[182] Doing something for the Catholic Poles as a way of ensuring their loyalty in the face of the threatened French invasion was one of the possibilities Alexander had entertained; Maistre would have been useful for that purpose. Once Napoleon crossed the Nieman on 24 June that possibility was set aside. It is also possible that Maistre had displeased the tsar by recommending Paulucci over Marshal Kutuzov.[183] Worth noting too is the fact that Count Rumiantsev, who seems to have initiated the attempt to acquire Maistre and who was supposed to serve as the intermediary between Alexander and Maistre, suffered a stroke on his way to Vilna in May. Although Rumiantsev continued as titular foreign minister, Alexander subsequently acted as his own minister and relied on Count Kurt Nesselrode to execute his wishes.[184] After his return to the capital, Maistre wrote to the tsar a couple of more times, but since there was no response, he eventually had to conclude that his adventure as the tsar's adviser was at an end.[185]

Curiously enough, although Maistre had been greatly worried that his agreement to serve the tsar (conditional though it was) might displease his own king, this does not appear to have been the case. When the court finally received his letters of March and April 1812 in which he had described the project, the response was that "the king approves."[186] Eventually, at Maistre's request, the king wrote to Alexander expressing his complete approval of his ambassador's service to the Russian tsar.[187] But by the time Victor-Emmanuel's letter arrived, it was far too late to make any difference.

Maistre's sojourn at Polotsk was nevertheless one of the more interesting episodes of his life. While there he had the pleasure and the honour of participating in elaborate inauguration ceremonies marking the official elevation of the Academy to its new status as a university.[188] For the Jesuits, and for Maistre himself, the occasion marked a great victory. Unfortunately, the triumph was short-lived. The inauguration took place on 22 June, just two days before the French invasion began. Polotsk, along with the rest of the region, would suffer from the war. More significantly, the great war with France brought a profound awakening of Russian national feeling. As Russian opinion became more conservative and xenophobic, the Jesuits were increasingly perceived as a threat to Orthodoxy, and within three years they were expelled first from St Petersburg and Moscow, and then, in 1820, from all of Russia. But this subsequent history, and its repercussions for Maistre himself, belongs to a later part of our story.

Despite his satisfaction at participating in the inauguration, Maistre found the time long at Polotsk. With nothing from Alexander, he busied himself with other correspondence, with reading, and with retouching the manuscript of his *Essai sur le principe générateur.*[189] But he revealed his frustration in a letter to his son:

> I cannot recall another time in my life when I was more alone, more isolated, more separated from every living being, and from all *consolation*. I pass entire days in my armchair, and leave it only to go to bed. The Jesuits have done the impossible for me; there is no imaginable courtesy that they have not done for me; without them I would not be able to stay here. They have furnished me with everything I need; their library and their company have been a great help to me, but I do not abuse the second.[190]

Maistre was also worried because he had received no news from his wife about her possible journey to St Petersburg. (In fact, she was unable to get a passport for travel through Austria, and remained in Turin until 1814.)[191] Whatever he had expected, Polotsk turned out to be a bittersweet experience.

In one sense Joseph de Maistre's direct influence on Russian politics would appear to have ended with the humiliating termination of his mission to Polotsk. It is true that after 20 April 1812, he no longer had immediate access to Tsar Alexander. But on the other hand, since Maistre's role as the tsar's adviser had been kept absolutely secret (except from two or three persons in Alexander's entourage and from his own court), his friendships with important and influential Russians seem not to have been affected by this adventure. From his return to St Petersburg in July 1812 until his final departure in the spring of 1817, Maistre continued to frequent the salons where he had won entry prior to 1812, and his letter register shows uninterrupted correspondence with high-ranking Russian friends. More significantly still, the years following 1811 saw a shift in Russian educational policies away from the reforms undertaken in the early years of Alexander's reign towards implementation of the kind of policies Maistre had recommended in his writings on Russian education.

One feature of Maistre's recommendations for Russian education failed to survive. The expulsion of the Jesuits from the capital and then from the entire country ended the role Maistre had foreseen for them in strengthening Russian loyalty to traditional political and religious values. But the difficulties encountered by the Jesuits in these later years were at least in part, ironically, the consequence of Maistre's success in helping Russian conservatives to formulate a coherent anti-reform ideology. With respect to educational policy, that ideology embodied almost all Maistre's recommendations.

Maistre's writings on Russian education had proposed a number of fundamental changes for Russian education. He advocated an emphasis on religious and moral education rather than instruction in modern science. This had implied a classical, rather than a utilitarian, curriculum, and he had cautioned against the risks of providing education for the lower classes. Maistre's cherished Jesuits fell into disfavour, but in the judgment of David W. Edwards, an historian who has studied the matter in some depth, his general ideas on education had a lasting influence "among the only 'public' that counted in Alexander's Russia – the gentry, the members of the court, and the officers of the government."[192] Edwards has traced how the education statutes of 1803 and 1804 were gradually modified and then completely replaced in 1828 by a new statute that "was largely an implementation of Maistre's recommendations."[193] He has also shown how these changes were, for the most part, proposed and implemented by men who had fallen under Maistre's influence. Beginning with Count Razumovsky, four of the five men who held the office of minister of public instruction in Russia from 1810 to 1848 were men who had been part of Maistre's intellectual circle. In addition to Razumovsky, the four included Prince Alexander Golitsyn, Admiral A.S. Shishkov, and Count S.S. Uvarov.

Golitsyn, who as over-procurator of the Holy Synod had recommended Maistre's writings to Alexander in the fall of 1811, replaced Razumovsky as minister of education in 1816, and in 1817 was placed in charge of a new combined ministry of spiritual affairs and education. Under his direction, the union of religion and education that Maistre had preached became official policy.

Maistre had met Shishkov in 1811 at the meetings of a group called the Lovers of the Russian Word.[194] The group became a centre of opposition to France, and Shishkov, whose speech "On Love of Country" expressed one of their burning interests, was apparently one of the leaders. As minister of public instruction from 1824 to 1828 he expressed a philosophy of education essentially the same as that of Joseph de Maistre. He maintained that the goal of education was the development of "true sons of the church, faithful subjects, people devoted to God and Tsar,"[195] and promoted an educational program in which the content was classical, the spirit religious, and the purpose national.[196]

Uvarov, who was the son-in-law of Count Razumovsky, had published a *Projet d'une Académie Asiatique* (1810), which had recommended that Russia establish an Asian Academy so that it could realize its potential in the Far East. This work elicited a long letter and commentary from Joseph de Maistre and initiated a correspondence that lasted until 1814.[197] Maistre congratulated Uvarov on his work and for professing "the good and ancient principles," but warned him of instances where he had "compromised" with the eighteenth century. Their subsequent correspondence revealed some differences of opinion between them, but they "both accepted an anti-revolutionary, anti-materialist ideology and both were enemies of the Enlightenment."[198] As curator of the St Petersburg school district in 1811, Uvarov eliminated political economy, commerce, esthetics, and philosophy from the curriculum of the gymnasium and introduced Russian language and religion.[199] This classical bias, which Maistre had advocated, soon spread to other schools. When Uvarov became the Russian minister of public instruction (1833–48), his tripartite formula "Orthodoxy, Autocracy, and Nationality" became the motto not only for his ministry but for the reign of Tsar Nicholas I as well.[200] Uvarov did his best to implement the conception of education based on religion in support of the state that Maistre had advocated so eloquently to his Russian friends.

Edwards concludes his study of Maistre's influence on Russian educational policy with this assessment:

These men, supported ideologically by Maistre, presided over the destruction of the system established early in the reign of Alexander. The original system was first drained of its substance and then completely abolished in 1828. The spirit of the new law indicated the influence of Joseph de Maistre on Russian domestic policy. Maistre left Russia in 1817, but his views on education would be incorporated into the official Russian policy which lasted until the reforms of Alexander II.[201]

No doubt other factors, such as Alexander's growing mysticism and conservatism and pressure from the nobility, whose social and economic interests had been threatened by the earlier reforms, were also involved in this shift in educational policy, but there seems no reason to deny the importance of Maistre's role in articulating and propagating a philosophy that served so well the needs of Russian conservatives.

SCHOLAR AND AUTHOR

Joseph de Maistre's energies and activities in St Petersburg were far from exhausted by his official and semi-official roles as Sardinian ambassador, consultant to the French pretender, and participant in Russian domestic politics. In the more private facets of his life, he played other social roles, remained the curious and serious scholar, and became an increasingly productive and effective author. Assiduous attendance at the capital's lively salons was a necessary part of Maistre's duties as a diplomat, but he enjoyed these social activities for their own sake. These occasions both stimulated him to develop his ideas and served as forums where his views could be exposed and tested. It was in this milieu too that Maistre exercised a kind of religious apostolate, especially with certain aristocratic ladies who either were Catholic or eventually converted to Catholicism.

The lively curiosity that had characterized Maistre's intellectual life as a young man in Chambéry was still evident in the busy ambassador. As he acknowledged to a friend he had known from Lausanne, he remained possessed by the desire for more knowledge: "I feel myself consumed more than ever by the fever to know. It is a paroxysm I cannot describe to you. The most curious books pursue me and hurry to place themselves in my hands. As soon as *ineffable* diplomacy allows me a moment's respite, I rush, despite all the calls of civility, to this cherished pasture, this kind of ambrosia that never satiates the mind."[202]

Maistre's ability to accomplish so much was due in part to a physical constitution that required little sleep.[203] He also disciplined himself with extremely regular habits that included scheduling time for his studies. This aspect of Maistre's life in St Petersburg is nicely depicted in one of Xavier's letters to their brother Nicolas:

He is in the pink of health. He has notably put on weight. His hair is white, but he has lost none. There is always the same activity of thought and elocution as formerly. This is an admirable man. The strongest microscope will find no fault in his private or public conduct. Also, he has the happiness of being known and appreciated here. If he had his family with him he would be perfectly happy. He sustains this separation, like the rest of his sorrows, with an admirable strength, and nothing deters him from his religious practices or his hours of work. That goes like the most perfect chronometer. This order and this rule would appear to lead to dryness; but no, his heart and his mind retain all their freshness.[204]

This portrait leaves a different impression than Joseph de Maistre's long letters of complaint to his court, but Xavier is probably correct in suggesting how well life in St Petersburg agreed with his brother's habits and interests.

The opening paragraphs of the *Soirées de Saint-Pétersburg* give us a charming description of many of the things Maistre found so attractive in the Russian capital. The scene is set on a warm evening in July 1809, with Maistre and his friends, the Russian Senator and the French Chevalier, ascending the Neva in a launch. Maistre notes how "reciprocal esteem, conformity of ideas, and some precious relations of service and hospitality have formed between us an intimate connection."[205] As they are rowed along, the friends delight in the scenery and the atmosphere: "Nothing is more rare, nothing is more enchanting than a beautiful summer evening in St Petersburg, whether the length of the winter and the rarity of these evenings, in rendering them more desirable, give them a particular charm, or whether, as I believe, they really are softer and calmer than those in more temperate climates."[206]

The long word picture of the beauty of the northern sunset that follows is indebted to Xavier's literary talents, which were of a different order than those of his elder brother.[207] The famous conversation of the *Soirées* has already begun as the boat approaches the landing and Count de Maistre points up to his balcony:

THE COUNT. You see before you, above the entrance of my house, a small terrace supported by four Chinese columns: my study opens directly onto that kind of belvedere, what you might call a large balcony. It is there, seated in an old armchair, that I peacefully await the moment of sleep. Struck twice by lightning, as you know, I no longer have a right to what is vulgarly called *happiness*: I even confess to you that before strengthening myself with salutary reflections, it often happened that I asked myself, *What is left for me?* But conscience, forcing me to answer ME, made me blush at my weakness, and for a long time I have not even been tempted to complain. It is there especially, in my observatory, that I find delicious moments. Sometimes I surrender myself to sublime meditations: the state where they lead me by degrees tends towards rapture. Sometimes, like an innocent magician, I evoke the venerable shades that were once for me terrestial divinities and that I evoke today as tutelary geniuses. Often they seem to signal to me; but when I rush towards them, charming memories remind me of what I still have, and life appears to me as beautiful as if I were still in the age of hope.

When my oppressed heart demands repose, reading comes to my assistance. All my books are there under my hand: I require few, for I have long been convinced of the perfect uselessness of a crowd of works that still enjoy a great reputation ... [208]

Among the volumes Maistre kept close at hand were the large notebooks in which he had entered the gleanings and reflections of a lifetime of reading. His books, his notebooks, and good friends in whose conversation he found enjoyment and stimulation – Maistre had in St Petersburg all he needed for a rich life of the mind.

His intellectual life continued to be nourished by remarkably broad and varied reading. As for earlier periods of his life, his notebooks provide evidence of the pattern and tempo of his scholarly habits during these years. In fact, since he became more meticulous in his practice of dating entries, it is at times possible to trace both his reading and the evolution of his thought on particular topics through the comments he appended to the citations and references he entered in his notebooks. In terms of volumes of works consulted and numbers of pages of citations and commentary, Maistre's most active years as a scholar were from 1805 through 1811; during these years he consulted, on average, more than 20 "new" works per year, and took an average of over 300 pages of notes per year. The high point occurred in 1806 when he took over 860 pages of notes from 29 different works.[209]

Turning from the general pattern of Maistre's reading to specific works he appears to have studied systematically, we can note only the highlights of his reading year by year. It was in 1803, for example, that he first consulted *The*

Works of Sir William Jones (London 1799, 6 volumes), a brilliant British orientalist whose scholarship provided Maistre with information on India and the Near East. The same year he also took extensive notes from Jean-François de La Harpe's *Lycée, ou Cours de littérature ancienne et moderne* (Paris An VII – An XIII, 19 volumes), a work Maistre used as a reference encyclopedia. In 1804, the only work from which he took any volume of notes was Joseph Black's newly published *Lectures on Chemistry* (Edinburg 1803, 2 volumes). For 1805, the work from which Maistre took the most notes was a *History of Hindostan* (London 1795, 2 volumes) by Thomas Maurice. Other works systematically consulted that year were Gottlieb S. Bayer's *Museum Sinicum* (St Petersburg 1730, 2 volumes) and Edward Gibbon's *Mémoires* (Paris, An V, 2 volumes).

It appears 1806 was the year Maistre did most of the research for his *Examen de la philosophie de Bacon*. He took 245 pages of notes on Jean André de Luc's *Précis de la philosophie de Bacon* (Paris 1802, 2 volumes) and 80 pages of notes from the 1803 London edition of *The Works of Francis Bacon* (10 volumes). Other dated entries from Bacon's own works are from 1806 through 1818, and other entries from Luc's *Précis* are from 1805 and 1807. (Maistre's manuscript of the *Examen de la philosophie de Bacon* carries the date 1816 on the title page,[210] but the work was not published until 1836.) The other work Maistre studied systematically in 1806 was John Locke's *Essay Concerning Human Understanding*. Maistre took most of his notes from Coste's French translation (Amsterdam 1729 edition), but he also consulted the English original.

It was also in 1806 that Joseph de Maistre put together two volumes of extracts from English journals.[211] As he explained in a prefatory "Letter to those who will page through this collection after my death," an English gentleman on leaving St Petersburg had left him an enormous package of English reviews. Maistre had finally decided, after neglecting the pile for a long time, to go through them and "extract the pieces that relate more or less to my tastes and studies." The journals in question had been published in handy octavo format, and Maistre had the selected pages bound in two neat volumes, adding a table of contents to each. The 170 items included extracts from the *Anti-Jacobin Review*, the *European Magazine*, and the *London Review*. The selections leaned heavily towards book reviews and theology.

In 1807, the work from which Maistre took the largest volume of notes was Malebranche's *De la Recherche de la Vérité* (Paris 1721, 2 volumes), but there are notes from this work from 1806 and 1809 as well.[212] Other works from which Maistre took a significant number of notes in 1807 include Jean-André de Luc's *Lettres sur l'histoire physique de la terre* (Paris 1798), the works of Hippocrates (in Greek), Antoine Ferrand's *L'Esprit de l'histoire* (Paris 1804, 4 volumes), and Louis Maimbourg's *Histoire de la décadence de l'Empire après Charlemagne ...*

In 1808, the two works to which Maistre appears to have devoted the most attention were Giovanni-Rinaldo Carli's *Lettres Américaines* (Paris 1788, 2 volumes) and Giuseppe Agostino Orsi's *Della origine del'Dominio a della Sovranita dei Romani Pontifici* ... (Rome 1754). The latter work was obviously relevant to his epistolary dispute with Blacas over Gallicanism. Works Maistre read in 1809 included the theological works of Leonard Lessius, the *Tripos in Three Discourses* (London 1684) by Thomas Hobbes, and two heavy works in German: *Der Triumph der Philosophie in Achtzehnten Jahrhunderte*, a denunciation of the Enlightenment published anonymously in 1803 by Joahann A. von Starck, and *Die Siegeschichte der christlichen Religion in einer gemeinnützign Erklärung der Offenbarun Johannis* (Nuremburg 1799), another anonymous work (in fact, by Joahann H. Jung-Stilling).

In 1810, judging from his notebooks, Maistre studied Jacob Bryant's *New System, or an Analysis of Ancient Mythology* (London 1774–6, 3 volumes), Bishop Fénelon's *Oeuvres spirituelles* (1740, 4 volumes), Madame Guyon's *Discours chrétiens et spirituels* (Paris 1790), a number of Plato's works (in Greek), and some of the works of Plutarch (also in Greek). One may perhaps speak of a trend towards more "spiritual" works in Maistre's reading from about 1809 onward.

The work from which Maistre took the most notes in 1811 was the *Theologicorum Dogmatum* (Paris 1644–50, 5 volumes) of the French Jesuit, Denis Petau; Maistre found Petau helpful for his own critique of John Locke. In this same year Maistre was also reading the *Summa contra gentiles* of Thomas Aquinas and Voltaire's historical works – the *Essai sur l'histoire générale* and the *Essai sur les moeurs*. A strange juxtaposition perhaps, but in some ways typical of Maistre's diverse interests.

Maistre appears to have spent less time reading (or at least taking notes) after 1811; from 1812 to 1817 the average number of "new" works we find cited in his notebooks drops to about eight per year, and the number of pages of notes to an average of about sixty per year. But it may still be of interest to note some of the works he was reading in these years. It was in 1812 that he read Condillac's *Essai sur l'origine des connaissances humaines* (Amsterdam 1746) and Newton's *Principia*. For 1813, we can note Madame du Deffant's letters and *An Essay on the Principles of Population* by Thomas Malthus. From 1814 through 1817 the references and citations are all relatively brief, so it would be hazardous to infer systematic study of any particular work. But the continuity of dated citations and dated marginal additions to earlier notes testify that Maistre persisted in his scholarly habits in these years. One need only peruse the extensive notes appended to his later works to appreciate the use to which he put his erudition.

Nor was Maistre's "research" limited to books and journals. The manuscript folio register (labeled "Russie") that contains the original manuscripts of his minor works dealing with Russia also contains some 117 anecdotes about Russia and prominent Russians.[213] What Maistre did, apparently, was enter here all the stories he heard from his Russian friends that seemed to him relevant to understanding Russia, and its history, government, and culture.[214]

Considering all his other activities in St Petersburg, Maistre's literary productivity during these years is quite astonishing. In addition to voluminous diplomatic and private correspondence (which included memoirs that were in themselves minor works), Maistre wrote five major works and more than a dozen minor works during his fourteen years in the Russian capital. Only two of these "Russian" works were published before his return to Italy in 1817 (ie, the *Essai sur le principe générateur,* which came out in both St Petersburg and Paris in 1814, and his translation of one of Plutarch's essays, which was published in Lyon in 1816 under the title *Sur les Délais de la justice divine*). The other major work published during his lifetime was *Du Pape,* which appeared in 1819.[215] *Les Soirées de Saint-Pétersbourg,* the work often considered Maistre's masterpiece, and *De l'Eglise Gallicane* were published only a few months after his death in 1821. The *Examen de la philosophie de Bacon* did not appear until 1836; the remaining minor works were brought out piecemeal from 1822 through 1884. So although it took some time for the full stature of these literary activities to become known, in retrospect we can see that these were Maistre's most productive years as an author.

As to why Maistre wrote so much during these years when the possibility of publishing what he produced seemed so uncertain, we have only these remarks in a letter to a Russian friend:

Since you left us, I have scribbled a lot, but I have not been tempted to make a visit to M. Antoine Pluchard.[216] There is no theatre here for speaking a certain language. The great theatre is now closed; and who knows *if* and *when* and *how* it will be re-opened?[217] While waiting, I work as if the world must give me an audience, but with no other prospect than that of leaving it all to Rodolphe. If by chance, while I am still strolling this poor planet, one of those apropos moments on which tact can scarcely be mistaken should present itself, I would say to my papers: *Depart you scraps!*[218]

The appropriate time came only with the author's return to Italy.

The circumstances in which some of these "Russian" works were written have already been noted, but in focusing on Maistre as an author I want to trace the chronology of his literary activities. Unfortunately, not all his manuscripts are dated, so in some instances it is easier to trace his reading than his writing. Most of the minor pieces were works of circumstance, written with a very specific purpose in mind, and are easy enough to date. The composition of some of his major works is harder to document.

In 1798, as was noted earlier, Maistre had begun a new notebook he titled "Religion E," and on the title-page he had written "Fragments on religion, or Collection of extracts and reflections relative to a work where the Catholic system will be envisaged from a new point of view." The notebook kept growing over the years, though in the end it was not one "work on the Catholic system," but a number of works that incorporated the extracts, reflections, and first draft passages that swelled its pages. The timing and circumstances prompting this shift remain unclear, but there is some evidence that suggests the decision was not made until some time after December 1805.

In the very first pages in this collection of materials on religion there is a copy of a "Mémoire à M. le Chevalier de H ... " which Maistre noted as having been sent off on 7 December 1805.[219] In it he described himself as a "Catholic who is thinking of a work against Protestantism," and requested the assistance of "some zealous Catholic" in collecting citations "to beat the Protestants with their own arms." Although he indicated he would be grateful for any texts ("two or a thousand"), Maistre spelled out his wish for three particular kinds of evidence: texts favourable to Catholicism by Protestant authors; passages relative to the education of youth (especially testimony to immorality in German universities); and texts by Protestant philosophers and theologians showing the extent to which "they have followed the general impulsion of their century."[220] Chevalier de H ... remains unidentified, and Maistre appears not to have received any response to his request for a German collaborator. The memoir seems to show, however, that at this point Maistre was still thinking in terms of one work on religion.

The "first draft" of what eventually became the concluding pages of *Du Pape* (a passage that develops the image of the Pantheon in Rome as temple of all the saints) appears in Maistre's notebook with the notation that it had been set down on 11 January 1806.[221] But here it is identified as a "fragment that will terminate the chapter on the cult of the saints." As we saw in tracing his relationship with the Count de Blacas and the court of the French pretender, it was not until 1813 that Maistre decided to write a book about the pope. In short, here is a passage that was originally envisaged as part of a general book on the Catholic system (a book which would have been directed against the Protestants), and which was eventually incorporated into a work designed to persuade Catholics to accept an ultramontane view of papal authority in the Church.

The first hint that Maistre was thinking of writing something like the *Soirées de Saint-Pétersbourg* appears in 1806 in a letter to an old acquaintance, the ex-bishop of Nancy who had shared his flight down the icy Po in the winter of 1799. Reflecting on the fortunes of empires in the light of Austerlitz and its consequences, Maistre told his friend: "For a long time, Monseigneur, I have been thinking of certain dialogues on Providence where

I would make it be seen clearly enough, I think, that all these hackneyed complaints about the impunity of crime are only sophisms and manifestations of ignorance. Unfortunately, I suffer from a sterile fecundity that never ceases imagining without executing. In truth, this is a shameful illness."[222]

Providentialism, of course, had been a feature of Maistre's thinking since at least 1794 (and his discourse on the death of young Eugène de Costa), but this is the first indication that he was considering the dialogue as an appropriate literary form for treating the theme. What Maistre himself identified as the "first thought" of his *Soirées* occurs in an 1808 notebook entry added to the first page of a collection of about a dozen pages of notes from Seneca and Plutarch all dealing with the ways of providence.[223] Since the opening scene of the *Soirées* is set on a summer evening in 1809, it is usually assumed that at least the first dialogues date from that year. In April 1813, Maistre described his "great work" as "far advanced."[224] We know that Xavier de Maistre provided suggestions for revision on most of the work before Joseph left Russia in the spring of 1817.[225] Others there were apparently allowed to read the manuscript as well.[226] Occasional references to the *Soirées* in his correspondence in the later years of his life, and the dates of publication of works cited in his footnotes, suggest that Maistre kept returning to his masterpiece and polishing it as long as he lived.

The *Essai sur le principe générateur* was a major work in terms of its importance although it was slight in volume. The circumstances of its composition in opposition to the constitutional schemes of Speransky have already been noted. We know from notes on the manuscript that Maistre revised the work during the weeks he spent at Polotsk in the spring of 1812. He added a preface in May 1814 when he had the work printed in a small edition (150 copies) in St Petersburg. This was the edition that was sent to Blacas and Bonald, and reprinted in Paris in the fall of 1814.[227]

But apart from the *Essai*, Maistre's other major "Russian" works were the product of many years of effort, and he appears to have set them aside and worked on other pieces from time to time when stimulated by particular circumstances.

The first of the minor "Russian" works, dating from 1807, was a lengthy "review" of a new edition of the letters of Madame de Sévigné.[228] In this case Maistre was provoked by the attempt of the editor to portray Madame de Sévigné as a sceptical forerunner of the Enlightenment. In his "observations," Maistre ridiculed the literary style and pretentions of the editor. The piece remained unpublished until it appeared in the Vitte edition of Maistre's works in 1884,[229] and it remains of interest today primarily as evidence of Maistre's traditional views on the role of women in society. Maistre's religious proselytizing activities among the aristocratic ladies of St Petersburg were the occasion for a letter "A une dame Russe sur la nature et les effets du schisme et sur l'unité Catholique" dated 20 February 1810.[230]

The identity of the lady to whom the letter was originally addressed remains unknown.[231] This letter, like the earlier 1797 letter "A une dame protestante," combines religious apologetics (with arguments similar to those found in *Du Pape*) with cautious advice to his potential convert to be prudent about announcing her conversion. Maistre was encouraged in these efforts at religious apologetics by his Jesuit friends.[232] The letters in question were first published, without Maistre's authorization, in 1820.[233]

Our author's literary activities in 1810 also included the preparation of a translation of an essay from Plutarch's *Moralia*, which he published in 1816 under the title *Sur les Delais de la justice divine*.[234] The subject of Plutarch's essay was similar to that of Maistre's *Soirées de Saint-Pétersbourg*, and it was probably this similarity that led him to undertake the translation. Maistre provided his work with a preface and lengthy notes in which he expounded a specifically "Christian" interpretation of the Greek author. North American readers may be amused to learn that a judicious assessment of Maistre's enterprise may be found in the memoirs of John Quincy Adams, the American ambassador to St Petersburg. His entry for 16 August 1811 reads:

> I received a note from Count Maistre, the Sardinian Minister, requesting me to return him his manuscript translation of Plutarch's treatise on the Delays of Divine Justice which he lent me some weeks ago. I have read it, and been pleased with the preface and notes. The translation is too much dilated. The argument against Wittenbach, to prove that the Christian Scriptures were known to Plutarch, is weak.[235]
>
> He commends Wittenbach's learning and ingenuity, but censures his infidelity. There are two points in the character of Plutarch's style which the French denominate *bonhomie* and *naîveté*; they are well represented in the old translation of Amyot, but I do not find them in that of Count Maistre. He has doubtless corrected some mistakes and elucidated some obscure passages. Plutarch reasons well, but leaves much of the mysterious veil over his subject which nothing but Christian doctrine can remove.[236]

Whatever the justice of Adam's remarks, Maistre's translation proved popular; it went through some twenty-one editions or reprintings between 1822 and 1885.[237]

Maistre's *L'Eclaircissement sur les sacrifices* is usually dated 1810 since Maistre included a quotation from it in the 1814 preface to his *Essai sur le principe générateur* and described it as having been written in that year.[238] In this essay on sacrifices, which is a systematic development of ideas he had first enunciated in his chapter "On the Violent Destruction of the Human Species" in the *Considérations*, Maistre mustered all the evidence he could find to demonstrate that men have always and everywhere believed in the expiatory power of the effusion of blood.

The circumstances that in 1810 and 1811 led Maistre to compose four works designed to influence Russian educational policies have already been described. Also a product of the Russian milieu were Maistre's critical reflections on an 1805 historical work on the first three centuries of Christianity by Methodius, the Russian Orthodox archbishop of Twer. Maistre's "Animadversiones," which were written in Latin and dated March 1812, were first published in 1851.[239] In the text itself, Maistre mentions that he had obtained the archbishop's work from Count Paul-Alexander Strogonov.[240] In substance, the work is a defence of Roman Catholic Christianity and papal authority as opposed to the position of the Eastern churches; the arguments are similar to those Maistre would later use in Book IV of *Du Pape*. Maistre's ostensible purpose, as stated in the text itself, was to persuade the learned archbishop of the error of his position. Presumably it was this purpose that led Maistre to prepare his reflections in Latin, the language used by the Russian churchman. But since there is no mention of the work in his surviving correspondence, we have no way of knowing what other purposes he may have had in mind, nor do we know whether the piece ever left his portfolio even in manuscript.

Also dating from 1812 is the preface Joseph de Maistre wrote for a new edition of his brother Xavier's *Voyage autour de ma chambre* that was published in St Petersburg that year; Joseph's preface does not appear in his works nor does it appear in subsequent editions of *Voyage autour de ma chambre*.[241]

In 1814 the defeat of Napoleonic France and the prospect of Piedmont-Sardinia's recovery of its mainland possessions inspired Maistre to prepare a sermon to celebrate the occasion.[242] He had planned to have a French priest memorize the piece for delivery at a planned Te Deum mass and to have it printed anonymously, when news of the First Peace of Paris and the partition of Savoy reached St Petersburg. Discouraged by the terms of a settlement that left Chambéry under French rule, Maistre regretfully abandoned his project. It was his own view that he had written "nothing better,"[243] but the piece was not published until 1851 (in the *Lettres et opuscules inédites*). While the declamatory style would probably not suit modern ears, the piece does include a brief eloquent statement of Maistre's conviction that prideful irreligion was the primary cause of the French Revolution and that a return to religion and austere morals was necessary for the restoration of a durable political order.

Much more readable are Maistre's "Letters on the Spanish Inquisition" which were written a few months later.[244] It is not known whether there really was a Russian gentleman to whom the letters were originally addressed or whether, as seems more likely, the epistolary form was adopted for stylistic reasons. In 1816 Maistre tried to make arrangements through a French bookseller in St Petersburg to have the piece published anonymously in Paris, but when delays ensued, he became fearful that it might be published under his name or in a drastically edited form, and requested an old acquaintance then resident in Paris, the Marquis Alfieri de Sostegno, to recover the manuscript and return it to him.[245] In the end, the letters were not published until 1822, the year after Maistre's death.

This little work is characteristically Maistrian, offering a vigorous defence of an institution that had been soundly condemned in the eighteenth century by Protestants and philosophes alike. Maistre took the position that the Spanish Inquisition had been grossly caricatured by these writers and he sought to set the record straight. In his interpretation, it was a mild and beneficent institution that had maintained national unity and preserved Spain from the the horrors of the religious upheavals and civil wars that had plagued Germany, France, and England, and from the catastrophe of anything like the French Revolution. Maistre's appreciation of Spanish civilization appears to have been derived in part from the Spanish ambassador to St Petersburg, General Bénito Pardo de Figueras.[246] Maistre admired Pardo as a Hellenist and art critic,[247] and it seems likely that it was from Pardo that he obtained documentation on the Inquisition. From the perspective of modern scholarship, of course, Maistre's interpretation requires revision, but at the time his little work provided a useful corrective to the anti-Spanish prejudices common north of the Pyrenees.

Maistre's manuscript for his *Examen de la philosophie de Bacon* carries the date 1816 on the title-page, but there is a pencilled marginal note on page 152 of the manuscript that reads: "I was writing these lines when my family arrived. 12(24) December 1814 at 9 o'clock in the evening."[248] We can safely conclude that the work was written in the period from 1814 through 1816, but we can only speculate as to why he never published this major work during his lifetime. Some clues can be found in a letter to a former French ambassador to St Petersburg, in which Maistre described the work in amusing terms and hinted that he despaired of finding a sympathetic audience: "I do not know how I find myself led to mortal combat with the late Chancellor Bacon. We boxed like two Fleet Street toughs, and if he pulled some of my hair, I am also sure his wig is no longer in place ... In any case, Mr Ambassador, I am only writing for my portfolio, and I am only thinking of a few friends. The rostrum where I could have spoken out is closed or overthrown."[249] Related to this discouragement about finding sympathetic readers was fear of ridicule.

In the very early pages of the "Notes sur Bacon pour servir de matériaux à l'examen de sa Philosophie," which he began in 1806, Maistre had set down what he felt were five fundamental truths about the relationship between science and religion.[250] Following this listing, he recorded his uncertainty about what to do with these ideas:

The development of these truths would produce a large book; but why should it be necessary to prove them? They are obvious of themselves; to see them it is only necessary to open one's eyes. They follow from the most evident principles. Metaphysics demonstrates them. History proclaims them. Sometimes I am tempted to exclaim *Filii hominum usquequo gravi corde?*[251] But I am afraid the disciples of Condillac, and even his schoolboys, would treat me like a *priest*; I do not want to expose myself.[252]

Perhaps another reason for Maistre's reluctance to publish his attack on Bacon was a certain ambivalence about the soundness of his critique of modern science.

In nearly all Maistre's writings one can find evidence of tension between, on the one hand, his natural curiosity and his admiration for the new knowledge of the physical world being discovered by science, and, on the other hand, profound disquiet and concern about the potentially disruptive moral and social consequences of modern science.[253] One can trace this theme in Maistre's notebooks and in his earlier works, but its full development appeared only in the *Soirées* and, especially, in the *Examen de la philosophie de Bacon*. It may not be accidental that these two works did not appear during Maistre's lifetime. His correspondence shows that he was uncertain about the wisdom of an overt attack on science. He once warned a clerical friend "be very careful ... of the objection taken from science. It is a very difficult point ... This is a subject about which I have meditated a great deal. Science is a plant that must be abandoned to its natural growth."[254] Maistre was also well aware of the audaciousness of his book on Bacon and expected it would "astonish" even such a like-minded spirit as Louis de Bonald.[255] Whatever the reason, the work stayed in the author's portfolio.

By May 1817 when Joseph de Maistre left St Petersburg to return to Turin by way of Paris, his portfolios were well stocked with manuscripts.[256] Some of these works, such as the essays written to influence Russian educational policy, were probably never intended for publication, but others were of major importance. If circumstances had not led to Maistre's return to Italy at this time, perhaps none of these works would have been published in his lifetime. Turin was not the ideal location for arranging the publication of books in France, but it was markedly more convenient than St Petersburg. From his homecoming in September 1817 until his death in February 1821, much of Maistre's time and energy would be devoted to assuring the publication of *Du Pape, De l'Eglise Gallicane*, and *Les Soirées de Saint-Pétersbourg*. He might have preferred to stay in Russia, but his influence and literary reputation undoubtedly gained from his recall to Turin.

RECALL TO TURIN

With the arrival of his wife and daughters on Christmas Eve 1814, Maistre would have been content to live out his life in Russia. His brother Xavier had married a wealthy Russian princess and Joseph entertained hopes of similar marriages for his children. His return to Turin in 1817 was the consequence of changing attitudes towards the Jesuits and Catholicism on the part of high-ranking Russian officials and the tsar himself. Following the Napoleonic invasion and its repulsion, Russians became more nationalistic, xenophobic, and conservative, and in this new climate of opinion, the Jesuits and Roman Catholicism were perceived as threats to Orthodoxy and the Russian identity. As a supporter and associate of the Jesuits, and as an ardent and articulate Catholic, Maistre found himself compromised when the Jesuits were suddenly expelled from St Petersburg in January 1816. At first Maistre thought he might weather the storm, but within a few months, both he and the tsar had requested Turin to arrange his recall.

The Russian decision to move against the Jesuits appears to have been prompted by a number of considerations. First, the conversion to Catholicism of several members of leading Russian families was attributed to the Jesuits and resented. Second, the Jesuits were blamed for their lack of enthusiasm for the work of the Bible Society, an association much favoured by the tsar and by Prince A.N. Golitsyn, over-procurator of the Holy Synod and president of the Russian branch of the Society. Third, the official restoration of the Jesuit order by Pope Pius VII in 1814 meant that the Jesuits in Russia now became subject to a foreign superior. So long as the Jesuits existed only in Russia, the Russian government remained confident it could control them. The new situation put this control in question and added to other tensions in the relationship between the papacy and the tsarist government. Alexander's perception of himself as the saviour of Europe from Napoleonic domination and as the leader of the Holy Alliance inevitably implied competition with the pope for the leadership of Christian Europe. In addition, the Jesuits had been in constant conflict with the Catholic Archbishop of White Russia (and, in effect, primate of all Latin Catholics in the Russian Empire), Stanislaus Siestrzencewisc. A "bizarre personality," in Maistre's characterization,[257] Siestrzencewicz had been in turn a Lutheran pastor, a Prussian officer, and a Polish officer before converting to Catholicism. He had won his position by the favour of Catherine the Great and the acquiesence of the papacy. Content to be a "Josephist" prelate, he participated in the Bible Society, despite papal warnings to desist. His attempts to control the Jesuits clashed with their traditional jealousy of their own autonomy and their loyalty to the papacy. These three factors – the conversions, the conflict over the Bible Society, and the ultramontane question – are the usual explanations given for the downfall of the Jesuits in Russia.[258]

A fourth factor, which remained invisible to Maistre and the Jesuits themselves at the time, was the extent to which the expulsion served Alexander's short-term political interests in an internal political struggle over the issue of educational policy.[259] In 1812, acceding to the request to elevate the Jesuit college at Polotsk had been a way of mollifying opposition to major reforms in the Russian educational system. By 1816, the conservative opponents of these reforms (who had supported the Jesuits in 1812) had come to see the Jesuits as a threat to "true" Russian values such as Orthodoxy and the Russian language. The Jesuits were Westerners (most of them French or Polish) and as Catholics, almost by definition, corrupters of Orthodoxy. The Russian conservatives opposed the state university system as a threat to Russian values because of its Western connections. Alexander continued to resist changes in the new universities, but he now appeased conservative opinion by expelling the Jesuits, who thus served as a pawn in a conflict over the direction of Russian education.

In his letter informing his own court of the decree expelling the Jesuits from St Petersburg, Maistre acknowledged that he himself was also suspected of having brought about conversions in high society.[260] A couple of days later, transmitting the text of the decree, he pointed out that while the Russian text had spoken of the conversion of "some persons of the weaker sex," the official French translation provided by the Russian government spoke of "some women of weak and illogical minds."[261] Maistre found this ludicrous since the women in question were, "as everyone knows perfectly well ... the most distinguished in virtue, in mind, and even in knowledge, without speaking of rank, which is nevertheless something."[262] This circle of aristocratic ladies was well known to Maistre, since he had frequented their salons for years. The group included Countess Rostopchin, wife of the governor of Moscow, Countess Tolstoy, wife of the grand marshal of the court, Countess Golovine, whose salon was the usual gathering place for these Catholic ladies and those sympathetic to their cause, a Princess Galitzine, a young widow with five children, and finally, Madame Sophie Swetchine, who later became an influential figure in French Catholic intellectual life.[263] Many had been Catholic before Maistre met them, but he played a role in the conversion of others. Manscript copies of his letters "A une dame protestante," and "A une dame russe," together with two letters by one of his Jesuit friends, were passed from hand to hand in this milieu.[264] Madame Swetchine, in particular, confided her doubts to Maistre when she was wrestling with her conversion decision in the summer of 1815; he told her that doubts were a sign of Protestant pride, but nevertheless sought to answer her objections on specific points relating to papal authority.[265]

Whatever Maistre's role in these conversions (in retrospect it is difficult to know whether it was his writings or his conversations that were the most influential), his "pastoral" activities had attracted the attention of the Russian government.[266] He now had to report that Count Nesselrode, the Russian foreign minister, had raised the matter with him at the tsar's request. According to Maistre's account, he assured Nesselrode of the benign nature of his religious activities: "With great promptness I seized this occasion to ask Count Nesselrode to please convey to his Imperial Majesty 'my word of honour that I have never attacked the faith of his subjects' (which is very true), adding nevertheless 'that if by chance some one of them had made certain confidences to me, honour and conscience would have kept me from telling him that he was wrong'."[267]

But these assurances seem not to have been sufficient. When Maistre finally had an interview with Tsar Alexander on 6 February 1816, his first since 1812, he immediately sensed the change in atmosphere: "It is not very easy to keep all the composure one needs on this sort of occasion. The emperor advances with twenty-six million men in his pockets (one sees them clearly), he presses you at close quarters, and even, since his hearing is poor, brings his head close to yours. His eye interrogates, his eyebrows are suspicious, and power comes out of his pores."[268]

After discussion of diplomatic questions relating to Sardinia, Alexander passed to the "big Catholic question" and Maistre repeated the explanation he had given to Nesselrode. But the tsar told him: "I have reason to believe, on good authority, that actually you have supported these gentlemen [the Jesuits]." When the tsar went on to talk about his ideas on the unification of all Christians, Maistre distracted him with a question about the Holy Alliance. Then, sensing that the interview was coming to an end, he tried to tell the tsar that he would request his own recall:

I said to his Imperial Majesty: "Sire, I beg Your Imperial Majesty to observe that my place here is no longer tenable with even the suspicion of having displeased you. I will be the first to write to Turin ... " He was a little way from me, and not having heard well, understood me to say, "I fear that Your Majesty has written to Turin." He quickly turned back to me saying, "Never, never have I written a word to Turin in this sense. You know how much I have always esteemed you, and it is precisely because of this esteem that I wanted to explain myself to you frankly. It is all finished now, and things will take their old course." With that, he seized my hand and very kindly shook it the English way.[269]

But Maistre soon realized that things could no longer be the same. He felt oppressed by the climate of suspicion against Catholicism that followed the decree against the Jesuits, and before the month was out requested Turin to arrange his recall, citing financial reasons as well as the disquiet aroused by the Jesuit affair.[270]

Aware that Maistre had asked to be recalled, Nesselrode now wrote to the Russian ambassador in Turin and instructed him to insist that Maistre be replaced. In the first of two letters dated 12 April 1816, Nesselrode noted that although there was good reason to believe that Maistre was not exempt from reproach with respect to his association with the Jesuits, the tsar nevertheless did not want to see him compromised with his own government, and requested the ambassador to assure the Sardinian government that Maistre had been forced to request his recall for financial reasons and that he merited a good post in Turin. A secret second letter was much harsher, blaming Maistre for his political views and religious convictions, for the extraordinary zeal with which he had frequented high society, and for having imagined himself the plenipotentiary of Catholicism.[271] Count Kozlovski, the Russian ambassador in Turin, was embarrassed by his charge. He was a Catholic convert himself, and had been in friendly correspondence with Joseph de Maistre. After discussing his problem with the French ambassador in Turin,[272] he approached the Sardinian foreign minister, Count de Vallaise, and corroborated Maistre's plea of financial problems as the reason he had requested his recall. When Vallaise, who disliked Maistre and had no wish to see him back in Turin, offered to double Maistre's salary to keep him in St Petersburg, Kozlovski had to admit that the Russian government also wanted him recalled. But he insisted on the tsar's wish that Maistre be granted a suitable post in Turin and managed to get Vallaise to arrange the affair without revealing the specific reasons for the recall demand. Kozlovski was told that Maistre would be named president of the commerce tribunal in Turin.[273]

Maistre disdainfully rejected the offer of the commerce tribunal post,[274] and there followed some months of wrangling over the conditions of his return and that of his son Rodolphe (with Maistre insisting that Rodolphe be accepted into the Sardinian army with his Russian rank of lieutenant-colonel). The Russian foreign office intervened again by writing directly to the Sardinian minister of foreign affairs to reiterate Alexander's wish that Maistre be given an honourable appointment.[275] Maistre himself indicated his wish not to return to the magistrature, and hinted that he would like to be named ambassador to the papal court in Rome.[276] It was November before these matters were more or less settled – with Rodolphe promised appointment at the requested rank and Maistre himself retention of his rank as Minister of State with a specific posting to be decided after his return.[277] In consideration of his age and the fact that he would be travelling with his wife and daughters, it was agreed that his departure could be delayed until the spring.

Maistre's departure from St Petersburg was both gratifying and bitter. Once the recall had been arranged Tsar Alexander showed him every kindness. Arrangements were made for the ambassador and his family to travel to Calais on a Russian warship that was going to France to retrieve Russian soldiers, and at Maistre's last audience the tsar presented him with a magnificent farewell gift, a box worth more than 20,000 rubles.[278] But as he described the scene to his superior, the actual leave-taking was heart-wrenching: "I cannot express … what I have experienced in leaving friends of fifteen years. I give this kind of eternal separation the name *amputation*. In truth, it is one. They accorded me many honourable tears, which I could only repay with my own, and which I will never forget."[279] Xavier de Maistre reported to their brother Nicolas that the "chagrin of leaving a country where he had been so well treated depressed him to the point that he aged ten years in the last month."[280]

At eleven o'clock on the morning of 27 May 1817, accompanied by Rodolphe, Xavier, his wife, his daughters, the Countess Razumovski, his valet, and his dog, Joseph de Maistre went aboard an imperial cutter for the trip from St Petersburg to Kronstadt. Xavier and Countess Razumovski were dropped at Kronstadt, and at six-thirty in the evening the cutter delivered the Maistre family to the *Hambourg*, which was anchored in the roadstead. When it was discovered that an important chest had been left in St Petersburg, Rodolphe was sent back by steamboat to recover it. The next morning, with the recovery of the chest and a final good-bye to Rodolphe, who returned to the capital to manage the affairs of the legation until the arrival of the new ambassador, the *Hambourg* set sail for the Baltic. Joseph de Maistre's Russian adventure was coming to an end.[281]

CHAPTER SEVEN

Turin

When Joseph de Maistre left Russia in the spring of 1817 he had less than four years to live, but he was in good health until the last few months of his life and remaxined active and productive almost to the end. After being left in suspense for over a year and half, he was finally confirmed as a minister of state and named Régent de la Grande Chancellerie (a position that put him at the head of the kingdom's judicial hierarchy) and so played a role in the Sardinian government until his health failed in late 1820. Intellectually as vigorous as ever, he continued to read and to add to his notebooks, to enjoy "philosophical" conversations, to occupy himself with the editing and publication of the major works he had written in St Petersburg, and to carry on an extensive correspondence.[1] Finally, there were family affairs to manage, such as Rodolphe's marriage and the purchase of a house and bit of land. While the final years of Maistre's life may lack the drama of some of his earlier adventures, they are nevertheless of interest for our understanding of the man, his work, and his reputation.

A PLACE FOR COUNT DE MAISTRE

The departure from St Petersburg had been a distressing experience, but Maistre's natural buoyancy soon reasserted itself and he interested himself in the details of a voyage aboard a Russian naval vessel. His diary noted such details as a man overboard, the weather, and successive stages of the journey – entrance into the Baltic, anchorages off Bornholm and Helsignör, sightings of the coast of Holland (Texel) and England (Yarmouth), and the final anchorage off Calais on the evening of 20 June 1817.[2] He later recalled the three-week voyage as "one of the most agreeable episodes" of his life.[3] The family was treated with great courtesy by the captain and the crew, and Maistre in turn entertained the captain with long expositions of his views on Russia.[4] The voyage was a fitting epilogue to the long Russian experience.

The Maistre party disembarked at Calais on 21 June 1817, and left immediately for Paris. Over sixty years later Constance de Maistre still recalled that it had been a famine year, and that her father had distributed bread or alms at each posting station.[5] They arrived in Paris on the evening of 24 June, and Joseph de Maistre was soon plunged into a whirl of social and tourist activities. He had particularly anticipated meeting Louis xviii, the monarch whose cause he had so long championed; before leaving St Petersburg he had written to Blacas of his joy at the thought of being presented "as one of his best foreign servants."[6] Twice presented, at a private audience on 7 July and at a dipomatic reception the following day,[7] Maistre was disappointed to find the king polite but cool. Believing that his *Considérations sur la France* had played a role in restoring the Bourbons, he was astonished to find that the king carefully avoided any mention of the work:

when I had the honour of being presented ... to this august person, he said not a word to me of this same book ... he even affected to talk to me of the *Voyage autour de ma chambre* ... It was an ingenious enough way of saying without saying: "As for you, I have nothing to say to you." In recalling all that had happened, I certainly had a right to be a little surprised. I attributed it all to my anti-constitutional confession of faith, so inappropriately reprinted, under my name, by some unknown enemy hand.[8]

There were other disappointments as well; a number of the people he had hoped to meet in Paris were absent from the capital during his visit. Blacas was serving in Rome as the French ambassador to the Holy See, Bonald was away at his family estate in southern France, and Chateaubriand was detained elsewhere by his wife's illness.

The royal welcome may have been a bit frosty, but the Bourbon apologist was more warmly received in the aristocratic salons of the Faubourg Saint-Germain, where he was introduced by old friends and acquaintances from Russia, such as the Duke de Richelieu and Madame Swetchine. The latter was especially close to the Duchess de Duras, whose salon was frequented by a number of leading monarchist intellectuals.[9] Expecting assistance and support for his publication projects in such a milieu, Maistre entrusted the manuscript of *Du Pape* to the Duchess de Duras with the understanding that it would be passed on to Chateaubriand on his return to Paris. Unfortunately, the Duchess forgot the precious manuscript on her desk for a couple of months. Recounting the story to Madame Swetchine, Maistre recalled how uncomfortable he had felt in the sophisticated salon of the Duchess: "I never think of her without remembering how poorly I succeeded in that hotel. I found myself awkward, embarrassed, ridiculed, not knowing to whom to speak, and understanding no one. It was one of the most singular experiences that I have had in my life."[10] For someone who had performed so brilliantly in the salons of Lausanne and St Petersburg, it must have been disconcerting to feel like a tongue-tied provincial.[11]

Maistre's attendance at a session of the Académie des Inscriptions was more flattering since he was recognized, offered an armchair, and invited to sit with the members.[12] He also visited the usual round of tourist attractions, including Versailles and the capital's renowned institute for deaf-mutes.[13] As he later described his Parisian experience to Bonald, he found it all quite hectic: "what happens to all strangers happened to me; the whirlwind seized me, and abandoned me only when I entered my carriage for Turin. The court, the city, the Tuileries, the varieties, the museums, the mountains, the ministers, the merchants, things and men so disputed my poor person that it seems to me now that I did nothing and saw nothing, and I am not even sure of having been in Paris."[14] After a stay of a little over six weeks, the Maistre family left Paris at six o'clock on the morning of 7 August.[15]

With short stopovers at the Château d'Hermé near Provins to visit the Marquis de Clermont Mont-Saint-Jean, his old classmate from the University of Turin, and Lyon, Maistre reached Chambéry on 14 August.[16] It had been over twenty-four years since he had left his native city in February 1793. Gratified to be feted by a host of relatives,[17] he was nevertheless depressed to find at least twenty noble houses closed, all his acquaintances dead or dispersed, and the "hideous buyers" of confiscated properties in the places of all he had known and loved.[18] He remained in Chambéry only a week; by 22 August 1817 he was in Turin where, except for short journeys to Genoa and Savoy, he would live out the remaining years of his life.

When Joseph de Maistre arrived in Turin, however, his future was far from decided. He was received kindly enough by the king, but nothing was said about an appointment and Maistre was at first reticent about forcing the issue.[19] He did have a preference, indeed a dream that he had entertained for some years. In 1814, as we saw, he had hinted to Blacas that he was interested in the possibility of representing France in Rome.[20] Blacas had ignored the hint and now occupied that post himself. The following year, in a letter to the papal nuncio in Vienna, Maistre had written openly of his desire for a position in Rome:

I would be very happy, Monseigneur, if you would again find and seize the occasion to place my person and my writings, my zeal and all the strength I possess, at the feet of His Holiness, whose very loyal philosophic, political, and theological subject I am, in the sense that I believe reason, politics, and religion equally interested in recalling him to the full and free exercise of his sublime functions, and in finally freeing the priesthood from the unjust chains with which we have very imprudently bound it. A new field is open to the wise and religious policy of the Sovereign Pontiff, and perhaps we, as men of the world, are in a position to present him with arms that are all the more useful for having been formed in the camp of the rebels. I have long sighed for a stay in Rome, where it seems to me that I would be able to occupy myself in a way that would conform at once to my studies, my inclinations, and the general interest.[21]

Did Maistre dream of an appointment from the pope himself? There are two bits of circumstantial evidence that point to the possibility. The first is a curious chapter in *Du Pape* where he tried to illustrate the reasonableness of his conception of papal power by describing a hypothetical application of its exercise. In this scenario the members of the estates-general of an unspecified kingdom petition the pope for release from their oath of fidelity to their monarch on grounds of his capriciousness and incompetence. In response to this request the pope "would then send to the country in question a man enjoying his fullest confidence, and qualified to treat such great interests. This envoy would interpose between the people and their sovereign."[22] Perhaps Maistre imagined himself in some such role.[23] Other evidence of a vague dream of papal service may be found in his correspondence where there are half-ironic comments about entering the religious life. In the spring of 1816, following his decision to ask for his recall, he had written to Henry Costa lamenting this new blow to his family's fortunes: "the edifice that I have built is overthrown, and it is necessary to begin again with the first stone." The letter continues: "Without my two daughters, I would ask my wife to become a nun, leaving me free to become a monk."[24] In January 1818, writing to a clerical friend, Maistre made a similar remark, this time in a clearly jocular way. Enumerating the familial and social obligations preventing him from completing his literary projects, he writes: "The misfortunes of a man of the world! Without this woman who is beside me, and who sends you her compliments, I would become a Jesuit. But she has no wish to become a religious, and I sense no eloquence to persuade her. And so I will scribble a few less pages in my life."[25] In holy orders, of course, Maistre would have been better placed to play the role of grey eminence to the papacy. But given the realities of his life, this idea could never have been more than a half-acknowledged vision. Much more practicable was the possibility of service as the Sardinian ambassador to Rome.

While still in Russia, Maistre had written to his government expressing repugnance at the idea of returning to the magistrature and an interest in Rome: "The greatness of the court I am leaving closes the door to the diplomatic career, Rome excepted perhaps, if the post were to be free."[26] When Blacas learned of his friend's recall and his disinclination to return to a judicial career, he immediately suggested that Maistre request the ambassadorship to Rome so that they could again be together.[27] In responding to Blacas, Maistre acknowledged that "nothing would suit me better than to go and finish my career and my days in the Eternal City." But he indicated that he felt constrained by his responsibilities to his children since he "could obtain a place in Turin that could much favour their establishment."[28] Writing from Paris a few weeks later, Maistre repeated his concern about establishing his children and noted another obstacle to the project – the fact that there already was a Sardinian ambassador in Rome: "God preserve me from displacing M. de Barbaroux."[29] Only if the latter freely retired would he give serious consideration to the possibility.

Once back in Turin, Maistre reported to Blacas that he found that nothing had been decided concerning his future, and that his fate appeared to be a matter of dispute between opposing factions at court. He pointed out that after twenty-five years of absence he was practically a stranger in Turin and that all his contacts were broken: "No voice is raised for me, except that of my feeble services and foreign voices that are sometimes harmful."[30] Blacas, in reply, wrote that the present Sardinian ambassador's mission was only temporary and that he would be ready to retire if a suitable place could be found for him. Maistre now offered three reasons why the project was impossible: separation from his son would be unbearable; the Roman posting would not pay enough for him to meet his financial obligations to his family; and it was the king, and not himself, who gave such places.[31] The third reason was obviously the operative one.

And yet the mirage of a posting in Rome lingered on for another year while Maistre's fate remained undecided. Blacas did his utmost to encourage and further the project. When Maistre admitted, in May 1818, that he was still "nursing" the idea of the Roman mission,[32] Blacas offered to enlist the help of Charles-Emmanuel (the previous king of Sardinia and brother of the current king, who had abdicated and retired to a monastery in Rome in 1802).[33] When Maistre rather hestitatingly agreed that this course might be worth pursuing,[34] Blacas went ahead and approached the retired king and the current ambassador as well (to be certain he was willing to accept another position in Turin).[35] But Maistre then reported, after "testing the terrain," that it seemed unlikely that the project could succeed in Turin and that he was now resigned to accepting a position in Chambéry as President of the Senate of Savoy.[36] His detailed explanation of the financial considerations that were weighing on his decision led Blacas to offer him a substantial loan.[37] Maistre now explained that his government's final settlement of the question of property that had been confiscated in Savoy during the French occupation (which he described as a "definitive spoliation ... under the veil of partial compensation") made his return to Chambéry impossible.[38] Finally, in early December 1818, Maistre let his friend know that it appeared likely he was to be appointed a minister of state and minister of the interior (but expressed strong misgivings about accepting the responsibilities inherent in the latter post).[39] Blacas reacted to this news with one last attempt to enlist the assistance of Charles-Emmanuel in obtaining the ambassadorship for his friend.[40] But before this effort could have had any practical effect, Maistre wrote to say that he had been named a minister of state and Régent de la Grande Chancellerie.[41]

For two years, until his failing health prevented him from attending meetings of the council of state, Maistre was again involved in the work of government. As he explained to Bonald, his position was equivilant to that of a vice-chancellor and put him at the head of the magistrature. The title of Minister of State involved neither particular duties nor direction of a department.[42] He complained of the cost in time, intimated that his position was largely honorary, and indicated that he kept at it only for the sake of his family: "Every day I see better that I am displaced; I have been thrown into affairs just at the moment when I should be retiring. I could still have served the good cause and flung some useful pages into the world instead of using all my time to sign my name, which meanwhile is no great affair. Unfortunately, I cannot unbind these chains, which are so precious for my family."[43]

Nevertheless he appears to have taken his official responsibilities quite seriously. His surviving papers contain memoirs (in French and Italian) dealing with the activities and organization of the council of state, with the last dated 24 September 1820, less than five months before his death.[44] According to accounts provided by his children, in one of his last appearances in the council he distinguished himself by his opposition to proposed constitutional changes. Here is the story as told by Constance:

At the time the Spanish Cortes had proclaimed a constitution that did not lack admirers in Turin. In a council of state composed of high officials and presided over by the king, the question of a modification in the form of government was raised. The ministers leaned towards a constitution, either that of the Cortes or the French charter. The king wanted neither one nor the other. My father stood up and talked at length against all change. In his discourse, which they say was admirable, there was this phrase: "The earth is trembling and you want to build." The king was charmed and in his first audience ... deigned to tell him: "You are truly a good subject and a perfectly honest man." "See, my children," our father told us, "I have served him for fifty years, and today is the only time he has recognized my zeal and fidelity, which means that I am going to die soon." His presentiment was only too correct.[45]

One suspects that the tale is coloured by the views of the teller (Constance was much more dogmatically reactionary than her father had been)[46] and the passage of time (her account was written sixty years after the incident), but it is probably accurate in reporting Joseph de Maistre's concluding phrase. His advice to the council was a fitting dénouement to his political career.

His immediate impact on Sardinian politics, however, was of minor importance compared to the long-term influence of his major literary works. In his last years in Turin, Maistre also found time for his studies and his writings – reading and annotating works sent him by friends and admirers, writing a couple of minor pieces, and editing and arranging publication of works written in Russia.

The "Russian" work that had top priority and that required the greatest amount of time and effort was *Du Pape*. When Maistre left the manuscript of his book on the pope with the Duchess de Duras in Paris, it was with the expectation that someone like Chateaubriand would be able to arrange its publication in a matter of a few months.[47] In the event it was almost two and a half years before *Du Pape* came off the presses in Lyon. Publication of a work so contradictory to prevailing Gallican opinions about papal authority proved to be much more difficult and complicated than Maistre had anticipated. Some of the delays were due to circumstances such as the forgetfulness of the Duchess de Duras, the illness of a collaborator, and the hazards of the postal service, but what took the most time were revisions requested of the author by advisers who were frightened by the temerity of the original manuscript. After a couple of false starts Maistre was extremely fortunate in finding an editor whose advice and assistance proved invaluable.

Maistre had sought help from Chateaubriand, requesting him to make appropriate corrections and to complete arrangements with a Parisian publisher with whom the matter had been discussed. But when the manuscript was finally passed on to Chateaubriand, he wrote to Maistre to say "that it was not for a student to tamper with the master's painting." He pleaded lack of time as well, but offered to deal with the publisher if Maistre wanted him to go ahead.[48] By the time Maistre received this letter he had been advised by interested friends that publication of the work would not likely be permitted in France because of its sharp attack on the "Gallican system," so he now asked Chateaubriand, if the least difficulty with the censor were foreseen, to return the manuscript.[49] When the work arrived in Turin, Maistre enlisted the assistance of émigré priests he had known in Lausanne.

He first consulted two priests in Chambéry, the Abbé de Thiollaz (with whom he had collaborated in editing Panisset's retraction in 1795) and the Abbé Rey (a knowledgeable Scripture scholar who was winning renown as a preacher).[50] These men submitted some suggestions for revisions and warned Maistre of theological errors in his work, but were unable to provide assistance in finding a publisher.[51]

Maistre then turned to another clerical friend from Lausanne, the Abbé Vuarin, now a parish priest in Geneva.[52] Vuarin had greatly admired Maistre's *Considérations sur la France* and was eager to assist in the project. But he was frightened by the "exaggerations" in Maistre's manuscript, and eventually, with the author's agreement, passed it on to the Abbé Besson in Lyon for corrections and publication.

Besson, who had also assisted in editing Panisset's retraction and who was now a parish priest in Lyon, undertook to make the necessary arrangements with a local publisher, Rusand. This publisher, who was well known for his services to the royalist cause and to the Church, had printed Maistre's translation of Plutarch's *Sur les délais de la justice divine* in 1816. Maistre had been upset when Rusand had published the work with his name on the title-page (despite his request for anonymity), but he now acquiesced in the choice.[53] Before delivering the manuscript to Rusand however, Besson reviewed it himself – and was also alarmed by the author's audacity. When he suggested revisions, Maistre readily agreed, provided no changes be made without his express permission.[54] But Besson found that he was much too busy to get involved in the details of correcting Maistre's lengthy manuscript and enlisted the assistance of a lay scholar named Guy-Marie de Place.[55] When Besson passed on his friend's first suggestions, Maistre seems to have immediately appreciated how helpful De Place's help could be and asked that his "genuine gratitude" be conveyed to the priest's "learned friend."[56] By mid-June 1818, Maistre was corresponding directly with De Place and there began an eighteen-month postal collaboration between author and editor that substantially modified the original text.

Guy-Marie de Place was a modest but highly capable scholar.[57] Born in Roanne in 1772, he had been a brilliant student at the local college. During the Terror the family's property had been pillaged and the father and sons imprisoned. Following Thermidor, Guy-Marie had settled in Lyon with the goal of rebuilding the family's fortune, but he was soon attracted to a life of scholarship and within a few years had won acceptance in the élite intellectual and artistic circles of his adopted city as a dedicated educator and talented journalist. During the Napoleonic years he had written for a local journal edited by Ballanche, and in 1814 and 1815 had published pamphlets attacking Napoleon's treatment of the Church. Following the second restoration in 1815, he had become a regular contributor to the Parisian ultra-royalist journal *Mémorial religieux, politique et littéraire* with articles attacking eighteenth-century ideas. De Place was a knowledgeable grammarian and well-read in philosophy, theology, the Church Fathers, and church history. Enthusiastic for Maistre's project but aware of French sensitivities, an excellent judge of the nuances of literary style, and tactful but not the least bashful about offering warnings and suggestions, he proved to be a zealous editor who proceeded to subject the Savoyard's manuscript to painstaking scrutiny.

Joseph de Maistre had written in Russia in the absence of adequate library resources and had often relied on memory and secondary sources for his citations. De Place brought factual errors to the author's attention, verified quotations, replaced second-hand citations by direct references, and tried his best to impose moderation on Maistre's ardent rhetoric. The author's letters to his editor show that he took all De Place's criticisms and suggestions with the utmost seriousness, revising and accommodating his text in countless ways.[58] Maistre's letters to De Place also provide interesting insights into his goals in publishing *Du Pape* and the specific purposes he had in mind in particular parts of the book, his attitudes towards authorship, polemics, and scholarship, and the contrast between his forthright literary style and his personal timidity.

Perhaps the most surprising thing revealed by this correspondence is Maistre's ambiguity about publishing the work at all. Already in his letters to Besson, he had declared his willingness to suppress the piece entirely if the priest so advised:

I believed the work would do some good, and I only believed so because others believed it, since I am excessively skittish myself. If the enterprise were to go foward smoothly and without any difficulty, I would be pleased humanly and moderately. But if you see more chance for evil than good, and especially if the publishers fear to expose themselves, I would not want to compromise anyone for a vainglory that any wise man would easily know how to forego ... Again, I put it to your Christian prudence to suppress the work if you judge it appropriate.[59]

Similar sentiments were expressed in one of his first letters to De Place: "Buffon said that 'the style is the man,' and I believe that in general he was right; however I find an exception in myself, for my style is sharp and decided – and I am as timid as a chicken ... Examine the thing again closely, Monsieur ... and if the utility of the work does not appear extremely probable to you, send it back to me without the least fear of irritating me."[60] De Place kept reassuring the author of the excellence and importance of his work, and predicted that its impact would be great in France and Europe.[61] Maistre, for his part, remained remarkably patient through the whole lengthy process of revision and final editing, despite his fear that excessive delays would weaken the impact of his book.[62]

As with his earlier works, Maistre insisted on at least the pretense of anonymity. It was only at the insistence of both De Place and the publisher that he allowed himself to be identified on the title-page as the author of the *Considérations sur la France*.[63] Part of the reason for this reticence was his fear, especially following his appointment to his new position in December 1818, of embarrassing his government, and part of the reason was his desire to avoid opening himself to public attack.[64]

While generally receptive to De Place's observations and suggestions, Maistre proved obdurate on two fundamental issues. In the first place, he remained convinced of the necessity of persuading French statesmen and churchmen to abandon their adherence to "Gallican liberties." He insisted he had no desire to shock anyone, but acknowledged that in "telling the truth" he was willing to make "them cry a little."[65] From the beginning, it had been Maistre's vigorous attack on the Gallican system and its apologists that had most upset those who had read his manuscript. He knew that in his section "on the Gallican Church in its relations with the Holy See" (Book IV of his original text) he had "put a stick into a wasp's nest," but, mixing his metaphors, insisted that "it was necessary to overturn this magic castle or nothing is accomplished."[66] When De Place exhorted him to "respect persons" (such as Bossuet) even though he had to attack their opinions, Maistre disagreed:

Be well persuaded, Monsieur, that this is a French illusion ... you have found me docile enough in general not to be scandalized if I tell you *that one can do nothing against opinions so long as one does not attack persons, because the authority of persons maintains opinions* ... Moreover, it is very certain that in France you have made a dozen apotheoses which have made it impossible to reason any more. In making all these gods descend from their pedestals to declare them simply *great men*, I do not believe one does them wrong, and one does you a great service.[67]

In the end, alerted by De Place as to just how controversial his polemic against Gallican theologians and historians was likely to prove and perhaps discouraged by the delays that would be involved in replying to all his editor's objections, he had the "sudden illumination" to drop the section on the Gallican Church from *Du Pape* with a view to publishing it later.[68] De Place warmly supported this course of action, pointing out how well the section could stand by itself.[69] (*De l'Eglise gallicane* was finally published in 1821 at the same time as a second edition of *Du Pape*.)

The second issue on which Maistre proved reluctant to acquiesce was the matter of the general style of the work. When Guy-Marie de Place kept sending him enormous volumes of observations, Maistre thanked him, told him that he was utilizing them as much as he could, but pointed out that some of the suggestions were inappropriate for the sort of work he had in mind: "I cannot say everything. My object is to get myself read by fashionable society, to elevate myself to general ideas in order to prove to good minds *that the Church only claims for itself a law of the world*."[70]

With this goal in mind, he refused to emasculate his provocative prose: "You will perhaps find in the responses I invent and in those you have suggested to me a light tinge of disdain; but I know men well. It is thus that one must respond. It is persuasion that persuades and persuasion never wavers, etc."[71] On another occasion, he told De Place that he was deliberately allowing some impertinent phrases to stand since impertinence was as necessary in certain works "as pepper in stews."[72]

Maistre was quite conscious that he was producing a work of "honest proselytism" (to borrow a phrase the author himself used in the work's "Preliminary Discourse")[73] and not simply another scholarly tome. Camille Latreille, who had access to the papers of Guy-Marie de Place,[74] found it easy enough to compile a long list of Maistre's sins against the canons of careful scholarship: faulty, second-hand, and inappropriate citations, citations taken out of context, neglect of certain "indispensable" works, unwillingness or inablity to take opposing opinions seriously enough.[75] But Latreille had to admit that Maistre accomplished his purpose: "A simple scholar would have redone Cardinal Orsi's treatise:[76] J. de Maistre laicized the questions of primacy and infallibility, conquered for them a secular public and launched them into the great current of public opinion."[77] Never the cold dispassionate scholar, Maistre remained the committed advocate ready to use all the rhetorical skills he had learned and exercised as a lawyer to persuade his readers to accept his case.

When Maistre's manuscript had first been delivered to Lyon, the concluding section had been a long "book" on the Gallican Church. But he soon revealed to his editor that he had another "book" that had not been ready when the manuscript had been sent off, and suggested that this section, which was entitled "Eglises Photiennes" and originally intended to precede the section on the Gallican Church, might serve as an addition to a second edition of *Du Pape* if the first succeeded.[78] But not long after, Maistre forwarded the section with an explanation of its purpose: "This book … is particularly directed against M. de Stourdza's book, which has done much harm in Russia, but the author is not named because of my old ties with his family and because of the protection the Emperor has given to the book. Rome counts a lot on its refutation."[79]

Alexandre Stourdza's book, *Considérations sur la doctrine et l'esprit de l'Eglise orthodoxe*, had been published in Germany in 1816, and Maistre had been aware of it and concerned about its influence since February 1817 when he had reported its appearance and significance to Cardinal Severoli in Rome. He had described the author as "a young man of much wit and instruction," noted his Moldavian origins, and the circumstance that the tsar had provided 20,000 rubles to subsidize publication of the work.[80] In closing his letter to Severoli, Maistre had mentioned the "bizarre circumstance" that he himself was on the point of completing a book on the pope:

While M. Stourdza was getting ready to publish his book against the pope, I have myself just completed one on the same subject, where I have brought together all that I know and all that I can do. The title is not long: *Du Pape* … It would be a singular spectacle, Monseigneur, that would display two lay athletes, the one a minister and the other a chamberlain, struggling before Europe, *in French*, on this great question.[81]

It is not known which papal spokesman encouraged Maistre to undertake the task of replying to Stourdza. But if what became Book IV of *Du Pape* (with the title "Du Pape dans son rapport avec les Eglises nommées schismatiques") was designed to refute Stourdza, it did so only in general terms and without specific reference to the Moldavian or his arguments. (It may be noted that the Maistre family archives contain the partial manuscript of a detailed refutation of Stourdza's work. But this document is in the handwriting of Rodolphe de Maistre, and from remarks in letters from Joseph de Maistre to his son and from Rodolphe to his sister Constance, it is evident that Rodolphe had attempted the work with his father's encouragement and assistance.)[82]

Maistre's correspondence with Guy-Marie de Place also reveals that Book II of *Du Pape* ("Du Pape, dans son rapport avec les souveraines temporelles") was directed "almost entirely against M. Ferrand."[83] Count Antoine Ferrand was the author of a book entitled *Lettres politiques et morales d'un père à son fils* (Paris 1803).[84] A royalist and émigré who had gotten into trouble with Napoleon's censors for his support of the Bourbon cause, Ferrand drew Maistre's ire because his interpretation of the history of the medieval papacy reflected the Gallican views of the old French parlements.[85] Maistre had read Ferrand's work in 1807,[86] and in 1810 he had warned his Russian friends against including it in the curriculum of a lycée being established by the tsar.[87] Following the Restoration in France, Ferrand had been named a minister of state and a peer, and consequently Maistre felt obliged to moderate his polemic. He now acknowledged that his antipathy to Ferrand had been excessive, undertook to weaken the passages that concerned him, and asked De Place to review the corrections to ensure the revisions reflected this intention.[88]

The softening of the attack on Ferrand is a good example of the ameliorating influence of Guy-Marie de Place on the text of Maistre's work. In the same letter in which he had discussed Ferrand's book, Maistre told De Place: "Your observations having led me to new reflections on my work, it is only now that I understand its deficiency. It had to be conceived in a foreign country to escape French prejudices; but it had to be corrected in France to know how to humour them. Moreover, the book is too polemical."[89]

Joseph de Maistre was quite aware of his debt to his learned editor; his letters to De Place contain numerous expressions of his gratitude. Within four months of the beginning of their postal collaboration, he told De Place that the work "belongs to you more than to me," and offered to cede it to him if it succeeded.[90] After the work was finally published, Maistre wrote again to express his appreciation: "But what do I not owe you, Monsieur, and what does my work not owe you? There is not, I think, a page that is not indebted to you and that was not returned to you ameliorated by your observations. I hope that you, on your side, always found me quite submissive and always ready to listen to your reasons, that is to say, Reason."[91]

Although the two men never met face to face, Maistre's letters show that he had come to regard his editor as an intimate friend. Moreover, their collaboration did not end with the publication of *Du Pape*; Maistre was delighted to enlist De Place's assistance in the final editing of *De l'Eglise gallicane* as well as the editing of the revised second edition of the first work. De Place's commitment in time and energy was certainly remarkable; he received no payment from the publisher, counting himself fortunate to have laboured for the good cause and for "one of the most distinguished writers in Europe."[92]

Apprehension about the reception of his audacious attempt to say something new about papal authority had troubled Joseph de Maistre since he had first sought to arrange publication of his book. From his correspondence with Blacas, with his French clerical friends, and with his editor, he had ample warning of possible adverse reactions in France. As the date of publication approached, he also experienced doubts about how his book might be received by the authority he sought to defend; discouraged by contemporary events in France, he exclaimed to De Place: "A handful of *fellow* keepers of the Vestal fire may perhaps welcome my ideas, but if I provoke twenty million men, is it worth the pain of writing? Everything is breaking up, Monsieur, everything is disappearing; soon we will be fighting for what is no more, and if Rome were to condemn my work I would not be surprised."[93] Nevertheless Maistre made arrangements for one of the first bound copies of his work to be sent to Pope Pius VII and for other copies to be sent to influential friends in Paris, to French journals, and to high-ranking clergymen in France and Piedmont-Sardinia.[94]

In the long run, of course, *Du Pape* proved to be one of Maistre's most important and influential works; in G.P. Gooch's judgment it was Maistre's "political testament, ranking among the classics of political and social philosophy with those of Burke and Locke, Rousseau and Marx, all of which were designed to change the outlook of Europe and have deeply influenced the course of history."[95] In the course of the nineteenth century some forty editions (and/or reprints) would be published in France, with translations into German (1832), Spanish (1847), and English (1850).[96] But during Maistre's lifetime, its reception brought the author only limited consolation.[97]

Maistre's prediction about *Du Pape*'s initial fortunes in France proved correct. There were prompt letters of congratulations and appreciation from a few sympathetic individuals – Chateaubriand,[98] Lamennais,[99] Marcellus,[100] Bonald,[101] and Lamartine.[102] These same men and their friends sought to ensure favourable reviews in ultra journals.[103] But apart from these papers, the first few months saw little published reaction. Maistre himself blamed the assassination of the Duke de Berry (13 February 1820) for distracting public attention from the appearance of his work.[104] There was never any mention of *Du Pape* in any of the major French journals of the time – the result, so Rusand reported, of official government policy.[105]

The timing of the book's appearance, in fact, was unfortunate. If it had come out in 1817, as had been Maistre's original intention, it would have coincided with the signing of a new concordat between the restored monarchy and the papacy – and perhaps had the kind of success Chateaubriand's *Le Génie du Christianisme* (1802) had enjoyed following the Napoleonic Concordat of 1801.[106] But Rome had overplayed its hand in 1817 (by too hastily publishing a bull establishing new French dioceses and nominating new bishops), and aroused Gallican susceptibilities. The French ministry had tried to mollify opinion by presenting the chamber with a new law (incorporating many of the provisions of Napoleon's Organic Articles that had been so offensive to the papacy) rather than the text of the concordat, but had to back down in the face of opposition from both the left and the right. The pope was offended by the maneuvre, and in the end it was the Concordat of 1801 that remained in force.[107] The last thing the government wanted in 1820 was publicity for ultramontane opinions.

If Maistre was disconcerted by reports of government-imposed silence, he also had more encouraging news from Paris. Bonald's compliment was generous, witty, and astute: "I cannot tell you how much reason, wit, sublimity, and new and original things I find in it; but as I have said, kings are not Christian enough to appreciate it, nor are bishops politicans enough. In order to sense the book's importance and to appreciate all its truth one must have considered religion in its great relationships with society."[108]

Bonald also reported that others, even those who because of Gallican opinions imbibed with their clerical or legal education were alarmed by some of Maistre's ideas, were dumbfounded with admiration for his genius, and named the Marquis de Fontanes, the Count de Marcellus, Cardinal de Bausset, and the Duke de Richelieu. Fontanes borrowed Bonald's copy and devoured it in twenty-four hours. Cardinal de Bausset was the author of a biography of Bossuet[109] from which Maistre had borrowed his Bossuet citations.[110] Maistre had sent Bausset a copy of *Du Pape*, and the cardinal responded with a long letter that combined gracious praise ("a work so remarkable, so extraordinary, so sparkling with wit, so full of erudition, so ably conceived and executed, that Bossuet himself would have smiled at the hardiness of the enterprise and admired the prodigious genius that was required to take his measure") with an attempt to persuade the author that he was mistaken in his judgment of Bossuet's role in French ecclesiastical history.[111]

Maistre also received a detailed assessment of the impression his work was making in Paris from Father Grivel, a Jesuit he had known in Russia who was now resident in the French capital. Grivel made careful distinctions among various classes of readers:

Bonald ... is content with it ... All the laymen in Bonald's circle think the same. The Parisian clergy do not appreciate it: the reason is simple, your work destroys the

Gallican system. However, the Abbé Frayssinous called it a *very strong* work; but he is a Sulpician and the Sulpicians approve it highly.[112] Is it also necessary to speak of our crew [ie, the Jesuits]? It has given us a singular pleasure and we believe it very good, very solid, and capable of doing much good, despite its opponents. Barruel alone blames what you say about infallibility. But we know why; he wished in his work, *Du Pape et ses Droits*,[113] to amalgamate Roman and Gallican views; he has his system and anything that deviates from it displeases him. However, he said: "Suppress certain things, change the title to *Of the Influence of the Popes on Society* (or civilization) and the work is excellent." ... Finally, Monsieur, I believe that it will be well received by the laity (except Mme Swetchine, who is passionate for Bossuet and a little less so for Fleury), by all those who are not passionate Sorbonnists, and by many eccelesiastics in foreign countries who are enlightened in these matters. No member of the clergy will write against you, except with moderation to defend Bossuet, who you treat, they say, disrespectfully; they will abandon Fleury to you. The lawyers will perhaps attack you on the temporal power of kings, a delicate point that, again they say, it would have been wise to omit. In any case, it is selling well, and Rusand's representative has reordered from Lyon. In summary, I think it will be little attacked, not because it does not merit the honours of persecution, but because public opinion is favourable to greater authority for the pope. It will be little defended for fear of appearing opposed to the authority of kings and to Bossuet. I am speaking here only of honest folk; if the liberals attack it, its fortune is made. In any hypothesis, I see it will win the bourgeoisie in France and will thereby do a lot of good.[114]

On the whole, Grivel's analysis proved to be fairly accurate. He perhaps underestimated the hostility Maistre provoked among French churchmen both by his temerity in treating a topic that had been more or less a clerical monopoly and because of the extent to which his ultramontane views challenged their traditional Gallican assumptions. Although none appeared before his death, the 1820s saw the publication of three substantial refutations.[115] But Maistre eventually got his hearing in France. The large number of editions of *Du Pape* appearing between 1850 and 1870 suggests that the book was especially popular under the Second Empire. The admirer who claimed that Maistre had been "a human preface" to the First Vatican Council[116] undoubtedly exaggerated his influence, but it seems clear he deserves credit for having helped prepare French Catholic opinion to accept the Council's declaration of papal infallibility.

If the Parisian clergy at first failed to appreciate *Du Pape*, as Father Grivel reported, there were other clergymen who did. The Abbé Rey wrote from Chambéry to pronounce the book "divine, Monsieur Count, yes incontestably divine."[117] Rey reported as well that one of the best educated ecclesiastics in Grenoble was having it read in the refectory of his seminary.[118] There was a gallant note from the Archbishop of Chambéry, thanking Maistre for the copy that had been personally delivered by Constance de Maistre: "I am French, and what is more Gascon, which you were perhaps not aware of, and consequently I must be against infallibles; but with God's help and your reasoning I hope to become what you desire."[119] The Bishop of Pinerolo (in Piedmont) wrote to say that in his judgment the work "ought to create an epoch in ecclesiastical history and, please God, in politics."[120] There was also a flattering note from Cardinal Morozzo, the Bishop of Novara.[121] But the approbation Maistre most desired was that of the Bishop of Rome.

The story of Joseph de Maistre's efforts to win the public approval of Rome for his work is rather complicated, and for a long time was poorly understood. The author himself appears to have died believing that he had been deceived by the papal nuncio in Turin and thereby denied papal recognition.[122] Only recently have historians consulted the relevant file in the Vatican's secret archives and thus been able to recontruct what happened.[123] The story that emerges is one of misunderstanding arising mainly as a consequence of Maistre's impatience and the dilatory habits of Vatican officials.

Shortly after Maistre had begun his correspondence with Guy-Marie de Place in the early summer of 1818, the Abbé Romualdo Valenti, the papal nuncio in Turin, reported to the papal secretary of state, Cardinal Consalvi, that he had met Count de Maistre, that he had been told by him that his book on the pope would be published in one of the most important French cities, and that editing and printing were in the hands of a capable and scholarly person.[124] Then in December 1819, Valenti reported that he had met Maistre again, learned that *Du Pape* would be published in Lyon within a month or two, and gave it as his view that there should be no doubts about the probity and principles of the author, and that the work would produce great results in favour of religion and the Holy See.[125] Maistre had arranged to have a specially bound copy of *Du Pape* delivered directly to Valenti, and as soon as the nuncio received it, he forwarded it to Rome with a note explaining that although the author did not dare send it directly, he hoped that the work would be brought to the attention of His Holiness.[126] Then on 25 January 1820 Maistre called on Valenti, delivered two more copies of his book, informed the nuncio that a second edition was already being planned, and solicited the criticisms of the Holy See with respect to modifications, additions, or notes.[127] Before this request for criticisms could have arrived in Rome, Consalvi had written to Valenti to say that "the Holy Father was extremely appreciative of the gift of the aforesaid work, which he proposes to read himself, not doubting that it measures up completely to the importance of the subject and the well-known merit of the author."[128] When Valenti advised Maistre of this reply, the latter was delighted,[129] and did not refrain from passing on the good news: "I have been highly approved in Rome. By a delicacy that you well understand, I had not wanted to send my book directly to the Holy Father. I made use of a minister, but I have lost nothing. The Pope said, 'Leave me that book, I want to read it myself'."[130] But with the crossed communications between the original gift and its acknowledgment, and Maistre's request for a critique, difficulties began. Once criticism (and, by implication, formal approval) was solicited, Consalvi appears to have become more cautious.

Having received an initial indication of approval, Maistre soon became impatient for a reply to his request. He showered Valenti with copies of letters and articles praising his book, and began visiting the nuncio almost every day looking for an answer.[131] It was not until 12 March 1820 that Rome informed Valenti that *Du Pape* was being examined by a capable theologian well versed in church history. The report would be passed on to Joseph de Maistre with the understanding that he could use it as he saw fit. The Holy See had not judged it appropriate to submit the work to formal examination by a Congregation since that was only done for books that might merit censure.[132] But before this report was completed and transmitted to Maistre, he had departed for his son's wedding at Valence in southern France, and taken with him (for transmittal to Lyon) revisions for the second edition. In reporting this development, Valenti expressed his fear that Rome's tardiness was irritating Maistre's perhaps too ardent zeal.[133] It seems likely the author completed his revisions for the second edition while spending some four weeks in Chambéry after Rodolphe's wedding; in any case, the new preface added to this edition is dated "Chambéry, 1 July 1820."[134]

The observations of Consalvi's theologian were completed and sent off to Turin on 3 June 1820, but were not given to Joseph de Maistre until 13 July following his return from Savoy.[135] The observations had been sent with a note pointing out that they were the advice of a private person and that Maistre was free to give them whatever weight he judged appropriate.[136] The text of this report has not survived,[137] but the Vatican theologian's comments can be deduced from Joseph de Maistre's comments on them,[138] and from a later minute by the same theologian.[139] Apart from a number of quibbles on minor points, the Vatican expert had three significant reservations about *Du Pape*: Maistre's argument gave the appearance of basing the infallibility of the Church and the pope on the fact that their judgments were without appeal; he had spoken with a great deal of exaggeration against the authority of general church councils; and he had maintained that all truly Catholic writers were of the opinion that the Church was a monarchy tempered by aristocracy.

Only the first of the three reservations touched on the essentials of Maistre's argument. What he had done in Book I of *Du Pape* was to try to lead his readers from their understanding and acceptance of the concept of sovereignty in the secular order to the logical necessity of acknowledging papal infallibility in the spiritual order. De Place had in fact warned him of the danger of confusing the practical impossibility of appealing the final decisions of a secular sovereign and the revealed doctrine of infallibility.[140]

In addressing the point in the preface of his second edition, Maistre acknowledged that his approach to infallibility had aroused fears that by "basing his doctrine on philosophical consideratons only" he had humanized it too much.[141] But he pointed out that he had made the essential distinction in his original edition when he had stated that "infallibility is on the one hand *humanly supposed* and on the other *divinely promised*."[142] In developing his argument in *Du Pape*, Maistre had presented it in the context of the more general proposition "that theological truths are no other than general truths manifested and divinized within the sphere of religion."[143] Defending this approach in his new preface, Maistre maintained that "the analogy of Catholic dogma and usages with the beliefs, traditions, and practices of mankind (if the subject is treated with suitable scope) would produce a work of controversy of a new genre that would be as convincing as any."[144] In contrast to traditional theologians, who usually based their arguments on divine revelation and sacred tradition, Maistre's method represented a philosophical or rationalist approach to religious questions.[145] It is not surprising that his slighting of traditional methods distressed the Vatican theologian.

When Joseph de Maistre and Valenti had a long interview to discuss the theologian's observations, Maistre complained of a certain acrimony in the critic's style, but acknowledged the justice of most of his points and promised to take them into account in his revised edition.[146] But he went on to indicate that he would have appreciated a personal letter from the Holy Father or Cardinal Consalvi. Then, dissatisfied with Valenti's excuses for the absence of such a letter, Maistre told the nuncio that he doubted whether his book had ever found its way to the Holy Father's desk. What had become a warm exchange ended with Valenti calming the author by offering to read him Consalvi's letters, and Maistre requesting that their disagreement remain confidential. In reporting the episode, the nuncio excused Maistre's conduct as a momentary display of the author's literary vanity.[147] Replying to this report, Consalvi explained that the theologian, who had the greatest esteem for Maistre's talents, had simply expressed himself with the customary frankness of a man of letters, and that it was never a matter of insisting that Maistre change any particular phrase judged false or inaccurate. He also indicated that if the book had been accompanied by a personal letter, the Holy Father would not have failed to reply, and that the pope continued to hold Maistre in high esteem.[148]

With Maistre's assurances that the Roman theologian's comments had been taken into account in the preface to the second edition and in certain revisions to the text,[149] the issue of Rome's criticisms or approval might have appeared closed. But then in early December 1820, Maistre approached Valenti with a request (both verbal and written) for permission to include a Latin letter of dedication to Pope Pius VII in his new edition. He said that while he thought that this dedication would add weight to his work, he would understand if His Holiness could not accept, and that it was "only a question of being useful and nothing more."[150] In passing on the request, Valenti suggested that the dedication was the author's oblique way of trying to win the pope's direct approbation.

Asked to comment on Maistre's request, Consalvi's expert theologian expressed some unhappiness about the extent to which Maistre had been willing to revise his text, but acknowledged that his errors, or rather inexactitudes, were only those of excessive zeal. However he recommended that the pope, for reasons of prudence, should decline the dedication.[151] This report is undated, and it is not known what action Consalvi took on the recommendation. Since Joseph de Maistre became incapacitated by his final illness in December 1820 and died 26 February 1821, it is unlikely he ever received a response to his last request.[152]

In short, while Joseph de Maistre may have been disappointed that his great work on the papacy was not more enthusiastically welcomed by Rome, there is nothing to suggest Vatican opposition in principle to the book, nor even anything in the way of an evasion of the issue on political grounds.[153] A slight error in etiquette in the way the book was presented, the habitual caution of papal officials, and Maistre's impatience were factors that led to tension between the author and the nuncio. What might have happened if Maistre had lived longer is impossible to say, but the important point is that there was never any question, either at that time or later, of condemnation of his work.[154] Maistre had concluded his second edition preface with an avowal of his willingness "to submit his work to the judgment of Rome, without the least possible reservation,"[155] and there seems no reason to doubt his sincerity.

While Maistre learned something of his book's reception in France and Rome, he appears to have been less successful in finding out about a third readership he had hoped to reach. Book IV of Du Pape, it will be recalled, was designed to refute Stourdza's defence of Orthodoxy. Shortly after publication, sharing reflections with his old friend Abbé Rey, Maistre admitted he most feared the reaction of the Russians:

I certainly believe there will be tempests, but the strongest will be from the north, and I regret in advance all the harm that it can do me. Believe me, the chapter on Russia will fall on St Petersburg like a bomb. Can they question the Russian *witnesses*? When they see this list, they will be struck with amazement, and then anger. But what will happen to the author? *I do not know.* Who knows if the one who spent 20,000 rubles to have us insulted by a child (in knowledge) will want to tolerate the reprisals?[156]

Maistre long entertained the hope that Tsar Alexander could be won to a more favourable policy towards Catholicism. In the spring of 1819, he had prepared a long letter "sur l'état du Christianisme en Europe."[157] Ostensibly addressed to "M. le Marquis ... ," it is clear from the contents that it was written for Alexander's benefit, and it is likely Maistre hoped to have it brought to the tsar's attention through the efforts of one or other intermediary.[158] Much of the piece was given over to describing how the "very good, very human, very pious Emperor of Russia" had struck serious blows against Christianity by the protection he had accorded to Geneva (ie, Calvinism), by the support he had given to the Bible Society, by his persecution of Catholicism and the Jesuits, and by his willingness to welcome the "German venom" of "universal Christianity." It is not known whether Maistre's letter was ever seen by the tsar. What is sure is that the Russian censorship prevented any mention of *Du Pape* in any Russian newspaper or journal.[159]

In another letter to the Abbé Rey, written just a few days after the letter cited in the previous paragraph, Maistre predicted that the importance of *Du Pape* would not be appreciated until many years later: "This book will give me little satisfaction in the short term; perhaps it will give me many annoyances. But it is written, it will make its way in silence. Perhaps Rodolphe will receive the compliments. The great explosion of *Considérations sur la France* occurred more than twenty-five years after its date of publication."[160] It was one of Maistre's more accurate prophecies since it was in the period following the mid-1840s that the popularity of *Du Pape* reached its peak.[161]

THE FINAL ACT

The mixture of satisfaction and disappointment afforded by *Du Pape* was echoed in other areas of Maistre's life during his last years. The joy of being reunited with brothers, sisters, and other relatives was dimmed by separation from Xavier and his family (who remained in Russia) and by the death of another brother, André. If Maistre was gratified by Rodolphe's prospering military career and advantageous marriage, he regretted his son's prolonged absence on garrison duty in Novara, and would never have the pleasure of knowing his grandchildren since he died within eight months of Rodolphe's marriage. The restoration of kings in Paris, Turin, and elsewhere had marked a setback for the revolutionary ideology Maistre had so long opposed, but he was under no illusions about its continuing vitality. And if he continued his literary activities through the last few months of his life, completing preparations for the publication of *De l'Eglise gallicane*, *Les Soirées de Saint-Pétersbourg*, and a revised edition of *Du Pape*, he never knew the satisfaction of seeing them in print.

Always a man with an extremely strong sense of family solidarity, Joseph de Maistre was undoubtedly very pleased to be among his extended family again. In addition to the week-long visit to Chambéry in the summer of 1817 on his return journey from St Petersburg, he travelled to Genoa that same fall to visit his sister Anne and her husband Count Alexis de Saint-Réal.[162] His delight at renewing his relationship with his brother André was heightened by the news that the latter had been named Bishop of Aosta. But this joy was short-lived. A banquet was planned for 19 July 1818 to celebrate his elevation, and members of the family had gathered in Turin for the occasion when André suddenly fell ill, and after four days died in Joseph's arms on 18 July.[163] It was a devastating blow; Joseph's letter to Madame Swetchine testifies to his respect for his brother and his sense of loss: "We are disconsolate, appalled, deader than he. Famous orator, apostle, theologian, man of the world, excellent brother, friend of my childhood, that is what I have lost."[164] Lamartine, who had known André through his friendship with Louis Vignet (nephew to André and Joseph), has left us a charming pen portrait of this somewhat eccentric cleric:

The Abbé de Maistre was at once very pious, very sprightly, and in his unexpected originality very like a Savoyard Sterne or a dean of St Patrick's. He was at least the equal of his two brothers in wit, singularity, and native energy … His personality corresponded to his character … The serious and the playful were mixed in such equal parts that one always saw a burst of laughter ready to betray the gravity of his lips.[165]

For Joseph, Andre's death was more than a blow to the heart. His brother's new status might have helped in his own search for a suitable position in Turin; as he remarked to Blacas: "My brother would have been able to push my bark a little."[166]

Friendships were nearly as important to Maistre as family, and the return to Turin meant the opportunity of renewing his ties with old friends such as the Marquis de Barol.[167] There is an account, by a visiting Frenchman who spent three months in Turin towards the middle of 1820, of evenings spent at Barol's home, where Maistre was an habitual figure who entertained the guests with his witty and gay conversations, and shared with them his views on contemporary events in France.[168] If the failure to arrange a meeting with Blacas was a disappointment, there was nevertheless a steady exchange of letters between Turin and Rome, where the latter continued to serve as French ambassador to the Holy See. It was Blacas whose interest-free loan made it possible for Maistre to purchase a house and some land a few months before his death.

Maistre was becoming a well-known literary figure, and his advice and support were solicited for diverse causes. An enthusiast for a newly invented system of writing, for example, tried to win Maistre's assistance in bringing the project to the attention of the academy of science in Turin. His replies to such impositions were polite and witty; in the case of *pasigraphie* Maistre acknowledged that if it worked it would eclipse printing, the compass, clocks, and fire engines in importance, but tactfully pointed out certain problems that made it quite impracticable.[169] The Royal Academy of Science of Turin did, however, honour Maistre himself by electing him to membership in January 1819.

There were other projects to which Maistre was willing to lend support. He joined a group called Amis catholiques, which had been established in Turin some years previously to publish and distribute cheap copies of "good books," and wrote on their behalf to Count Friedrich Leopold zu Stolberg about an Italian translation of one of the latter's historical works, which they were proposing to publish.[170] Maistre also supported the work of a similar group called the Société des bons livres by contributing a piece of anti-Protestant propaganda to one of their publications.[171]

However, judging from its salience in his correspondence with Rodolphe during the last three years of his life, it appears that the topic most on Joseph de Maistre's mind was a suitable marriage for his only son. For a man of his class and belief, ensuring a patrimony and descendants to cherish and augment the family heritage were matters of the utmost importance. In earlier years there had been discussion of possible marriages for one or the other of his daughters, but once the uncertainty concerning his own position had been resolved, he focused his attention on Rodolphe's marriage prospects.

Many factors had to be taken into account. His love for his son was deep and his concern for the young man's personal happiness genuine; he would not pressure Rodolphe to accept anyone for whom he had no strong inclination.[172] But on the other hand, the family's financial situation remained worrisome. The Revolution had robbed them of the property that had accumulated from his inheritance from his father and his own marriage settlement; in the long hard years of exile in Switzerland, Italy (except for the three years in Sardinia), and Russia it had been nearly impossible to do anything about rebuilding the family's fortune. So it was extremely important to parlay all their non-monetary assets into a marriage that would strengthen the family's financial and social status. Maistre's standing as the former ambassador to the court of the tsars and his position as minister of state and Régent de la Grande Chancellerie, as well as his literary renown, were counters to be bargained carefully. Rodolphe's status as a highly decorated veteran of the Napoleonic wars, his standing as the youngest lieutenant-colonel in the royal army, his linguistic skills, and his diplomatic experience as his father's secretary were all advantages to be used in the search for the dowry that could restore the family's finances.[173] Another consideration, given Joseph de Maistre's great admiration for French language and culture and his status as one of the greatest living writers of French prose, was the nationality of the bride. He believed, moreover, that Frenchwomen made better wives than Italians,[174] and that the long-term possibilities for the family's ascension were higher in a great nation than in a small Italian kingdom.[175] Finally, Joseph de Maistre was fully aware of how important a wise choice of partner had been for his father and for himself. Both his mother and his wife had brought to their marriages strength of character, financial assets, and family alliances that had benefited himself and his children.[176] He wanted no less for Rodolphe.

Although Maistre's preference was for France, the net was cast as wide as possible. Relatives and clerical friends were enlisted to help with the search.[177] Rodolphe had to be counselled to give up a "half-bourgeois Margoton,"[178] and a young Russian countess the young man had known in Russia and who showed up in Turin in December 1818.[179] When a possible match was discovered in Lyon, Rodolphe was sent off for a visit, with business with the publisher of *Du Pape* as an excuse for his journey. Other possible brides included a girl from Chambéry and one originally from Milan.

By the fall of 1819 the search had been narrowed down to a choice between the Milanese and the daughter of a Marquis de Plan de Sieyès, a former French naval officer who had a château near Valence in southeastern France. But just when Joseph de Maistre was about to write to his son to tell him decisive good news about the second candidate, Rodolphe wrote from Novara to announce his engagement to the Italian girl. His father was dumbfounded; his reply reveals his frustration as well as many of the factors he was considering:

Ah! My God, what have you done? Dear Rodolphe. My head is spinning. Did you not give us carte-blanche? ... You tell me "Why didn't you notify me immediately?" Good God! Should we have tormented you before being sure? Mlle de Syeyes[180] is young, beautiful, virtuous, and vivacious; she is as beautiful as the other and better educated. She speaks Italian well; she has 125,000 livres and the sure expectation of another 50,000 ... We only wanted to wait a few days to have the pleasure of surprising you and to spare you painful and useless anguish – and during this short delay you become engaged! ... I have nothing to say of her merit, and less of her nobility, but I distinctly remember my dear cousin adding "that one is not rich." Finally, you, my dear son, who does not lie, you told me rich *enough*? No doubt 80,000 Milanese livres for example; that is to say very little and much less than we need. I have 104,000 livres but I owe 10 or 12 to your good mother: you are three – count. As for the question of nation, I do not know what more I can tell you, but I must repeat, take care! *Man entraps himself.* To refuse a woman because she belongs to a particular nation has always appeared to me to be the height of folly. Everywhere, happily, there are superior women. But each nation having a distinctive trait, that of the French is ascendancy and action. This trait is softened among the women, but still strong, and this is precisely what we need ... Marry a Laplander if she can make you happy, but rescue me from the horrible position in which you have put me. It is a question of honour ... I cannot describe to you the state we are in. What strange luck I have! The letter I awaited like roses from heaven will perhaps poison my life. I do not know where I am at. For – I do not know what to tell you. I embrace you tenderly.[181]

Somehow, we do not know how, Rodolphe was able to withdraw from whatever commitment he had made to the Milanese, and subsequently gave his consent to serious negotiations with the Sieyès family.

However, it was a number of months before all the financial arrangements for Rodolphe's marriage to Azélie de Sieyès could be worked out. The most difficult problem seems to have been the fact that Joseph de Maistre owned practically no real estate (except a few remnants in Savoy that had finally been returned as part of a post-restoration settlement). It was a difficulty that was not easy to resolve. Until a decision had been reached on his own situation, he was unsure as to whether he should try to purchase property in the Turin area or in Savoy.[182] The idea of owning and passing on property in land had become almost an obsession with him; in a letter in which he had requested the assistance of the Abbé Rey in finding a suitable bride for Rodolphe, Maistre had written: "but I never cease to cry like the sailors, Land! Land!"[183] As he explained to Rodolphe, the difficulty was that to acquire land, a dowry was required, and to obtain a dowry, one needed land. "We are trapped in a completely vicious circle."[184] A dowry would make it possible to meet the payments on a purchase, but until they held land, it was hard to get agreement on a marriage contract. Although Joseph de Maistre was still complaining to Rodolphe about this problem in late April 1820,[185] agreement was finally reached (with only the promise to purchase, apparently).[186] In any case, Maistre himself was present at Rodolphe's wedding in Valence on 5 June 1820.[187]

He was still fussing over the financial settlement when he returned to Turin in July (after a long visit in Chambéry). The Maistre family had expected that Azélie would be provided by her parents with such items as silver and linen, and Joseph resented having to provide such things for Rodolphe's establishment.[188] Nevertheless everyone was delighted by the personal qualities of Rodolphe's bride. In Maistre's last surviving letter to his son and his new wife, his satisfaction is more than evident:

Your cardinal [ie, Cardinal Morozzo, the bishop of Novara] has just written to me and spoken to me admiringly of your better half. It does my heart good. I see that this girl is succeeding everywhere. What honour for the entire family. This is a great, this is an immense blessing from heaven. Dear Azélie, come quickly so that I may embrace you at my ease. You will not find me well – and you are the cause, since it is you who are making me a grandfather and grandfathers must be ponderous.[189]

Maistre died before Azélie had really made him a grandfather, but she and Rodolphe eventually had eleven children, of which seven survived to adulthood. Since Joseph's daughters married late in life and had no children, and since none of his brothers had children who survived their own deaths, it was Rodolphe's marriage to Azélie de Sieyès that ensured a numerous Maistre progeny down to our own time.

"The year 1820 has been for me a climacteric year that has put an end to my long youth."[190] With the receipt of printed copies of *Du Pape* in January and with Rodolphe's marriage in June, Joseph de Maistre seems suddenly to have felt himself growing old. Part of it was failing health; in this same letter he went on to describe the weakness he was feeling in his legs. He had had a serious fall, and although the women in the family blamed the accident for the weakness, Maistre himself believed "the fall was the effect and not the cause."[191] Perhaps linked to the health problems was a growing pessimism about the direction of public affairs in Piedmont-Sardinia, in France, and in Europe generally.

Passionate interest in political, intellectual, and religious developments, always so characteristic of Maistre's intellectual life, never diminished. His letters for this whole period, from those written on his return from Russia to the last few dictated to Constance after his hand had become too weak for him to hold the pen himself, testify to a continuing sense of involvement in the life of his time. Although his reactions to contemporary events varied with his mood and the successive turns events appeared to take, in general he became increasingly less hopeful about the course of European politics, but retained his faith in a future regeneration of religion and morality through the efforts of a revitalized French Catholicism in fruitful communion with Rome.

Maistre remained fascinated by things French.[192] Louis XVIII's Charter, as we have seen, had left him singularly unimpressed. He had been willing to admit, at least in a private letter to his brother in March 1817, that the king may have followed the course of political wisdom: "You made me burst out laughing with the description you gave me of the *French Charter*. If some fools believed in it or still believe in it, too bad for them. The king, however, may well have done the right thing ... It is necessary to do many things in politics for *the crowd*; while waiting, minds will calm down. Contrary elements will amalgamate, and *that will be it* [*ça ira*]."[193]

But from his passage through France in the summer of 1817, from his correspondence with Frenchmen, and from his reading of the French press, he found ample evidence to convince himself that the ideas on which he blamed the Revolution remained alive and well in Paris. Comparing the France he had left at the height of the Terror in 1793 (ie, French-occupied Savoy), and France under the Restoration, he concluded that the political situation remained unstable. In a letter to the Count de Noailles, the restored French monarch's ambassador to Russia whom he had gotten to know during his last years in St Petersburg, Maistre offered this analysis:

When I left, heads were falling; today they are turning. I do not find any other differences. You will perhaps tell me that we have already gained much by the one difference – but in truth ... I do not know about that. It is a matter of arithmetic, and God alone knows the answer. The falling of ten heads, for example, could be less fatal for the state than a thousand heads turning. So it is a matter of numbers – and who knows the numbers.[194]

What really upset Maistre, it becomes evident in a letter written a few months later to another French acquaintance, was that the heads which had been turned included too many of the old aristocracy:

Many people have done me the honour of addressing the same question to me that I read in your letter: "Why do you not write on the present situation in France?" I always have the same reply: in the time of the *canillocratie*,[195] I could at my risk and peril, tell the truth to those inconceivable *sovereigns*; but today those who are mistaken are of too good houses for one to be permitted to tell them the truth. The revolution is much more terrible than in Robespierre's time; in ascending it has refined itself.[196]

Ultra correspondents, such as Bonald, Marcellus, and Lamennais, and the ultra press, served to confirm Maistre in his black perception of the political situation in France.

Nor did he find the prospect any brighter in Piedmont-Sardinia. In the same letter in which he had given the Count de Noailles his diagnosis of heads turning in Paris, Maistre sketched a similar scene in Turin: "Arriving home ... I found only a miniature of the great painting I had just seen. The influence that you [ie, the French] continue to exercise on us is a strange phenomenon, which would furnish me with a fine text for one of our philosophical tête-à-têtes."[197] Unlike France, which remained a great power, Piedmont-Sardinia faced not only the persistent threat of renewed revolutionary agitation, but the old threat of Austrian domination. In one of his last letters to Blacas, undated but written at about the time of the Congress of Troppau (which met in November 1820 and authorized great power intervention in smaller states to reverse revolutionary changes), Maistre voiced his habitual distrust of the Hapsburg power: "Today we are in a situation that makes us tremble. I say we, I mean we subjects of the king of Sardinia. Who knows what is being schemed at Troppau? Of what use is wisdom, moderation, and foresight when the folly or ambition of the foreigner can ruin us? In thinking about certain positions and the lack of equilibrium, I shudder."[198]

Maistre was not imagining phantoms. In January 1821 there was violent student agitation in Turin, which led to reprisals,[199] and in the second week of March, just days after Maistre's death, agitation and rebellion by army officers and aristocrats in Alessandria and Turin led to the abdication of

Victor-Emmanuel ɪ and the attempt to establish a liberal constitutional regime. It required vigorous action by Charles-Félix, Maistre's old nemesis from Sardinia who now succeeded his brother on the throne,[200] and the intervention of the Austrian army to defeat the attempted coup.

The most often quoted of Maistre's expressions of discouragement from these years appears in a letter to the Count de Marcellus in which he exclaimed: "I die with Europe, I am in good company."[201] However this statement should be put in context; Maistre was writing less than three weeks after the death of his brother André, and the cited phrase follows an evocation of that event: "Since I lost the bishop of Aosta ... I am only half alive." While Maistre's remark in this case may reveal his recognition of the irrevocable passing of the old monarchical and Catholic Europe whose memory he cherished, it must be emphasized that his political pessimism remained balanced by faith in a future religious renaissance of some kind or other. The providentialism that had forged a prophecy of monarchical restoration in the darkest days of the Terror now provided Maistre with a consoling hope that was more purely spiritual.

This combination of political pessimism and religious hope found expression in a number of Maistre's letters during this period. Already in January 1815, he had predicted important religious events: "All of Europe is in a fermentation that is carrying us towards a religious revolution that will be forever remembered and of which the political revolution we have just witnessed was only a dreadful preface."[202] In 1819, in the same letter in which he had described the ideological situation as being worse than in Robespierre's time, he had gone on to predict that France would somehow play a crucial role in ushering in a new epoch in the history of Christianity:

The revolution being completely Satanic, as I said in the book that you have had the goodness to reread, it can only be really killed by the contrary principle. The counter-revolution will be angelic or we will not have one ... Europe is in an extraordinary and violent state that announces an inevitable change ... Contrary to all imaginable appearances, the movement will begin in France, and the astonishing proselytism of this people will win them pardon for all the harm they have done.[203]

Apparently Maistre was even freer with his predictions in salon conversations than in his correspondence. The visiting Frenchman who encountered him at the home of the Marquis de Barol in the summer of 1820 reports that Maistre predicted that "the royal family would be chased out of France again," but then grew extremely animated and went on to prophecy the eventual defeat of the revolution:

On the return of France to the truth, on the epoch of that return, on the causes that will lead to it, I cannot be as precise as the misfortunes I foresee; but I have in me a secret instinct that it will occur at a given moment like *a last-but-one revelation of truth in the minds of the masses.* All will be astonished to see and understand that what had been sought in the discomfort of discussions and disputes is simple and easy, and on that day *the revolution will be ended.*[204]

But it was in his books that were published a few months after his death that Maistre's faith found its most fervent expression. *De l'Eglise gallicane* was one long argument aimed at persuading French clergymen to sacrifice their Gallican prejudices and so prepare for the providential role for which they were destined. And it was in the last dialogue of *Les Soirées de Saint-Pétersbourg*, as Maistre told Bonald, that he had "gathered together ... all the signs that announced some great event in the sphere of religion."[205]

Work on *De l'Eglise gallicane* had gone forward steadily from September 1819 when the decision had been made to separate it from *Du Pape*. Maistre assured De Place that all his comments on what had been Book v of the first work were being taken into account,[206] agreed with De Place's advice for "less vivacity in style and expression," and said that he "would willingly use a buffer on all the harsh expressions."[207] Book v was understood to have been included in the original contract with Rusand, and the publisher now pressed for its publication as a separate work.[208] The author's preface is dated August 1820, and by mid-September the revised manuscript had been sent directly to Rusand.[209] Maistre believed that his work on the Gallican Church "would necessarily produce a great explosion,"[210] but he did not live to hear the echoes. Like *Du Pape,* the sequel enjoyed its greatest popularity in the four decades following 1840.[211]

But *Les Soirées de Saint-Pétersbourg* was the "cherished work" into which Maistre had "poured his head."[212] The nearly completed manuscript had been in his "Russian portfolio" when he returned to Turin in 1817. The following June he told De Place that it could be ready with a month's work, and described its ambitious scope and purpose: "It does a turn, so to say, around all the great questions of rational philosophy, and can shock no one, except the ideologues and the Lockists. The work is designed to achieve the solemn wedding of philosophy and the Gospel, and its principal purpose is to restore to our language the sceptre so foolishly ceded by our people in the past century."[213]

But as with *Du Pape*, Maistre appears to have been uncertain about the wisdom of publishing and the likelihood of success. At least one extra copy was made of the manuscript, and a number of people were asked to read all or parts of the initial draft.[214] In requesting an opinion from De Place, Maistre revealed both his pride in what he had accomplished and his reasons for hesitating:

This book is *all that I can do and all that I can know.* But what can I do and what do I know? That is not for me to decide ... However, as a certain confidence in one's ideas is not a crime, provided it be modest and always ready to retract, I would be willing to launch the book into space without any other security than this interior confidence in the truth, a little reaffirmed, and animated by the effect the manuscript has produced on certain minds ...

the work is addressed ... to everyone. You will see, Monsieur, how I have set about making philosophy (ancient philosophy especially) walk with theology, and how I have made the work dramatic and even sentimental. In short, Monsieur, this is *my* great work; unfortunately, the possessive pronoun spoils everything, since one man's great work may only be an atom before universal reason.[215]

Again we sense the tension between Maistre's audacious pen and a certain timidity in action.

Publication of *Du Pape* and his many other activities apparently kept Maistre from doing much about completing the *Soirées* until after Rodolphe's wedding. It was only in September 1820 that the project was again mentioned in his correspondenc with De Place.[216] Later that month he was busy revising the famous portrait of Voltaire that appears in the fourth dialogue of the work.[217] Negotiations with Rusand had been opened in 1818, but finally, in December 1820, Maistre informed De Place that he had decided against the Lyon publisher. There had been some disagreements over the publication of the works on the papacy and the Gallican Church, and Maistre concluded that Rusand was "beneath the enterprise." Moreover, the author had made a gift of the work to his wife, and she preferred to have it published in Paris. In this same letter to De Place, Maistre reported that the first volume was already "complete and perfect" and "had taken flight towards the great *Lutèce.*"[218] A few days later he informed Rodolphe that "everything was underway for the printing of the *Soirées* where all that is lacking is the ending, that it so say the most difficult part."[219] But illness overtook the author, and he died before he could complete the manuscript of the second volume. As published by the Librarie Grecque, Latin et Française in Paris in 1821, the last dialogue of the *Soirées* remains unfinished.[220] But Maistre's *Eclaircissement sur les sacrifices* was published as an addendum, and has usually been published with subsequent editions of the *Soirées*. This was probably the author's intention, since it is bound with the second volume of the manuscript copy of the latter work that survives in the Maistre family archives.

For most of his life Joseph de Maistre had enjoyed robust good health. Until his final illness, the only problem that had given him much concern was a disconcerting tendency to fall asleep briefly in embarrassing situations. It 1815, concerned that rumours about his health might be getting back to Turin, Maistre wrote to his superior to explain what was involved:

For the past half dozen years more or less, I have been subject to entirely inexplicable accidents of sleep, which often surprise me in society, and of which I am the first to laugh. These are only a flash, and what is strange, this sleep has nothing in common with night-time sleep. By nature, I sleep very little: three hours out of twenty-four or even less are sufficient for me, and the least worry deprives me of that … What is the origin of this sudden and passing sleep of a minute or two? This is something I have never understood. For several months, these *sleep attacks* (for I do not know what else to call them) have greatly diminished, and I certainly hope that I will soon be entirely free of them.[221]

The problem did not disappear, of course. Xavier de Maistre had observed the symptoms and realized that Joseph's "sleep attacks" might be used against him in Turin:

My brother's sleep worried me very much in its beginnings while he was still here. But it is certain that his health is perfect despite it and that his mind is in no way weakened. But I would not answer for his sometimes falling asleep in council. This disposition can only give arms to the malevolent, without however being able to affect his affairs, which he will study with a pure conscience and a facility that few people can match.[222]

There is in fact no evidence that these episodes, probably a form of narcolepsy, affected Joseph's capacity for work prior to the fall of 1820.

Constance de Maistre was later to report that her father had been preoccupied with the thought of his death during the last year of his life,[223] but it was only in September 1820 that Maistre's correspondence reveals serious concern. Writing to Rodolphe, he acknowledged that he had not been feeling well for some time; he explained that he had a weakness in his legs and had had a bad fall.[224] By mid-December, he admitted that his health "had been badly shaken."[225]

Maistre's final illness involved a creeping paralysis that began in his legs and then gradually spread upward through the rest of his body. In its early stages it became difficult for him to walk; he sometimes staggered like a drunken man and he fell a number of times. As it became difficult to swallow his appetite disappeared.[226]

Finally, after struggling against the disease for some time, he took to his bed on 1 January 1821.[227] Except for being placed in his armchair, or carried to his carriage two or three times for brief outings in the warm sunshine, he had become bedridden. Maistre's mind, however, remained quite lucid, and he continued to dictate letters until two days before he died. Nor did his wit abandon him; in a letter to an old friend he described his symptoms in these terms: "A bizarre humour to which they give different names has attacked my legs and deprived me of them. There are neither sores, nor pain, nor swelling, nor is there in any fever, but finally there are two legs fewer, and that is a lot for a biped."[228]

He joked with his daughter that "one of these days you will find only a mind in my bed."[229] On 21 February he dictated a substantial and nuanced letter on the problem of Italian unification,[230] and on 24 February a very important letter to Lamennais warning him that the second volume of his *Essai sur l'indifférence en matière de religion* had advanced some dangerous principles.[231]

Joseph de Maistre's last days were eased by the consolations of his religion. He often asked that the Gospel of St John, the *Imitation of Christ*, and the psalms be read to him. The Eucharist was brought to him as well.[232] On the evening of 25 February he refused to accept any more medicine, saying "Let me die in peace." At two o'clock the following morning he tried to swallow a bit of soup, but then fell into a coma and died about ten o'clock. He was surrounded by his wife and daughters, but Rodolphe did not arrive from Novara until later that day.[233]

Among the papers in the Maistre family archives is the undated draft of a will that Joseph de Maistre drew up sometime after his appointment as Régent de la Grande Chancellerie in December 1818. The first paragraph reads:

I affirm that I die in the bosom of the apostolic and Roman Catholic Church that I have always professed and even defended from the errors of my century according to my strength. I recommend myself to the infinite goodness of my creator, very humbly entreating him to want to save his creature and to receive me among the number of his elect.[234]

Maistre died as he had lived, the ardent self-appointed champion of Catholicism, the paladin of throne and altar.

CHAPTER EIGHT

Epilogue

When Joseph de Maistre died in 1821 his writings were just becoming well known in Europe and his person was scarcely known at all. Of his major works, only half had yet been published. Although two of the remaining three appeared in the months following his death, it was fifteen years before the third was published and thirty years before the first extensive publication of his letters began to reveal the private man to his readers. It was not until the 1880s that an edition of his "complete works" was brought out. Biographical studies were also slow to appear. There were brief obituaries and a eulogy immediately following his death, relatively brief "literary portraits" by Saint-Beuve in 1843 and Lamartine in 1849, and Rodolphe de Maistre's "Notice Biographique" in 1851, but it was not until the last two decades of the century that professional scholars began to be allowed very limited access to materials in the possession of the Maistre family. A full-scale treatment of Joseph de Maistre's reputation and influence would require another book, but we can scarcely appreciate how he has been generally perceived without at least a brief look at this posthumous fortunes, both literary and biographical.

Among the ironies surrounding Joseph de Maistre and his literary reputation, perhaps none is more piquant than the fact that his notoriety is due in part to writings published after his death. The author himself distrusted posthumous publications. Reflecting on what had happened to Bossuet, Maistre had written:

All posthumous works are suspect, and it has often occurred to me that it would be desirable to prohibit their publication without public authorization. Every day we write things we afterwards condemn. But we hold on to what we have written, and especially if the work is considerable and if it contains useful pages we hope to turn to account, it is difficult to decide to destroy it. Meanwhile death comes, and always unexpected since no man believes he will die today. The manuscript falls into the hands of an heir, a buyer, etc., who publishes it. It is usually a misfortune and sometimes a crime.[1]

Since many of the manuscripts remaining in Maistre's portfolio had been written in reaction to specific circumstances and with particular purposes in mind, he probably had his own situation in mind in writing these lines.

De l'Eglise gallicane, however, could not fall into the category of suspect works. It had been thoroughly revised in collaboration with Guy-Marie de Place and the manuscript sent off to Rusand in Lyon some months before Maistre's death. As with the first edition of *Du Pape*, the title-page advised that the work was by "the author of *Considérations sur la France*." In the preface, Maistre acknowledged that the book had originally been prepared as part of *Du Pape* and informed his readers that "this work, like that from which it is detached, was written in 1817, five hundred leagues from Paris and Turin."[2] The veil of anonymity was perfectly transparent. Since *De l'Eglise gallicane* appeared at the same time as a second edition of *Du Pape* and while opinions on the first edition of the latter were still being formulated, it is practically impossible to disentangle French reactions to the two works. Maistre's sequel was encompassed in the refutations of *Du Pape* that appeared in the 1820s.[3] Addressed to a more restricted audience than the first book (ie, to the French clergy rather than to the French generally), *De l'Eglise gallicane* appears to have been only about half as popular (as measured by the number of editions and reprints) as the first book. Together, and as refracted through the writings of Lamennais in the 1820s and Louis Veuillot (in his journal, *L'Univers*) in the 1850s and 1860s, these two works undoubtedly made a significant contribution to the ultramontane cause in France. Just as *Du Pape* helped prepare Catholic lay opinion to accept the first Vatican Council's proclamation of papal infallibility, so *De l'Eglise gallicane* played a role in weaning French clergymen from Gallican doctrines.[4]

The case of *Les Soirées de Saint-Pétersbourg* is more complicated. As we have seen, a first manuscript volume had been sent off to Paris two months before the author's death. Although Maistre died before he had the opportunity to complete the second to his satisfaction, it seems that about all that remained unfinished was an appropriate closing scene. The very short "Esquisse du morceau final," first published in 1851, consists of farewell remarks by the Count to his interlocutors, the Chevalier and the Senator.[5] It is probably impossible at this date to discover what editing Maistre's manuscript may have received from other hands after his death.[6] As published, the work includes twenty-seven "Editor's notes" in addition to a very large number of other notes not so identified. But except for about a half dozen, the content and style of these specially identified notes reflect

Maistre's erudition and characteristic raillery, which suggests that they are most likely the author's own.[7] In any case, there is no evidence to suggest that Saint-Victor's role went beyond contributing the laudatory preface that adorns the work.

Apart from cases that had occurred without his authorization, this was the first of Maistre's works to appear with his name (and all his titles) on the title-page.[8] Although the *Soirées* received generally favourable reviews on publication,[9] it eventually provoked an industrious abbé to produce a three-volume refutation.[10] Like the books on the papacy and the Gallican Church, the work did not really become popular until after 1850.[11]

Given the subject-matter, the influence of the *Soirées* was obviously much more diffuse and is thus much more difficult to estimate than that of the previous two books. As Saint-Victor had noted in this preface, "In his book *Du Pape*, M. de Maistre developed only one truth," while in his new book:

the field is more vast, or to put it better, without limits; it is man that he considers in his relations with God; it is free will and the divine power that he tries to reconcile; it is the great enigma of good and evil that he wants to explain; these are the innumerable truths, or rather these are all the great and useful truths that he has laid hold of as his own, to defend as a legitimate possession against the pride and impiety that has attacked them all.[12]

It might be easier to trace the impact of particular themes than that of the book as a whole. The powerful pages on the "divinity of war" from the seventh dialogue, for example, were picked up in various ways by such diverse writers as Leo Tolstoy, Pierre Joseph Proudhon, and Louis Veuillot, and have been reprinted separately during times of war.[13] But whatever reservations critics at the time or since have had about the theorizing in the work, few have questioned its status as a veritable showpiece of Maistre's literary and rhetorical skills.[14] Unfortunately, no one has yet attempted an English translation of Maistre's great work, and we are still waiting for a critical French edition.[15]

The long delay in the publication of the *Examen de la philosophie de Bacon* (Paris 1836) has never been satisfactorily explained.[16] A comparison of the manuscript copy in the Maistre family archives and the printed text reveals some editing at the time of publication, but it is not known who was responsible.[17] Like the *Soireés*, the *Examen* contains some of Maistre's best writing, at least from a literary point of view: "In none of his other books ... does M. de Maistre show himself more brilliantly and more profoundly himself. The chapters on 'final causes' and 'the union of science and religion' include passages on the order and proportion of the universe, on art, on Christian painting, on the beautiful, that are, certainly, some of the finest pages that have ever been written in a human language."[18] Judgments on the content of the work have always been more ambiguous.

Maistre's indictment of Bacon contained much that was picayune and trivial, but there were two principal charges that he pressed most effectively. In the first place, he accused Bacon of trying to reduce all knowledge and science to physics, both methodologically, by promoting the method of physics as the only true method of discovering truth, and materially, by assuming that all truth is essentially the truth of physics – its data and propositions. Second, Maistre contended that Bacon's radical reduction of all science to physics must inevitably promote materialism and atheism, a consequence he judged foolish as well as blasphemous. Baconian "materialism," in his view, threatened to annihilate all notions of human dignity. Maistre had convinced himself that Bacon was "an idol that must come down,"[19] and in the *Examen* he mounted a sustained attack designed to demolish Bacon's reputation as an innovator in scientific method, to demonstrate the childishness of his scientific opinions, and to prove his teachings destructive of philosophy and religion.[20]

Perhaps the impact of the *Examen* would have been considerable if it had been published in the early years of the Restoration, but by 1836 the mood of revulsion against the Enlightenment was fading, and the appearance of this new Maistrian opus aroused no great stir. It was praised by some,[21] but the reviewer in the Catholic journal whose establishment had been inspired by Maistre himself[22] was of the view that "the work has arrived too late; what it was supposed to do has already been done, the idol has been broken."[23] Nevertheless the book was popular during the Second Empire and later, with ten editions appearing by 1880.[24]

To turn now to Maistre's minor posthumously published works, the first to be published after his death was the *Lettres à un gentilhomme russe sur l'inquisition espagnole*, which was brought out in Paris in 1822. We have no evidence whatsoever as to the circumstances of publication. The thesis of the piece could only appear shocking to nineteenth-century liberals. Nevertheless there were new editions in 1844 and 1846, and it was reissued another fifteen times before 1880.[25]

It was Louis Veuillot who facilitated the publication of the next batch of Maistre's unedited works together with the first significant collection of his letters.[26] Veuillot learned through an Abbé Cazali, who had discussed the matter with Constance de Maistre in Nice, that Rodolphe was thinking of publishing more of the materials remaining in his father's portfolio. In his initial letter to Rodolphe in February 1847, Veuillot described himself as an experienced editor and stressed his esteem for the author: "I profoundly admire the writings of M. Count Joseph de Maistre ... They have contributed more than anything else I have ever read in affirming my reason in the Christian way. God made me a Catholic, M. de Maistre made me Roman. My gratitude equals my admiration."[27]

Veuillot told Rodolphe that he thought he could do nothing more worthwhile for religion than to publish more of Maistre's writings, offered to handle all the details of publication, and intimated that he was also thinking of writing a biography of the great writer. Rodolphe replied promptly and described what might be involved in the project: "Among my father's works that are still in portfolio, the most important part, in my opinion, is a collection of philosophical, political, religious, and family letters, then some memoirs on different subjects still agitating the world at present and that will probably retain for a long time what modern style calls actuality."[28]

Rodolphe suggested that it would perhaps be useful to join to these materials some previously printed pieces, discouraged Veuillot's biographical project on the grounds that it was his father's "literary and philosophical career" that had been important, reported that he was seriously occupied with putting his father's papers in order, and promised to send a list with appropriate indications.[29]

Although initiated in the spring of 1847, this publication project did not come to fruition until 1851. Two circumstances appear to have contributed to the delay. In the first place, all the participants were distracted by the revolutions that swept France, Piedmont-Sardinia, and the rest of Europe in 1848.[30] Second, Rodolphe found the task of editing his father's letters for publication a formidable one:

It is not as though I am not tormented with doubts: sometimes an anecdote that could shock, sometimes a paragraph that is a little too official, sometimes praise of certain personages whose only claim to respect is their standing on the royal list. In short, I sometimes have difficulty deciding since I want to change nothing; I have only suppressed some paragraphs ... so as not to *lose an entire letter*.[31]

In another letter he indicated that his father's letters to the Abbé Vuarin were in Constance's possession, but that in any case were not suitable for publication since they all had "extremely confidential passages on men and affairs."[32] In short, this collection of Maistre's letters was carefully edited to avoid the release of material that might reflect unfavourably on the author or cause embarrassment to the family.

As published by Vaton Frères in 1851, the *Lettres et opuscules inédits du Comte J. de Maistre* included a "Notice biographique" by Rodolphe (about which more later), some 195 letters, a few previously published pieces that had long been unavailable and were thus practically unknown (of which the "Discours à Mme de Costa" was the most significant), and a half-dozen previously unpublished minor works.[33] Of the latter, the "Cinq lettres sur l'éducation publique en Russie," was the piece that revealed the most "reactionary" facet of the author's thinking; one suspects that Maistre would not have written in the same way for a French audience as he did in trying to persuade Count Razumovsky. But given the inherent interest of the new material, and the new wave of revolutions that had rocked Europe in 1848 and given renewed "actuality" to the opinions and theories of the author, it is perhaps not surprising that this two-volume collection went through five editions in the years of the Second Empire.[34] A few years later Rodolphe also facilitated publication of his father's "Quatre chapitres sur la Russie,"[35] another of the author's more "reactionary" compositions.

The publication in 1858 of an important collection of Maistre's diplomatic correspondence was quite beyond the control of the Maistre family. It was Count Cavour, the prime minister of Piedmont-Sardinia who authorized Albert Blanc of the University of Turin to consult the state archives.[36] The editing was governed, not by family sensitivities, but by the wish of Blanc and his patron to exploit Joseph de Maistre's anti-Austrian and pro-French views for the purpose of enlisting French support for their contemporary campaign to evict Austria from the Italian penninsula.[37] Perhaps because this cause had largely succeeded by 1860, the two additional volumes of diplomatic correspondence Blanc published in that year were simple collections with few omissions and no commentary.[38] Whatever their deficiencies, all three volumes were important additions to known Maistre material.

While Maistre's writings enjoyed their greatest popularity under the Second Empire, it was not until the second decade of the Third Republic that the task of publishing a "complete edition" of his works was taken up. By this time his immediate descendants had died (Adèle in 1862, Rodolphe in 1865, and Constance in 1882), and it was Joseph's grandson, Count Charles de Maistre, who made the arrangements.[39] This new "complete" edition reprinted all of Maistre's major works, most of his minor works, the unedited pieces released by Rodolphe in 1851 and by Charles de Maistre in 1870, all the letters edited by Rodolphe in 1851, additional letters from the family archives, many of the letters that had been published by Blanc, and a selection of letters addressed to Joseph de Maistre. While extremely useful, the collection suffers from the faults of its parts. Except for Amédée de Margerie's introduction to the *Examen de Bacon*, the works appear without any critical apparatus, and the editing of the correspondence leaves a great deal to be desired. But despite its shortcomings, this edition became an indispensable tool for Maistrian scholarship, which could now begin to come of age.

The story of the slow unveiling of the fascinating details of Joseph de Maistre's personal life is another intriguing tale. Beginning with the great writer himself, the family was for a long time extremely reticent about allowing outsiders access to the very human man behind the persona of the author, to his private papers, to anything that might reflect unfavourably on a figure they soon elevated to the status of a latter-day Father of the Church. The ironic consequence was that until recently chances for accurate and objective biographical studies of this generally very attractive and admirable personality were greatly reduced. Without access to Maistre's personal papers, both admirers and critics of the author too often indulged in the creation and perpetuation of myths.

From the beginning of his career as a young magistrate, Joseph de Maistre had made a careful distinction in his own mind between the personage that the public was allowed to see (and the responsibilities inherent in playing a public role in society) and the private person who could indulge in all kinds of intellectual adventures in the privacy of his study or in the company of intimate friends. He had lectured his Senate colleagues on the importance of winning and retaining public confidence in the rectitude and wisdom of the magistrature. As a counter-revolutionary propagandist in Switzerland, he confided grave doubts about the viability of the Sardinian monarchy to his friend Vignet des Etoles at the same time his pamphlets were proclaiming its virtues. In St Petersburg, playing the prestigious role of ambassador to the court of the tsars, he had been careful to avoid revealing his private penury.[40] Literally working himself to death in his last years as Régent de la Grande Chancellerie,[41] he willingly accepted the sacrifice for the sake of the standing the post provided and for what it meant for the social advancement of his children.

Critics have too readily denounced Joseph de Maistre's preoccupation with status and public image as the product of vanity and hypocrisy.[42] What can be forgotten is that Maistre lived out his life in a traditional hierarchical society in which the sense of rank was imbred and conventional. One played a role in "the great theatre of the world," and what went on backstage was not the business of the audience. Maistre's works, especially the *Soirées*, could be intensely personal, but the author was in control, presumably, of what was revealed. The public image Maistre chose to leave to posterity was that of the distinguished ambassador enveloped in titles and decorations, the witty erudite Count whose St Petersburg conversations would continue to win high society down through the years. The private man of intimate and loyal friendships, the personal anguish of intellectual doubts and hard-tried monarchical fidelity, the undignified squabbling between the able but touchy civil servant and an often petty court, the delightful and charming personal correspondent, these were facets of his personality and life that Maistre and his family were careful to veil from public scrutiny. There were no scandalous secrets to hide, but a certain conception of personal and family honour demanded the projection and protection of a protagonist without the frailties of ordinary humanity.

One might have expected that Joseph de Maistre's nephew, Louis Vignet, would have been his first biographer. He respected Vignet's literary judgment, since he sent him a manuscript copy of the *Soirées* for comment. As a journalist and friend of Lamartine, Vignet would have been the logical family member for the task, but for whatever reasons, perhaps because he died relatively young in 1837, Vignet never published anything about his uncle.

The first published account of the life of our author was by a native of Chambéry, a physician and scholar who had known Maistre personally. But George Marie Raymond's "Eloge historique de S. Excellence le comte J. de Maistre" appeared in the austere pages of a learned journal of very restricted circulation.[43] As laudatory as the genre prescribed, Raymond's address, which was delivered on 3 January 1822 to the late Count de Maistre's colleagues of the royal academy of science in Turin, did reveal a few details that could only have come from personal conversation with the subject or members of his family – such as Maistre's living accommodations as a refugee in Venice, his sessions with the learned Lithuanian professor of oriental languages in Cagliari, and his donation of some 200 remaining volumes of his pre-revolutionary library to the Chambéry public library. But Raymond's tribute to Maistre's personal character and scholarly achievements could do little more than review the public highlights of his judicial and diplomatic careers.

Apart from his own works and letters, Maistre's image in nineteenth-century France probably owes more to Saint-Beuve than to anyone else. A self-proclaimed sceptic, the great literary critic was repelled by most of Maistre's doctrines, disliked his aristocratic attitudes, and was angered by his cavalier treatment of Pascal and the Jansenists of Port-Royal, but he was nevertheless fascinated, seduced even, by the Savoyard's literary talents.[44] Saint-Beuve acknowledged that he suffered "involuntarily to see a man who speaks such a beautiful French express sentiments that are so little ours,"[45] but admitted that what "Maistre has is his marvellous language; with all its rigidity and brittle tones, it is incomparable, and we inevitably surrender to it each time we hear it or read it."[46]

Although Saint-Beuve returned to the topic to comment on the editions of letters and unedited works published in 1851 and 1860, his essential article on Joseph de Maistre was the literary portrait he published in the *Revue des Deux Mondes* in 1843. He utilized Raymond's "Eloge," calling it "the most exact notice that has yet been written on the life that concerns us,"[47] but also consulted people who had known Maistre personally. "They have told me" is the locution Saint-Beuve used to introduce a number of his stories about his subject, including a delightful tale about Joseph's prodigious memory as a schoolboy, an anecdote about the young Maistre and some of his friends meeting the Abbé Raynal at Aix-les-bains, and Maistre's promise to Madame Huber never to use his pen to attack her cousin, Jacques Necker.[48] Saint-Beuve named only one of his oral sources,[49] but his informants may have included members of the Maistre family since his article revealed such intimate details as the anecdote about young Joseph and his mother on the occasion of the expulsion of the Jesuits from France, the fact that Maistre had worked on his famous portrait of Voltaire during the last six weeks of his life, and the information that Maistre had written "*Plato putrefactus*" on the title page of his copy of Kant.[50] Saint-Beuve mentioned too his own personal relations with "the respectable and modest scholar" (De Place) who had "tempered" many things in Maistre's "terrible" *Du Pape*.[51] Although he knew, or at least wrote nothing, about such matters as Maistre's career as a Freemason, his difficulties as Regent in Sardinia, or the reasons for his recall from Russia, Saint-Beuve was able to enliven his account with enough personal details to give life to his portrait. He sensed the person behind the author, citing one of Maistre's relatives or friends to the effect that the "most beautiful part of his life is the part that is hidden and about which nothing is said."[52]

As a literary critic, Saint-Beuve devoted most of his attention to an appreciation of Maistre's writings. He knew the early *Eloge de Victor-Amédée III* and the "discourse on virtue" Maistre had delivered to the Senate in 1777. He also mentioned the counter-revolutionary pamphlets Maistre wrote in Lausanne, but admitted that he had been able to find only the fourth of the "Savoyard letters." He understood the importance of the "Discours à Mme Costa," citing the key passage about the Revolution being an "epoch" and not an "event" with the comment that all "the work, the philosophical and theosophic work of De Maistre was going to come from this: this was the first moment when one saw it sprout."[53] Saint-Beuve also recognized Maistre's *Considérations sur la France* as "the cornerstone of all that he later tried to build."[54] Although he disagreed with Maistre's thesis on papal authority, he acknowledged that "after him one will never write on the papacy as it was permitted to write before."[55] As for *De l'Eglise gallicane*, Saint-Beuve declined to comment in his literary portrait, saying only that he was going to refute Maistre's chapter on Port-Royal in his own book on the subject.[56] Maistre's "most beautiful, most durable book," in the great critic's judgment, was *Les Soirées de Saint-Pétersbourg*.[57] He found Maistre's style in that work "firm, elevated, simple ... one of the great styles of the time."[58]

Saint-Beuve was able to contrast the author with the private man by including a number of citations from Maistre's letters, shown him by their recipients.[59] These included letters Maistre had written from St Petersburg in the years from 1812 to 1814 (put at his disposal by the "precious benevolence" of the addressee, Countess d'Edling – not named),[60] the letter in which Maistre had told the Chevalier d'Orly (not named) in 1818 that under the Restoration the Revolution was more terrible than in Robespierre's time,[61] and the letter to Marcellus (also not named) in which Maistre had written of "dying with Europe."[62] Saint-Beuve also quoted from a letter from an unidentified correspondent who had observed and described Maistre's final illness.[63]

The literary portrait concluded with remarks that were both a compliment to Joseph de Maistre and a sharp rejoinder to many who claimed to be his disciples:

M. de Maistre appears to me, of all writers, the least made for the servile disciple who would take him literally: he misleads him. But he is especially for the intelligent and sincere adversary: he provokes him, he straightens him out ... the disciple who attachs himself to Maistre's very terms and follows him to the letter is *stupid* ... But let us quickly quit this unfortunate and perfectly unworthy following of such a noble and great subject; let us remain in the presence of his lofty, integral, and venerable figure ... most particularly let us apply to him in full certitude the beautiful phrase Saint Cyran used about St Bernard: "This is *a true Christian gentleman.*"[64]

Since some of Saint-Beuve's later comments on Maistre would be much less generous, this conclusion is the characterization worth remembering.

There were some minor factual errors in Sainte-Beuve's account, and one could dispute some of his judgments, such as his contention that "for the most part, M. de Maistre's writings were, in effect, composed in solitude, without a public, as by an ardent animated thinker talking to himself ... who almost never was warned, who almost never encountered anyone in conversation who said to him *Hallo!*"[65] Maistre had, after all, sought readers for his manuscripts, and taken their comments very seriously. Still, despite the hostility to what Maistre stood for, Saint-Beuve had revealed something of the human being as well as the author, had shown that Maistre had a "youth," that he had been hostile to absolutism before the Revolution, and that his Catholicism was a deeply held and lived belief. His article confirmed Maistre's status as a master of French prose, but also popularized the view that Maistre was best understood as a brilliant spokesman for an outworn cause. The magic of Saint-Beuve's own literary style ensured that his portrait of Joseph de Maistre became so well known and so often cited that even today it is hard to see the Savoyard except through his eyes.

The magic of style also gave verisimilitude to Lamartine's pen portraits of Joseph de Maistre. The first occurs in *Confidences,* a novelistic version of Lamartine's own early life, which appeared in *La Presse* in 1849 before being published as a book the same year. Here, in the course of writing of his friendship with Louis Vignet, Lamartine recounted a visit to Chambéry and the Maistre family in 1815 (at a time when Joseph was still in Russia). After painting a charming picture of the family's life at the Château de Bissy, Lamartine went on to offer what purported to be an intimate description of the most famous Maistre brother:

It was on another occasion that I knew there Count Joseph de Maistre, the eldest of all these brothers, the Levi of this tribe. I heard from his mouth the reading of his *Soirées de Saint-Pétersbourg* before their publication. Friends and enemies of his philosophy know equally little of the man beneath the writer.

The Count de Maistre was a man of great height, a handsome and male military figure, with a high and open forehead where there floated, like the debris of a crown, some beautiful locks of silver hair. His eye was lively, pure, frank. His mouth had the habitual expression of subtle pleasantry that characterized all the family; he had in his attitude the dignity of his rank, his thought, and his age. It would have been impossible to see him without halting and without suspecting that one was before something great.

Young when he came down from his mountains, he had first lived in Turin, then commotions had flung him to Sardinia, then Russia, without ever passing through France, England, or Germany. He had been removed from his usual surroundings from his youth. He knew nothing except through books, and he read very few of those. Thus the marvellous eccentricity of his style. This was a raw soul, but a great soul; a poorly disciplined intelligence, but a vast intelligence; a rude style, but a strong style. Abandoned thus to himself, all his philosophy was only the theory of his religious instincts. The holy passions of his mind became his state of faith. He made dogmas of his biases. That was all his philosophy. The writer in him was much superior to the thinker, but the man was as superior to the writer as the latter to the thinker. His faith, which he too often gave the vestment of sophism and the attitude of reason-defying paradox, was sincere, sublime, and fecund in his life. This was an antique virtue, or rather a rude virtue with the great features of the Old Testament, like Michelangelo's Moses whose members still bear the imprint of the chisel that formed them. Thus the genius was only roughed out, but it had great proportions. This is why M. de Maistre is popular. More harmonious and more perfect, he would be less pleasing to the crowd, which never looks closely. This is an alpine Bossuet.[66]

Given what is now known of Maistre's life and work, Lamartine's portrait must be characterized as caricature.

How and why Lamartine was led to pen such an inaccurate likeness of Joseph de Maistre is a long story.[67] The ideological bias is obvious, but the essential fact is that Lamartine had never had the opportunity to get to know Maistre personally, since he met the Savoyard only once, briefly (for a day in company with all Maistre's relatives), when Maistre had visited Chambéry on his return journey from Russia in 1817. Maistre himself remembered meeting Lamartine for only a moment.[68] There most certainly would never have been the opportunity to hear the author read his *Soirées*. It is thus perhaps not surprising that Lamartine managed to make so many factual errors, beginning with his description of Maistre as being of great height – we know from one of his passports that he was only five foot six (165 cm).[69] As to the nature of Maistre's doctrines and compositions, one has the feeling that all Lamartine did was parody Saint-Beuve's characterizations.

When Lamartine came to treat Joseph de Maistre in his *Cours familier de littérature* (Volume vii) in 1859, he had much more to work with, since by this time Rodolphe de Maistre had published the first important collection of his father's letters and a biographical notice, and Albert Blanc had published the first volume of Maistre's diplomatic correspondence. What Lamartine did with this new material was produce an imaginative elaboration of his first portrait. Although he corrected some of his factual errors, he continued the fiction of personal acquaintance with his subject by describing long walks in which Maistre had supposedly chatted with him at length about his experiences in Sardinia and Russia and recited his favourite poetry. He also invented a spurious anecdote about Maistre's attendance at his own wedding in which Maistre is portrayed as employing an ingenious stratagem to avoid signing the marriage contract in public in circumstances inappropriate to his status as a minister of state – and thus displaying his vanity.[70] In short, Lamartine's second treatment of Maistre is no more trustworthy than the first. Unfortunately, his bad coin has long been accepted at face value.[71]

When Rodolphe de Maistre came to write his "biographical notice" about his famous father, he had the immense advantage of possession of Joseph de Maistre's personal papers.[72] But if Rodolphe approached his task without the vanity and ideological bias that distorted Lamartine's picture, he was not without his own presuppositions. When Louis Veuillot had raised the possibility of himself writing a biography of Joseph de Maistre, Rodolphe had discouraged the idea, and in doing so revealed his own attitude by the way he characterized the essential points to be kept in mind: "A wise and studious youth followed by a long exile devoted entirely to the service of an unfortunate prince, some interesting but in no way dramatic episodes, some important affairs in which my father had been involved secretly, others less grave but which saturated with bitterness the last years of his life and over which we must extend a respectful veil."[73] In the event, it was Rodolphe himself and not Veuillot who prepared the notice that prefaced the 1851 edition of Maistre's letters and unedited works, and it appears that he followed his own advice.

Rodolphe's short article (some thirty-eight pages) reflected his filial piety, but nevertheless provided many personal details about his father's life that had not been revealed before. Despite errors (such as the astonishing one of advancing his father's birthdate by a year to 1754), Rodolphe's own memories and frequent citations from his father's letters enabled him to produce an interesting and attractive portrait. He disclosed that his father had been a Freemason (but characterized Maistre's lodge as "a perfectly insignificant simple white lodge"),[74] that he had been so moderate in his political views in the early days of the Revolution that he had been suspected of Jacobinism, and that he had been a life-long opponent of Austria's Italian ambitions. He revealed as well that his father had had enemies at court who had been ready to use his health problems, his "sleep attacks," against him. Rodolphe's narration of some of the more controversial episodes in his father's life – such as his tenure as Regent in Sardinia, his attempt to secure an interview with Napoleon, and the proselytizing activities that led to his recall from St Petersburg – placed his actions in the most favourable light possible. In short, if Rodolphe revealed much that had been unknown, he did it in a way designed to enhance his father's reputation as a loyal monarchist, able magistrate and diplomat, courageous Catholic apologist, and tender and loving spouse and father.

Rodolphe also took pains to contrast the rigid principles of the author with the tolerance of the private man:

Count de Maistre, inflexible in his principles, was, in social relations, gracious, easy, and immensely tolerant: he listened calmly to opinions most opposed to his own, and combatted them with composure and courtesy and without the least bitterness ... He was pleased to estimate men by their commendable side ...

Count de Maistre was easy to approach, sprightly in conversation, constant in his conduct as in his principles, a stranger to any kind of artifice, firm in the expression of his opinions; he remained distrustful of himself, docile to criticism, without any other ambition than that of an irreproachable accomplishment of all his duties.[75]

One suspects, of course, that some of these remarks were intended to refute the characterizations of Saint-Beuve and Lamartine.

Rodolphe concluded his biographical notice with an explanation of his motives in publishing his father's letters. He cited first "the utility they might possess in virtue of the truths they defended and the sane doctrines they contained," and second, "the desire to trace a living and animated portrait of Count de Maistre to make him loved by those who only admired him."[76] The letters, Rodolphe thought, would constitute "a simple and noble monument to the memory of a venerated father."[77] The biographical notice and the release of a substantial number of Joseph de Maistre's letters was an important contribution to a better understanding of the author's person and thinking, but it was another generation before the family began allowing carefully selected scholars very limited access to Maistre's personal papers.

In 1868, a Jesuit of Russian origin, Father J. Gagarine, was allowed to edit and publish some "Russian anecdotes" that Joseph de Maistre had entered in a manuscript volume.[78] Gagarine was aware that Maistre's notebooks were still "conserved by his family with religious respect,"[79] but there is no reason to believe that he had the opportunity to consult them.

In 1882, Amédée de Margerie, a professor of philosophy and the dean of the Catholic faculty of letters at Lille, published a substantial study of Joseph de Maistre that gave the appearance of being based on work in the family archives.[80] In a note introducing his first unpublished document, a Latin inscription young Joseph de Maistre had composed in his mother's memory in 1774, Margerie made a point of thanking Joseph's grandson: "I owe it, as well as the other unpublished documents that will give this study its principal merit, to the extreme kindness of Count Charles de Maistre."[81] But the fact of the matter is that the other documents cited by Margerie (with the exception of an exchange of Latin letters with Father Brzozowski, the Jesuit superior in Russia, and a couple of letters Constance had written in 1821) had either appeared in the 1851 *Lettres et opuscules inédites* or would appear in the 1884 *Oeuvres complètes*. Margerie describes seeing Maistre's notebooks, but his comment made it clear that he had not been allowed to use them systematically: "I have had under my eyes and with a pious respect thumbed through these volumes which are large folio registers, polyglot registers where he deposited the essence of his immense Greek, Latin, French, Italian, English, and German reading. Theology, philosophy, history, politics, literature, linguistics, and the sciences are all represented there."[82]

The suspicion that Margerie was entirely dependent on what Charles de Maistre chose to give him is confirmed by a letter in which Margerie requested the assistance of the latter in finding manuscript materials that could help refute a recently published suggestion that many of Joseph de Maistre's ideas had been borrowed from the "unknown philosopher," Saint-Martin.[83] Margerie's refutation of this "accusation," which he added as an appendix to his book, cites only published materials.[84]

Despite its title and pretentions, Margerie's work revealed practically no details on Maistre's life that had not already been covered by Rodolphe's biographical notice or could not have been gleaned from the published correspondence.[85] Moreover, despite his academic credentials, Margerie was quite frank in presenting his work as ammunition for the cause of royalism and ultramontane Catholicism:

[Joseph de Maistre] represented, at the beginning of our century, a new manifestation of the spirit that in the Middle Ages produced chivalry and the crusades, and which, today, under the control and with the blessing of the Holy See and the episcopate, fights for their mother [ie, the Church] in the fields of science, philosophy, history, and social and political questions. To tell the truth, our Catholic universities have no goal more precious than to form and enlarge this army of the modern crusade. The honour I have of belonging to one of them perhaps gives me a particular reason for occupying myself with this great soldier, who in his time fought almost alone for the cause they defend, and who, if he returned to the world, would be their foremost captain.[86]

Much of Margerie's book was given over to defending Joseph de Maistre against the likes of Lamartine and various liberal critics who were doing their best to make Maistre's name a byword for obscurantism and blind reaction, and to demonstrating how astute Maistre had been in condemning the Revolution and predicting the inevitable outcome of attempts to implement its principles. Contemporary political, ideological, and religious divisions were too deep and bitter to allow the luxury of objective scholarship, or so it seemed.

The publication of the "complete edition" of Joseph de Maistre's works in the mid-1880s reinforced the stream of articles, book-length studies, and biographies that continues to this day. But for a long time these studies had to be based almost exclusively on already published materials since little more was released by the family. There were, it is true, a couple of things that saw the light in the 1890s. In 1895, Clément de Paillette published the two unfinished memoirs on the French parlements that Maistre had written in 1788, noting that he owed them to a communication from the author's grandson.[87] Paillette had seen Maistre's famous notebooks, but apparently was not allowed to study them in any meaningful way, and in reporting his brief examination cast doubt on their usefulness: "Perhaps there would be something to collect in this quantity of notes. An unfortunately too rapid reading did not permit us to inform ourselves on this point as we would have liked. However, we doubt that they could throw light on the thought of our author: all their substance passed into his works."[88] Later in the 1890s, Father Dominique de Maistre, Joseph's great-grandson, published his ancestor's response to the Vatican theologian who had written a report on *Du Pape*.[89] But for the most part scholars looking for new materials on Joseph de Maistre had to look elsewhere.

One who did look to other archival resources with great success was François Descostes, who published important studies on *Joseph de Maistre avant la Révolution* (Paris 1893) and *Joseph de Maistre pendant la Révolution* (Tours 1895). Descostes based his work on research in the state archives in Turin, parish and municipal archives, the archives of the Senate of Savoy, and the private archives of Maistre's friends and relatives.[90] Descostes also had access to Maistre's diary, which he called the *Journal intime*, and indicated the Maistre family archives as the source of the document. We now know, however, that this diary was one of the relatively few Maistre documents that remained at the Castello di Borgo (the estate near Turin acquired by the husband of Constance de Maistre, the Duke Eugène de Montmorency-Laval) after the bulk of his papers had been moved to the Château de Beaumesnil in Normandy (an estate Rodolphe inherited from Constance's husband). Descostes corresponded with Charles de Maistre, who then controlled the Beaumesnil archives, and learned some details about a portrait of Joseph de Maistre done in St Petersburg by the German artist, Vogel von Vogelstein,[91] but it is evident he had no success in gaining access to this most important collection of Maistre papers.

It was only in the 1920s, the centennial decade of the death of Joseph de Maistre, that this archival collection (by then moved to the Château de Saint-Martin-du-Mesnil-Oury, also in Normandy) was cautiously opened to certain scholars who were allowed to use selected materials for specialized studies. Georges Goyau consulted Maistre's notebooks and a dossier labeled *"Illuminées"* for his study of Maistre's religious thought,[92] Emile Dermenghem used the same materials to study Maistre's relationship to Martinism, illuminism, and Masonry,[93] and Canon J.M. Montmasson found the notebooks helpful for his work on Maistre's providentialism.[94] It was in this same decade as well that Count Xavier de Maistre published Joseph de Maistre's diary.[95]

When Robert Triomphe undertook his massive doctoral study in the years following World War II, he was initially allowed to see some of the material in the family archives,[96] but the family soon concluded that he was "dogmatic" and "unobjective," and denied him further access.[97] It is only since the formation of the Institut des études maistriennes in 1976 that qualified scholars have been able to consult these materials in a really systematic way. The result has been a new era in Maistrian scholarship with the establishment of a review and the undertaking of a new critical edition of Maistre's works.

The present study is the first full biography to benefit from this change in family policy. With the advantage of access to the family archives and to the work of other members of the Institut it has been possible to present a detailed account of Maistre's intellectual life, his relationship to his milieu, and his interaction with the momentous events of the Revolutionary and Napoleonic epoch. It is to be hoped that we can now look forward to better informed and more judicious studies of the thought and influence of this powerful and seminal writer.

Notes

ABBREVIATIONS

Most titles of books and articles have been cited in shortened form following
the first citation. Full titles appear in the bibliography at the end of the volume.
The following abbreviations have been used in the notes:

AS	Archivio di Stato (Turin)
BN, MSS, n.a.f.	Bibliothèque Nationale, Département des Manuscrits, Fonds Nouvelles Acquisitions Françaises
M.f.a.	Maistre family archives
OC	*Oeuvres complètes de Joseph de Maistre*
REM	*Revue des études maistriennes*

INTRODUCTION

1 It was his belief that good French style required his name to be used in this
form when not preceded by first name or title: "Will you permit me, Monsieur,
to have a small grammatical quarrel with you? The particle *de*, in French,
cannot be joined to a proper name beginning with a consonant unless it follows
a title. Thus, you can very well say, 'The Viscount de Bonald said,' but not
'De Bonald said'; one must say, 'Bonald said,' and yet one says, 'D'Alembert
said.' Grammar orders it so." Maistre to M. de Syon, 14 November 1820.
Oeuvres complètes de J. de Maistre (Lyon 1884–6; hereafter cited as *OC*),
14:243.

2 For a good review of English-language literature on Maistre, see E.D. Watt,
"The English Image of Joseph de Maistre," *European Studies Review*, 4
(1974): 239–59. Since the date of Watt's article, Charles M. Lombard's *Joseph
de Maistre* (New York 1976), a volume in Twayne's World Authors series, has
helped fill the gap. While quite useful as an introduction, this is a brief

treatment based entirely on printed sources and concerned primarily with Maistre's place in literary history. Lombard concludes with the observation that "Joseph de Maistre is in need not only of reevaluation but of rediscovery" (p 129).

3 *Joseph de Maistre: étude sur la vie et sur la doctrine d'un matérialiste mystique* (Geneva 1968). Triomphe completed his work as a doctoral thesis in 1955, but it was not published until 1968.

4 Jean Nicolas, *La Savoie au 18e siècle: noblesse et bourgeoisie* (Paris 1978).

5 Systematically in *Throne and Altar: The Political and Religious Thought of Joseph de Maistre* (Ottawa 1965), and on particular aspects of his thought in articles and papers cited in this book.

6 I am in complete agreement with the view of my colleague, Jean-Louis Darcel: "The work of the historian rightly consists in extricating the foundations of a work, especially if they seem hidden from the sight of the reader. If Maistre has often been the victim of inexact or simplified interpretations it is perhaps because insufficient care has been taken in following closely – that is to say starting from the texts – the evolution of the man, the politician, and the philosopher in contact with the unheard-of events with which the Chamberian senator found himself brutally confronted when the duchy of Savoy entered in its turn into the era of revolutionary upheavals." "Cinquième lettre d'un Royaliste Savoisien à ses compatriotes," *Revue des études maistriennes* (hereafter cited as *REM*), no. 4 (1978): 9–10.

7 "I know by numerous experiences that I am *dystraduisable* (as it is elegantly said in Greek). *Difficult to translate*, not only because of a style that is altogether French, but because of frequent allusions and citations that my memory is always recalling." Maistre to Rodolphe de Maistre, 22 September 1819. Maistre family archives (hereafter cited as M.f.a.).

8 *Les Grands Ecrivains français; XIXe siècle: philosophes et essayistes* (Paris 1930), 119.

CHAPTER ONE: SAVOYARD ROOTS

1 The particle "de" was not added to the family name until the time of Joseph's residence in Russia.

2 See Robert Triomphe, *Joseph de Maistre*, 36–8, for a full discussion of this "legend." Triomphe provides a critical discussion of a work by Aristide Donnadieu, *Les Origines languedociennes de Joseph de Maistre* (Chambéry 1942), which tried to make the case for noble French ancestry. The closest that Donnadieu came to documentary evidence was an act, dated 21 September 1815, in which Joseph de Maistre declared that there was a public tradition that his family was descended from a Jean de Maistre "established in the states of the king of Sardinia since the beginning of the seventeenth century" and "that Jean claimed to be a son of Louis [de Maistre] and a native of Languedoc"

(document cited from Donnadieu by Triomphe). The Maistre family archives contain a document labelled "Traduction de la Déclaration Judicaire de cinq Gentilhommes de Nice sur la Maison Maistre," dated 10 February 1787, which attests to this same public tradition.

3 Again, see Triomphe, *Joseph de Maistre*, 39 n19, for details from the study by Georges Doublet, "Gli antenati Nizzardi del Savoiardo Giuseppi De Maistre," *Bollettino dell'Associazioni fra Oriundi Savoiardi e Nizzardi Italiani*, no. 17, December 1928. Jean Rebotton believes that Doublet presents the best evidence, but acknowledges that obscurities remain. Rebotton was unable to find any documents in the archives in Turin that might shed light on the origins of the family. This seems unusual because ordinarily the king, before granting hereditary nobility as he did to François-Xavier Maistre, would have ordered an inquiry into the family's origins. *Etudes maistriennes: nouveau aperçus sur la famille de Maistre et sur les rapports de Joseph de Maistre avec Monsieur de Stedingk* (Aosta 1974), 8–10.

4 See Triomphe, *Joseph de Maistre*, 39 n18.

5 In fact, François-Xavier Maistre was the only Niçois Senator to be named to the Chambéry court in the eighteenth century. See Nicolas, *Savoie au 18e siècle*, 672–3.

6 The document is cited in François Descostes, *Joseph de Maistre avant la Révolution* (Paris 1893) 1:49–50.

7 Rebotton, *Etudes maistriennes*, 25, 427.

8 The letters patent are reproduced in Rebotton, *Etudes maistriennes*, 432–4.

9 Nicolas, *Savoie au 18e siècle*, 902–3 nn363, 364.

10 See Descostes, *Maistre avant la Révolution*, 1:69 n1, for their "marriage act."

11 Insofar as Joseph de Maistre's brothers and sisters played significant roles in his life, it seems worthwhile to record here the essential biographical information: Marie-Christine (1755–1837) married Pierre-Louis Vignet, also a Senator, in 1778. Their youngest son, Louis Vignet, was a close friend of Lamartine. Nicolas (1756–1837) served as an officer in the Piedmontese army. André (1757–1818) followed an ecclesiastical career. At the time of his death he had just been named Bishop of Aosta. Anne (1758–1822) married Count Alexis Vichard de Saint-Réal in 1796. Saint-Réal served as an intendant on the island of Sardinia for many years (including the years Joseph spent there as the island's chief magistrate). Marthe-Charlotte (1759–1826) entered the Ursuline convent in Chambéry as Sister Eulalie. Jeanne ("Jenny") (1762–1834) married the Chevalier Charles de Buttet, who served, until his death in 1797, as the Director of the Arsenal in Turin. Xavier (1763–1852), also a renowned author, began his career as an army officer. In 1799, in advance of Joseph's diplomatic assignment to St Petersburg, Xavier migrated to Russia, where he settled and married. Thérèse (1765–1832) married an army officer, the Chevalier Constantin de Moussy, in 1792. Victor-André (1771–1801) was a young army officer at the time of his premature death (Triomphe, *Joseph de Maistre*, 58

n95). There were at least two more babies who died in early infancy, one in 1754 and another in 1760. See Rebotton, *Etudes maistriennes*, 21 n55, and 49, 384.

12 See Rebotton, *Etudes maistriennes*, 15–20.

13 See Descostes, *Maistre avant la Révolution*, 1:126–7, for a moving description by a close family friend of the consternation of the president and his children.

14 Rodolphe de Maistre, "Notice biographique," in J. de Maistre, *OC*, 1:vii.

15 Ibid.

16 Maistre to Nicolas de Maistre, 14 February 1805. *OC*, 9:335.

17 Maistre to Adèle de Maistre, 1804. *OC*, 9:303. The reference is to Louis Racine the poet, not Jean Racine the playwright.

18 See, for example, *OC*, 4:163–4.

19 Descostes, *Maistre avant la Révolution*, 1:79.

20 Rebotton, *Etudes maistriennes*, 54.

21 The official title was the Confrérie de la Sainte-Croix et de la Miséricorde. Four times a year, completely covered with black hoods with only two eye-openings in the cowl, with large rosaries in their horsehair belts, the *pénitents noirs* marched barefoot through the town in the evening hours, singing psalms as they went. See Jean-Louis Darcel, "Des pénitents noirs à la franc-maçonnerie: Aux sources de la sensibilité maistrienne," *REM*, no. 5–6 (1980): 75–80.

22 "I was a *pénitent noir* in Chambéry ... My grandpapa gave me my book and my habit in 1768." Maistre to Abbé Rey, 20 February 1820. *OC*, 14:202.

23 See Jean-Louis Darcel, "Les Bibliothèques de Joseph de Maistre, 1768–1821," *REM*, no. 9 (1985): 11, for the text of the will. Darcel emphasizes the value and importance of the bequest.

24 "Notice biographique," *OC*, 1:vii.

25 This anecdote was passed on to Robert Triomphe by Joseph de Maistre's great-grandson, old Count Ignace de Maistre, who had heard it from Constance. Triomphe, *Joseph de Maistre*, 40 n26.

26 See Rebotton, *Etudes maistriennes*, 38, for an excellent photograph of this bust. From Joseph de Maistre's diary we learn that the bust was made by an artist in Turin, after a model done some time in the 1780s by Joseph's brother Xavier (who was an artist as well as an author), and that the bust was delivered to Joseph in July 1791, two years after his father's death. *Les Carnets du Comte Joseph de Maistre*, published by Count Xavier de Maistre (Lyon 1923), 6.

27 Rebotton reproduces 140 letters from François-Xavier Maistre (dating from 1749 to 1769) to magistrates serving in the Val d'Aosta, as well as official documents associated with the elder Maistre's career (*Etudes maistriennes*, 228–413). Using these documents as well as other bits of relevant evidence, Rebotton has produced the most detailed study to date of Joseph's father and of the relationship between the two. What follows is based on Rebotton's work.

28 "Discours sur le caractère extérieur du Magistrat," *OC*, 7:3–34.

29 Laurent Chevailler, *Essai sur le Souverain Sénat de Savoie, 1559–1793* (Annecy 1953), 127. Cited in Rebotton, *Etudes maistriennes*, 37.

30 Rebotton, *Etudes maistriennes*, 37.

31 Ibid., 37–40.

32 Maistre to Nicolas de Maistre, 14 February 1805. *OC*, 9:336.

33 Rebotton, *Etudes maistriennes*, 16–18, 41–3.

34 F.-X. Maistre's description of this incident is in a letter to Jacques Salteur, 23 July 1755. Rebotton, *Etudes maistriennes*, 325.

35 François-Xavier Maistre to Nicolas, 11 August 1774. M.f.a.

36 Maistre to Chevalier de Rossi, May 1808. *OC*, 11:109.

37 *"élevé dans toute la sévérité antique."* Maistre to Count de Marcellus, 13 March 1820. *OC*, 14:208.

38 Rebotton, *Etudes maistriennes*, 45.

39 Ibid., 54–5.

40 Maistre to Nicolas de Maistre, 18 August 1789. M.f.a.

41 "Extracts F," 297. M.f.a. A description of Maistre's notebooks is provided in the next section.

42 Xavier de Maistre, *Voyage autour de ma chambre*, Chapter 38, cited by Rebotton, *Etudes maistriennes*, 45.

43 Maistre to his sister, Thérèse Constantin, 7 May 1814. *OC*, 12:426. Similar expressions may be found in a number of his letters.

44 Maistre to Jeanne de Buttet, 10 August 1816. *OC*, 13:417.

45 Nicolas, *Savoie au 18e siècle*, 390.

46 "The Jesuits … were Joseph's educators." Descostes, *Maistre avant la Révolution*, 1:81.

47 Maistre to King Victor-Emmanuel, 12 November 1811. *OC*, 12:76.

48 Maistre to Count de Vallaise, 2 January 1816. *OC*, 13:204.

49 Maistre to Chevalier de Saint-Réal, September 1816. *OC*, l:vi.

50 "from his tenderest childhood he gave himself to his studies, with a marked taste, under the direction of the Jesuit Fathers." Rodolphe de Maistre, "Notice biographique." *OC*, 1:vi.

51 It may be significant that when the time came, Maistre engaged an ex-Jesuit as a tutor for his own son. See his letter to the Marquis de Barol, 13 April 1804, in Clément de Paillette, *La Politique de Joseph de Maistre d'après ses premiers écrits* (Paris 1895), 84.

52 Nicolas, *Savoie au 18e siècle*, 932–3, 952–3.

53 Jean Rebotton, "Nouveaux aperçus sur l'éducation et l'attitude religieuses du jeune Maistre," *REM*, no. 3 (1977): 8 n17, and Darcel, "Des Pénitents noirs," 82.

54 Darcel, "Des Pénitents noirs," 81–5.

55 In an unpublished letter to his daughter Adèle, dated Chambéry, 1 July 1820 (when he had returned to his native city for a visit), Maistre described

reminiscing with an old classmate from fifty-eight years before (which would take us back to about 1762, when Joseph would have been nine or ten). This old classmate (General de Boigne, who had made a fortune in India and who is memorialized with the "fountain of elephants" that still embellishes one of Chambéry's central intersections) had "verified the dates, the names of professors, and every imaginable circumstance, and he found that we had made all our studies together, a thing I had completely forgotten" (M.f.a.). René Johannet and François Vermale in the introduction to their edition of Maistre's *Considérations sur la France* (Paris 1936), xii n2, cite this letter as proof that Maistre attended the *collège royal*. But there is nothing in the letter to indicate if they were classmates at the Jesuit school or at the college.

56 Nicolas, *Savoie au 18e siècle*, 932–3. Maistre himself, in his *Eloge de Victor-Amédée III* of 1775, may have been registering his dissatisfaction when he spoke of "the education of youth, so neglected among us." Cited by Nicolas.

57 Nicolas, *Savoie au 18e siècle*, 933.

58 Bernard Secret, *Joseph de Maistre, Substitut et Sénateur* (Chambéry 1927), 7.

59 Descostes, *Maistre avant la Révolution*, 1:113–15. Curiously enough, one of the two theses that Maistre presented for his *licence* dealt with the relationship between the civil power and papal authority. See Descostes for the Latin titles of the theses.

60 "Notice biographique," *OC*, 1:vii.

61 "Extraits F," 357–9, and "Extraits G," 15.

62 "Extracts F," 89, 137.

63 C.J. Gignoux, *Joseph de Maistre; Prophète du passé, historien de l'avenir* (Paris 1963), 22.

64 Rebotton, "Nouveaux aperçus," 9.

65 Descostes, *Maistre avant la Révolution*, 2:288.

66 F.-X. Maistre to a high official in the justice ministry or to the minister himself. AS Lettre particolari, Mazzo 9, cited by Rebotton, "Nouveaux aperçus," 9.

67 Rebotton, "Nouveaux aperçus," 11. Rebotton reproduces passages from both sorts of documents.

68 "Cinq Lettres sur l'éducation publique en Russie," *OC*, 8:190–2.

69 Cited by Rebotton, "Nouveaux aperçus," 11.

70 In an *Apologie générale de l'Institut et de la doctrine des Jésuites* (1763), cited by Rebotton, "Nouveaux aperçus," 11.

71 Rebotton, "Nouveaux aperçus," 11–12, citing a study by Marc Perroud, *Le Jansénisme en Savoie* (Chambéry 1945).

72 Perroud, cited by Rebotton, "Nouveaux aperçus," 11–12.

73 Darcel, "Des Pénitents noirs," 89–90, citing the work of Philippe Ariès, *L'Homme devant la mort* (Paris 1977), 296–7.

74 See Darcel, "Des Pénitents noirs," 75–80.

75 *Joseph de Maistre*, 67–82.

76 Rebotton, "Nouveaux aperçus," 5–23, and Jean-Louis Soltner, "Le christianisme de Joseph de Maistre," *REM*, no. 5–6 (1980): 99–100.

77 "Des Pénitents noirs," 92–4.

78 A detailed description and analysis may be found in Richard Lebrun, "Les Lectures de Joseph de Maistre d'après les registres inédits," *REM*, no. 9 (1985): 126–94.

79 *OC*, 4:118–19.

80 "Extracts F," 111.

81 Ibid.

82 "Extracts F," 297. The cross-reference to the first entry clearly links the two together.

83 Ibid.

84 "Des Pénitents noirs," 93.

85 Ibid., 92–3.

86 See Philippe Ariès, *L'Homme devant la mort*, and John McManners, *Death and Enlightenment: Changing Attitudes to Death among Christians and Unbelievers in Eighteenth-Century France* (Oxford 1981)

87 "Extracts F," 137. Deletions (words, phrases, and sentences rendered completely illegible) have been indicated because it appears that Maistre at some later date exercised a kind of self-censorship. There are numerous cases of such deletions in the notebook materials dating from the 1770s. Evidence of such self-censorship suggests that the young Maistre may have been even more "liberal" than the surviving passages would indicate.

88 Peter Gay, *The Enlightenment: An Interpretation. The Rise of Modern Paganism* (London 1967), 104.

89 See, for example, *OC*, 4:108.

90 "Extracts F," 456–8.

91 Ibid., 87–92.

92 *OC*, 1:236.

93 "Extracts F," 209.

94 "Extracts F," 117.

95 *OC*, 4:14.

96 "Extracts F," 174.

97 Ibid., 304.

98 Ibid., 314–15.

99 "All things considered, when one compares what he was in his youth with what he will proclaim when he becomes a writer, nothing is so definitively striking, with some minor qualifications, as the continuity of his attitudes, his endeavours, and his faith." Rebotton, "Nouveaux aperçus," 23.

100 "Extraits F," 183.

101 Nicolas, *Savoie au 18e siècle*, 81.

102 Cited in Rebotton, *Etudes maistriennes*, 56–7.

103 Secret, *Maistre, Substitut*, 14.

104 Cited in Rebotton, *Etudes maistriennes*, 57.

105 Ibid., 57–8.

106 Triomphe, *Joseph de Maistre*, 84–5, and Rebotton, *Etudes maistriennes*, 58–60.

107 See Albert Blanc, *Mémoires politiques et correspondance diplomatique de J. de Maistre* (Paris 1858), 14, and François Vermale, *Joseph de Maistre émigré* (Chambéry 1927), 12.

108 Nicolas, *Savoie au 18e siècle*, 612.

109 *Joseph de Maistre*, 87.

110 Secret, *Maistre, Substitut* reproduces some 30 of Maistre's official letters to the secretary of state for internal affairs. The letter on hospital administration is dated 3 February 1790 (pp 24–5).

111 Ibid., 7–8.

112 Nicolas' study, *Savoie au 18e siècle*, provides a remarkably full and well-documented economic, social, institutional, and intellectual portrait of Savoy in the eighteenth century. What follows is based almost exclusively on his work.

113 Ibid., 11.

114 Ibid., 16.

115 Ibid., 45.

116 Ibid., 138.

117 Ibid., 154–6.

118 Ibid., 201–2.

119 Ibid., 220–1.

120 Ibid., 248–9.

121 Ibid., 250.

122 Stuart Woolf, *A History of Italy 1700–1860: The Social Constraints of Political Change* (London 1979), 66–7.

123 Gignoux, *Joseph de Maistre*, 15.

124 Maistre to Count de Blacas, 14 April 1813. Cited in Ernest Daudet, *Joseph de Maistre et Blacas* (Paris 1908), 243.

125 *Savoie au 18e siècle*, 120.

126 Ibid.

127 Ibid.

128 Ibid., 539.

129 On this remarkable ruler and his achievements, see the new biography by Geoffrey Symcox, *Victor Amadeus II: Absolutism in the Savoyard State, 1675–1730* (London 1983).

130 *History of Italy*, 67.

131 Ibid.

132 Ibid.

133 Nicolas, *Savoie au 18e siècle*, 594.

134 Ibid.

135 Ibid., 595–6.

136 *History of Italy*, 68.
137 Ibid., 110.
138 See Nicolas, *Savoie au 18e siècle*, 641–8.
139 Woolf, *History of Italy*, 68.
140 Ibid., 69.
141 Ibid., 121.
142 Nicolas, *Savoie au 18e siècle*, 642–6.
143 Ibid., 947, 979.
144 Ibid., 1036.
145 P. 39. This eulogy was published privately; whether or not it was ever delivered or brought to the king's attention is unknown. See Triomphe, *Joseph de Maistre*, 92.
146 Symcox, *Victor Amadeus II*, 223–4.
147 *Savoie au 18e siècle*, 1026.
148 Ibid.
149 Conclusions of a judgment dated 28 July 1784. Cited by Nicolas, *Savoie au 18e siècle*, 1028.
150 *Carnets*, 26, entry for 27 March 1791. Unfortunately, the report does not appear to have survived.
151 Ibid., 5, and Maistre's letter of 19 October 1791 to the Secretary of State, in Secret, *Maistre, Substitut*, 36–7.
152 *Savoie au 18e siècle*, 783.
153 Ibid., 850–1.
154 Ibid., 915.
155 Nicolas has traced this salary history through President Maistre's correspondence with the government in Turin. *Savoie au 18e siècle*, 612–13.
156 Unpublished document from the Maistre family archives, cited by Descostes, *Maistre avant la Révolution*, 2:250 n1.
157 But of this amount Joseph received only 3,000 livres immediately; an amount of 6,000 livres was to be paid to creditors of Joseph and his father, 10,000 would be paid on his mother-in-law's death, and 3,000 on the death of his wife's aunt. Nicolas, *Savoie au 18e siècle*, 799, citing notarial records.

CHAPTER TWO: ADVENTURES OF THE
MIND

1 *OC*, 4:11.
2 Eugène Burnier, *Histoire du Sénat de Savoie* (Chambéry 1864), 2:334, identifies the two as Gaspar Millo de Casagiate and Théophile Langasco. Nicolas, *Savoie au 18e siècle*, 673, establishes their origin.
3 "Extraits G," 213–14.
4 Darcel, "Bibliothèques de J. de Maistre," 81, 95.
5 "Extraits F," 183.

6   Thomas Berry, *Grammaire générale de la langue angloise* (Paris 1746). This book was in Maistre's library. See Darcel, "Bibliothèques de J. de Maistre," 59.

7   "Extraits F," 213–14.

8   Ibid., 228–9.

9   Lebrun, "Lectures de J. de Maistre," 143.

10 Darcel, "Bibliothèques de J. de Maistre," 43–101.

11 Lebrun, "Lectures de J. de Maistre," 143.

12 Classical historians read in these years included Plutarch, Tacitus, Livy, and St Augustine. Roman "antiquities" were represented by Johann Rossfeld, *Antiquitatem romanorum corpus absolutissum* (Geneva 1632). In medieval and modern history the titles included Enquerrant de Monstrelet's *Chroniques*, Charles-F.-F. Hénault's *Nouvel abrégé chronologigue de l'histoire de France* (Paris 1751), Carlo Denina's *Révolutions d'Italie* (Paris 1771–5), Viscount Henry St. John Bolinbroke's *Letters on the Study and Use of History* (Paris 1788), and Robert Henry's *History of Great Britain* (London 1781). Ecclesiastical history was represented by the works of Paolo Sarpi and by Claude Fleury's massive *Histoire ecclésiastique* (Paris 1691–1738, 36 volumes). Citations from Cornelius de Pauw's *Recherches philosophiques sur les Egyptiens et les Chinois* (Berlin 1773) signal Maistre's budding interest in oriental history and culture.

13 "Extraits G," 131.

14 Ibid., p. 120. The reference is to the work cited in note 12.

15 Ibid., 157.

16 Ibid., p. 312.

17 Ibid.

18 There is, however, no evidence that he perceived Sarpi as the secret atheist portrayed by David Wootton in his recent *Paola Sarpi: Between Renaissance and Enlightenment* (Cambridge 1983)

19 "Extraits G," 316.

20 "Extraits F," 18.

21 "Extraits G," 12.

22 Ibid., 14. The entry is dated 1774. There is a marginal comment dated 1811: "Youth."

23 Ibid., 216–17.

24 Ibid., 210. Maistre's enthusiasm for the American cause was also evident in his 1775 *Eloge de Victor-Amédée III.*

25 Ibid.

26 Ibid., 249.

27 Ibid., 322.

28 *OC*, 1:226–7.

29 "Extraits F," 175–81. An appended note dated 8 June 1812 reads: "This is what I was pleased to write in 1772. I knew nothing at all. Today I laugh at reading what I wrote then on the origins of poetry. This question has always

occupied me, and today I have the pleasure of knowing no more than I did then."

30 "Extraits G," 117.
31 "Extraits F.," 315–16.
32 Ibid., 75–6.
33 "Nouveaux aperçus," 16.
34 The reference is to Pierre *Charron's Les Trois Vérités contre Tous Athées, Idolâtres, Juifs, Mahumétans, Hérétiques et Schismatiques* (1593), a book we know Maistre possessed. See Darcel, "Bibliothèques de J. de Maistre," 73.
35 "Extraits G," 16–17.
36 Ibid.
37 "Extraits F," 313.
38 Darcel, "Bibliothèques de J. de Maistre," 26.
39 Lebrun, "Lectures de J. de Maistre," 142.
40 "Extraits G," 188. There is an added note dated 1807 that reads: "It is understood of course that I was one of the three."
41 A marginal note dated 1809 reads: "What nonsense."
42 Ibid., 149–50. Montesquieu used Correggio's famous line, "I too am a painter," as an epigraph for his *De l'Esprit des lois.*
43 Maistre to Baron de Rubat, 16 January 1785. Cited in François Descostes, *Necker, écrivain et financier, jugé par le Comte de Maistre* (Chambéry 1896), 12–13.
44 "Extraits G," 126.
45 *OC*, 1:72.
46 Ibid., 73 n1.
47 See Descostes, *Maistre avant la Révolution,* 1:218–29, and Jean Rebotton, *Ecrits maçonniques de Joseph de Maistre* (Geneva 1983) 14–22.
48 Triomphe, *Joseph de Maistre*, pp. 92–100, and Rebotton, *Ecrits maçonniques*, 19–22.
49 *Eloge*, 35.
50 Ibid., 37–8.
51 Ibid., 39–40.
52 Ibid., 50
53 Ibid., 61.
54 Ibid. 41.
55 Ibid., 42.
56 Ibid., 21.
57 Ibid., 53.
58 Ibid.
59 Ibid., 54–5.
60 Ibid., 51.
61 Ibid., 71. Curiously enough, Maistre and Panisset crossed paths again in Lausanne in 1796, when Maistre edited the latter's "retraction" for having accepted election as a constitutional bishop in French-occupied Savoy.

62 Descostes, *Maistre avant la Révolution*, 1:312.

63 Ibid., 2:38–52. The discourse is reproduced in François Descostes, *Joseph de Maistre orateur* (Chambéry 1896), 13–27.

64 *Maistre orateur*, 26–7.

65 Ibid., 14.

66 Ibid., 24.

67 Ibid., 14.

68 Descostes, *Maistre avant la Révolution*, 2:53–84, reproduces letters from Salteur and Maistre to Roze, as well as much of their seventeen-page commentary (in Maistre's hand) on Roze's draft. Maistre's letter is dated 11 November 1779.

69 Ibid., 73.

70 Ibid., 75.

71 Ibid., 101–23.

72 These fragments are reproduced in Descostes, *Maistre avant la Révolution*, 1:225–9. Unfortunately, Descostes gave no indication of his source. Jean Rebotton, who has gathered together practically all the surviving texts bearing on Maistre's Masonic career, was unable to locate the original of this letter. The archivist of Freemasons' Hall in London could find no trace of its existence. *Ecrits maçonniques*, 31–2.

73 Rebotton, *Ecrits maçonniques*, 15 n8.

74 Maistre to Vignet des Etoles, 9 December 1793. *OC*, 9:59.

75 In Maistre's own description, a "*société de plaisir.*" In his "Mémoire sur la Franc-Maçonnerie" (1793). *Ecrits maçonniques*, 125.

76 Pierre Chevallier, *Histoire de la Franc-Maçonnerie française* (Paris 1974), 111, cited in Rebotton, *Ecrits maçonniques*, 17.

77 See Nicolas, *Savoie au 18e siècle*, 1017–20. It was Daquin, more than any other person, who was responsible for establishing a public library in Chambéry; he also introduced smallpox vaccination to the city, and when Joseph de Maistre had his daughter, Adèle, vaccinated in May 1791, he entrusted the task to Daquin. *Carnets*, 3–4.

78 Clement XII in the bull *In Iminenti* (1738) and Benedict XIV in the bull *Providas* (1751). Rebotton, *Ecrits maçonniques*, 15 n7.

79 See Darcel, "Des Pénitents noirs," 69–95.

80 Rebotton, *Ecrits maçonniques*, 18.

81 René Le Forestier, *La Franc-Maçonnerie templière et occultiste* (Paris 1970), 22, published by Antoine Faivre.

82 "Mémoire sur la Franc-Maçonnerie," *Ecrits maçonniques*, 136.

83 Darcel identifies fifteen *congréganistes* in 1778. "Des Pénitents noirs," 86.

84 *Ecrits maçonniques*, 56.

85 Ibid., 57.

86 Ibid., 31.

87 Ibid., 20. Rebotton cites as evidence in support of this suggestion Maistre's comment, in a 1793 letter, that "England had never heard of" the Trois Mortiers. Ibid., 31–2.

88 See Rebotton, *Ecrits maçonniques*, 22–3, and Antoine Faivre, "Joseph de Maistre et l'illuminisme: rapports avec Willermoz," *REM*, no. 5–6 (1980), 125.

89 Willermoz to Charles de Hesse, 12 October 1781. Cited in Le Forestier, *La Franc-Maçonnerie*, 300.

90 Rebotton, *Ecrits maçonniques*, 23.

91 Le Forestier, *La Franc-Maçonnerie*, 300.

92 Ibid.

93 Faivre, "Maistre et Willermoz," 126.

94 Rebotton, *Ecrits maçonniques*, 24–5.

95 Rebotton, *Ecrits maçonniques*, 32, citing Alice Joly, *Un Mystique lyonnais (J.B. Willermoz) et les secrets de la Franc-Maçonnerie* (Mâcon 1938), 137.

96 Faivre, "Maistre et Willermoz," 126.

97 *OC*, 5:249.

98 These letters, dated 9 July 1779, 9 June 1780, and 3 December 1780, are among the documents reproduced in Rebotton, *Ecrits maçonniques*, 61–72.

99 By Antoine Faivre as an appendix to Le Forestier, *La Franc-Maçonnerie*, 1023–49.

100 This précis follows Rebotton, *Ecrits maçonniques*, 33–5.

101 "Instruction secrète," in Le Forestier, *La Franc-Maçonnerie*, 1026.

102 Ibid., 1049.

103 Ibid.

104 *Ecrits maçonniques*, 70, 73.

105 Ibid., 74. Rebotton points out that the dangers alluded to by Willermoz were of a political and religious nature. In claiming to be heirs of the Templars, Masons risked being accused of plotting against the monarch and the papacy – for it was Philip the Fair and Pope Clement v, who had destroyed the Templars. Ibid., n7.

106 See Faivre, "Maistre et Willermoz," 131–2, for a systematic analysis of their personal relations and a comparison of their psychological and doctrinal positions and views on Masonry generally.

107 See Rebotton, *Ecrits maçonniques*, 37–48, and Emile Dermenghem, *Joseph de Maistre mystique* (Paris 1946), 59–60, for more details on Brunswick and his attempts to bring order to the badly divided Stricte Observance Templière. This Duke of Brunswick was a nephew of the duke who was defeated at the Battle of Valmy in 1792.

108 Dermenghem, *Joseph de Maistre mystique*, 38.

109 "Mémoire au duc de Brunswick," *Ecrits maçonniques*, 80.

110 Georges Goyau, *La Pensée religieuse de Joseph de Maistre d'après des documents inédites* (Paris 1921), 50. Maistre's copy of the memoir was found

among his papers and first used by Goyau. The document was then published by Emile Dermenghem in 1925. It has now been republished in a critical edition by Jean Rebotton in *Ecrits maçonniques*, 77–120. Subsequent citations are from the latter edition.

111 Ibid., 82. Maistre's peremptory dismissal of the great Crusading order probably derives from reading Paolo Sarpi. Later, in *Du Pape*, Maistre wrote of the Crusades with unqualified approval.

112 Ibid., 83–4. Maistre cites Henry's *History of Great Britain* (London 1781) from newspaper excerpts. Most modern historians, of course, agree with this view.

113 Ibid., 85.

114 Ibid., 88–97.

115 Rebotton identifies this line as verse 36, stanza 3, of Louis Racine's poem, *La Religion.* Ibid., 97 n52.

116 Ibid., 97.

117 Ibid., 88.

118 Rebotton, *Ecrits maçonniques*, 38.

119 "Mémoire au duc de Brunswick," 98.

120 Ibid.

121 Ibid. This schema would have accommodated the reformed Scottish rite hierarchy of Willermoz, with its three introductory grades, three intermediate grades, and secret higher ranks.

122 Ibid., 99.

123 Ibid., 99.

124 Ibid., 100.

125 Ibid., 99–100.

126 Ibid., 101.

127 Ibid., 102.

128 Ibid.

129 Ibid., 103.

130 Ibid.

131 *OC*, 1:228–9.

132 "Mémoire au duc de Brunswick," 104.

133 Rebotton opts for the first view. *Ecrits maçonniques*, 40–1.

134 "Mémoire au duc de Brunswick," 105.

135 Ibid., 105–6.

136 Triomphe, *Joseph de Maistre*, 103.

137 Le Forestier, *La Franc-Maçonnerie*, 619 n16.

138 "Mémoire au duc de Brunswick," 106–7.

139 Ibid.

140 Ibid.

141 Ibid.

142 Ibid.

143 Ibid., 109.

144 Ibid., 112.

145 Ibid., 109.

146 Emile Dermenghem, in a note in his edition of Joseph de Maistre, *La Franc-Maçonnerie: Mémoire inédit au duc de Brunswick* (Paris 1925), 105 n1.

147 *Joseph de Maistre*, 111.

148 "Mémoire au duc de Brunswick," 113.

149 Ibid.

150 François Vermale argued that this passage showed Maistre to be an advocate of all-out Gallicanism and Josephism. *Joseph de Maistre émigré* (Chambéry 1927), 20.

151 Rebotton acknowledges that young Maistre appears to have been influenced by Paolo Sarpi's defence of civil and political rights against papal interventions, but argues that he never became an immoderate Gallican. He notes that the three countries cited by Maistre in this passage were not at this date examples of extreme Gallicanism. In contrast to the anti-papal radicalism of the Parlement of Paris, the Senate of Savoy usually followed a very moderate course. (Here Rebotton cites Laurent Chevailler, *Essai sur le Souverain Sénat de Savoie, 1559–1793*, 68–9.) Moreover, in the eighteenth century the French crown needed papal support in its efforts to suppress Jansenism. And in Austria, the struggle between Joseph II and the papacy did not reach its climax until about 1783 (ie, after the date of Maistre's memoir). *Ecrits maçonniques*, 113–14 n69.

152 "Mémoire au duc de Brunswick," 115.

153 Ibid., 118.

154 Ibid., 119. The underlined portion of the quotation is a paraphrase of the pope's formulation of the question.

155 Ibid.

156 See Richard Lebrun, "Joseph de Maistre et la loi naturelle," *REM*, no. 8 (1983): 117–35.

157 Rebotton, *Ecrits maçonniques*, 44.

158 Ibid., 45.

159 Savaron to Maistre, June 24, 1782. In *Ecrits maçonniques*, 134.

160 *Ecrits maçonniques*, 45.

161 See Le Forestier, *La Franc-Maçonnerie*, 709–11.

162 "Mémoire sur la Franc-Maçonnerie," in *Ecrits Maçconniques*, 134.

163 See Jean Rebotton, "Maistre, alias Josephus a Floribus, pendant la Révolution: repères et conjectures," *REM*, no. 5–6 (1980): 146–7.

164 Darcel, "Bibliothèques de J. de Maistre," 60.

165 *Ecrits maçonniques*, 93.

166 Maistre to Thérèse de Maistre, 12 July 1791. *OC*, 9:9.

167 *Carnets*, 26.

168 Ibid., 126.

169   *OC*, 5:249.

170   "Mémoire sur la Franc-Maçonnerie," in *Ecrits maçonniques*, 138.

171   Maistre to Count de Vallaise, 7 May 1816. *OC*, 13:331–2.

172   *Joseph de Maistre*, 114 n156.

173   The extract from this document, *Aus den Tagebüchern Friedrich Münters* (Ed.
      by Ojvind Andreasen, Copenhagen, Leipzig 1937) has been published in
      French translation by Jean Nicolas as an appendix to his "Noblesse, élites et
      Maçonnerie dans la Savoie du XVIIIe siècle," *REM*, no. 5–6 (1980): 65–8.
      Descended from a German family that had settled in Denmark, Münter was a
      linguist and a theologian, and well-versed in ancient languages, archeology,
      and numismatics. He was sent to Italy by his government to search out ancient
      texts in ecclesiastical archives and libraries. But he had a dual mission since he
      had also been charged by German "Strict Observance" Masons to contact their
      Italian brothers. His visit to Chambéry came at the end of a three-year journey.
      Ibid., 65 n.a.

174   Ibid., 66. Maistre described to Münter how he had taught himself how to read
      English.

175   Ibid., 66–7.

176   Rebotton, *Ecrits maçonniques*, 139 n49.

177   *Ecrits maçonniques*, 141.

CHAPTER THREE: ON THE EVE OF
UPHEAVAL

1   "Prospectus de l'expérience aérostatique de Chambéry." The manuscript,
    which carries a note indicating it was approved for printing on 3 April 1784,
    survives in the Maistre family archives. It is printed as an appendix in Charles
    de Buttet, *Aperçu de la vie de Xavier de Maistre* (Grenoble 1919), 193–200.

2   This whole episode is described in detail in Descostes, *Maistre avant la
    Révolution*, 1:125–69, with generous quotations from both Joseph's
    "Prospectus" and Xavier's description of the flight.

3   Maistre to Monsieur ***, 20 February 1786. *OC*, 9:1–3.

4   Descostes, *Maistre avant la Révolution*, 2:193–4.

5   Maistre's name appears on a 1787 membership list. Nicolas, *Savoie au 18e
    siècle*, 1089–91, and plate 162.

6   Descostes, *Maistre avant la Révolution*, 1:146.

7   Ibid., 145–50, 166–75.

8   Salteur to Roze, 12 November 1779. Cited in Descostes, *Maistre avant la
    Révolution*, 1:150–1.

9   Ibid., 151.

10 Ibid., 155–7.

11 Letter of Lovera de Maria, 6 November 1790, cited in Nicolas, *Savoie au 18e
    siècle*, 1026–7.

12 Descostes, *Maistre avant la Révolution*, 1:154 n1.
13 Maistre's diary and letterbooks show 31 letters to Salteur between 1793 and 1810.
14 Maistre to Costa, 14 April 1816. *OC*, 13:314.
15 Nicolas, *Savoie au 18e siècle*, 805–7. Henry Costa later complained that his father had endangered the family's patrimony by trying to implement his "dangerous speculations."
16 Triomphe, *Joseph de Maistre*, 117 n9.
17 Maistre to Costa, 7 December 1789. Cited in Charles-Albert Costa de Beauregard, *Un Homme d'autrefois* (Paris 1910), 91. By Henry Costa's grandson, this volume includes otherwise unedited correspondence between the two men.
18 Maistre to Costa, 14 April 1816. *OC*, 13:315. The reference is to Maistre's "Le caractère extérieure du magistrat," delivered before the Senate on 1 December 1784.
19 Costa de Beauregard, *Un Homme d'autrefois*, 20–36.
20 "Le Caractère extérieur du Magistrat ou les moyens d'obtenir la confiance publique," *OC*, 7:1–34.
21 In Descostes, *Maistre Orateur*, 21
22 *OC*, 7:11.
23 Costa to Maistre, undated. *OC*, 7:3–4.
24 From "Of great places." One of Maistre's notebooks contains a lengthy extract from Bacon's essay "Of Judicature" along with Maistre's translation. A marginal note dated 1809 read: "one of my first English translations." "Extraits G," 105–14.
25 *OC*, 7:11.
26 Ibid., 30.
27 Ibid., 25.
28 Maistre to Vignet des Etoles, 9 December 1793. *OC*, 9:58.
29 *OC*, 7:26.
30 Ibid., 30.
31 Ibid.
32 Paris 1784. Maistre had this work in his library. See Darcel, "Bibliothèques de J. de Maistre," 70.
33 The entire letter, dated 16 January 1785, is reproduced in Descostes, *Necker, écrivain*, 11–34.
34 Cited by Descostes, ibid., 16 n1.
35 Ibid., 16–17.
36 Ibid., 24–5.
37 Ibid., 29.
38 Ibid., 17.
39 Ibid., 31.
40 Ibid., 20, 31.

41 Ibid., 23–4.
42 Ottavio Falletti, Marquis de Barolo. We do not know how Maistre made Barol's acquaintance – perhaps at the University of Turin – but we do know that they continued to correspond over the years.
43 Giovanni-Rinaldo Carli was an Italian scholar. Maistre's notebooks contain many references to the French translation of Carli's *Lettres américaines* (Paris 1788) as well as to the Italian edition of his works (Milan 1784–94).
44 "*parturient montes et nascetur ridiculus mus.*" Horace, *Epistola ad Pisones* [*Ars Poetica*], l 139. "The mountain will labour and bring forth a ridiculous mouse."
45 Cited in Clément de Paillette, *Politique de Joseph de Maistre*, 7–8.
46 Ibid., 7.
47 Only one of his letters to his wife, from June 1808, has been found – in a copy in one of his letterbooks in the family archives. But we know from his journal and his letter registers that during their years of separation (some thirteen in total between 1793 and 1814) he wrote over 350 letters to her. See Jean-Louis Darcel, "Registres de la correspondance de Joseph de Maistre," *REM*, 7 (1981): 13–14.
48 Maistre to Costa, 8 September 1786. *OC*, 9:4–5.
49 *Joseph de Maistre*, 82.
50 Five years previously, in a letter to a friend whose new wife had been badly received by his parents, Maistre remarked: "If my fortune permitted me to take a wife at the present time, they [Maistre's family] would receive her with open arms." Maistre to Joseph de Juge, 13 August 1781. Cited in Descostes, *Maistre avant la Révolution*, 2:196.
51 There is suggestive evidence in Maistre's journal and in one of his letters of another romance that never came to fruition. A diary entry for 22 December 1797 (in Turin) notes seeing Apollonie de St Barthélemi, now Mme Buschetti, who he had not seen since eight o'clock in the evening on 3 December 1778. *Carnets*, 126. A letter of 9 August 1806, to his cousin, Baron de Paulini in Nice, describes the 1778 and 1797 meetings with precision and includes a request to be remembered to the "amiable Apollonie." *OC*, 10:170–1. Maistre had evidently met Apollonie on one of his visits to Nice; we have no information to suggest why this romance came to naught.
52 Descostes, *Maistre avant la Révolution*, 2:243. Descostes reproduced Maistre's wedding certificate, which refers to the bride's father as the "late noble Jean-Pierre Morand" – so despite the wording of Maistre's letter to Costa cited above, Françoise's father must have been dead by the time of the marriage.
53 Ibid., 248–9.
54 Ibid., 249, 251.
55 Ibid., 2:255.
56 Maistre to Mme Huber-Alléon, 26 September 1806. *OC*, 10:206–7.

57 M.f.a. The letterbook copy carries the date "May 1808," but this would be the date by the Julian calendar. Maistre's "*registre de correspondance*" has the following entry for 9 June 1808: "to my wife (without no.) of 27 May (8 June): confidential letter of 24 pages, enregistered and delivered to Baron departed the … (P.S. departed in the month of March 1809)." Darcel, "Registres de la correspondance," 136.

58 Maistre to Guy-Marie de Place, 9 August 1819. C. Latreille, "Lettres inédites de Joseph de Maistre," *Revue bleue*, 50 (1912): 356.

59 Vermale cites a third-party letter dated 19 April 1788, to the effect that "Count Maistre, who has been in Turin, for some time, will be named a supernumerary Senator." *Maistre émigré*, 24.

60 Maistre retained the manuscripts in his papers and they still exist in the family archives. They were published by Descostes in *La Politique de Joseph de Maistre*, 36–47, 11–17. These documents will be cited later as important evidence of Maistre's political views on the eve of the French Revolution.

61 Ibid., 47.

62 Rebotton reproduces the royal letters patent "conferring the office of Senator" on Joseph de Maistre. *Etudes maistriennes*, 57–8.

63 Maistre to Henry Costa, 6 January 1792. *OC*, 9:20.

64 Maistre to Nicolas de Maistre, 14 February 1805. *OC*, 9:331–2.

65 *Carnets*, 5–6.

66 Maistre to Costa, 6 January 1792. *OC*, 9:19–20.

67 Cited in Descostes, *Maistre avant la Révolution*, 2:288.

68 Ibid., 291–302.

69 *Carnets*, 9, 15, 16.

70 Darcel, "Registres de la correspondance," 15–16.

71 The values given for Maistre's properties, unless otherwise indicated, are the amounts for which they were sold during the Revolution. Triomphe has gathered together, from a variety of sources, all the available information on Maistre's fortune. *Joseph de Maistre*, 54 n84.

72 *Carnets*, 6.

73 Inherited from his uncle, Guillame-François Demotz. François Descostes, *Joseph de Maistre pendant la Révolution* (Tours 1895), 50.

74 Maistre's diary records a visit to Montmeillant and the bottling of 68 bottles of his wine on 8 February 1791. *Carnets*, 2–3.

75 Descostes, *Maistre avant la Révolution*, 2:247.

76 *Carnets*, 207.

77 Ibid., 11.

78 Ibid., 14.

79 Ibid., 207.

80 Ibid., 7, 207. Maistre had visited this eighty-six year old priest on his sickbed during the last few weeks of his life (ibid., 4–5), but relatively little is known

about him. In his will, Victor identified himself as a Canon of Warsaw, a counsellor of the court of Saxony, and the previous tutor of the reigning Elector of Saxony. The will, dated 6 May 1777, is cited in Darcel, "Bibliothèques de J. de Maistre," 13.

81 Ibid., 29, 99–101.
82 Ibid., 28.
83 Ibid., 26.
84 *Savoie au 18e siècle,* 1001. There were probably larger collections (for example, Maistre's Masonic acquaintance, Dr Daquin, had some 30,000 livres invested in his library), but no usable inventories for them have survived. Ibid., 1002.
85 Darcel, "Bibliothèques de J. de Maistre," 15.
86 Ibid., 26.
87 Ibid., 27. Nicolas provides a subject-matter tabulation of the holdings of 28 other private libraries in Savoy. *Savoie au 18e siècle,* 1004–5.
88 "Bibliothèques de J. de Maistre," 32.
89 Ibid.
90 Ibid., 101.
91 Ibid., 100.
92 Ibid., 32–3.
93 "La vénalité des charges," cited in Paillette, *La Politique de Joseph de Maistre,* 39. All citations from these two memoirs will be from Paillette.
94 Ibid., 41.
95 Ibid., 42–3.
96 Ibid.
97 Ibid., 40.
98 Ibid., 41.
99 Ibid., 45.
100 Ibid.
101 Ibid., 45–6.
102 Ibid.
103 Ibid., 47.
104 Cited in Paillette, *La Politique de Joseph de Maistre,* 11.
105 Ibid.
106 Ibid., 12–13.
107 Ibid.
108 Ibid., 11–12, 14.
109 Ibid., 17.
110 *Joseph de Maistre,* 127.
111 This document has now been printed as an appendix to Lebrun, "Maistre et la loi naturelle," *REM,* no. 8 (1983): 136–44. This piece may be what won Maistre admission as an *associé libre* of the Académie Delphinale of Grenoble in early 1790. The Maistre family archives contain an exchange of letters with the secretary of the Academy. Maistre was told that "the *enchantillon* from

your portfolio, which my son has shared with me, and which I will keep secret, suffices to establish your literary reputation." (Gagnon to Maistre, 21 March 1790) In his reply, Maistre wrote: "This flattering distinction cannot be justified by a shapeless essay that you have read with indulgence, and that, moreover, must not see the light of day." (Maistre to Gagnon, 5 April 1790)

112 These questions are discussed in detail in the article cited in the previous note.

113 For details on Dupaty and Séguier, see *Nouvelle Biographie générale* (Paris 1853–66), 12:256–63 and 41:465, and William Doyle, *The Parlement of Bordeaux and the End of the Old Regime* (London 1974), 39, 136.

114 Cited from "Annexe," Lebrun, "Maistre et la loi naturelle," 137.

115 Ibid., 142–3.

116 Ibid., 137–9.

117 Ibid., 140. The president's epigraph for Turgot would appear to be an adaptation from Vergil's *Aeneid*, VI, ll. 870–1, which read "*ostendent terris hunc tantum nec ultà/esse senent.*" The lines are about the premature death of Marcellus; Maistre's adaptation might be translated: "the fates will give France only a glimpse of him, but deny him survival."

118 Ibid., 144.

119 Jean-Louis Darcel, "Joseph de Maistre et la Révolution française," *REM*, no. 3 (1977): 30–3.

120 Maistre to Count de Vallaise, 2 January 1816. *OC*, 13:204.

121 See Triomphe, *Joseph de Maistre*, 133.

122 Cited in Costa de Beauregard, *Un Homme d'autrefois*, 83.

123 M.f.a.

124 M.f.a.

125 Undated letter to Henry Costa. Cited in Descostes, *Maistre avant la Révolution,* 2:332–4.

126 Since Costa de Beauregard, who transcribed this letter, says that Maistre was so carried away as to allow himself the use of vulgar language, we may assume that he censored the phrase "the ... of the third."

127 Maistre to Costa, 7 December 1789. Cited in Costa de Beauregard, *Un Homme d'autrefois*, 89–90.

128 Ibid.

129 Ibid.

130 Darcel, "Maistre et la Révolution française," 33–4.

131 Ibid., 34.

132 Letter of 3 February 1790. In Secret, *Maistre, Substitut*, 24–5.

133 Ibid., 25.

134 M.f.a.

135 Maistre to Thérèse de Maistre, 12 July 1790. *OC*, 9:10.

136 M.J. Sydenham, *The French Revolution* (London 1965), 72.

137 Maistre to Thérèse de Maistre, 12 July 1790. *OC*, 9:10.

138 Maistre to Costa, 21 January 1791. *OC*, 9:11.

139 Ibid., 12–13.

140 This line, which is from Molière (*Le Misanthrope*, Act 1, Scene 1), continues, "when I see men converse together in the manner they do; I find nothing anywhere, but base flattery, but injustice, interest, treachery, and knavery."

141 *OC*, 9:13.

142 "Maistre et la Révolution française," 34.

143 In more than 5,000 pages of Maistre's *registres de lectures*, I have found only four brief references to the *Reflections*, three to Burke's "Letters on the Proposal for Peace with the Regicide Directory of France," and one to Burke's "Letter to a noble Lord on the attacks made on him ... by the Duke of Bedford." It must be admitted, however, that there is a significant gap in this material, with no dated entries between July 1776 and May 1793. Lebrun, "Lectures de J. de Maistre," 131.

144 *The Rage of Edmund Burke: Portrait of an Ambivalent Conservative* (New York 1977).

145 Frederick Holdsworth, *Joseph de Maistre et Angleterre* (Paris 1935), 246–9. For a similar interpretation that emphasizes the divergence of their views and influences, see Michel Fuchs, "Edmund Burke et Joseph de Maistre," *Revue de l'Université d'Ottawa*, 54 (1984): 49–58.

146 See, for example, Triomphe, *Joseph de Maistre*, 139–40.

147 *Maistre et l'Angleterre*, 246.

148 *Joseph de Maistre*, 140.

149 Maistre to Costa, 17 February 1791. *OC*, 9:15.

150 Ibid., 16. "Who God would destroy He first makes mad." Euripides, *Fragments*. Latin version attributed to James Duport, a seventeenth-century English classicist.

151 Letter of 23 March 1791. Cited in Secret, *Maistre, Sustitut*, 26.

152 Ibid., 27.

153 Letter of 29 March 1791. Ibid., 28.

154 Darcel, "Maistre et la Révolution française," 34.

155 This would seem to be the incident referred to in Maistre's diary entry of 15 March: "Stupid brawl in Chambéry by young ruffians, excited by French scoundrels, and whose probable effect will be to put us in the wrong with the king and procure for us a regime of iron in place of mild government." *Carnets*, 3.

156 Letter of 29 March 1791. Secret, *Maistre, Substitut*, 29.

157 Ibid.

158 Letter of 23 April 1791. Ibid., 31.

159 Ibid.

160 Ibid., 32.

161 Ibid., 34.

162 Maistre had been charged with preparing memoirs on current royal projects to buy out remaining feudal rights and the tithes in Savoy.

163 Letter of 15 May 1791. Secret, *Maistre, Substitut*, 34.

164 *Joseph de Maistre*, 142–3.

165 At this point Vignet des Etoles had just been charged with the reform of the justice system in Savoy. Following the French invasion, he was to serve as the Sardinian ambassador to Berne; Maistre would be much involved with him in this latter capacity.

166 Maistre to Vignet des Etoles, 8 July 1791. Cited in Darcel, "Maistre et la Révolution française," 35.

167 Vermale, *Maistre émigré*, 36.

168 Maistre to Costa, 27 April 1792. *OC*, 9:26.

169 Ibid.

170 Ibid., 28.

171 Ibid., 29.

172 Ibid.

173 Ibid., 30.

174 *Carnets*, 16.

175 Ibid.

176 By Jean-Philippe Dutoit-Membrini, a Swiss mystic. See Rebotton, "Josephus a Floribus," 161, 164.

177 *Carnets*, 11–16.

178 Darcel, "Maistre et la Révolution française," 36.

179 *Carnets*, 17.

180 Ibid., 18.

181 Darcel, "Maistre et la Révolution française," 36.

182 *Carnets*, 18.

183 Ibid.

184 Jean-Louis Darcel, "Introduction" to Joseph de Maistre, *Considérations sur la France* (Geneva 1980), Edition critique, 21.

185 Maistre to Victor-Emmanuel I, 16 June, 1814. Archivio di stato (Turin) (hereafter cited as AS). Letteri ministri Russia. Mazzo 9. A similar explanation occurs in another letter of the same period. "The kings did not ask us to leave; they did not forbid us to return. I left the States of the King to satisfy myself, and I keep a close watch not to esteem myself more than those that did otherwise." Maistre to Count de Vallaise, 31 July 1814. In Albert Blanc, *Correspondance diplomatique de Joseph de Maistre* (Paris 1860), 1:390.

CHAPTER FOUR: LAUSANNE

1 We know from his diary and from his letter register that Maistre wrote at least 2,096 letters between his departure from Chambéry in September 1792 and his departure from Lausanne at the end of February 1797; of these letters about 150 have been published (in whole or in part), while another 58 remain in the Maistre family archives. Of the approximately 208 letters thus available, 152 are to Baron Vignet des Etoles, who was both a good friend of Joseph de

Maistre, and, as the Sardinian representative in Bern, his immediate superior for most of these years. Particularly for the period from May 1793 through November 1795, Maistre's letters to Vignet des Etoles are of great value for following his reaction to events and his thinking. The most important of these letter have been published by Jean-Louis Darcel in his "Les Années d'apprentissage d'un contre-révolutionnaire: Joseph de Maistre à Lausanne, 1793–1797," *REM*, no. 10 (1986–87): 7–135.

2 *Carnets*, 19.

3 Letter of 28 July 1804. This letter is identified in Maistre's *OC*, 10:442, as to Count Diodati. This identification, however, is most likely in error. The same letter is printed in Fédor Golovkine, *La Cour et le règne de Paul Ier* (Paris 1905), 401, as being to Count Fédor Golovkine. The copy in Maistre's letterbook (M.f.a.) carries no indication of addressee, but his letter register lists a letter to Count Théodore Golowkin for this date. See Darcel, "Registres de la correspondance," 124.

4 Ibid. On Favrat, see Nicolas, *Savoie au 18e siècle*, 615, 673, 902, 1047. On Favrat and Giraud, see as well, Rebotton, "Josephus a floribus," 149–50.

5 *Carnets*, 20.

6 Darcel, "Maistre et la Révolution," 36.

7 Maistre to Vignet des Etoles, 27 May 1793. M.f.a.

8 On the Marquis de Sales and his influence in Aosta, see Vermale, *Maistre émigré*, 40, and Descostes, *Maistre pendant la Révolution*, 178–85.

9 Vermale, *Maistre émigré*, 39.

10 Descostes, *Maistre pendant la Révolution*, 163–4.

11 "Adresse de quelques parents des militaires savoisiens à la Convention Nationale des Français," *OC*, 7:49.

12 Undated letter cited in Descostes, *Maistre pendant la Révolution*, 179.

13 *Carnets*, 20.

14 According to his diary entry for 19 November, between 10 October and that date he had read the following works: Winckelmann's history of art (in an Italian translation), Young's *History of Athens*, Cesarotti's *Saggio su la lingua italiana*, the letters of a Spanish Jesuit concerning his travels in Italy (three volumes in Spanish), and extracts (in Italian) of Aristotle's *Rhetoric*. *Carnets*, 20–1.

15 Ibid., 22–3.

16 Ibid., 23.

17 Ibid., 23–4.

18 "Notice biographique," *OC*, 1:ix–x. Judging from the details given in Rodolphe's account (down to the quoted phrase about fear of finding Madame de Maistre in some little cabin), it is clear that Rodolphe took the story from a draft letter in his father's papers. In 1802, Joseph de Maistre wrote to the French ambassador in Naples requesting exemption from the law of 6 Floréal (26 April 1802), which again required all French émigrés (including

Savoyards) to return under penalty of the loss of their property. The draft letter (to accompany a memoir on the subject) argues that his return to Savoy in 1793 had been the consequence of "painful" circumstances, that he had never given the least evidence of wishing to become French, and that therefore he should not be treated as an émigré. M.f.a.

19 He noted receipt of letters from both as well as eight letters to Thérèse, two to her husband, and two to Marie-Christine. *Carnets*, 19–22.

20 Ibid., 22.

21 Ibid., 24. The Latin appears to be an adaptation of a famous line from Vergil's *Eclogues* (IV, l. 5): "*Magnus ab integro saeclorum nascitur ordo.*" Maistre's version may be translated: "A new order is born."

22 Ibid.

23 Cited in Descostes, *Maistre pendant la Révolution*, 254–5. Descostes gives no date, but internal evidence and Maistre's letter register permit the establishment of the date given.

24 Maistre to Hauteville, 7 September 1793. Cited in Francesco Lemmi, "Giuseppe de Maistre a Losanna," *Fert*, 7 (1936): 209.

25 See Descostes, *Maistre pendant la Révolution*, 212–15, for a detailed description of these changes.

26 "Notice biographique," *OC*, 1:x. These details also come from Joseph de Maistre's 1802 draft letter to the French ambassador to Naples. M.f.a.

27 Descostes, *Maistre pendant la Révolution*, 224–6.

28 Maistre's diary records his observation of these events. On 15 February he noted: "Birth of the schism," and on 16 February: "Civic oath of 17 priests."*Carnets*, 26.

29 Ibid., 25. Entries for 2 and 4 February.

30 Maistre to Count de Vallaise, 8 October 1814. Blanc, *Correspondance diplomatique*, 2:34.

31 A diary entry for 15 February notes that he was studying German. *Carnets*, 26. The thought of refuge in Germany will recur during subsequent times of uncertainty in Maistre's life. His old friend, Abbé Victor (from whom, it will be recalled, Maistre had inherited a substantial library in 1791), had made a career at the court of the Elector of Saxony, and perhaps his example suggested the possibility of something similar.

32 *Carnets*, 26. Entry for 19 February.

33 Ibid., 26–9.

34 Ibid., 26–8.

35 *OC*, 7:46–81.

36 Maistre to Mallet du Pan, 28 February 1793. Cited in the edition of Mallet du Pan's works entitled *Mémoires et correspondance pour servir à l'histoire de la Révolution française* (Paris 1851), 1:339.

37 *OC*, 7:37.

38 The execution of Louis XVI.

39 "something absolutely fundamental."

40 Maistre to Mallet du Pan, 28 February 1793. Cited in Mallet du Pan, *Mémoires*, 1:340.

41 The story of the "Constantin affair" was uncovered by Jean Rebotton. See his *Etudes maistriennes*, 77–101.

42 *Carnets*, 26.

43 *OC*, 7:53–7.

44 Rebotton, *Etudes maistriennes*, 84–5.

45 Maistre to Sales, 2 April 1793. Cited in Descostes, *Maistre pendant la Révolution*, 229–30.

46 Rebotton, *Etudes maistriennes*, 88 n37.

47 Ibid., 88–101.

48 Maistre to Sales, 2 April 1793. Cited in Descostes, *Maistre pendant la Révolution*, 255.

49 Ibid., 282–3.

50 Maistre to Mallet du Pan, 28 February 1792. Cited in Mallet du Pan, *Mémoires*, 1:339.

51 *Joseph de Maistre*, 156.

52 Vermale, *Maistre émigré*, 47–8.

53 *Carnets*, 30. D'Erlach, who was known to be favourably disposed towards the émigrés, exercised the authority of Bern in Lausanne.

54 The text of this document is now easily available in Rebotton, *Ecrits Maçonniques*, 123–39. Rebotton, following Vermale, says that Maistre also sent this memoir (or other memoirs on the same topic) to the king and other high officials on the same day (ibid., 46). This view appears to be based on a misreading of Maistre's diary. The relevant entry reads: "30. j'ai donné à Mr le Baron Vignet un mémoire sur la Franc-Maçonnerie écrit au Roi, à M. de Cravanzane (avec un mémoire) à M. le Cte de Hauteville, à Mr le Chev. Radicati" (*Carnets*, 30). There is really nothing here to justify the assumption that the memoir on Freemasonry was sent to anyone other than to Vignet; a glance at other entries reveals that Maistre often neglected punctuation marks and that the form "écrit à" was his standard way of recording letters. All the entry says is that Maistre gave the Baron a memoir and that he wrote to the people listed. The memoir to Cravanzane (the war minister) could have been on any topic.

55 *Ecrits Maçonniques*, 48.

56 Ibid., 134.

57 Ibid.

58 Ibid., 133.

59 Ibid.

60 Ibid., 135.

61 Ibid., 133.

62 Maistre to Vignet des Etoles, 9 December 1793. *OC*, 9:59.

63 *Carnets*, 31–9.
64 *Ecrits Maçonniques*, 138.
65 Maistre to Vignet des Etoles, 14 May 1793. M.f.a.
66 Maistre to Vignet des Etoles, 21 May 1793. Darcel, "Maistre à Lausanne," 27. He added that his brother in Turin had discovered that Hauteville was painting him as a democrat because he knew English and ordered English books!
67 Maistre to Vignet des Etoles, 9 July 1793. Darcel, "Maistre à Lausanne," 36.
68 Cited by Maistre in his letter to Vignet des Etoles of 16 July 1793. M.f.a.
69 Ibid.
70 *OC*, 7:155–7.
71 This fundamental conservative dilemma has been explored by a number of scholars. But see, in particular, Everett E. Hagen, *On the Theory of Social Change* (Homewood, IL 1962).
72 *OC*, 7:159.
73 Ibid., 132–3.
74 Ibid., 84.
75 Ibid., 88. It seems evident that these passages describe Maistre's own reactions.
76 Ibid., 89.
77 Ibid., 82.
78 Ibid., 39.
79 Ibid., 148.
80 Ibid., 154.
81 Ibid., 152.
82 In one letter he writes, "I have heard from the Abbé Bigex that the second Savoyard letter has had a marvellous effect at Annecy. The good party has been greatly consoled by it, and Defresne who was the national treasurer handed in his resignation immediately." Letter of 9 July 1793. Darcel, "Maistre à Lausanne," 36.
83 Maistre to Vignet des Etoles, 24 July 1793. Ibid., 37.
84 As Maistre wrote to Vignet des Etoles, "Events have rendered fairly ridiculous a number of passages in my letters and the second letter entirely so." Letter of 8 October 1793. Ibid., 62.
85 *Carnets*, 30.
86 He told Vignet des Etoles that this amount would cover about two-thirds of his expenses. Letter of 9 August 1793. Darcel, "Maistre à Lausanne," 43.
87 Descostes, *Maistre pendant la Révolution*, 532–3, and *Carnets*, 40
88 Vermale, *Maistre émigré*, 54–6.
89 Descostes, *Maistre pendant la Révolution*, 500–8.
90 Maistre to Vignet des Etoles, 4 September 1793. *OC*, 9:49–50.
91 Maistre to Vignet des Etoles, 17 September 1793. Darcel, "Maistre à Lausanne," 52.
92 Maistre to Vignet des Etoles, 24 September 1793. Ibid., 57.

93   Maistre to Vignet des Etoles, 8 October 1793. Ibid. 62.

94   *Carnets*, 44. Entry for 24 October 1793.

95   Maistre to Vignet des Etoles, 11 November 1793. M.f.a.

96   Maistre to Vignet des Etoles, 9 December 1793. *OC*, 9:58–9.

97   Maistre to Vignet des Etoles, 6 January 1794. Darcel, "Maistre à Lausanne," 67.

98   Ibid., 73.

99   Ibid.

100   *Carnets*, 50.

101   Vignet des Etoles to Hauteville, 31 January 1794. Cited in Triomphe, *Joseph de Maistre*, 161.

102   Hauteville to Vignet des Etoles, 8 February 1794. Ibid.

103   Maistre to Vignet des Etoles, 12 December 1793. M.f.a. There are a few unpublished pages on hereditary aristocracy in one of Maistre's folio registers, but he never published anything specific on the topic. "Souveraineté Fragmens," 431–6 and 445–7. M.f.a.

104   Maistre to Vignet des Etoles, 19 March 1794. M.f.a.

105   *Carnets*, 55. Maistre never published a "fifth letter," and there has been some confusion about this reference. In 1895, Clément de Paillette revealed the existence of a "fifth letter," published extracts that he said were from its unpublished manuscript, and indicated that the piece entitled "Fragments sur la France," which had been first published in the *Lettres et Opuscules inédits du comte Joseph de Maistre* (Paris 1851), had also been drawn from the same manuscript. (See Paillette's *La Politique de Joseph de Maistre*, 19–20, and *OC*, 1:187–220.)

   With the publication of Maistre's diary in 1923, subsequent scholars assumed that the entry for 24 March 1794 referred to the same document. But Jean-Louis Darcel's careful study of Maistre's manuscripts reveals that they contain two documents carrying the title "Cinquième Lettre d'un Royaliste Savoisien," and that the document Maistre sent to the bishop in March 1794 was one that he later retitled "De la Souveraineté du Peuple. Discours Préliminaire." The material published under the title "Fragments sur la France" was taken from the second manuscript. Darcel provides critical editions of both manuscripts. See his "Cinquième lettre," 7–89.

106   Maistre to Vignet des Etoles, 21 June 1794. Darcel, "Maistre à Lausanne," 92.

107   Bovet to Maistre, 13 April 1794. Cited in Darcel, "Cinquième lettre,"81.

108   This work was published in the *Oeuvres complètes* under the incorrect title, *Etude sur la souveraineté*. 1:311–554. See Darcel, *REM*, 2 (1976): 3.

109   Darcel, "Cinquième lettres,"20.

110   First published in the *Oeuvres complètes* under the title "Examen d'un Ecrit de J.-J. Rousseau sur l'inégalité des conditions parmi les hommes," 7:509–66. Jean-Louis Darcel has established the correct title of this piece and published a critical edition. See *REM*, 2 (1976): 6, 58–99.

111   "Although my work is not absolutely complete, I have already spoken to a

publisher; but there will be great difficulties, and probably it will remain in my portfolio. I will not be so foolish as to print it at my own expense, and if I were dupe enough to give it away, it is doubtful if they would want to publish it." Maistre to Vignet des Etoles, 28 July 1795. Darcel, "Maistre à Lausanne, 121.

112 Maistre to Vignet des Etoles, 22 March 1794. Ibid., 79.

113 Maistre to Vignet des Etoles, 26 April 1794. Ibid., 84–5.

114 Maistre to Vignet des Etoles, 2 May 1794. *OC*, 9:60.

115 Maistre to Vignet des Etoles, 5 May 1794. Darcel, "Maistre à Lausanne," 88.

116 *Carnets*, 60–1.

117 Ibid., and Maistre to Henry Costa, 31 May 1794. *OC*, 9:61–3.

118 Undated letter, cited in Costa de Beauregard, *Un Homme d'autrefois*, 242. Maistre had brought Madame Costa back to Lausanne to stay with his family for about ten days. *Carnets*, 61.

119 "Discourse à Madame le Marquise de Costa," *OC*, 7:234–78.

120 M.f.a. Darcel has reproduced the most critical passage in the "Introduction" to his critical edition of Maistre's *Considérations sur la France*. But there are two additional suppressed pages that are also of interest.

121 *OC*, 7:241–2.

122 *Considerations on France*, translated by Richard A. Lebrun (Montreal and London 1974), 80. All citations from the *Considérations* are from this translation.

123 *OC*, 7:375–6.

124 *OC*, 4:206–10.

125 *OC*, 1:306–97. But without credit to the Archbishop of Tarantaise.

126 *OC*, 7:273–4.

127 These two paragraphs should be compared to the opening paragraphs of the *Considérations sur la France*, which begin: "We are all attached to the throne of the Supreme Being by a supple chain that restrains us without enslaving us." See *Considerations on France*, 23.

128 Louis XVI's sister, guillotined 10 May 1794.

129 Cited by Darcel, "Introduction," 31–3.

130 Darcel, "Introduction," 33. Maistre's diary entry for 6 February 1798 contains the following lines: "Before leaving Turin, I burned the manuscript of my *Lettres savoisiennes* composed at an epoch when I had not the least *illumination* on the French, or better, the *European Revolution*. Despite the upright views that dictated them, I have taken an aversion to them as a fruit of ignorance." *Carnets*, 127.

131 Darcel offers an intelligent and well-informed discussion of both questions. "Introduction," 33–4.

132 I have noted, for example, his attention to apocalyptic and prophetic literature in February 1793. *Carnets*, 26–7.

133 The work was translated into English in the same year. This translation is now available in a reprint version with an introduction by Paul H. Beik. Jacques Mallet du Pan, *Considerations on the Nature of the French Revolution* (New

York 1974).

134   Maistre to Vignet des Etoles, 4 September 1793. *OC*, 9:50.

135   *Considerations on the Nature of the French Revolution*, iii.

136   Maistre to Vignet des Etoles, 1 October 1793. M.f.a.

137   "I have read M. Young's book with great pleasure." Maistre to Vignet des Etoles, 12 December 1793. M.f.a.

138   "Mélanges A," 565.

139   Darcel, "Introduction," 33.

140   Fernand Baldensperger, *Le Mouvement des idées dans l'émigration française* (1789–1815) (Paris 1925), 65–97, 182–217.

141   Triomphe, *Joseph de Maistre*, 165, citing an anonymous merchant from Lyon who was resident in Lausanne in late 1793.

142   Ibid., 168.

143   Ibid., 165.

144   "the work has had all the success here that I could have hoped for." Maistre to Vignet des Etoles, 26 August 1794. Darcel, "Maistre à Lausanne, " 100.

145   Ibid.

146   Marquise de Nav … to Maistre, 10 May 1795. *OC*, 7:279–80.

147   Maistre to Vignet des Etoles, 7 May 1793. Darcel, "Maistre à Lausanne," 25.

148   "Introduction," 20.

149   Vermale, *Maistre émigré*, 64. Maistre's diplomatic correspondence with the ministry of foreign affairs in Turin for this period has disappeared. But according to a eulogy published shortly after Maistre's death by an acquaintance, Napoleon found a collection of Maistre's letters from 1793 to 1797 in the archives in Venice and read them "with as much surprise as admiration." J.M. Raymond, "L'Eloge de Comte Joseph de Maistre," *Memoire della Reale Academia delle Scienze di Torino*, 27 (1823): 178.

150   Maistre to Vignet des Etoles, 23 December 1794. *OC*, 9:85.

151   *Carnets*, 75.

152   "Mémoire sur le Projet d'unir la Savoie au Corps helvétique." This memoir has been published with an introduction and notes by Robert Triomphe, both in the *Bulletin de la Faculté des Lettres de Strasbourg*, January–February 1961, and as a separate publication with the title, *Mémoire sur l'union de la Savoie à la Suisse 1795* (Strasbourg 1961).

153   In the light of Maistre's later fulminations against written constitutions however, it is amusing to observe that in this case he was ready to envisage a written "fundamental law" to guarantee the Savoyard nobility as a "constitutional element of the government." *Mémoire sur l'union*, 33.

154   Vermale, *Maistre émigré*, 68.

155   He suspected these consequences as soon as he heard the news of the French victories. His diary entry for 30 April 1796 records his near despair: "Terrible news arrived from Italy today. *All appears lost for me*, no longer having either country, fortune, or even a sovereign, properly speaking." *Carnets*, 113.

156   Although both the manuscript and printed versions carry the date "C …

[Chambéry?] 15 July 1796," Maistre's diary entries note the dispatch of portions of the manuscript to Abbé Noiton and Vignet des Etoles in Bern in August and September, and it is only on 18 November 1796 that there is an entry indicating that copies of the memoir have been sent to people in Paris (including a member of the Council of Elders) asking them to make it known there (*Carnets*, 114–17). The memoir concluded with this appeal to the Directory: "Members of the Directory executive! Seize the noble initiative that is presented to you, honour in a solemn way the cradle of the Republic in giving to the most just claims the imposing weight of this message: misfortune to governments that begin by proscriptions! It is justice that produces love and it is love that perpetuates Empires." Cited in Triomphe, *Joseph de Maistre*, 173 n116.

157   *Carnets*, 114–20.

158   Maistre to Vignet des Etoles, 16 December 1794. Darcel, "Maistre à Lausanne," 108. One of Maistre's notebooks contains notes on this work ("Mélanges A," four pages following p 180), and there is a sarcastic reference to it in Maistre's *Considerations on France* (p 101). The book in question was the work of the same General Montesquiou who had commanded the French forces at the time of the invasion of Savoy in 1792 and who had since become an émigré.

159   "I am working on a great catalogue of the Enragés and their products." Maistre to Vignet des Etoles, 19 March 1794. Darcel, "Maistre à Lausanne," 78. This compilation of extracts from the *Moniteur* and some twenty other newspapers collected between 1794 and 1799 was published in the *Oeuvres complètes* under the title "Bienfaits de la Révolution française," *OC*, 7:385–500.

160   Maistre to Vignet des Etoles, 1 November 1794. M.f.a.

161   Maistre to Vignet des Etoles, 18 November 1794. M.f.a.

162   "Introduction," 36–8.

163   Ibid., 38–9.

164   "Josephus a floribus," 173–5. But it should be noted that Rebotton does not appear to have been aware of the suppressed pages of Maistre's 1794 discourse.

165   Ibid., 176.

166   *OC*, 1:325.

167   Rebotton, "Josephus a floribus," 161–3.

168   In the memoir on Freemasonry that he submitted to Vignet des Etoles in April 1793, Maistre had been able to tell his friend that the local Masonic lodge in Lausanne was in correspondence with a lodge in Constantinople. *Ecrits Maçonniques*, 139.

169   *Carnets*, 117.

170   Rebotton, "Josephus a floribus," 179.

171   Descostes, *Maistre pendant la Révolution*, 610–11.

172   The text of the retraction is reproduced as an appendix to Maistre's *Carnets*, 226–9.

173 Pius VI to Panisset, 1 June 1796. Cited in *Carnets*, 229–30.

174 In 1796, in a letter to Cardinal Costa, he described Panisset as a weak and false head whose "tic" was to be a bishop. Cited in Descostes, *Maistre pendant la Révolution*, 612–13. The characterization of Panisset as a wretch occurs in a letter to Abbé Rey, 9 February 1820. *OC*, 14:203.

175 Triomphe, *Joseph de Maistre*, 168–9, and René Johannet and François Vermale in the introduction to their critical edition of Maistre's *Considérations sur la France* (Paris 1936), XV.

176 "We have already had a little tussle on the subject of the retraction of that poor wretch Panisset, which he had drafted and which I redid from one end to the other ... Today, here is another disagreement." Maistre to Abbé Rey, 9 February 1820. *OC*, 14:203.

177 Author's note, *OC*, 7:350.

178 "Adresse du maire de Montagnole à ces Concitoyens," *OC*, 7:351–67.

179 Author's note, *OC*, 7:350.

180 Darcel, "Introduction," 40.

181 Some years later, in a letter to a friend who also knew her, Maistre recalled the chats he had had with the "extraordinary" Madame de Staël: "Not having studied together either theology or politics, we had some scenes in Switzerland that would have made you die of laughter, but never really falling out. Her father, still alive then, was a relative and friend of people I loved with all my heart, and for all the world I would not have wanted to vex him ... there was always between that family and me *peace* and *friendship* despite the difference in banners" (Maistre to Marquise de Priero, August 1805. *OC*, 9:444). Maistre revealed his feelings about Constant in a letter to Count d'Avaray, where he referred to him as "that funny little Constant." Letter of 30 August 1797. Cited in Daudet, *Maistre et Blacas*, 9.

182 Maistre to Vignet des Etoles, 12 May 1795. M.f.a.

183 Maistre to Vignet des Etoles, 21 May 1795. Darcel, "Maistre à Lausanne," 119.

184 "Introduction," 41.

185 Maistre to Avaray, 30 August 1797. Cited in Daudet, *Maistre et Blacas*, 9.

186 Darcel, "Introduction," 43–4. There seems no way of knowing if Maistre offered his services or was asked.

187 Ibid.

188 Maistre's original title had been *Considérations religieuses sur la France*. Maistre's note on the title-page of the manuscript reads: "M. Mallet du Pan wrote to me apropos this title: 'if you let the epithet *religious* stand, no one will read you.' One of my friends (M. Baron Vignet des Etoles) had substituted *moral*; but I suppressed all epithets." Darcel edition, 62.

189 The work is available in a critical English translation. See *Considerations on France*, translated by Richard A. Lebrun (Montreal and London 1974). All citations that follow are taken from this translation. For those who read French,

Jean-Louis Darcel's critical edition (Geneva 1980) is indispensible. In addition to Darcel's extremely valuable introduction and notes, this edition also offers a helpful "Avant-propos" by Jean Boissel.

190 *Considerations*, 23. Subsequent references to this translation will be given in parentheses in the text.

191 *OC*, 5:126

192 See Jean-Louis Soltner, "Le Christianisme de Joseph de Maistre," *REM*, 5–6 (1980): 109–10.

193 This appears to have been intended as a direct refutation of Benjamin Constant's chapter on "Objections Drawn from Experience against the Possibility for a Republic in a Large State."

194 Ibid., 81. Maistre's original manuscript had gone on at some length on this theme. See Ibid., 82 n5.

195 See especially, "Réflexions sur le Protestantisme dans ses rapports avec la Souveraineté," *OC*, 8:63–97. This work, which is dated Turin 1798, was not published during Maistre's lifetime. The essence of the argument is summed up in these two lines: "Sovereignties only have strength, unity, and stability in proportion as they are *divinized* by religion. Moreover Christianity, that is to say Catholicism, being the cement of all European sovereignties, Protestantism, in taking Catholicism away from them without giving them another faith, has mined the foundations of all those that had the misfortune to embrace the reform in that sooner or later it left them in the air." Ibid., 94. This same theme, that Protestantism must be blamed for the abasement of sovereignty in Europe, finds expression in all Maistre's later works. See Lebrun, *Throne and Altar*, 138–41.

196 Ibid., 89. In his original manuscript Maistre had first cited the Latin phrase that had appeared on old French coinage, "*Christus regnat, vincit, imperat,*" and had then substituted the French, "*Le Christ commande, il règne, il est vainqueur.*" M.f.a.

197 Citations from Maistre's *Essai* are from the excellent translation by Elisha Greifer entitled *On God and Society* (Chicago 1959). The passage cited here is from pp xxviii–xxix.

198 Ibid., xxx.

199 Ibid., xvi–xxvi.

200 Ibid.

201 "Lecture de Joseph de Maistre," *Mémoire*, 1 (1984): 36

202 Maistre to Count Potocki, 28 October 1814. *OC*, 12:461.

203 Maistre was quite upset when an editor decided to omit this chapter from the 1814 edition of the work. See Maistre to Bonald, 19 November 1819. *OC*, 13:192.

204 *Soirées*, *OC*, 4:248. On the use made of Hume by counter-revolutionary writers, see L.L. Bongie, *David Hume, Prophet of Counter-Revolution* (Oxford 1965).

205 Darcel, "Introduction," 44–56, provides a detailed review of all the editions that appeared during Maistre's lifetime.

CHAPTER FIVE: ITALIAN INTERLUDE

1 We know from his letter register that he wrote at least 1,361 letters between the time he left Lausanne and the date of his departure from Cagliari, but only 14 have been published. The Maistre family archives and the state archives in Turin have another 10.
2 *Carnets*, 121.
3 Ibid.
4 J. Mandoul, *Joseph de Maistre et la Politique de la Maison de Savoie* (Paris 1899), 35–44, and Blanc, *Mémoires politiques*, 45–8.
5 Mandoul, *Maistre et la Maison de Savoie*, 32.
6 Costa to his wife, undated. Costa de Beauregard, *Un homme d'autrefois*, 405–6.
7 *Carnets*, 122.
8 Ibid., 122–3.
9 Ibid. One of Maistre's notebooks contains a draft essay entitled "Intorono allo stato del Piemonte rispetto alla Carto-moneto." ("Miscellanea," 133–77. M.f.a.) This manuscript essay is dated Venice, 13 March 1799, but it seems likely that it covers the same ground as the memoir he had sent to Barol.
10 *Carnets*, 123–4.
11 Ibid.
12 Vermale, *Maistre émigré*, 73–4, and Goyau, *Pensée religieuse*, 101.
13 Gignoux, *Joseph de Maistre*, 96.
14 Daudet, *Maistre et Blacas*, 3–4.
15 Maistre to Avaray, 30 August 1797. Ibid., 5, 15.
16 Ibid., 12.
17 Ibid., 21.
18 Ibid., 13.
19 *Carnets*, 124.
20 Ibid., 125. The Order of St Maurice and St Lazare was the Piedmontese equivalant to the British Order of the Garter.
21 Gignoux, *Joseph de Maistre*, 96.
22 *Carnets*, 125.
23 Avaray to Maistre, 28 September 1797. Daudet, *Maistre et Blacas*, 23–4.
24 Maistre to Avaray, 28 October 1797. Ibid., 30. Daudet misdates the letter to 20 October.
25 Maistre to Avaray, 12 November 1797. Ibid., 32.
26 Ibid., 35.
27 *Carnets*, 126. Years later, on 21 February 1810, in St Petersburg, Maistre penned these comments on the discourses in question: "They were read more

than twenty years ago in Lyon, in a society of men much occupied with the matter that make up their subject matter. The author, who I never knew even by name, made a present of them to a Piedmontese gentleman who communicated them to me in Turin in 1797. Profiting from the sad leisure that circumstances had given me, I copied them by hand. The task was completed on 4 December of that year, as I see by my journal." (Cited in Paillette, *La Politique de Joseph de Maistre*, 56.)

There followed a number of comments on illuminism and Saint-Martin. These comments were later reworked by Maistre and inserted into his *Soirées* (*OC*, 5:248–51). Finally, a note dated 1812 adds: "Since the date of this note, I have found these three discourses printed among the posthumous works of Saint-Martin" (Paillette, 58). The titles of the works in question were: "Les voies de la sagesse," "Les Lois temporelles de la justice divine," and "Le traité des bénédictions." Ibid., 56 n1.

28 Dated entries for 1797 include some 31 works and 395 pages of notes; for 1798, there are some 44 works and 333 pages of notes. For 1795 and 1796 respectively, there are dated references to 5 and 6 works with 14 and 60 pages of notes. For 1799, the number of authors drops to 13 and the pages of notes to 91. This is a rough analysis made from a computer listing of first or most lengthly citations of works cited by Maistre in his *registres de lectures*. It should be noted that a great many of the notebook entries are undated.

29 For an index of all these references, see Lebrun, "Lectures de J. de Maistre," 149–94.

30 "Religion E"

31 See Goyau, *Pensée religieuse*, 101.

32 *OC*, 8:129–38. In the printed version this letter is dated 9 December 1809, but the manuscript is dated 10 August 1797. M.f.a.

33 *OC*, 8:63–97.

34 Ibid., 66. See Lebrun, *Throne and Altar*, 138–42, for a more detailed analysis of Maistre's argument and its implications.

35 *OC*, 8:99.

36 "I knew that the tempest had not been calmed." *Carnets*, 126.

37 Ibid., 127.

38 Ibid.

39 Ibid., 128.

40 Ibid.

41 Ibid., 128–9.

42 Ibid., 131–2.

43 *OC*, 1:xiii–xv.

44 *Carnets*, 132. See also Maistre's *Soirées*, OC, 5:119, where the scenes with the French bishop are recalled.

45 *OC*, 7:501.

46 Ibid.

47 See ibid., 502–6, for Maistre's account of Maury's views on the two great pre-revolutionary French academies, languages, the English, the French, and books and libraries.

48 See *Carnets*, 133, and Triomphe, *Joseph de Maistre*, 182 n181.

49 Triomphe, *Joseph de Maistre*, 181. One of Maistre notebooks contains a little four-page printed leaflet entitled "Soldats François," which appealed to French soldiers to withdraw their support from the Directory. It carries a note in Maistre's hand that reads: "Venice, April 1799. The imperial commissioners asked me for this address at Count de Kevenhüller's." M.f.a.

50 *Carnets*, 134.

51 Ibid.

52 Ibid., 138.

53 Ibid., 139.

54 "Melanges A" has a number of references to this work dated from September 1798 to May 1799.

55 *OC*, 7:368.

56 "Philosophie D," 653–72. The first two pages are in another hand, but with revisions in Maistre's hand. The last 18 pages are all in Maistre's own hand. This essay has never been published, but a number of the citations and ideas that appear in it found their way into the *Soirées* and the *Eclaircissement sur les sacrifices.*

57 "Philosophie D," 653–4. In a previous chapter we noted how some of the earliest entries in Maistre's notebooks revealed his scepticism towards any approach that tended to "degrade" man. This will remain a major theme in his later critiques of science. See Richard Lebrun, "Joseph de Maistre, Cassandra of Science," *French Historical Studies*, 6 (1969): 214–31.

58 "Philosophie D," 654. The same statement will be found in the *Soirées* in a slightly different context. *OC*, 5:178.

59 "Philosophie D," 655. The quotation is from Hebrews 11:3. Maistre cites the original Greek in a footnote and points out that translators have provided different versions of this text. The same passage is cited in the *Soirées*, *OC*, 5:178, and there, in an appended note, Maistre provides the texts of eight variant translations in Latin, French, Slavonic, and German. 5:218–19.

60 From Bonnet's *Palingénésie philosophique* (1769), Part XIII, Chapter 2. Maistre used this same quotation in the *Soirées*, *OC*, 5:178.

61 "Philosophie D," 660.

62 Ibid., 659. In the *Soirées* Maistre used similar arguments to defend the possibility of esoteric knowledge. The references in his diary and his correspondence to "his star" suggest that his belief in astrology was not entirely theoretical.

63 "Philosophie D," 660–1. For a systematic treatment of Maistre's developed epistemology, see Richard Lebrun, "L'Epistémologie maistrienne: rationalité et connaissance transcendante," *REM*, no. 5–6 (1980): 225–39.

64 "Philosophie D," 661.

65 Ibid., 662–3.

66 Ibid., 669. The argument here recalls the chapter in the *Considérations* on the "violent destruction of the human species," and foreshadows part of the argument in the *Eclaircissements sur les sacrifices* where the same citations are used. *OC*, 5:297–9.

67 "Philosophie D," 669.

68 Ibid., 670–1.

69 Ibid., 671–2. The citation is from Baruch, 3:34–5.

70 We know that Maistre reread this manuscript in 1813, since there is a quotation from Saint-Martin added to one of the notes dated "September 1813, St Petersburg."

71 *Carnets*, 134.

72 Ibid., 134–6.

73 Ibid.

74 Maistre to Challembert, 28 July 1799. M.f.a.

75 *Carnets*, 139–40. The salary, in fact, turned out to be 20,000 livres.

76 See Alfred Bertier, *Xavier de Maistre* (Paris 1918), 73–4.

77 *Carnets*, 141.

78 François Descostes, *Joseph de Maistre inconnu* (Paris 1904), 22.

79 "The King recalls with pleasure, Monsieur, that you have constantly given him proofs of zeal, fidelity, and a particular attachment, that as a consequence of these laudable sentiments you have sacrificed your future in Savoy, that your services in the magistrature as well as in diplomacy in Switzerland have been distinguished, and wishing to give you a testimony of his approval, His Majesty has deigned to decorate you with the Cross of the Order of St Maurice and St Lazare." Count de Challembert to Maistre, 28 October 1799. M.f.a.

80 *Carnets*, 141.

81 Ibid. Sannazar was a famous sixteenth-century Italian poet.

82 "Lettre d'un sujet de S.M. à M. *** sur une question de Droit publique et de jurisprudence criminelle." Unpublished manuscript in a volume untitled "Miscellanea." M.f.a. The document carries the following marginal notation: "This letter was addressed to the Count de la Tour. We were both in Florence in October 1799."

83 *Carnets*, 141.

84 Ibid., 142.

85 His letters to his superiors and to the king himself were quite outspoken on the subject. See *OC*, 9:12–121, 410–11, 415–16, 457–63.

86 *Carnets*, 142. Entry for 14 January 1800.

87 Ibid.

88 Mandoul, *Maistre et la Maison de Savoie*, 34.

89 Challembert to Maistre, 15 August 1799. M.f.a.

90 Descostes, *Maistre inconnu*, 46.

91 See Triomphe, *Joseph de Maistre*, 186–91, for ample citations from the Viceroy's letters of complaint. Triomphe accepts all these complaints at face value, and gives a very one-sided account of Maistre's career as Regent.

92 Challembert to Maistre, 12 October 1801. M.f.a.

93 François Gabet to Maistre, 12 October 1801, and Challembert to Maistre, 12 October 1801. M.f.a.

94 See Darcel, "Registres de correspondance," 66–79.

95 Maistre recorded the news of her death in his diary, and added: "This death must have political consequences for us." *Carnets*, 147.

96 "Maistre is a good magistrate and a good diplomat, but he understands nothing of what makes a military state strong." Victor-Emmanuel I to Chevalier Rossi, 18 August 1804. Cited in D. Perrero, *I Reali di Sardegna nell' esilio (1799–1806)* (Turin 1898), 260.

97 Triomphe, *Joseph de Maistre*, 191. The Viceroy's letter was dated 20 August 1802, and the letters informing Maistre of the St Petersburg appointment were written in Rome on 28 September 1802 (not 8 September, as Triomphe states). Maistre did not receive the letters until 23 October, and in his diary misdates them to 7 September. (*Carnets*, 149.) The letters in the Maistre archives (two from Challembert and one from Gabet) are clearly dated 28 September 1802.

98 *Carnets*, 142.

99 Ibid., 143.

100 Ibid., 146–7, and Maistre to Count Napione Coconato, 20 January 1802. *OC*, 9:104–5. Nicolas married and settled down at the Château de Bissy on the outskirts of Chambéry.

101 *Carnets*, 148.

102 Ibid., 148–9. Maistre recorded their sad leave-taking on 25 September 1802 and added: "Since the beginning of the Revolution, I do not recall having experienced such a bitter moment ... It seemed to me that we were separating for ever. I cannot vanquish the black presentiments that rise in my heart."

103 Maistre's papers and letterbooks contain drafts and copies of both the letter and the memoir. All are dated 25 August 1802. (M.f.a.) But according to his letter register, they were sent from Cagliari on 12 September. Darcel, "Registres de correspondance," 75–6.

104 See Blanc, *Mémoires politiques*, 66–9. Maistre had to explain to his government that he had not solicited the last favour.

105 Descostes, *Maistre inconnu*, 29–30.

106 Unpaginated notes. M.f.a.

107 Ibid. For a detailed study of the relationship between Barruel and Maistre, see Michel Riquet, "Joseph de Maistre et le Père Barruel," *REM*, no. 5–6 (1980): 283–95.

108 "Philosophie D," 568.

109 One of his notebooks, entitled "Miscellanea," contains the title page and introduction to this piece. His letter register indicates that in April 1802 he

sent copies of the harangue to friends and relatives. Darcel, "Registres de correspondance," 72.

110 It appears that this decree was part of a deliberate strategy aimed at forcing Victor-Emmanuel to accept the permanent loss of his mainland provinces and to retire to Sardinia. Mandoul, *Maistre et la Maison de Savoie*, 49–54.

111 *Carnets*, 149. Maistre's Latin phrase may be translated as "when foes are friends."

112 Challembert responded on 29 November to Maistre's letters of 23 and 26 October, and 1 November; Maistre did not receive Challembert's reply until 23 December. M.f.a.

113 Count de Roburent to Maistre, 21 December 1802. M.f.a.

114 *Carnets*, 150–60.

115 Ibid., 153.

116 Ibid., 155.

117 Ibid., 158.

118 Letter cited (without date or address) by Blanc, *Mémoires politiques*, 71. Maistre to Gabet, 24 July 1803, describes the same meeting, but in less detail. AS Letteri ministri Russia. Mazzo 6.

119 Alquieur to Talleyrand. Cited in Mandoul, *Maistre et la Maison de Savoie*, 11.

120 See Triomphe, *Joseph de Maistre*, 230–3.

121 "It is necessary to write a book on Rome or not to talk of it at all." *Carnets*, 160.

122 Maistre to the Countess Trissino de Salvi, 20 November 1805. *OC*, 9:509–10.

123 Maistre to Adèle, 10 March 1803. *OC*, 9:112.

124 *Carnets*, 161. The Allobroges were the ancient Gallic people occupying the present Dauphiné and Savoy.

CHAPTER SIX: ST PETERSBURG

1 In contrast to Maistre's earlier life, the sources for these years are relatively abundant; in addition to the numerous works written during this period (some published only years after his death) there are his diary, his letter registers, his notebooks, and a large volume of correspondence. From Maistre's letter registers, we know that he wrote over 3,000 letters between the date he left Cagliari in 1803 and the time he left St Petersburg in 1817. Approximately 550 have been published at one time or another, and an additional 650 more are to be found in either the Archivio de stato in Turin or the Maistre family archives (in many cases in both, with the original in the state archives and a copy in Maistre's letterbook). This means that more than a third of his letters for this period are accessible. The great bulk of this material is diplomatic correspondence, but much of it is still of interest for Maistre's intellectual life. Moreover, since Maistre became a well-known figure in St Petersburg, there are also third-party references to him in the correspondence and memoirs of others of the time.

2 Mandoul, *Maistre et la Maison de Savoie*, 47–9.
3 Maistre to Rossi, 10 October 1803. AS Letteri ministri Russia, Mazzo 6. At this time Rossi was an assistant to François Gabet, the secretary of state for foreign affairs, but he soon advanced to the latter post himself. Maistre's personal relationship with Rossi was excellent, but Rossi seems to have had only a secondary role at court. Most of Maistre's diplomatic correspondence from 1804 to 1814 was addressed to Rossi.
4 Mandoul, *Maistre et la Maison de Savoie*, 56–7.
5 Ibid., 51–2.
6 Gabet to Maistre, 15 July 1803. M.f.a. The first minister, Roburent, later told Rossi: "In the name of God, write to Count Maistre to write dispatches and not dissertations." Roburent to Rossi, 14 July 1804. Perrero, *I Reali de Sardegna*, 269.
7 Maistre to Gabet, 30 August 1803. AS Letteri ministri Russia, Mazzo 6.
8 Maistre to Gabet, 30 October 1803. Ibid.
9 See Mandoul, *Maistre et la Maison de la Savoie*, 58–71, and Triomphe, *Joseph de Maistre*, 211–15.
10 Maistre to Rossi, 7 December 1804. AS Letteri ministri Russia, Mazzo 6.
11 See especially, Triomphe, *Joseph de Maistre*, 211–24.
12 "A one month stay in this country has convinced me of the absolute impossibility of living here with 20,000 livres." Maistre to Challembert, 11 June 1803. AS Letteri ministri Russia, Mazzo 6.
13 Maistre to Victor-Emmanuel I, 9 June 1803. Ibid.
14 Blanc reproduces this memoir but without giving the date, which was 25 March 1804. *Mémoires politiques*, 164–79.
15 Maistre to Victor-Emmanuel I, 6 February 1806. *OC*, 10:50–5.
16 Triomphe, *Joseph de Maistre*, 219–23.
17 The other letters have all disappeared, perhaps destroyed by Madame de Maistre herself. (There are, however, among Maistre's letters to his daughter Adèle, a few scattered notes to his wife. M.f.a.) From his letter registers, we know that he remained a faithful correspondent during their long years of separation. See Darcel, "Registres de la correspondance," 13–14.
18 The letter was dated 8 June 1808, but according to Maistre's letter register it did not leave St Petersburg until March 1809. Ibid., 136.
19 The queen was a Hapsburg, and Maistre was always quite outspoken in his criticism of Austrian policies in Italy.
20 Maistre to his wife, 8 June 1808. M.f.a.
21 Ibid.
22 Ibid.
23 Maistre's reiterated denunciations of Austrian policies and actions in Italy are the evidence used by Louis Blanc, *Mémoires politiques* (see especially 173–96), and J. Mandoul, *Maistre et la Maison de la Savoie*, to try to portray him as a great Italian statesman and precursor of Cavour.

24 Discussing the English in one of his early dispatches from St Petersburg, he
   wrote: "I admire their government (without believing, however, that one must
   or even that one can transport it elsewhere). I prostrate myself before their
   criminal laws, their arts, their science, their public spirit, etc., etc. But all that is
   spoiled in foreign policy by insufferable national prejudices and a pride
   without measure and without prudence that revolts other nations and prevents
   them from uniting with them for the good cause." Maistre to Rossi, 11
   December 1803. AS Letteri ministri Russia, Mazzo 6.
25 See Alan Palmer, *Alexander I: Tsar of War and Peace* (New York 1974) and
   Patricia Kennedy Grimsted, *The Foreign Ministers of Alexander I* (Berkeley
   1969).
26 See R.R. Palmer, *The Age of Democratic Revolution* (Princeton 1959),
   1:249–51.
27 Rossi to Maistre, 15 October 1803. AS Letteri ministri Russia, Mazzo 6.
28 Maistre to Rossi, 11 December 1803. Blanc, *Mémoires politiques*, 105–6.
29 Maistre to Rossi, 11 December 1803. AS Letteri ministri Russia, Mazzo 6.
   (Blanc omitted this portion of Maistre's letter.)
30 In 1816, reacting to the proselytizing of the Jesuits and Joseph de Maistre,
   Stourdza published (in excellent French) a book entitled *Considérations sur la
   doctrine et l'esprit de l'Eglise orthodoxe*, in which he defended the Russian
   Orthodox Church against the attempts of heterodox foreigners to raise doubts
   about the purity of its dogmas.
31 *Oeuvres posthumes* (Paris 1859), 3:170–1.
32 Maistre to the Baroness de Pont, 20 May 1805. *OC*, 9:400.
33 Triomphe, *Joseph de Maistre*, 282.
34 Maistre to Rossi, 28 December 1808. *OC*, 11:167.
35 Ibid.
36 Maistre to Serra-Capriola, 29 May 1804. Cited in Benedetto Croce, "Il duca di
   Serra-Capriola e Giuseppe de Maistre," *Archivio Storico per le Province
   Napoletane*, 57 (1922): 347.
37 Maistre to his wife, 8 June 1809. M.f.a.
38 Maistre to Challembert, 23 July 1803. AS Letteri ministri Russia, Mazzo 6.
39 *Carnets*, 162.
40 Rebotton, *Etudes maistriennes*, 143–218, provides a well-documented and
   detailed study of the relationship between Maistre and Stedingk; what follows
   is drawn mostly from this work.
41 Stedingk had been received into a lodge in Stockholm in 1777, and continued
   his Masonic involvement into the period of his acquaintance with Joseph de
   Maistre (ibid., 164–5). Rebotton cites one of Maistre's letters to Stedingk
   (from the period after the latter had returned to Sweden) as evidence that
   Maistre was an active participant in a lodge in St Petersburg in these years.
   However his interpretation of the relevant passage is open to question.
   Commenting, in a bantering way, on Stedingk's Masonic activities back in

Sweden, Maistre remarks: "Qu'il me seroit doux, M. le Maréchal, d'être reçu encore dans votre loge!" (Maistre to Stedingk, 16 December 1811. ibid., 21). Taken literally ("How pleasant it would be for me ... to be received in your lodge again."), the passage would mean that Maistre had been received previously in Stedingk's lodge. But given the context (the passage is followed by regret that they had probably been parted forever: "mais hélas! il n'y a pas d'apparence que je vous revoie jamais [but alas! It does not appear I will ever see you again]"), Maistre very likely intended "votre loge" as a reference to the Swedish ambassador's residence in St Petersburg, where he had so often been a guest. In the absence of any other documentary evidence of Maistre's participation in Masonic activities in the Russian capital, this ambiguous comment cannot be taken as proof of such involvement. In a long letter to Rossi the year before, in which he had reported on Swedish politics and Masonic activities in Sweden and Russia, Maistre had remarked: "If by chance they invited me to one of these assemblies, I would go without any difficulty, but I would let the emperor know the next day." Maistre to Rossi, 10 June 1810. Blanc, *Mémoires politiques*, 358.

42 Rossi to Maistre, 15 October 1803. AS Letteri ministri Russia, Mazzo 6.

43 Maistre to Rossi, 9 December 1803. Cited in Rebotton, *Etudes maistriennes*, 200.

44 Triomphe, *Joseph de Maistre*, 211.

45 Rebotton, *Etudes maistriennes*, 154.

46 Maistre to Victor-Emmanuel I, undated. Blanc, *Mémoires diplomatiques*, 152.

47 Maistre to Rossi, 30 April 1804. *OC*, 9:166–7.

48 Maistre to Victor-Emmanuel I, 14 February 1805. *OC*, 9:321–2.

49 Maistre even cultivated the ambassador of the American republic, John Quincy Adams, who served in St Petersburg from 1809 through 1814. Adam's memoirs for these years have a number of references to the Sardinian ambassador (*Memoirs of John Quincy Adams* [Philadelphia 1874], volume 2). When Adams first met Maistre in November 1809, he found him "a man of sense and vivacity in conversation" (p 64). At a diplomatic dinner in May 1810, he sat next to Maistre and discussed the "Slavonian language" with him (p 126). Maistre lent Adams his manuscript copy of his translation of Plutach's treatise on the delays of divine justice (296) and one of the works of the seventeenth-century Jesuit theologian, Denis Petau (p 582). In March 1814, on returning the Petau and other books, Adams recorded his final impressions of Maistre: "The Count is a religious man, a Roman Catholic, with all the prejudices of his sect. He is a great admirer of Malebranche, and has Locke and Condillac in horror. He thinks it a very sublime idea of Malebranche's, that God is the *place* in which spirits exist, as space is the place of bodies. So differently are the minds of men constituted, that this comparison conveys to my understanding no idea at all. It rather detracts from the idea I have of the

Deity, because it takes away its most essential characteristic, *intelligence*. It draws closely to the absurdities of the Greek philosophers, who thought water, air, fire, and what not, God. The Count was particularly harsh upon Locke for his doctine that we have no innate ideas. He insists that all our ideas are innate, and that a child can never learn anything but what he knows already. He expressed a mean opinion of Locke's genius, and said he was the origin of all the materialism of the eighteenth century; that Condillac was the corrupter of France; that Kant, the German metaphysician, though an atheist himself, had gone far to demolish Locke's pretence that experience was the source of our ideas; and that there is now wanting only a *coup de pied* to demolish such fellows as Locke and Condillac altogether" (pp 582–3)

50 Maistre acknowledged the fact of his naturalization in a letter to Blacas (24 August 1813), but we know nothing of the date or the precise circumstances. Daudet, *Maistre et Blacas*, 259.

51 In 1805, writing about a forthcoming Russian diplomatic initiative, Maistre remarked: "no one has yet understood how to deal with Bonaparte. He has only been confronted gingerly and with terror, and yet he can only be vanquished by audacity" (Maistre to Victor-Emmanuel I, 10 June 1805. *OC*, 9:420). According to Triomphe's tendentious interpretation of the evidence, Maistre's avowed purpose of advancing the interests of the Sardinian king was only a pretext for the interview, and the real motive was a highly romantic and mystical notion of himself as the "necessary man" who would "overturn" Napoleon. *Joseph de Maistre*, 231–3.

52 "I ardently desired to confront Tamerlaine in private; I know what I would have said to him." Maistre to Rossi, August 1807. *OC*, 10:453.

53 See Maistre's *Carnets*, 182–3, and Maistre to Rossi, 1 November 1807, *OC*, 10:509–14, in which all this activity is described.

54 Maistre to Savary (with the memoir), 27 October 1807. *OC*, 10:488–92.

55 Ibid., 490.

56 The only reference to Maistre to be found in Savary's correspondence for this period is a brief rather derogatory comment dated 23 August 1807 (ie, before Maistre's interview and before his memoir had been submitted). See Triomphe, *Joseph de Maistre*, 232 n208.

57 Rossi to Maistre, 15 February 1808. AS Letteri ministeri Russia, Mazzo 7. Writing to the Sardinian ambassador in London, Rossi decried Maistre's imprudence: "It is unfortunate that an indiscreet zeal and unlimited presumption so carries away in this way a man who otherwise has talents and knowledge of more than one kind." Rossi to Count de Front, 16 February 1808. AS Letteri ministeri Inghilterra, Mazzo 101.

58 Maistre to Rossi, 10 August 1813, and 18 September 1813. Blanc, *Correspondance diplomatique*, 1:334–7 and 352–4.

59 Rossi to Maistre, 29 November 1813. AS Letteri ministri Russia, Mazzo 9.

60 Maistre to Rodolphe, 8 October 1813. M.f.a.

61 Maistre to Rodolphe, 5 December 1813. M.f.a.

62 Rodolphe to his father, May 1814. M.f.a.

63 Ibid.

64 Rodolphe to his father, 8 June 1814. M.f.a.

65 Ibid.

66 The bulk of the most interesting portions of this correspondence has been published. The first volume appeared in 1858, authorized by Cavour with the purpose of publicizing Maistre's anti-Austrian and pro-French views. (See Albert Blanc, *Mémoires politiques et correspondance diplomatique de J. de Maistre*, 3.) Blanc's 1858 volume was highly selective, with "explanations and historical commentaries" (to give the work's subtitle). But in 1860, he published two additional volumes (without commentary), which included the more important letters from Maistre's later years in Russia (*Correspondance diplomatique de Joseph de Maistre*, 1811–1817 [Paris 1860]). Volumes 9 through 14 of the Vitte 1884 edition of Maistre's *Oeuvres complètes* reprinted most (but not all) of the letters Blanc had published, and added others Blanc had omitted. The additional letters that survive in the Archivio di stato in Turin and in the Maistre family archives deal mainly with Maistre's personal affairs (ie, repetitious complaints) and the affairs of private individuals whose problems came to Maistre's attention in his official capacity. The Blanc and Vitte editions both suffer from faulty editing; some letters are misdated, portions of letters are transposed to incorrect dates, and ellipses are not indicated. In the Vitte edition, in particular, there seems to have been a concerted effort to suppress passages that might reflect unfavourably on Joseph de Maistre. For a recent assessment of Maistre's diplomatic correspondence, see Edouard-Félix Guyon, "Joseph de Maistre, diplomate Sarde, témoin et juge de son temps, 1792–1817," *Revue d'histoire diplomatique*, 97 (1983): 75–107.

67 Maistre to Rossi, August 1807. *OC*, 10:454.

68 "I am annoyed that it has not occurred to you to write to me of this in code and to put it in the post in Vienna. It would have been decoded and read here, and this would have been one of the best ways to make it known to the Russian minister. I have used this method for my own account very advantageously." Maistre to Rossi, 26 March 1807. M.f.a.

69 Darcel, "Registres de la correspondance," 47.

70 Daudet, *Maistre et Blacas*, 50, 78.

71 A misdated letter in Maistre's *OC*, 9:113–19, has led to confusion on this matter. This letter, in which Maistre informed Rossi of his exchange of correspondence with Louis XVIII and Avaray, is there incorrectly dated 3 August 1803. It should have been dated 1804. The error must be blamed on Maistre himself, since the original in the Archivio di stato carries the date 3 August 1803, in Maistre's own hand, at the end of the letter. But at the head it is dated 1804 and from the context it had to have been written in 1804. In the

letter there is reference to an enclosed copy of a letter to Avaray, and this copy, which is also to be found in the same file, is dated 15 July 1804. The published version appears to have been taken from Maistre's letterbook copy (in a secretary's hand), which was also misdated. (M.f.a.) Triomphe accepted the 1803 date, which somewhat confused his narrative. *Joseph de Maistre*, 225.

72 Louis XVIII to Maistre, 25 June 1804. *OC*, 14:296. And Avaray to Maistre, 26 June 1804. M.f.a.

73 Maistre to Rossi, 23 March 1804. AS Letteri ministri Russia, Mazzo 6.

74 Maistre to Rossi, 16 June 1804. *OC*, 9:187–8 (wrongly dated as July 1804).

75 "An event I loath."

76 Ibid., 188–91. For a discussion of the implications of Maistre's belief in "duration" as the essential criterion of political legitimacy, see Lebrun, *Throne and Altar*, 65–70.

77 Maistre to Rossi, 3 August 1804. *OC*, 9:118.

78 Maistre to Avaray, 15 July 1804. AS Letteri ministri Russia, Mazzo 6. Blanc provides portions of this letter, but omits this opening sentence. *Mémoires politiques*, 127–31.

79 See Blanc, *Mémoires politiques*, 127–8. Avaray's letter had been ambiguous as to whether the request was for a draft or for advice in editing.

80 Ibid., 128.

81 Maistre refers to his *Considérations sur la France*.

82 Maistre to Avaray, 15 July 1804. AS Letteri ministri Russia, Mazzo 6.

83 Blanc, *Mémoires politiques*, 131. Near the end of the letter, in a passage omitted by Blanc, he again wrote of his uncertainty: "Harassed by all the devils of my imagination, veritably split apart by Society and by books that pull me in a contrary sense (what torture for a royalist!) I no longer know to whom to listen. I conform a little to the one, a little to the other, and I have the bittersweet prospect of being counted wrong by everyone."

84 Ibid., 128.

85 Maistre to Rossi, 10 October 1804. *OC*, 9:236–7.

86 Maistre to Avaray, 3 October 1804. *OC*, 9:229–33.

87 Maistre to Rossi, 5 April 1807. *OC*, 10:371.

88 Daudet, *Maistre et Blacas*, reproduces 44 of the 53 letters Maistre is known to have written to Blacas between 1808 and 1820. Four additional letters may be found in the Vitte edition of Maistre's works.

89 Maistre to Blacas, 3 July 1811. Daudet, *Maistre et Blacas*, 125–6.

90 Ibid., 127.

91 Blacas to Maistre, 20 October 18ll. Ibid., 143–4.

92 "There is an essential article on which our ideas are fundamentally opposed, this is the famous declaration of the clergy of 1682. You have really frightened me by telling me that 'the descendants of the great king know nothing of his repentance and disavowal'." Maistre to Blacas, 2 January 1812. Ibid., 152.

93 Maistre to Blacas, 22 May 1812. *OC*, 12:430.

94 "do me, I beg you, a great and veritable favour. Send back to me all that I wrote to you on the papacy. I am meditating a great work on this subject, the most important and the most ignored of our century" (Maistre to Blacas, 16 November 1813. Daudet, *Maistre et Blacas*, 281). Despite Maistre's plea that he had neglected to make copies of these letters and his promise to return them in three months, Blacas failed to respond to Maistre's request, and the latter did not dare repeat it. See Maistre to Vallaise, 2 February 1815. *OC*, 13:35–6.

95 Blacas to Maistre, 20 March 1812. Daudet, *Maistre et Blacas*, 173.

96 Ibid., 232.

97 Maistre to Blacas, 14 April 1813. Ibid., 232–6.

98 Maistre to Blacas, 16 November 1813. Ibid., 279–82.

99 Maistre to Blacas, 24 August 1813. Ibid., 258–9.

100 Blacas to Maistre, 19 February 1814. Ibid., 290.

101 Maistre to Blacas, 22 May 1814. *OC*, 12:434.

102 Guillaume de Bertier de Sauvigny, *The Bourbon Restoration* (Philadelphia 1966), 61.

103 Blacas to Maistre, 14 August 1814. Daudet, *Maistre et Blacas*, 292.

104 Blacas to Maistre, 10 November 1814. M.f.a.

105 We know from his letter register that he wrote at least four letters to Blacas during this period. Darcel, "Registres de la correspondance," 203–10.

106 Maistre to Blacas, 8 January 1815. M.f.a. Most of this letter may be found in *OC*, 13:4–7, but the above passage is omitted from the printed version.

107 This work had been composed in 1809 as a consequence of Maistre's involvement in Russian politics; the circumstances of its genesis will be described in the next section.

108 Maistre to Bonald, 13 July 1814. *OC*, 12:437–8.

109 Maistre to Blacas, 25 February 1815, and Maistre to Bonald, 25 February 1815. *OC*, 13:41–4, 45–8.

110 Ibid., 42.

111 Ibid., 43.

112 We know, however, that Maistre had at first been scandalized by the conditions on which Louis XVIII had been restored. In July 1814 he had written of the event in these terms: "they are infinitely deceived if they believe that Louis XVIII has remounted the throne of his ancestors. He has only mounted the throne of Bonaparte." Maistre to Vallaise, 18 July 1814. Blanc, *Correspondance diplomatique*, 1:379.

113 Blacas to Maistre, 14 December 1814. Daudet, *Maistre et Blacas*, 295–8.

114 Maistre to Blacas, 8 February 1816. *OC*, 13:243–4.

115 Maistre to Blacas, 23 August 1818. Daudet, *Maistre et Blacas*, 350.

116 *OC*, 9:125–56.

117 *Carnets*, 167.

118 Maistre to Monsignor de la Fare, 10 September 1805. *OC*, 9:464.

119 "We are lost … and it is the Emperor of Russia who has dealt us the fatal blow." Maistre to Count de Front, 10 January 1806. *OC*, 10:13.

120 Memoir, 2 January 1806, *OC*, 10:1–13; Maistre to Victor-Emmanuel I, 31 January 1806, ibid., 28–9, 39; and Maistre to Rossi, 27 February 1806, ibid., 64.

121 The most helpful study in English of Maistre's involvement in Russian domestic affairs is David W. Edwards, "Count Joseph Marie de Maistre and Russian Educational Policy," *Slavic Review*, 36 (1977): 54–75. Briefer treatments in English include Alexander Vucinich, *Science in Russian Culture: A History to 1860* (Stanford 1963), 227–31, James A. Billington,*The Icon and the Axe* (New York 1966), 271–6, and Donald W. Treadgold, *The West in Russia and China* (Cambridge 1973), 1:136–40. The most detailed study in French is Triomphe, *Joseph de Maistre*, 241–325. Both Triomphe and Edwards made extensive use of Russian language sources. What follows is based on their work.

122 James J. Flynn, "The Role of the Jesuits in the Politics of Russian Education," *The Catholic Historical Review*, 66 (1970): 253.

123 Ibid., 253–4.

124 See James T. Flynn, "The Universities, the Gentry, and the Russian Imperial Services, 1815–1825," *Canadian Slavic Studies*, 2 (1968): 486–92.

125 Flynn, "The Role of the Jesuits in Russian Education," 253.

126 Palmer, *Alexander I*, 166.

127 Ibid., 168. See as well Marc Raeff, *Michael Speranski: Statesman of Imperial Russia, 1772–1839* (The Hague 1957).

128 "what is sure, is that a new law, which they call constitutional, has just turned the country completely upside down, and made of it an entirely new Empire." Maistre to Victor-Emmanuel I, 18 January 1810. *OC*, 11:384. Misdated in the printed version to December 1809.

129 Ibid., 386.

130 This is the date indicated at the end of the manuscript. See Robert Triomphe's critical edition (Strasbourg 1959), 109.

131 Maistre to Victor-Emmanuel I, 18 January 1810. *OC*, 11:386–7.

132 Ibid.

133 Edwards, "Maistre and Russian Educational Policy," 62–3.

134 According to Maistre's own account, conversations with the new minister led the latter to ask Maistre to submit his ideas in writing. See *OC*, 8:161–3, and Maistre to Rossi, 26 September 1810, ibid., 10:493.

135 Edwards, "Maistre and Russian Educational Policy," 68.

136 These letters, dated June and July 1810, may be found in the Vitte edition of Maistre's works under the title "Cinq lettres sur l'éducation publique en Russie." *OC*, 8:161–232.

137 Edwards, "Maistre and Russian Educational Policy," 68–9.

138 Razumovsky's note is bound with Maistre's manuscript of his reply. M.f.a.

139 On Fessler, see Triomphe, *Joseph de Maistre*, 552.

140 "Observations sur le Prospectus Disciplinarum ou Plan d'étude proposé pour le Séminaire de Newsky par le Professeur Fessler." *OC*, 8:230–65.

141 Triomphe, *Joseph de Maistre*, 251, and Edwards, "Maistre and Russian Education Policy," 68.

142 Maistre to Rossi, 19 December 1810. *OC*, 11:522–3.

143 *OC*, 8:245.

144 Ibid., 242.

145 See Lebrun, "L'Epistémologie maistrienne," 230–41.

146 *OC*, 8:240–1.

147 Ibid.

148 A few additional remarks on Kant may be found in Maistre's notebooks and papers. (See Lebrun, "L'Epistémologie maistriennes," 227–8.) For trenchant criticisms of Maistre's critique of Fessler and Kant, see Triomphe, *Joseph de Maistre*, 552–6.

149 For a brief review in English of the story of the Jesuits in Russia, see Treadgold, *The West in Russia*, 1:131–40. In French, see Triomphe, *Joseph de Maistre*, 199–210, and Daniel Beauvois, "Les Jésuites dans l'Empire russe, 1772–1820," *Dix-huitième siècle*, 8 (1974): 257–72.

150 Treadgold, *The West in Russia*, 1:131–2.

151 Triomphe, *Joseph de Maistre*, 199, 204.

152 Treadgold, *The West in Russia*, 1:136.

153 Ibid.

154 Joseph de Maistre developed a close friendship with Gruber and deeply regretted his untimely death. See Triomphe, *Joseph de Maistre*, 307–8.

155 Ibid., 208.

156 Flynn, "The Role of the Jesuits in Russian Education," 254–5.

157 Ibid., 257–8.

158 *OC*, 8:267–75, and *Carnets*, 193.

159 Flynn, "The Role of the Jesuits in Russian Education," 258. Maistre noted in his diary that the decision was unanimous except for Baron Campen-Hausen, a German Protestant. One must presume that his information came from either Razumovsky or Golitsyn. *Carnets*, 193–4.

160 Flynn, "The Role of the Jesuits in Russian Education," 258.

161 Decree cited by Flynn, 258–9. This meant that Polotsk would function like a "university" in the sense of being the administrative centre of a "district" (ie, of all the Jesuit schools in Russia). The Academy was not empowered to grant degrees in law or medicine.

162 Ibid., 256–9.

163 *Carnets*, 194.

164 *OC*, 8:277–360. This work had been undertaken at Golitsyn's request prior to the composition of the shorter memoir on public instruction. Maistre to Victor-Emmanuel I, 12 November 1811. Blanc, *Correspondance diplomatique*, 1:42–3.

165 Maistre to Victor-Emmanuel I, 14 February 1812. *OC*, 12:80.

166 Maistre himself believed they made the crucial difference. Maistre to Victor-Emmanuel I. 14 February 1812. Blanc, *Correspondance diplomatique*, 1:49–50.

167 For a detailed but tendentious treatment of these events, see Triomphe, *Joseph de Maistre*, 256–67.

168 *Carnets*, 194.

169 Maistre to Rossi, 4 March 1812. *OC*, 12:91. Interestingly enough, Maistre had already written to his wife on 25 February alerting her of a possible trip to St Petersburg. Darcel, "Registres de la correspondance," 175.

170 Maistre to Rossi, 4 March 1812. *OC*, 12:91.

171 *Carnets*, 194–5. Entry for 8 March 1812.

172 Maistre to Rossi, 21 April 1812. Blanc, *Correspondance diplomatique*, 1:64.

173 *Carnets*, 195. Entry for 17 March 1812. According to the longer account in Maistre to Rossi, 21 April 1812, this conversation took place on 29 March. Blanc, *Correspondance diplomatique*, 1:65.

174 Ibid.

175 Ibid., 67–8.

176 Darcel, "Registres de la correspondance," 195, and Maistre to Rossi, 21 April 1812, Blanc, *Correspondance diplomatique*, 1:73.

177 Ibid., 89, and *Carnets*, 195, where there is also a list of the topics that were discussed. A longer account of this interview may be found in Maistre to Rossi, 9 May 1812. *OC*, 12:126–34.

178 Maistre to Rossi, 21 April 1812. Blanc, *Correspondance diplomatique*, 1:89.

179 Darcel, "Registres de la correspondance," 180. Entry for 25 April 1812.

180 Maistre to Victor-Emmanuel I. 18 July 1812. *OC*, 12:158.

181 Ibid., 159.

182 Palmer, *Alexander I*, 219–24.

183 See Triomphe, *Joseph de Maistre*, 266, 290.

184 See Palmer, *Alexander I*, 219–20.

185 Maistre to Victor-Emmanuel I. 27 December 1812. *OC*, 12:318.

186 Rossi to Maistre, 7 July 1812. AS Letteri ministri Russia, Mazzo 8.

187 Maistre to Alexander, 1 April 1813. *OC*, 12:343–54.

188 Maistre's own description of the festivities may be found in his letter to Victor-Emmanuel I. 24 July 1812. *OC*, 12:145–6. For a fuller description drawn from a Russian-language account, see Triomphe, *Joseph de Maistre*, 262–3. Maistre was evidently favourably impressed by what the Jesuits had accomplished at Polotsk; writing to the Neapolitan ambassador he described what he found in these terms: "the Jesuit establishment is very considerable. They support no less than 500 persons of all kinds – religious, novices, brothers, and pensioners included. All the necessary mechanical arts of all kinds are part of the establishment; otherwise they could not survive. They even have among the priests a great violinist who is a German. Everywhere

they have the same order and the same characteristics that we used to observe at home. The mistress of the house I am occupying told my valet: 'Without them we would be beasts.' In effect, they educate all these young people, and instead of asking for money from them, they give it to them, since their alms are immense." Maistre to Serra-Capriola, 20 May 1812. Cited in Benedetto Croce, "Due lettere inedite di Joseph de Maistre al Duci di Serracapriola," *Etudes italiennes*, 5 (1923): 195.

189 Triomphe, *Joseph de Maistre*, 261.

190 Maistre to Rodolphe, 7 June 1812. *OC*, 12:138.

191 "Your poor mother believes in good faith … that there is no other impediment to our reunion than the lack of passport and the circumstances of the war … Poor woman! … This is one of the most terrible moments of her life and of mine." Maistre to Rodolphe, 14 November 1812. M.f.a.

192 Edwards, "Maistre and Russian Educational Policy," 71.

193 Ibid., 68.

194 Ibid., 60.

195 Cited in Edwards, 73.

196 Ibid.

197 Maistre's initial letter of 8 December 1810 may be found in Uvarov's *Etudes de philologie et de critique* (Paris 1847), 53–66.

198 Edwards, 60–1. When Maistre sent Uvarov a copy of his *Considérations*, the latter responded with an enthusiastic letter of praise: "Reading this has produced in me such a lively feeling that I cannot prevent myself from communicating to you the ideas that it has awakened. Your work … is an axiom of the class of those that are not proved because they need no proofs, but that are felt because they are the rays of natural knowledge" (Uvarov to Maistre, 5 January 1815. M.f.a.). This letter appears as a preface to the 1884 Vitte edition of *Considérations sur la France*, but with the author identified only as "M.O … ." and with the Julian date, 24 December 1814. *OC*, 1:xlix–liv.

199 Edwards, 71.

200 See Nicholas V. Riasonosvsky, *Nicholas I and Official Nationality in Russia, 1825–1855* (Berkeley and Los Angeles 1965).

201 Edwards, 71.

202 Maistre to Baroness de Pont, 30 March 1805. *OC*, 9:361.

203 He claimed he needed only three hours out of every twenty-four. See Maistre to Vallaise, 2 February 1815. *OC*, 13:37.

204 Xavier de Maistre to Nicolas de Maistre, 25 January 1810. Félix Klein, "Lettres inédites de Xavier de Maistre à sa famille," *Le Correspondant*, 219 (1902): 918–19.

205 *OC*, 4:2.

206 Ibid.

207 Berthier, *Xavier de Maistre*, 234–48.

208 *OC*, 4:8–9.
209 These statistics are from a computer assisted analysis of dated first or most extensive citations.
210 M.f.a.
211 "Recueil d'anecdotes. Extraits et pièces fugitives tirés de Journaux Anglois."M.f.a.
212 On Maistre's judgment of Malebranche, see Richard Lebrun, "Joseph de Maistre et Malebranche." *REM*, forthcoming.
213 M.f.a.
214 Most of these anecdotes, rearranged in topical order, were published by Father J. Gagarine, "Anecdotes recueillies à Saint-Pétersbourg par le comte Joseph de Maistre," *Etudes*, 21 (4th series, vol. 2, 1868): 533–8, 777–98, and 22 (4th series, vol. 3, 1869): 84–99.
215 Two other minor works (religious apologetics in the form of letters) were published without Maistre's permission in 1820.
216 Pluchard was a St Petersburg printer-publisher.
217 Maistre undoubtedly means Paris.
218 Maistre to Countess d'Edling (née Stourdza), undated. *OC*, 14:277.
219 "Religion E," 3–6.
220 Triomphe reproduces the complete memoir (*Joseph de Maistre*, 517–19). For some reason Triomphe reads this memoir as evidence that Maistre contemplated "an entire book against Germany, mother of Protestantism and irreligion." Ibid., 517.
221 "Religion E," 161–2.
222 Maistre to Monsignor de la Fare, 25 May 1806. *OC*, 10:112.
223 In a register entitled "Manuscrits," 455. M.f.a.
224 Maistre to Abbé Nicole, 17 April 1813. Cited in Z. Frappaz, *Vie de l'abbé Nicole*, 97.
225 For a detailed treatment of Xavier's comments and Joseph's responses, see Berthier, *Xavier de Maistre*, 236–48, 353–6.
226 Alexander Stourdza claimed to have read it under the title "Principes des institutions humaines," but one wonders if his reference is not to the *Essai sur le principe générateur. Oeuvres posthumes*, 3:192.
227 See Triomphe's critical edition, xviii–xix.
228 *Lettres de Mme de Sévigné à sa fille et à ses amis*, ed. by Ph.-A. Grouvelle (Paris 1806), 11 volumes.
229 "Observations critiques sur une édition des lettres de Madame de Sévigné," *OC*, 8:1–59.
230 *OC*, 8:139–57. In this edition this letter is preceded by a letter "A une dame protestante sur la maxime qu'un honnête homme ne change jamais de religion" dated 9 December 1809 (pp 129–38). However, the manuscript of the second letter carries the date 10 August 1797. M.f.a.
231 Triomphe follows Rouët de Journal, *Une Russe catholique: Mme Svétchine*, 93, in suggesting that it was addressed to Countess Rostoptchine. *Joseph de Maistre*, 306 n651.

232 A note discussing the letter "A une dame protestante" concludes: "Therefore I conclude that it is of the greatest importance that those to whom God has given a clear and penetrating voice like yours must not allow themselves to be stifled by fear." Father Robert d'Ervelange-Vitry SJ to Maistre, 17 May 1811. M.f.a. See, as well, the Latin letter from Father Brzozoswki (3 January 1814) cited in Amédée de Margerie, *Le Comte Joseph de Maistre* (Paris 1882), 53–6.

233 Maistre complained bitterly that the letters were "absolutely secret pieces touching on what are called *matters of conscience*," suspected that Madame Swetchine (a Russian lady whose conversion was at least partly the consequence of Maistre's influence) had imprudently released the letters, and worried that their publication had compromised him "in the most terrible way with the irascible Alexander" (Maistre to Rodolphe, undated, but 1820. M.f.a.). See also Maistre to Lamennais, 1 May 1820 (*OC*, 14:227) where he complained to Lamennais as one of the editors of the offending journal, *Le Défenseur*. In his reply (18 May 1820, ibid., 367–8), Lamennais apologized with the explanation that the letters had simply been reprinted from a little review published in Rome. It has now been established that it was Maistre's nephew, Louis Vignet, who passed the letters on to Lamartine, another of the editors of *Le Défenseur*. See Jean Rebotton, "Lamartine et la famille Maistre," *REM*, no. 4 (1978): 108–9.

234 *OC*, 5:361–470. The Maistre family archives contain two manuscripts of the work. The first, a preliminary draft, is to be found in "Extraits F," 356:408ix; the second is a separately bound calligraphic copy. Both are dated 1810.

235 Maistre had cited Daniel Albert Wyttenbach's 1795 Oxon edition of Plutarch's *Moralia*.

236 *Memoirs*, 2:296–7.

237 *Catalogue Général des livres imprimés de la Bibliothèque Nationale* (Paris 1930), 104:66.

238 *OC*, 1:233. However the manuscript of the work carries the date 4 April 1813. M.f.a.

239 Maistre's original Latin version accompanied by a French translation by the editors appeared in the 1851 *Lettres et Opuscules inédits*, 2:453–525. The French title is "Réflexions critiques d'un Chrétien dévoué à la Russie sur l'ouvrage de Méthode, Archevêque de Twer." Both the Latin and French versions may also be found in *OC*, 8:361–417.

240 Ibid., 414. Paul Strogonov was one of Tsar Alexander's close companions in the early years of his reign.

241 It was, however, reprinted in Buttet, *Xavier de Maistre*, 213–16.

242 "Discours pour le Retour de Roi de Sardaigne dans ses états de terre ferme," *OC*, 8:451–68.

243 Ibid., 452. From an explanatory note Maistre had left attached to his manuscript.

244 The printed version is entitled *Lettres à un gentilhomme Russe sur l'Inquisition Espagnole* (*OC*, 3:283–401), but the manuscript title was "Lettres de

Philomathe de Civarron à un Gentilhomme Russe sur l'Inquisition Espagnole." The six individual letters are dated from 23 June 1815 through 27 September 1815, but the manuscript carries two notes at the end: "St Petersburg, 27 September 1815," and "work completed 15 September 1815" (M.f.a.). In the printed version the letters are datelined "Moscow." The reason for this revision is unknown. This little work has the distinction of having been thrice translated into English in the mid-nineteenth century. The first was by the Reverend John Fletcher and published in London in 1838. The second translation (Boston 1843), by T.J. O'Flaherty (the "Catholic pastor of Salem"), has recently been reprinted by Scholars' Fascimiles & Reprints (Delmar, NY 1977) with an introduction by Charles M. Lombard. The third translation (London 1851) was made by Aeneas McD. Dawson, who also translated Maistre's *Du Pape* (London 1850).

245 Maistre to Carlo-Emanuele Alfieri di Sostegno, letters of 11 November and 11 December 1816 and 4 February 1817. Nada Narciso, "Tra Russia e Piemonte (Lettere inedite de Giuseppe de Maistre a Carlo Emanuele Alfieri de Sostegno 1816–1818," in *Miscellanea Walter Maturi* (Turin 1966), 309–13.

246 See Triomphe, *Joseph de Maistre*, 281–2.

247 See, for example, Maistre to Rossi, 8 December 1808. *OC*, 11:168–70.

248 M.f.a. Maistre's note refers to the arrival of his wife and daughters from Turin after more than twelve years of separation.

249 Maistre to Count de Noailles, 6 November 1815. *OC*, 13:178.

250 The points were all incorporated into the *Examen* in the chapter on the "Union of Science and Religion." *OC*, 6:450–87.

251 "Sons of men, how long will you be hard of heart." Psalm 4:3.

252 "Philosophie D," 7.

253 See Lebrun, "Maistre, Cassandra of Science," 214–31.

254 Maistre to Abbé Vaurin, 26 January 1818. *OC*, 14:123.

255 Maistre to Bonald, 10 July 1818. *OC*, 14:138.

256 The manuscript of the *Examen de la philosophie de Bacon*, however, was forgotten in St Petersburg (Maistre to Rodolphe, 6 June 1817. M.f.a.). Although Rodolphe would have brought it to Turin when he returned from Russia a few months later, perhaps the fact Joseph de Maistre did not have this manuscript with him when he was in Paris that summer may help explain his failure to achieve prompt publication.

257 *OC*, 8:509.

258 The decrees of expulsion charged that the Jesuits had undermined the Orthodox Church and refused co-operation with the government. Maistre's accounts (see his letters to Count de Vallaise, 2 February 1816, *OC*, 13:202–4, and to Archbishop Severoli, 23 February 1816, ibid., 382–4) and those of the Jesuits themselves (see, for example, M.J. Rouët de Journal, *Un Collège de Jésuits à Saint-Pétersbourg* [Paris 1922], 207–300) emphasize the conversion issue.

259 For a well-argued case for the importance of this fourth issue, see Flynn, "The Role of the Jesuits in Russian Education," 251–65.

260 Maistre to Vallaise, 2 January 1816. *OC*, 13:204.

261 "quelques femmes d'un esprit faible et inconséquent."

262 Maistre to Vallaise, 5 January 1816. *OC*, 13:209.

263 For more details on this social circle and Maistre's relationships with most of these women, see Triomphe, *Joseph de Maistre*, 296–308.

264 Ibid., 308.

265 Maistre to Madame Swetchine, 12 August 1815. *OC*, 13:119–25. Perhaps it is not surprising that she later described the character of Maistre's religious beliefs in the following terms: "Answering all the exigencies of his reason, satisfying to all the needs of his genius, the Catholic system was always for him in a state of living demonstration; and never, perhaps, has the power of Catholicism known a greater or more absolute exercise. The faith had become so much the very nature of his mind that outside it he could consciously admit only ignorance, limited intelligence, bad faith or mysterious chastisement. In him, the idea ruled all and subdued his heart, which was more honest and righteous than naturally pious." Letter of 3 June 1851. Cited in Alfred de Falloux, *Madame Swetchine, sa vie et ses oeuvres* (Paris 1875), 1:429–30.

266 Eight days after the expulsion decree, an imperial secretary noted that "Count de Maistre, a bigot and more than a Jesuit, is accused of having contributed to this proselytism; it is certain that it was he who introduced them [the Jesuits] into our best houses." Cited by Triomphe, *Joseph de Maistre*, 315.

267 Maistre to Vallaise, 12 January 1816. *OC*, 13:211–12.

268 Maistre to Vallaise, 24 February 1816. *OC*, 13:280–1.

269 Ibid., 283–4.

270 Maistre to Vallaise, 27 February 1816. *OC*, 13:293–5.

271 Nesselrode to Count Kozlovski, 12 April 1816. Cited in Triomphe, *Joseph de Maistre*, 320–1.

272 See Count de Gabriac to the Duke de Richelieu, 10 June 1816. Cited in *Les Carnets du Joseph de Maistre*, 232–5.

273 Triomphe, *Joseph de Maistre*, 322–3.

274 Maistre to Vallaise, 9 July 1816. Blanc, *Correspondance diplomatique*, 2:244–5.

275 Capodistra to Vallaise, 6 August 1816. AS Letteri ministri esteri, Russia, Mazzo 1.

276 Maistre to Vallaise, 27 August 1816. Blanc, *Correspondance diplomatique*, 2:254–5. Writing to his old friend Henry Costa, Maistre expressed considerable chagrin at having to leave Russia: "pray for the dead. You no doubt are going to say to me: 'Is it you who are to be taken for dead?' Undoubtedly, my dear Marquis, for if His Majesty sends me walking with only my pension, am I not dead? And if, after fifteen years of a free, liberal, and almost libertine life, my master again sinks me in papers up to my ears, will I not also be dead?" Maistre to Costa, 1817. François Descostes, *Lettres inédites de J. de Maistre* (Chambéry 1899), 25.

277 Maistre to Vallaise, 11 November 1816. Blanc, *Correspondance diplomatique*, 2:279–80.
278 Maistre to Vallaise, letters of 9 May 1817 and 7 June 1817. Ibid., 365–7.
279 Ibid., 366–7.
280 Xavier to Nicolas de Maistre, 28 May 1817. Klein, "Lettres inédites de X. de Maistre," 1104.
281 *Carnets*, 201.

CHAPTER SEVEN: TURIN

1 We have evidence of at least 296 letters written between his departure from Russia in late May 1817 and his death 26 February 1821. But since Maistre stopped keeping his letter register at the end of December 1816 and discontinued his diary after his arrival in Turin at the end of August 1817, we have no way of knowing the total volume of his correspondence in these years. Some 122 letters from this period have been published (in various places), another 86 are to be found in the Maistre family archives (55 of these letters are to Rodolphe), and another 6 in the Archivio di Stato in Turin.
2 *Carnets*, 201–3.
3 Maistre to Karaoulov, 20 July 1819. *OC*, 14:179. Karaoulov had been the captain of the *Hambourg*.
4 Ibid., 180.
5 In a letter written 2 March 1881, responding to the questions of one of Joseph de Maistre's great-grandsons, a young Jesuit. "Un portrait de Joseph de Maistre tracé par sa fille Constance," *Etudes*, 125 (1910): 500. Although written when Constance was 88 years old and obviously hagiographic, this letter is nevertheless valuable because of the details it provides. Constance served as her father's secretary during his last years.
6 Maistre to Blacas, 8 May 1817. *OC*, 14:88.
7 *Carnets*, 203.
8 Maistre to Blacas, 23 August 1818. Daudet, *Maistre et Blacas*, 349–50.
9 See Falloux, *Madame Swetchine*, 1:173.
10 Maistre to Madame Swetchine, 26 October 1817. Falloux, *Madame Swetchine*, 1:210.
11 But over twenty years later, when Xavier de Maistre visited Paris, he found that his brother was still remembered: "his memory is living everywhere. All who are *bien pensant* and old in the Faubourg Saint-Germain approached me to talk to me and to boast of having known him." Xavier de Maistre to Adèle de Maistre, 23 April 1839. Félix Klein, *Lettres inédits de X. de Maistre à sa famille* (Paris 1902), 74.
12 "Portrait de J. de Maistre," 500.
13 *Carnets*, 205.
14 Maistre to Bonald, 15 November 1817. *OC*, 14:112–13.
15 *Carnets*, 205.

16 Ibid.

17 "I passed six days in a kind of continual enchantment, surrounded by brothers, sisters, nephews, nieces, cousins and cousins, caressed, feted, celebrated, and spoiled in an inconceivable way." Maistre to Madame Swetchine, 26 October 1817. Falloux, *Madame Swetchine*, 1:209.

18 Maistre to Blacas, 23 August 1818. Daudet, *Maistre et Blacas*, 351.

19 Maistre to Blacas, 3 September 1817, ibid., 320; Maistre to Constance de Maistre, 6 September 1817, *OC*, 14:101; and Maistre to Bonald, 15 November 1817, ibid., 115.

20 Maistre to Blacas, 22 May 1814. *OC*, 12:434.

21 Maistre to Severoli, 13 December 1815. *OC*, 13:191–2.

22 *OC*, 2:279.

23 Triomphe argues strongly for this interpretation. *Joseph de Maistre*, 347–51.

24 Maistre to Costa, 14 April 1816. *OC*, 13:317. 125 Maistre to Abbé Vuarin, 26 January 1818. *OC*, 14:124.

26 Maistre to Vallaise, 27 August 1816. Blanc, *Correspondance diplomatique*, 2:255.

27 Blacas to Maistre, 9 February 1817. Daudet, *Maistre et Blacas*, 306.

28 Maistre to Blacas, 5 April 1817. Ibid., 308.

29 Maistre to Blacas, 20 July 1817. Ibid., 316.

30 Maistre to Blacas, 3 September 1817. Ibid., 321. The reference to "foreign voices" probably alludes to the tsar's efforts to ensure that Maistre be given a suitable position.

31 Maistre to Blacas, 26 December 1817. Ibid., 327–8.

32 Maistre to Blacas, 16 May 1818. Ibid., 340.

33 Blacas to Maistre, 29 May 1818. Ibid., 343.

34 Maistre to Blacas, 10 June 1818. Ibid., 344–5.

35 Blacas to Maistre, 8 August 1818. Ibid., 347.

36 Maistre to Blacas, 23 August 1818. Ibid., 351.

37 Blacas to Maistre, 26 September 1818. Ibid., 359–60.

38 Maistre to Blacas, 10 October 1818. *OC*, 14:171–3.

39 Maistre to Blacas, 5 December 1818, and another letter undated, but clearly written just a few days later. Daudet, *Maistre et Blacas*, 362, 365–6.

40 Blacas to Maistre, 16 December 1818. Ibid., 368–9.

41 Maistre to Blacas, 19 December 1818. Ibid., 370.

42 Maistre to Bonald, 22 March 1819. *OC*, 14:160.

43 Maistre to Abbé Rey, 9 February 1820. *OC*, 14:201. Writing to his son, Maistre was even more deprecatory: "As for the position I am presently occupying, I can assure you that nothing is less significant. It is a position that is absolutely null for the state in that it gives no influence of any kind. The phrase *Grande Chancellerie* dazzles the provincials, but take it for certain it means nothing" (Maistre to Rodolphe, 5 April 1819. M.f.a.). On the other hand, the Austrian ambassador to Turin ranked Maistre among the three or four most influential people in the government: "One can only congratulate the country to thus see

three essential places filled by persons of such talent, merit, and recognized probity as Messieurs de Saint-Marsan, de Maistre and de Balbe." Staremberg to Metternich, 15 September 1819. *Le Relazioni diplomatiche fra l'Austria e il regno di Sardegna,* edited by Narciso Nada (Rome 1964), 1:404.

44 In a manuscript volume entitled "Mémoires – Notes – Relations." M.f.a.

45 "Portrait de J. de Maistre," 502. According to Rodolphe's version, his father had argued that the proposed changes were good, even necessary, but that the time was not opportune. "Notice biographique," *OC*, 1:xli.

46 On the personality and views of Constance, see Jacques Lovie, "Constance de Maistre: éléments pour une biographie," *REM*, no. 4 (1978): 141–63.

47 "From all appearances … the work … will be introduced to the world within four months." Maistre to Count de Noailles, 29 July 1817. A.G. Brahan, "Six Lettres inédites de Joseph de Maistre au comte de Noailles," *Revue d'histoire littéraire de la France*, 67 (1967): 128.

48 Chateaubriand to Maistre, undated, but apparently in mid-September 1817. Cited in Camille Latreille, *Joseph de Maistre et la papauté* (Paris 1906), 99.

49 Maistre to Chateaubriand, October 1817, *OC*, 14:109–10. This letter is here mistakenly identified as to Bonald.

50 On the Abbé Rey, see Lovie, "Constance de Maistre," 148–9.

51 Latreille, *Maistre et la papauté*, 101–2.

52 On the Abbé Vuarin, see Lovie, "Constance de Maistre," 172, note.

53 Latreille, *Maistre et la papauté*, 103.

54 Maistre to Besson, 18 April 1818. Camille Latreille, "Lettres inédites de Joseph de Maistre," *Revue bleue*, 50 (1912): 258.

55 Latreille, *Maistre et la papauté*, 104.

56 Maistre to Besson, 2 May 1818. Latreille, "Lettres inédites," 1 259.

57 On De Place, see Latreille, *Maistre et la papauté*, 107–18, and Louis Trenard, "Joseph de Maistre et ses amis Lyonnais," *REM*, no. 8 (1983): 46–58. Despite Joseph de Maistre's rule about the use of particles, which has been followed here for his own name, Guy-Marie de Place signed his name De Place, and this is how his name was used by contemporaries (including Maistre).

58 Latreille's "Lettres inédites de Joseph de Maistre" includes twenty-seven letters dating from June 1818 through December 1819, when *Du Pape* was finally published, and another nine letters written in 1820. Eighteen letters from De Place to Maistre remain in the Maistre family archives.

59 Maistre to Besson, 3 June 1818. Latreille, "Lettres inédites," 261.

60 Maistre to De Place, 20 or 23 June 1818. Ibid., 262. The point was repeated in another letter, 28 September 1818. Ibid., 296.

61 De Place to Maistre, letters of 24 May 1818, 8 December 1818, and 26 April 1819. M.f.a.

62 At least he restrained his impatience in his letters to De Place; his letters to Rodolphe express bitter feelings of frustration over his dealings with De Place, Besson, and Rusand. M.f.a.

63 Maistre to De Place, 8 February 1819. Latreille, "Lettres inédites," 235.

64 Maistre to De Place, 15 July 1818. Ibid., 294.

65 Maistre to De Place, 20 or 23 June 1818, Ibid., 262.

66 Maistre to De Place, 29 June 1818. Ibid., 292.

67 Maistre to De Place, 28 September 1818. Ibid., 295.

68 Maistre to De Place, 18 September 1819. Ibid., 359.

69 De Place to Maistre, 11 November 1819. M.f.a.

70 Undated letter to De Place, cited by Latreille, *Maistre et la papauté*, 94.

71 Maistre to De Place, 8 February 1819. Latreille, "Lettres inédites," 326.

72 Maistre to De Place, 28 September 1818. Ibid., 296.

73 *Du Pape, OC*, 2:xxiii.

74 Including unedited manuscripts of *Du Pape* and Maistre's letters to De Place –
    which have since disappeared apparently. See the introduction by Jacques
    Lovie and Joannes Chetail to their critical edition of *Du Pape* (Geneva
    1966), ix.

75 *Maistre et la papauté*, 40–95.

76 *De irreformabili Romani Pontificis in definiendis fidei controversis Judicio*
    (Rome 1771). Giuseppe Agostino Orsi was an ultramontane writer whose work
    Maistre cited against Bossuet.

77 *Maistre et la papauté*, 95.

78 Maistre to De Place, 29 June 1818. Latreille, "Lettres inédites," 292.

79 Maistre to De Place, 28 September 1818. Ibid., 296.

80 Maistre to Severoli, 23 February 1817. *OC*, 14:56–7. In other letters to his
    government and to a Jesuit friend, Maistre described his friendship with the
    Stourdza family, expressed his admiration for the remarkable linguistic talents
    of the young author (who wrote a pure French), analyzed the contents of the
    book, and speculated about a refutation. Maistre to Vallaise, 27 April 1817, *OC*,
    14:82–4, and Maistre to Rosaven, 16 May 1817, ibid., 95–7.

81 Maistre to Severoli, 23 February 1817. *OC*, 14:59.

82 Maistre to Rodolphe, letters of 9, 21, 26, and 30 October 1819, 11 and 17
    November 1819, and 20 January 1820, and Rodolphe to Constance, 19 January
    1819. M.f.a. There are also references to this "anti-Stourdza" in the letters of
    the papal nuncio in Turin, the Abbé Romualdo Valenti, and in one of Maistre's
    letters to Abbé Vuarin. In a letter dated 12 December 1819, Valenti reported
    that Maistre had discussed with him publication of a refutation of Stourdza's
    book (Cited in Bernard Jacqueline, "Le Saint-Siège et la publication de *Du
    Pape*," *REM*, no. 8 (1983): 62). In another letter dated 4 January 1820, Valenti
    said that Maistre had come to see him and told him that the Sardinian king
    would not authorize publication of the Stourdza piece in his kingdom. Valenti
    advised Maistre to contact Abbé Vuarin with a view to publishing in
    Switzerland (ibid.). Maistre evidently acted on this suggestion, since there is a
    mention of the project in one of his surviving letters to Vuarin: "It is well
    understood that if we take in hand our *Anti-Stourdza* all the pieces will be
    returned to you; but in truth the thing goes slowly enough" (25 March 1820,

OC, 14:212). Finally, in a letter to Valenti (which was transmitted to Rome on 2 December 1820) Maistre wrote: "It is not all my fault if the refutation of our great friend Stourdza has not been ready sooner. My affairs and my son's marriage have stopped everything. Let me know, I beg you, if the Court of Rome still counts on this refutation; my part is all done, and I believe as well that my son could complete his work in two months at most" (Cited in Jacqueline, "Le Saint-Siège et *Du Pape*," 68). This was only three months before Maistre's death, after which the project appears to have been abandoned.

83 Maistre to De Place, 9 July 1818. Latreille, "Lettres inédites," 292.

84 This work is also known under the title *Esprit de l'histoire*.

85 On Ferrand, see Latreille, *Maistre et la papauté*, 57–60.

86 "Religion E" contains over 50 pages of notes on this work.

87 *OC*, 8:183.

88 Maistre to De Place, 9 July 1818. Latreille, "Lettres inédites," 292. In the printed text of *Du Pape* there are seven specific references to Ferrand's book. The author is not named, but Maistre added a footnote referring to Ferrand's new status as a minister and peer, and begging "the respectable author to permit me to contradict him from time to time." *OC*, 2:214 n1.

89 Maistre to De Place, 9 July 1818. Latreille, "Lettres inédites," 292.

90 Maistre to De Place, 7 September 1818. Ibid., 293.

91 Maistre to De Place, 22 January 1820. Ibid., 390. Included in the same letter, Maistre sent along a separate sheet that he asked De Place to paste in one of his copies of the work. It read: "To M. De Place Senior whose learned and indefatigable assistance powerfully favoured the publication of this work. The author begs him to accept this copy and to preserve it as a feeble monument to his limitless esteem and gratitude." Ibid., 393.

92 De Place to Maistre, 16 October 1820. M.f.a.

93 Maistre to De Place, 9 August 1819. Latreille, "Lettres inédites," 356.

94 Maistre to De Place, 8 December 1819 and 3 January 1820. Ibid., 359–61.

95 *French Profiles: Prophets and Pioneers* (London 1961), 175–6.

96 The English translation by Aeneas McD. Dawson (London) has recently been reprinted with an introduction by Richard A. Lebrun (New York 1975).

97 For a dated but still valuable assessment of *Du Pape's* reception and influence, see Latreille, *Maistre et la papauté*, 239–354.

98 Chateaubriand to Maistre, 25 January 1820. Cited in Jacqueline, "Le Saint-Siège et *Du Pape*," 76.

99 Lamennais to Maistre, 5 February 1820. *OC*, 14:365.

100 Marcellus to Maistre, 5 February 1820. M.f.a.

101 Bonald to Maistre, 14 February 1820. *OC*, 14:351–4.

102 Lamartine to Maistre, 16 March 1820. Ibid., 362–3. At the suggestion of Maistre's nephew, Louis Vignet, Lamartine had been sent a copy of the book along with a flattering covering letter. See Rebotton, "Lamartine et la famille de Maistre," 100–2.

103 There were articles in *L'Amie de la religion et du roi* (issues of 22 January, 4 March, 15 April, and 27 May 1820), *Le Défenseur* (by Lamennais in June 1820), and *Le Drapeau blanc* (19 January 1820 and 29 July 1821).

104 Maistre to Constance de Maistre, 21 February 1820, *OC*, 14:206, and Maistre to Bonald, 25 March 1820, ibid., 214.

105 Maistre to Rodolphe, 23 February 1820. M.f.a. Lamartine made the same report. (See Lamartine to Maistre, 17 March 1820. *OC*, 14:363.) Apparently some journals imposed self-censorship. Bonald had indicated to Maistre that he intended to write of *Du Pape* in the *Conservateur*, but doubted whether the editorial board would allow him to do so (Bonald to Maistre, 14 February 1820. Ibid., 352–3). Constance de Maistre, who met Lamartine in Chambéry in April 1820, passed this story along to her father: "When *Du Pape* appeared, the editors of the *Conservateur* held a great council, at which M. de Lamartine was present, where they deliberated on speaking of your work, and after a great debate it was decided that the word *charte* on the masthead of the paper would not permit approbation of a book that attacked the liberties of the Gallican Church, consecrated by the great constitutional act, and as they did not want to say anything bad, they resolved to say nothing." Letter of 15 April 1820. Cited in Lovie, "Constance de Maistre," 165.

106 Latreille, *Maistre et la papauté*, 251.

107 See Bertier de Sauvigny, *The Bourbon Restoration*, 304–5.

108 Bonald to Maistre, 14 February 1820. *OC*, 14:352.

109 *Histoire de J.-B. Bossuet* (Paris 1815). Bausset had sent a copy of his work to Maistre, who replied with a charming letter of acknowledgment (Maistre to Bausset, 16 October 1816. *OC*, 13:436–9). Maistre had admired Bausset's earlier *Histoire de Fénelon* (Paris 1808), which he described as "a work dictated by the purest talent, the most severe impartiality, and the highest wisdom" (Maistre to Bonald, 13 December 1814. Ibid., 12:470), but found his second work too Gallican: "If you are curious to know to what point the modern spirit has penetrated the French episcopate, read, I beg you, the *Histoire*, or better said, the *Panégyrique de Bossuet*, by M. de Bausset; the chapter on the Declaration of 1682 will seem to you to have been written by an unrestrained *parlementaire*." Maistre to Severoli, 13 December 1815. Ibid., 13:187.

110 De Place had insisted that these be replaced with direct references to Bossuet's works. De Place to Maistre, 17 August 1819 (M.f.a.), and Maistre to De Place, 7 September 1819. Latreille, "Lettres inédites," 356.

111 Bausset to Maistre, 15 March 1820. M.f.a.

112 Interestingly enough, Frayssinous went on to become the Minister of Ecclesiastical Affairs and Education (1824–8) and an articulate opponent of the variety of ultramontanism then being propagated by Lamennais. See Bertier de Sauvigny, *The Bourbon Restoration*, 318, 349.

113 *Du Pape et son droit religieux à l'occasion du Concordat* (Paris 1803).

Augustin de Barruel was eighty years old at this point; he died a few months later. See Riquet, "Maistre et Barruel," 294.

114 Grivel to Maistre, 29 February 1820. M.f.a.

115 The Cardinal de la Luzerne's *Sur la déclaration de l'assemblée de France en 1682* (Paris 1821) was directed in part against Maistre. Their titles describe the works by the Abbé Baston, *Réclamation pour l'Eglise de France et pour la vérité contre l'ouvrage de M. le comte de Maistre intitulé "Du Pape," et contre la suite ayant pour titre "De l'Eglise gallicane ..."* (2 volumes, Paris 1821, 1824) and the Abbé Pierre-Elie Senli, *Purgatoire de feu M. le comte J. de Maistre pour l'expiation de certaines fautes morales qu'il a commis dans ses derniers écrits* (Paris 1823).

116 Canon Lecigne, *Joseph de Maistre* (Paris 1914), 252.

117 Rey to Maistre, 24 January 1820. M.f.a.

118 Rey to Maistre, 12 February 1820. M.f.a. Rey also reported that members of the Senate were amusing themselves by digging in their archives to pit Maistre the young magistrate against the author of *Du Pape*.

119 22 January 1820. M.f.a.

120 6 February 1820. M.f.a.

121 2 February 1820. M.f.a.

122 At least this was the impression that survived in his family. Writing some sixty years later, Constance de Maistre described the nuncio as a "a bad rascal belonging to the sect of the *Carbonari*" who had lied to her father about requesting the pope's approval of a "letter to dedication" to Pius VII that he had proposed to place at the head of a second edition. "Not even that consolation before dying," is how she reported her father's disillusioned comment. "Portrait de J. de Maistre," 504.

123 Archivio Vaticano. Segretaria di Stato, 1818 to 1821, No. 257, 3 and 4. Correspondence with the Abbé Valenti. See the introduction to their critical edition of *Du Pape* by Jacques Lovie and Joannès Chetail, xxiii–xxxiv, and Jacqueline, "Le Saint-Siège et *Du Pape*," 61–82, where the relevant documents are cited in both the original Italian and in French translation.

124 Valenti to Consalvi, 7 July 1818. Cited in Jacqueline, "Le Saint-Siège et *Du Pape*," 61–2.

125 Valenti to Consalvi, 12 December 1819. Ibid., 62.

126 Valenti to Consalvi, 19 January 1820. Ibid.

127 Valenti to Consalvi, 26 January 1820. Ibid.

128 Consalvi to Valenti, 27 January 1820. Ibid. It should be noted that the Vatican archives file contains only the "minutes" of Consalvi's replies.

129 Valenti to Consalvi, 1 February 1820. Ibid.

130 Maistre to Rey, 9 February 1820. *OC*, 14:202–3.

131 Valenti to Consalvi, letters of 14 February and 1 March 1820. Jacqueline, "Le Saint-Siège et *Du Pape*," 63.

132 Consalvi to Valenti, 12 March 1820. Ibid.

133 Valenti to Consalvi, 22 May 1820. Ibid.

134 See Lovie and Chetail's critical edition, 10.

135 Valenti to Consalvi, 17 July 1820. Jacqueline, "Le Saint-Siège et *Du Pape*," 64.

136 Minute of the Vatican Secretary of State, 3 June 1820. Ibid.

137 However, extracts of the report, sent by Valenti to a correspondent in France, may be found in the Bibliothèque National, Département des Manuscrits, Fonds Nouvelles Acquisitions Françaises (hereafter cited as BN, MSS, n.a.f.) no. 24745, p 74.

138 Maistre's comments, written in Italian and dated 29 October 1820, have been published in French translation by Dominique de Maistre under the title "Un écrit inédit de Joseph de Maistre: Amica Collatio ou échange d'observations sur le livre françois intitulé: DU PAPE," in *Etudes*, 73 (1897): 7–32.

139 The Italian text of this second document appears as an appendix to Jacqueline, "Le Saint-Siège et du pape," 71–4. A French translation of this same minute may be found in Lovie and Chetail's introduction, xxxi–xxxxiv.

140 De Place to Maistre, 11 January 1819. M.f.a.

141 *OC*, 2:ix.

142 Ibid., 157.

143 Ibid., 1–2.

144 Ibid., xii.

145 Whence Triomphe's caustic comment: "Catholic intelligences must have remained prisoners to the atheism of the previous century to have greeted with enthusiasm these exclusively temporal proofs of eternal dogmas." *Joseph de Maistre*, 337.

146 Valenti to Consalvi, 27 July 1820. Jacqueline, "Le Saint-Siège et *Du Pape*," 64.

147 Ibid., 64–5.

148 Consalvi to Valenti, 9 September 1820. Ibid., 66, 79.

149 Assurances provided to Valenti verbally in their heated interview and later at a diplomatic dinner (Valenti to Consalvi, 9 August 1820, ibid., 65–6) as well as in the "Amica collatio" of 29 October 1820.

150 Valenti to Consalvi, 2 December 1820, citing Maistre's undated letter of request. Ibid., 67.

151 Undated minute. Ibid. 68–9, 71–4.

152 The 1821 edition of *Du Pape* appeared without a dedication to Pius VII. The 1884 Vitte edition printed one version of the proposed letter (*OC*, 2:v–vii); Lovie and Chetail offer as well a second version found in the Vatican archives (pp 11–13). The Maistre family archives hold manuscript copies of these two versions plus a third, but since none of them are in Maistre's hand, it seems impossible to know why the 1884 editors chose their particular version.

153 Jacqueline, "Le Saint-Siège et *Du Pape*," 69.

154 It should be noted, however, that a Swiss scholar who reviewed these same files reached the conclusion that "Rome through refusal of the dedication indirectly condemned Maistre's apologetic writings." Max Huber, *Die Staatsphilosophie von Joseph de Maistre im Lichte des Thomismus* (Basel and Stuttgart 1958), 283.

155 *OC*, 2:xv.

156 Maistre to Rey, 26 January 1820. *OC*, 14:199–200.

157 *OC*, 8:485–519. This letter was first published in the 1851 edition of Maistre's *Lettres et opuscules inédites*.

158 See Latreille, *Maistre et la papauté*, 289–90. Latreille discovered a copy of Maistre's letter in the papers of the Abbé Vuarin with extracts and a note indicating that the whole had been transmitted to Tsar Alexander in 1820. Latreille thought it probable Vuarin used as his intermediary a Russian-born Polish countess who sometimes resided in Geneva.

159 Ibid., 288 n2.

160 Maistre to Rey, 9 February 1820. *OC*, 203.

161 There appear to have been at least 32 editions (and/or reprintings) of Du Pape during the 37 years between 1843 and 1880. *Cataloque de la Bibliothèque Nationale*, 104:64.

162 Maistre to Madame Swetchine, 26 October 1817. Falloux, *Madame Swetchine*, 1:209.

163 Details from Maistre's letter to Madame Swetchine, 22 July 1818. Ibid., 216.

164 Ibid. See also, Maistre to Blacas, 23 August 1818 (Daudet, *Maistre et Blacas*, 348), where he describes the experience as one of the most painful of his life and declares that he "remains almost dazed by it."

165 *Cours familier de littérature* (Paris 1859), 7:408–9. Lamartine had spent a week with Louis Vignet as the guest of Nicolas de Maistre at the Château de Bissy in 1815; André was also staying there at the time and Lamartine had the opportunity to observe him at leisure. Consequently there is no reason to question the integrity of this description. However, Lamartine's famous pen portraits of Joseph de Maistre cannot be trusted. See Rebotton, "Lamartine et la famille Maistre," 91–139.

166 Maistre to Blacas, 25 August 1818. Daudet, *Maistre et Blacas,* 356.

167 Barol had published a study of contemporary philosophy (Turin, 1817) and at his friend's request Maistre read the work and prepared a forty-page commentary on it. "Observations sur le livre *Apperçus philosophiques.*" Unpublished manuscript, M.f.a.

168 See "Extrait d'une conversation entre J. de Maistre et M. Ch. de Lavau," *OC*, 14:284–6.

169 See Maistre's letters to Dumont of 3 January and 27 February 1818. *OC*, 14:119–21, 126–9. The Maistre family archives contain Dumont's letter of request and a brochure describing the invention.

170 Maistre to Stolberg, December 1817. *OC*, 14:116–18. Interestingly enough, Stolberg's reply included a long and favourable report on the activities of the Bible Society in Germany (Stolberg to Maistre, 2 June 1818. M.f.a.). Perhaps it was this testimony that led Maistre, in the very last pages of the *Soirées*, to qualify his condemnation of the Bible Society. *OC*, 5:257.

171 "Lettres à M. le Marquis … sur la fête séculaire des Protestantes," dated 14 January 1818. *OC*, 8:471–81. This letter was originally published in a collection entitled *Nouvelles anecdotes chrétiennes*.

172 He told Rodolphe he wanted to leave "the thing completely at the disposition of Monsieur your well-counselled heart." Maistre to Rodolphe, 17 October 1818. M.f.a.

173 Writing to the Abbé Rey in connection with a possible marriage to a Zoé de Vidau, Maistre set forth Rodolphe's assets in the following terms: "For my part, I am not a wholly insignificant man: my name has been pronounced in the world, especially in Zoe's country; but I am ashamed to speak of myself; without self-conceit I can only speak of my son. He is the youngest colonel in the army: he made seven campaigns; he was present at all the battles that decided the state of the world from Moscow to Montmarte. He wears the Cross of St Maurice from his king, that of St Louis of France, that of the merit of Prussia, and St André from Russia as well as the Sword of Gold for valour (that is the inscription) given to him by his Russian general on the battlefield. He speaks French, Italian, Latin, German, Russian, and English." Maistre to Rey, 21 May 1819. Cited in Jean Nicolas, "Quelques lettres inédites de Joseph de Maistre," *Cahiers d'Histoire*, 10 (1965): 322.

174 "I am telling you and I am repeating to you that France is certainly the country of superior women." Maistre to Rodolphe, 14 March 1818. M.f.a.

175 "*It is necessary to marry into a great country* and create chances for the family." Maistre to Rodolphe, undated but from the context evidently in March 1818. M.f.a.

176 "I hope that she [Rodolphe's hoped for bride] will maintain the honour of our family which has always shone by its women." Maistre to Rodolphe, 25 October 1819. M.f.a.

177 Clergymen who were involved included the Abbé Besson in Lyon, the Abbé Rey in Chambéry, and the bishop of Pinerolo.

178 Maistre to Rodolphe, 14 October 1818. M.f.a.

179 Maistre to Rodolphe, 6 December 1818. M.f.a. In this case, Maistre wrote to alert his son of the visit, told him he could arrange military leave for him to return to Turin if he wished, but emphasized all the disadvantages of marrying a Russian girl.

180 Maistre spelled the name "Syeyes," but the accepted modern spelling appears to be "Sieyès." This Sieyès family was not related to the Abbé who played such a prominent role in th French Revolution.

181 Maistre to Rodolphe, 23 October 1819. M.f.a.

182 Maistre to Rodolphe, 14 February 1818. M.f.a. Apparently General de Boigne, Maistre's old classmate who had returned from India a wealthy man, was buying up all available property in Chambéry.

183 Maistre to Rey, 21 May 1819. BN, MSS, n.a.f. no. 24635.

184 Maistre to Rodolphe, 23 February 1820. M.f.a.

185 Maistre to Rodolphe, 22 April 1820. M.f.a.

186 It seems that the agreement was completed on the strength of the promise of a loan from Blacas. See Maistre's undated letter to Blacas in which he accepts the latter's offer of loan of a thousand louis (ie, 20,000 francs) on the eve of his departure for Rodolphe's wedding (Daudet, *Maistre et Blacas*, 385–6). Later that summer after his return to Turin, Maistre purchased a garden with a house for some 130,000 livres. Maistre to Blacas, undated, Ibid., 392.

187 "This past Monday the 5th in Valence, my son married Mlle Azélie de Sieyès, oldest daughter of the Marquis de Sieyès, former captain of the king's ships. She is a charming and excellent person who unites all the desirable qualities. The Château du Valentin from where I am writing to you is a beautiful property belonging to her father. The marriage, without being what one could call *rich*, is nevertheless good enough to satisfy me. As the daughter of a first marriage, the young lady is her mother's sole heir for 120,000 livres without paternal rights. I have enough." Maistre to De Place, 7 June 1820. Latreille, "Lettres inédites," 393.

188 Maistre to Rodolphe, 19 July 1820. M.f.a.

189 Maistre to Rodolphe, 19 December 1820. M.f.a. By this date Joseph de Maistre's health was failing rapidly.

190 Maistre to Rodolphe, 27 September 1820. M.f.a.

191 Ibid.

192 "I am without contradiction the foreigner who is most French and the most attached to French legitimacy, as I believe I have well proven." Maistre to Bonald, 22 March 1819. *OC*, 14:159.

193 Maistre to André de Maistre, 24 March 1817. M.f.a.

194 Maistre to Noailles, 18 April 1818. Branan, "Six lettres inédites," 131.

195 Word coined by Joseph de Maistre to mean rule of the *canaille*, the mob.

196 Maistre to the Chevalier d'Orly, 5 September 1818. *OC*, 14:148.

197 Maistre to Noailles, 18 April 1818. Branan, "Six lettres inédites," 131. The same image occurs in a letter to Blacas where Turin is described as a "miniature" affected by the same winds as Paris. Maistre to Blacas, 16 May 1818. Daudet, *Maistre et Blacas*, 341.

198 Maistre to Blacas. Undated. Daudet, *Maistre et Blacas*, 384.

199 When Joseph de Maistre was told the police had wounded one of the students, he is reported to have said: "Madame, that was a small misfortune, a private misfortune. The important thing is that force be retained by authority." "Un portrait de J. de Maistre," 502.

200 With the full support, ironically, of Constance and Rodolphe de Maistre. See Lovie, "Constance de Maistre," 151–3.

201 Maistre to Marcellus, 9 August 1819. *OC*, 14:183.

202 Maistre to the Count de Bray, January 1815. *OC*, 13:27.

203 Maistre to Orly, 5 September 1818. *OC*, 14:148–9. A similar avowal occurs in a letter to Blacas in which Maistre told his friend: "I persist in believing that France will extricate itself [from its present situation] to the profit of humanity and that it will accomplish as much good for the world as the harm it has done it" (Maistre to Blacas, undated, but from 1818. Daudet, *Maistre et Blacas*, 365). And in a letter to De Place: "France will rise again, preach, and convert Europe." Letter of 10 May 1819. Latreille, "Lettres inédites," 328.

204 See "Extrait d'une conversation entre J. de Maistre et M. Ch. de Lavau." *OC*, 14:216.

205 Maistre to Bonald, 4 December 1820. *OC*, 14:216.

206 Maistre to De Place, 22 January 1820. Latreille, "Lettres inédites," 390.

207 Maistre to De Place, 3 April 1820. Ibid., 391.

208 Maistre to De Place, 22 April 1820. Ibid., 393.

209 Maistre to De Place, 18 September 1820. Ibid., 394.

210 Maistre to Vuarin, 22 January 1821. *OC*, 14:253.

211 There appear to have been some 18 editions (and/or reprints) of *De l'Eglise gallicane* in the years between 1844 and 1886. *Cataloque de la Bibliothèque Nationale*, 104:55.

212 Maistre to De Place, 11 December 1820. *OC*, 14:250.

213 Maistre to De Place, 20 or 23 June 1818. Latreille, "Lettres inédites," 263.

214 Maistre requested the Abbé Besson and De Place to examine the work, noting that his children had made an extra copy he could send to them (Maistre to Besson, 18 July 1818. Ibid., 293). Constance later described how "we three copied it: Rodolphe the dialogue on war, my sister the exposition on sacrifices, and myself the attack on Locke's philosophy, etc." ("Portrait de J. de Maistre," 498). Joseph de Maistre's brother-in-law read a fragment (Saint-Réal to Maistre, 12 August 1818. M.f.a.) and his nephew, Louis Vignet, the bulk of the manuscript (Vignet to Maistre, 18 November 1820. M.f.a.).

215 Maistre to De Place, 9 July 1818. Latreille, "Lettres inédites," 293.

216 Maistre to De Place, letters of 2 and 18 September 1820. Ibid., 394–5.

217 Maistre to Rodolphe, 7 September 1820. M.f.a. The portrait of Voltaire is entirely absent from the manuscript copy in the Maistre family archives.

218 Maistre to De Place, 11 December 1820. Latreille, "Lettres inédites," 395–6. "Lutèce" is a French version of the Latin name for Paris, "Lutetia."

219 Maistre to Rodolphe, 18 December 1820. M.f.a. He reported as well that it appeared there would be no quibble over the proposed price of 40,000 livres: "For my life I would not have asked such a price. It was Constance who took charge of this negotiation with ineffable *disinvoltura* [aplomb]."

220 A short "Esquisse du morceau final" was published in the 1851 *Lettres et opuscules inédites,* and appeared in the 1884 Vitte edition as well (*OC*,

5:279–82). A preface was provided by Louis de Saint-Victor. Louis Vignet had involved Saint-Victor in the search for a suitable publisher in Paris (Vignet to Maistre, 18 November 1820. M.f.a.), and it seems likely that Saint-Victor was enlisted for this task as a result of Vignet's initiative.

221 Maistre to Vallaise, 2 February 1815. *OC*, 13:37.

222 Xavier de Maistre to Sr Eulalie de Maistre, 11 January 1819. Klein, *Lettres inédites de X. de Maistre*, 47.

223 Constance de Maistre to De Place, 28 May 1821. C. Latreille, "Les derniers jours de Joseph de Maistre racontés par sa fille Constance de Maistre," *Quinzaine*, 16 July 1905, p 158.

224 Maistre to Rodolphe, 27 September 1820. M.f.a.

225 Maistre to Rodolphe, 18 December 1820. M.f.a.

226 Modern medicine would probably diagnose Maistre's final illness as a form of Guillain-Barre's syndrome. I am indebted to my daughter, Dr Connie Lebrun, for this suggestion.

227 Constance de Maistre to De Place, 24 February 1821. Latreille, "Les derniers jours," 153–4.

228 Maistre to the Duchess des Cars, 5 February 1821. *OC*, 14:254.

229 Constance de Maistre to De Place, 28 May 1821. Latreille, "Les derniers jours," 158.

230 Maistre to the Marquis d'Azegio, 21 February 1821. *OC*, 14:256–9.

231 See Louis Le Guilou, "Joseph de Maistre et Lamennais en 1820–1821," *REM*, no. 8 (1983): 99–100.

232 Constance de Maistre to De Place, 24 February 1821. Latreille, "Les derniers jours," 152.

233 Constance de Maistre to De Place, 28 May 1821. Ibid., 159.

234 M.f.a. None of Maistre's biographers have found his actual will, but there is no reason to think its provisions differed significantly from the draft document, which made provisions for his wife and daughters and named Rodolphe as his principal heir.

CHAPTER EIGHT: EPILOGUE

1 *De L'Eglise gallicane*, *OC*, 3:171.

2 Ibid., vi–vii.

3 However, Henri Grégoire, the revolutionary abbé who had become a constitutional bishop and who in 1819 had been denied a seat in the chamber of deputies, published a brief pamphlet entitled *Observations critiques sur 'De l'Eglise gallicane'* … (Paris 1821).

4 See Latreille, *Maistre et la papauté*, 239–354, and Austin Gough, *Paris and Rome: The Gallican Church and the Ultramontane Compaign 1848–1853* (Oxford 1986), 60, 68, 96.

5 *OC*, 5:279–82.

6 Since the manuscript in the Maistre family archives does not include the famous portrait of Voltaire, which we know was from Maistre's own pen, we can surmise that the actual printing was done from a different manuscript.

7 Discussing possible publication of his *Soirées* with De Place, Maistre mentioned points that could be "cast into the notes of an imaginary editor." Maistre to De Place, 9 July 1818. Latreille, "Lettres inédites," 293.

8 "Par M. Le Comte Joseph de Maistre, Ancien ministre de S.M. Le Roi de Sargaigne à la Cour de Russie, Ministre d'Etat, Régent de la Grande Chancellerie, Membre de l'Académie des Sciences de Turin, Chévalier Grand'Croix de l'Ordre religieux et militaire de S. Maurice et de S. Lazare."

9 *Le Défenseur*, for example, welcomed it as the work of "one of those powerful geniuses who, rescuing peoples from the edge of the abyss, reinstall them forever in the conservative paths from which they have been diverted by pride and miserable perversity." 5 (1821): 423. However, the Abbé Féletz published a much more critical review in the *Journal des Débats* (issues of 18 July, 1 and 2 August 1821).

10 J.-B.-M. Nolhac, *Soirées de Rothaval ... ou Réflexions sur les intempérances philosophiques de M. de Comte Joseph de Maistre dans ses Soirées de Saint-Pétersbourg* (Lyon 1843, 2 volumes), and as volume 3, *Nouvelles Soirées de Rothaval, ou Réflexions sur les intempérances théologiques de Joseph de Maistre* (Lyon 1844).

11 The 1821 edition was followed by a second edition in 1822, but then only four further editions up to 1850. But the thirty years from 1850 to 1880 saw some 22 editions or reprints. See *Cataloque de la Bibliothèque Nationale*, 104:63–6.

12 *OC*, 4:vx–xvi.

13 See Lebrun, "Maistre's 'Philosophic' View of War," 50–2.

14 See Margrit Finger, *Studien zur literarischen Technik Joseph de Maistres* (Marburg 1972), 236–78, and a shorter version under her married name, Margrit Zobel-Finger, "Quod semper, quod ubique, quod ob omnibus ou L'art de fermer la bouche aux novateurs," in *Joseph de Maistre tra Illuminismo e Restaurazione*, edited by Luigi Marino (Turin 1975), 70–9. See also Barbara Sampson, "La Rhétorique de l'essai dialogue chez Joseph de Maistre," McGill University M.A. thesis, 1977.

15 Now in preparation by members of the Institut des études maistriennes.

16 However, Rodolphe de Maistre's letters to his sister Constance (of 3 September 1834 and 3 October 1835) suggest that the postponement may have been due at least in part to attempts to negotiate more profitable terms with publishers. M.f.a.

17 Perhaps it was Rodolphe, who arranged publication, or Constance, whose intelligence and literary gifts more nearly matched those of her father. See Lovie, "Constance de Maistre," 151–63.

18 Sainte-Beuve, *Revue des Deux Mondes*, 3 (13th year, new series, 1843): 387.

19 *Soirées*, OC, 4:275.

20 For more detailed treatments of Maistre's critique of Bacon, see A. de Margerie's preface to the 1884 Vitte edition of the *Examen* (6:vii–xxxvi), Holdsworth, *Maistre et l'Angleterre*, 63–92, and Richard A. Lebrun, "Joseph de Maistre's Critique of Francis Bacon," in *Maistre tra Illuminismo et Restaurazione*, 80–90.

21 Fredéric Ozanam, *Deux Chanceliers d'Angleterre: Bacon de Verulum et Saint Thomas de Canterbéry* (Paris 1836), 97, and François Huet, "Le Chancelier Bacon et le comte Joseph de Maistre," *Nouvelles archives historiques, philosophiques et littéraires*, 1 (1837): 65–94.

22 See Louis Foucher, *La Philosophie catholique en France au XIXe siècle* (Paris 1955), 65.

23 A. Combiguilles, *Annales de philosophie chrétiennes*, 15 (1837): 408.

24 *Cataloque de la Bibliothèque Nationale*, 104:57–9.

25 Ibid., 104:59.

26 For a listing of the Maistre letter collections published between 1843 and 1967, see Triomphe, *Joseph de Maistre*, 604–5.

27 Veuillot to Rodolphe de Maistre, 9 February 1847. BN, MSS, n.a.f., no. 24223, p 124. On Maistre's importance for Veuillot, see Gough, *Paris and Rome*, 87.

28 Rodolphe de Maistre to Veuillot, 5 March 1847. BN, MSS, n.a.f., no. 24635, pp 63–4.

29 The dates of this exchange of letters show that Jean Rebotton was mistaken in his speculation that it was the publication of Lamartine's first (and quite inaccurate) "literary portrait" of their father in 1849 that provoked the decision of Rodolphe and Constance to undertake publication of their father's letters. "Lamartine et la famille de Maistre," 127–8.

30 The events cost Rodolphe de Maistre his position as the governor of Nice in February 1848. As a consequence of writing a letter to the editor of the local newspaper defending the Jesuits, he was relieved of his post and retired to private life. (See Margerie, *Le Comte Joseph de Maistre*, 422–6.) Following his initial contact with Rodolphe, Veuillot also entered into epistolary and personal relations with Constance. The letters exchanged between Veuillot and Constance during this year of crisis show her to have been far more ready to condone vigorous action against the revolutionaries than her correspondent. BN, MSS, n.a.f., no. 24635, pp 49–136.

31 Rodolphe to Veuillot, 19 April 1850. Ibid., 73–75.

32 Rodolphe to Veuillot, undated. Ibid.

33 The collection appeared without preface or introduction, and with no indication of Louis Veuillot's assistance. Saint-Beuve, however, was aware of Veuillot's role, and mentioned it in his review in *Le Constitutionnel*, 2 June 1851.

34 *Catalogue de la Bibliothèque Nationale*, 104:50–1.

35 *Quatre chapitres inédites sur la Russie* (Paris: Vaton 1859).

36 *Mémoires politiques et correspondance diplomatique de J. de Maistre avec explications et commentaires historiques* (Paris 1858), 3.

37 Even Dupanloup, the bishop of Orléans and the vigorous opponent of Veuillot's ultramontanism, was scandalized by this attempt "to make M. de Maistre a liberal who demanded political and religious renovations ... and to make this ardent Catholic a kind of rebel who did not fear outraging Pius VII by the grossest epithets and who prophesized a kind of new revelation of the resurrection of the Church ... and a precursor of the Saint-Simonians." Letter of 7 October 1858. No addressee indicated. BN, MSS, n.a.f., no. 24745.

38 *Correspondance diplomatique de Joseph de Maistre, 1811–1817* (Paris 1860).

39 See Triomphe, *Joseph de Maistre*, 12–13. Vaton Frères had published a ten-volume edition of Maistre's *Oeuvres* in 1853, and an additional volume of *Oeuvres inédites* in 1870 (material released by Charles de Maistre), so the first "complete" edition carried the following full title: *Oeuvres complètes de J. de Maistre, nouvelle édition, Contenant ses Oeuvres posthumes et toute sa Correspondance inédite*. Published by Vitte et Perrussel of Lyon between 1884 and 1886, the edition contained eight volumes of "works" and six volumes of correspondence. Long unavailable, it has been reissued recently in a seven-volume photographic reproduction (Geneva: Slatkine 1979).

40 In the long confidential letter sent to his wife by private courier, Maistre had warned her about open reference to their limited finances: "Sums must never be expressed clearly, seeing that our exiguity would cause laughter in the countries where we are read ... You will appreciate that in such a country [as Russia] we must not speak in ordinary letters of dowries for our children or of our income." Letter of 18 June 1808. M.f.a.

41 "I am frightened by all you are doing, you are using yourself, you are killing yourself." Constance de Maistre to her father, 29 January 1820. Cited in Lovie, "Constance de Maistre," 147.

42 This is a constant theme in Triomphe's work.

43 *Memorie della Reale Academia delle Scienze di Torino*, 27 (1823): 173–91. Later published as a brochure (Chambéry 1827).

44 Saint-Beuve wrote about Joseph de Maistre on a number of occasions. Except for his critique of *De l'Eglise gallicane* in his study of Port-Royal, Saint-Beuve's comments appeared first in periodicals before being published in his multi-volume series *Causeries du Lundi* (15:67–83) and *Portraits littéraires* (2:287–466). These pieces have been brought together and annotated by Maurice Allem in Saint-Beuve, *Les Grands Ecrivains français: XIXe siècle, philosophes et essayistes* (Paris 1930), 1:1–163. For the sake of convenience, this latter edition will be cited here.

45 Ibid., 121.

46 Ibid., 131.

47 Ibid., 2, note.

48 Ibid., 4, 15, 56.

49 Count Eugène de Costa, described as "M. de Maistre's compatriot." Ibid., 4, note. This was obviously a different Eugène de Costa than the young man who had been the subject of Maistre's eulogy.

50 Ibid., 2, 87, 78.

51 Ibid., 67–8. Although De Place was not named in the original 1843 article, Saint-Beuve later did a review of a biographical article about De Place that was published after the latter's death that same year (along with seven of Maistre's letters to De Place). Ibid., 134–9.

52 Ibid., 8.

53 Ibid., 8.

54 Ibid., 27, note.

55 Ibid., 39.

56 Ibid., 68–9. The relevant extract from Saint-Beuve's *Port-Royal* (livre III, ch. XIV) is reprinted in this same collection. Ibid., 142–63.

57 Ibid., 69.

58 Ibid., 72.

59 Some are letters that were later published, but for others Saint-Beuve's citation is the only knowledge we have of the letters in question. Unfortunately, he did not cite addressees and dates.

60 Ibid., 81–5. The identification is possible because these same letters were published by Rodolphe de Maistre in 1851.

61 Ibid., 85–6.

62 Ibid., 86.

63 Ibid., 87–8.

64 Ibid., 89

65 Ibid., 50.

66 *Oeuvres de A. de Lamartine* (Paris 1886–7), 8:427–9.

67 See Rebotton, "Lamartine et la famille de Maistre."

68 Maistre to Lamartine, 28 January 1820. Cited in Rebotton, "Lamartine et la famille de Maistre," 101.

69 The passport listed him at "5 pieds un pouce," but this would have been old French measure, with the "pied" equal to 32.5 cm. See Ibid., 121 n102.

70 In fact, Joseph de Maistre never signed the document in question, and there is some doubt as to whether he attended the ceremony. See ibid., 136–7.

71 Triomphe, for example, cites Lamartine's story about his wedding as solid evidence of Maistre's personal character. *Joseph de Maistre*, 354–7.

72 The manuscript of Rodolphe's "Notice biographique" survives in the Maistre family archives; marginal notations (which do not appear in the printed version) show that Rodolphe made systematic use of his father's letters.

73 Rodolphe to Veuillot, 5 March 1847. BN, MSS, n.a.f., no. 24635.

74 *OC*, 1:viii.

75 Ibid., xxiv, xl.

76 Ibid., xlii–xliii.

77 Ibid., xliii.

78 "Anecdotes recueillies à Saint-Pétersbourg par le comte Joseph de Maistre," *Etudes*, 21 (4th series, vol. 2, 1868): 533–8, 777–98, and 22 (4th series, vol. 3, 1869): 84–99.

79 *Revue du Monde Catholique*, (1868), 533.

80 *Le Comte Joseph de Maistre; sa vie, ses écrits, ses doctrines, avec des documents inédits* (Paris 1882).

81 Ibid., 8–9 n4.

82 Ibid., 17.

83 Margerie to Charles de Maistre, 1 May 1881. M.f.a. The suggestion of plagiarism was in an article by Adolphe Franck, "Sur l'Histoire de la philosophie en France, de Ferraz," *Journal des Savants* (April 1880), 246–56, and (May 1880), 269–76.

84 *Le Comte Joseph de Maistre*, 429–42.

85 He did, however, include a helpful appendix on Rodolphe's life. Ibid., 415–28.

86 Ibid., 2.

87 *La Politique de Joseph de Maistre d'après ses premiers écrits* (Paris 1895), 11.

88 "Joseph de Maistre, Conférence à l'Institut Catholiques de Paris, 1891–92," *Bulletin de l'Institut Catholique* (March 1892), 82.

89 "Un écrit inédit de Joseph de Maistre: Amica Collatio ou échange d'observations sur le livre français intitulé: DU PAPE," *Etudes* 73 (1897): 5–32.

90 The private archives mentioned in his notes include those of Costa de Beauregard, Charles de Buttet, Demotz de la Salle, Hector Laracine, Juge de Pieulieut, Pierre Goybet, Salteur de la Serraz, Baron Moran, Abbé Feyge, Claudius Blanchard, Emile Raymond, Edouard de Buttet, André Perrin, Jacques Bourgeois, Albert Metzger, Claudius Bouvier, and Joseph Coppier. See *Maistre avant la Révolution*, 1:7 n. 1.

91 Ibid., 2:41 n1.

92 *La Pensée religieuse de Joseph de Maistre* (Paris 1921).

93 *Joseph de Maistre, mystique* (Paris 1923).

94 *L'Idée de Providence d'après Joseph de Maistre* (Lyon 1928).

95 *Les Carnets du Comte Joseph de Maistre: Livre Journal 1790–1817* (Lyon 1923).

96 *Joseph de Maistre*, 16 n34.

97 Personal communication from Jacques de Maistre.

Bibliography

This bibliograpy lists only items cited in the text or used in its preparation.

ARCHIVAL SOURCES

Archives de Savoie, Chambéry. Holds some papers relating to the Maistre family and the archives of the Senate of Savoy.
Archivio di Stato, Turin. Holds Maistre's diplomatic correspondence.
Biblioteca Civica, Turin. Holds a few Maistre letters.
Bibliothèque Nationale, Département des Manuscrits, Fonds Nouvelles Acquisitions Françaises. Letters of Joseph de Maistre, Rodolphe de Maistre, Constance de Maistre, Louis Veuillot, and Bishop Dupanloup.
Maistre family archives. Private collection held near Paris.

PRINTED SOURCES

The Works of Joseph de Maistre

Collected and Critical Editions by Date of Publication

Lettres et opuscules inédites du comte Joseph de Maistre. 2 vols. Paris: A. Vaton 1851.
Mémoires politiques et correspondance diplomatique. Published with explanations and historical commentaries by Albert Blanc. Paris: Librairie Nouvelle 1858.
Correspondance diplomatique, 1811–1817. 2 vols. Collected and published by Albert Blanc. Paris: Librairie Nouvelle 1860.
Oeuvres complètes. 14 vols. Lyons: Vitte et Perusssel 1884–6.
Joseph de Maistre et Blacas: leur correspondance inédite et l'histoire de leur amitié, 1804–1820. Introduction, notes, and commentary by Ernest Daudet. Paris: Plan-Nourrit 1908.

Les Carnets du Comte Joseph de Maistre: Livre Journal 1790–1817. Published by Comte Xavier de Maistre. Lyon: Vitte 1923.

La Franc-Maçonnerie: mémoire au duc de Brunswick. Published with an introduction by Emile Dermenghem. Paris: Rieder 1925.

Considérations sur la France. Ed. by René Johannet and François Vermale. Paris: Vrin 1936.

Des Constitutions politiques et des autres institutions. Ed. by Robert Triomphe. Strasbourg: Publications de la Faculté des Lettres de l'Université de Strasbourg 1959.

Mémoire sur l'union de la Savoie à la Suisse, 1795. Published by Robert Triomphe. Strasbourg: Publications de la Faculté des Lettres de Strasbourg 1961.

Du Pape. Critical edition with an introduction by Jacques Lovie and Joannès Chetail. Geneva: Droz, 1966.

De l'Etat de Nature. Text established, presented, and annotated by Jean-Louis Darcel. *REM*, 2 (1976): 1–170.

Considérations sur la France. Critical edition by Jean-Louis Darcel. Geneva: Slatkine 1980.

Ecrits maçonniques de Joseph de Maistre et de quelques-uns de ses amis franc-maçons. Critical edition by Jean Rebotton. Geneva: Slatkine 1983.

English Translations

Considerations on France. Translated by Richard A. Lebrun. Montreal: McGill-Queen's University Press 1974.

Essay on the Generative Principle of Political Constitutions. Reprint of 1847 edition. Delmas, NY Scholars' Facsimiles and Reprints 1977.

Letters on the Spanish Inquisition. Reprint of 1843 edition. Delmas, NY: Scholars' Facsimiles and Reprints, 1977.

On God and Society: Essay on the Generative Principle of Political Constitutions and Other Human Institutions. Ed. by Elisha Greifer and translated with the assistance of Lawrence M. Porter. Chicago: Regnery 1959.

The Pope. Translated by Aeneas McD. Dawson. Reprint of 1850 edition with an introduction by Richard A. Lebrun. New York: Howard Fertig 1975.

Other Works Cited or Utilized

Adams, John Quincy, *Memoirs of John Quincy Adams.* Vol. 2. Philadelphia: Lippincott 1874.

Baldensperger, Fernand, *Le Mouvement des idées dans l'émigration française (1789–1815).* 2 vols. Paris: Plon-Nourrit 1925.

Beauvois, Daniel, "Les Jésuites dans l'Empire Russe, 1772–1820." *Dix-huitième siècle,* 8 (1976): 257–72.

Berthier, Alfred, *Xavier de Maistre*. Paris: Vitte 1918.

Bertier de Sauvigny, Guillaume de, *The Bourbon Restoration*. Philadelphia: University of Pennsylvania Press 1966.

Billington, James A., *The Icon and the Axe*. New York: Knopf 1966.

Bongie, Laurence L., *David Hume, Prophet of Counter-Revolution*. Oxford: Clarendon Press 1965.

Branan, A.G., "Six Lettres inédites de Joseph de Maistre au comte de Noailles." *Revue d'histoire littéraire de la France*, 67 (1967): 128–34.

Burnier, Eugène, *Histoire du Sénat de Savoie*. 2 vols. Chambéry: Puthod 1864.

Buttet, Charles de, *Aperçu de la vie de Xavier de Maistre*. Grenoble: Allier 1919.

Chevailler, Laurent, *Essai sur le Souverain Sénat de Savoie (1559–1793)*. Annecy: Gardet 1953.

Chevallier, Pierre, *Histoire de la Franc-Maçonnerie française*. Paris: Fayard 1974.

Costa de Beauregard, Charles-Albert, *Un Homme d'autrefois*. Paris: Plon 1910.

Croce, Benedetto, "Due Lettere inedite di Joseph de Maistre al Duca de Serracapriola." *Etudes italiennes*, 5 (1923): 193–5.

–, "Il duca di Serra-Capriola et Giuseppe de Maistre." *Archivio storico par le Province Napoletane*, 57 (1922): 340–57.

Darcel, Jean-Louis, "Les Années d'apprentissage d'un contre-révolutionnaire; Joseph de Maistre à Lausanne, 1793–1797." *REM*, no. 10 (1986–87): 7–135.

–, "Cinquième lettre d'un Royaliste Savoisien à ses compatriotes." *REM*, no. 4 (1978): 7–89.

–, "Joseph de Maistre et la Révolution française." *REM*, no. 3 (1977): 29–43.

–, "Des Pénitents noirs à la franc-maçonnerie: aux sources de la sensibilité maistrienne." *REM*, no 5–6 (1980): 69–95.

–, "Les bibliothèques de Joseph de Maistre, 1768–1821." *REM*, no. 9 (1985): 5–118.

–, "Registres de la correspondance de Joseph de Maistre." *REM*, no. 7 (1981): 9–266.

Dermenghem, Emile, *Joseph de Maistre mystique: ses rapports avec le martinisme, l'illuminisme et la franc-maçonnerie, l'influence du doctrines mystiques et occultes sur sa pensée religieuse*. Paris: La Colombe 1946.

Descostes, François, *Joseph de Maistre avant la Révolution: souvenirs de la société d'autrefois, 1753–1793*. 2 vols. Paris: Picard 1893.

–, *Joseph de Maistre inconnu: Venice–Cagliari–Rome (1797–1803)*. Paris: Champion 1904.

–, *Joseph de Maistre pendant la Révolution: ses débuts diplomatiques, le marquis de Sales et les émigrés, 1789–1797*. Tours: A. Mame et fils 1895.

–, *Joseph de Maistre orateur*. Chambéry: Perrin 1896.

–, *Lettres inédites de J. de Maistre*. Chambéry: Perrin 1899.

–, *Necker, écrivain et financier, jugé par le comte de Maistre*. Chambéry: Perrin 1896.

Donnadieu, Aristide, *Les Origines languedociennes de Joseph de Maistre*. Chambéry: Dardel 1942.

Doublet, Georges, "Gli antenati Nizzardi del Savoiardo Giuseppi De Maistre." *Bollettino dell'Associazioni fra Oriundi Savoiardi e Nizzardi Italiani*, no. 17, December 1829. Resumé by F. Vermale, "L'Ascendance niçoise de Joseph et Xavier de Maistre." *Mémoires et documents publiés par la Société savoisienne histoire et d'archéologie*, 66 (1929): 281–9.

Doyle, William, *The Parlement of Bordeaux and the End of the Old Regime*. London: E. Benn 1974.

Edwards, David W., "Count Joseph de Maistre and Russian Educational Policy, 1803–1828." *Slavic Review*, 36 (1977): 54–75.

Faivre, Antoine, "Joseph de Maistre et l'illuminisme: rapports avec Willermoz." *REM*, no. 5–6 (1980): 125–32.

Falloux, Alfred-F.-P. de, *Madame Swetchine, sa vie et ses oeuvres*. 2 vols. Paris: Didier 1875.

Finger, Margrit, *Studien zur literarischen Technik Joseph de Maistres*. Marburg 1972.

Flynn, James J., "The Role of the Jesuits in the Politics of Russian Education." *The Catholic Historical Review*, 56 (1970): 249–65.

–, "The Universities, the Gentry, and the Russian Imperial Services, 1815–1825." *Canadian Slavic Studies*, 2 (1968): 486–503.

Foucher, Louis, *La Philosophie catholique en France au XIXe siècle*. Paris: Vrin 1955.

Frappaz, Z., *Vie de l'abbé Nicolle*. Paris: Lecoffre 1857.

Fuchs, Michel, "Edmund Burke et Joseph de Maistre," *Revue de l'Université d'Ottawa*, 54(1984):49–58.

Gagarine, J., "Anecdotes recueillies à Saint-Pétersbourg par le comte Joseph de Maistre." *Etudes*, 21 (4th series, vol. 2, 1868): 533–8 and 777–98, and 22 (4th series, vol. 3, 1869): 84–99.

Gay, Peter, *The Enlightenment: An Interpretation. On the Rise of Modern Paganism*. London: Weidenfeld and Nicolson 1967.

Gignoux, G.-J., *Joseph de Maistre: prophète du passé, historien de l'avenir*. Paris: Nouvelles Editions Latines 1963.

Golovkine, Fédor, *La cour et le régne de Paul Ier*. Paris: Plon 1905.

Gooch, G.P., *French Profiles: Prophets and Pioneers*. London: Longmans 1961.

Gough, Austin, *Paris and Rome: The Gallican Church and the Ultramontaine Campaign, 1848–1853*. Oxford: Clarendon Press 1986.

Goyau, Georges, *La Pensée religieuse de Joseph de Maistre d'après des documents inédites*. Paris: Perrin 1921.

Grimsted, Patricia Kennedy, *The Foreign Ministers of Alexander I*. Berkeley: University of California Press 1969.

Guyon, Edouard-Félix, "Joseph de Maistre: diplomate sarde, témoin et juge de son temps, 1792–1817," *Revue d'histoire diplomatique*, 97 (1983): 75–107.

Hagen, Everett E., *On the Theory of Social Change*. Homewood, IL: Dorsey 1962.

Holdsworth, Frederick, *Joseph de Maistre et Angleterre*. Paris: Campion 1935.

Huber, Max, *Die Staatsphilosophie von Joseph de Maistre im Lichte des Thomismus*. Basel: Helbing and Lichtenhaln 1958.

Jacqueline, Bernard, "Le Saint-Siège et la publication de *Du Pape*." *REM*, no. 8 (1983): 59–75.

Klein, Félix, "Lettres inédites de Xaxier de Maistre à sa famille." *Le Correspondant*, 219 (1902): 899–936, 1103–31.

–, *Lettres inédites de X. de Maistre à sa famille*. Paris 1902.

Kramnick, Isaac, *The Rage of Edmund Burke: Portrait of an Ambivalent Conservative*. New York: Basic Books 1977.

Lamartine, Alphonse de, *Oeuvres de A. de Lamartine*. 13 vols. Paris: Lemerre 1886–7.

Latreille, Camille, "Les Derniers Jours de Joseph de Maistre raconté par sa fille Constance de Maistre." *Quinzaine*, 16 July 1905, pp 149–61.

–, *Joseph de Maistre et la papauté*. Paris: Hachette 1906.

–, "Lettres inédites de Joseph de Maistre." *Revue bleue*, 50 (1912): 257–63, 290–6, 323–30, 355–61, 390–6.

Lebrun, Richard, "L'Epistemologie maistrienne: rationalité et connaissance transcendante." *REM*, no. 5–6 (1980): 225–39.

–, "Joseph de Maistre, Cassandra of Science." *French Historical Studies*, 6 (1969): 214–31.

–, "Joseph de Maistre's Critique of Francis Bacon." In *Joseph de Maistre tra Illuminismo et Restaurazione*. Ed. by Luigi Marino. Turin: Centro Studi Piemontesi 1975.

–, "Joseph de Maistre et la loi naturelle." *REM*, no. 8 (1983): 117–35.

–, "Joseph de Maistre's 'Philosophic' View of War." *Proceedings of the Annual Meeting of the Western Society for French History*, 7 (1981): 43–52.

–, "Les Lectures de Joseph de Maistre d'après les registres inédits." *REM*, no. 9 (1985): 126–94.

–, *Throne and Altar: The Political and Religious Thought of Joseph de Maistre*. Ottawa: University of Ottawa Press 1965.

Le Forestier, René, *La Franc-Maçonnerie templière et occultiste aux xviiie et xixe siècles*. Published by Antoine Faivre. Paris: Aubier-Montaigne 1970.

Le Guillou, Louis, "Joseph de Maistre et Lamennais, 1820–1821." *REM*, no. 8 (1983): 85–100.

Lemmi, Francesco, "Giuseppe de Maistre a Losanna." *Fert*, 7 (1936): 185–215.

–, "Giuseppe de Maistre in Sardegna." *Fert*, 3 (1931): 240–68.

Lombard, Charles M., *Joseph de Maistre*. New York: Twayne 1976.

Lovie, Jacques, "Constance de Maistre: éléments pour une biographie." *REM*, no. 4 (1978): 141–63.

–, "Les Dernières Années de Joseph de Maistre (1817–1821)." *REM*, no. 10 (1986–87): 139–67.

–, *Mémoires et correspondance pour servir à l'histoire de la Révolution Française*. Paris: Amyot 1851.

Maistre, Dominique de, "Un Ecrit inédit de Joseph de Maistre: Amica Collatio ou échange d'observations sur le livre françois intitulé: DU PAPE." *Etudes*, 73 (1897): 5–32.

Mallet du Pan, Jacques, *Considerations on the Nature of the French Revolution.* Reprint of 1793 edition, introduction by Paul H. Beik. New York: Howard Fertig 1974.

Mandoul, J., *Joseph de Maistre et la politique de la maison de Savoie.* Paris: Alcan 1899.

Margerie, Amédée de, *Le Comte Joseph de Maistre: sa vie, ses écrits, ses doctrines, avec des documents inédits.* Paris: Librairie de la Société Bibliographique 1882.

Montmasson, J.M., *L'Idée de Providence d'après Joseph de Maistre.* Lyon: Vitte 1928.

Nada, Narciso, Ed., *Le Relazioni diplomatiche fra Austria e il regno di Sardegna.* Rome: Institut Storica Italiano 1964.

–, "Tra Russia e Piemonte (Lettere inedite di Giuseppe de Maistre a Carlo Emanuele Alfieri di Sostegno 1816–1818)," in *Miscellanea Walter Maturi.* Turin: Gioppichelli 1966.

Nicolas, Jean, "Noblesse, élites et Maçonnerie dans la Savoie du XVIIIe siècle." *REM,* no. 5–6 (1980): 47–68.

–, "Quelques lettres inédites de Joseph de Maistre." *Cahiers d'histoire,* 10 (1965): 315–25.

–, *La Savoie au 18e Siècle: Noblesse et Bourgeoisie.* Paris: Maloine 1978.

Nouvelle Biographie générale. 46 volumes. Paris: Didot 1853–66.

Paillette, Clément de, "Joseph de Maistre, Conférence à l'Institut Catholique de Paris." *Bulletin de l'Institut Catholique* (March 1892), pp 81–90 and (April 1882), pp 128–32.

–, *La Politique de Joseph de Maistre d'après ses prémiers écrits.* Paris: Picard 1895.

Palmer, Alan, *Alexander I: Tsar of War and Peace.* New York: Harper and Row 1974.

Palmer, R.R., *The Age of Democratic Revolution.* Princeton; Princeton University Press 1959.

Perrero, D., *I Reali di Sardegna nell'esilio (1799–1806).* Turin: Fratelli Bocca 1898.

"Portrait de Joseph de Maistre tracé par sa fille Constance, Un," *Etudes,* 125 (1910): 493–507.

Raeff, Marc, *Michael Speransky: Statesman of Imperial Russia, 1722–1839.* The Hague: Martinus Nijhoff 1957.

Raymond, George M., "L'Eloge de Comte Joseph de Maistre." *Memorie della Reale Academia della Scienza di Torino,* 27 (1823): 173–91.

Rebotton, Jean, *Etudes maistriennes: nouveau aperçu sur la famille de Maistre et sur les rapports de Joseph de Maistre avec Monsieur de Stedingk.* Aosta: Bibliothèque de l'Archivum Augustanum 1974.

–, "Lamartine et la famille Maistre." *REM,* no. 4(1978):91–139.

–, "Maistre, alias Josephus a Floribus, pendant la Révolution: repères et conjectures." *REM,* no. 5–6 (1980): 141–81.

–, "Nouveau aperçus sur l'éducation et l'attitude religieuses du jeune Maistre." *REM,* no. 3 (1977): 5–23.

Rials, Stéphane, "Lecture de Joseph de Maistre." *Mémoire*, 1 (1984): 21–48.

Riasonovsky, Nicholas V., *Nicholas I and Official Nationality in Russia, 1825–1855*. Berkeley and Los Angeles: University of California Press 1965.

Riquet, Michel, "Joseph de Maistre et le Père Barruel." *REM*, 5–6 (1980): 283–95.

Rouët de Journal, M. J., *Un Collège de Jésuites à Saint-Pétersbourg*. Paris: Perrin 1922.

Saint-Beuve, Charles A., *Les Grands Ecrivains français: XIXe siècle; philosophes et essayistes*. Ed. by Maurice Allem. Paris: Garnier 1930.

Sampson, Barbara, "La Rhétorique de l'essai dialogue chez Joseph de Maistre." McGill University M.A. thesis 1977.

Secret, Bernard, *Joseph de Maistre, Substitut et Sénateur*. Chambéry: Dardel 1927.

Siedentop, Larry Alan, "The Limits of the Enlightenment: A Study of Conservative Political and Social Thought in Early Nineteenth-century France with Special Reference to Maine de Biran and Joseph de Maistre." Oxford University D.Phil. thesis 1966.

Soltner, Jean-Louis, "Le Christianisme de Joseph de Maistre." *REM*, no. 5–6 (1980): 97–110.

Stourdza, Alexandre, *Considérations sur la doctrine et l'esprit de l'Eglise Orthodox*. Stuttgart: Cotta 1816.

–, *Oeuvres posthumes*. 5 vols. Paris: Dentu 1859.

Sydenham, Michael J., *The French Revolution*. London: Batsford 1965.

Symcox, Geoffrey, *Victor Amadeus II: Absolutism in the Savoyard State, 1675–1730*. London: Thames and Hudson 1983.

Treadgold, Donald W., *The West in Russia and China*. Cambridge, Eng.: Cambridge University Press 1973.

Trenard, Louis, "Joseph de Maistre et ses amis Lyonnais." *REM*, no. 8 (1983): 46–58.

Triomphe, Robert, *Joseph de Maistre: Etude sur la vie et sur la doctrine d'un matérialiste mystique*. Geneva: Droz 1968.

Uvarov, Serge S., *Etudes de Philologie et de Critique*. Paris: Didot 1847.

Vermale, François, *Joseph de Maistre émigré*. Chambéry: Dardel 1927.

Vucinich, Alexander, *Science in Russian Culture: A History to 1860*. Stanford: Stanford University Press 1963.

Watt, E.D., "The English Image of Joseph de Maistre." *European Studies Review*, 4 (1979): 239–59.

Woolf, Stuart, *A History of Italy 1700–1860: The Social Constraints of Political Change*. London: Methuen 1979.

Wootton, David, *Paolo Sarpi: Between Renaissance and Enlightenment*. Cambridge: Cambridge University Press 1983.

Zopel-Finger, Margrit, "Quod semper, quod ubique, quod ob omnibus ou L'art de fermer la bouche aux novateurs." In *Joseph de Maistre tra Illuminismo e Restaurazione*. Ed. by Luigi Marino. Turin: Centro Studi Piemontesi 1975.

Index

Absolutism: JM's opposition to, 93, 153
Adams, John Quincy, 218, 316n49
"Adresse ... à la Convention Nationale" (Maistre), 116
"Adresse du maire de Montagnole à ses Concitoyens" (Maistre), 145
Alexander I (of Russia), 187, 210; advised by JM, 3, 175, 189, 204–6; and anti-French coalitions, 181, 222; and Catholicism, 246; defeat at Austerlitz, 197; and domestic reforms, 198; and the Jesuits, 203–4, 222; and JM, 185, 187, 194, 197, 207–8, 222, 224–5; and Louis XVIII, 193; as own foreign minister, 207; and Rodolphe de Maistre, 179; and Speransky, 199; and the Treaty of Tilsit, 186; and the Tsarskoe Selo Lycée 200
Alexander II (of Russia), 210
Alfieri de Sostegno, Marquis Carlo-Emanuele, 220
Alquier, Charles, 173
America: cited by JM as an example, 49
Ami des hommes (Mirabeau), 20, 42
"Amica Collatio ou échange d'observations ..."

(Maistre), 244, 272, 336n138
Amis catholiques, 248
Année litteraire (Freron), 37
Anti-Jacobin Review, 213
Anti-Lucretius (Cardinal de Polignac), 20
Antraigues, Count d', 143
Aquinas, St Thomas, 214
Arnauld, Antoine, 159
Assemblée nationale des Allobroges, 112
Association des Amis de Joseph et Xavier de Maistre, x
Augustine, St, 148, 159
Austria, JM's suspicion of, 181, 188
Avaray, Count Antoine d': and draft royalist statement, 192; favourite of Louis XVIII, 190, 195; and JM, 157–8, 191, 196

Babeuf, François-Emile, 141, 147
Bacon, Francis, 39, 75, 97, 261, 291n24
Balbo, Chevalier Gaëtano, 187–8
Ballanche, Pierre-Simon, 234
Barol, Marquis de (Ottavio Falletti), 78, 83, 156, 247, 253, 292n42, 337n167
Barruel, Augustin, 170, 241,

312n107
Barthélemi, Apollonie de, 292n51
"Batonocracy": JM's opposition to, 129
Bausset, Cardinal Louis-François de, 240, 334n109
Bavarian illuminism, 171
Bayer, Gottlieb S., 213
Bayle, Pierre, 86
Beccaria, Cesare, 18, 31
Bellegarde, Jean-François de, 55, 120
Benedict XIV (pope), 67
Bentham, Jeremy, 21
Berry, Duke de, 241
Berthier, General, 161
Besson, Abbé, 234–5, 338n177, 340n214
Bianconi, Gian Battista, 171
Bible Society, 222, 246, 338n170
"Bienfaits de la Révolution française" (Maistre), 143, 305n159
Bigex, Abbé, 139, 301n82
Blacas, Count Pierre-Louis de: and draft royalist statement, 192; as French ambassador to Rome, 228; and Gallicanism, 193, 214; and JM, 190, 193–4, 196, 216–17, 228–31, 239, 247, 257, 320n94, 339n1386; and the Restoration (1814), 195